VANCOUVER
AND VICTORIA

JOHN GOTTBERG

1ST EDITION

PRENTICE HALL PRESS

New York □ London □ Toronto □ Sydney □ Tokyo □ Singapore

Published by Prentice Hall Press
A division of Simon & Schuster Inc.
15 Columbus Circle
New York, NY 10023

ISBN: 0-13-337999-X
ISSN: 1045-9316

Manufactured in the United States of America

CONTENTS

MAPS

A Disclaimer

Readers are advised that prices fluctuate in the course of time and that travel information changes under the impact of the varied and volatile factors that affect the travel industry. The author and publisher cannot be held responsible for the experiences of the reader while traveling. Readers are invited to write the publisher with ideas, comments, and suggestions for future editions.

INTRODUCING CANADA'S PACIFIC COAST

1. HISTORY, GEOGRAPHY, AND PEOPLE
2. ART AND ARCHITECTURE
3. SUGGESTED READING

Few places on Earth are as tailor-made for vacationers as Canada's spectacularly beautiful southwestern corner.

Focused around one of the world's great metropolises, Vancouver, and one of its most charmingly quaint and walkable cities, Victoria, this is a region where worldly sophistication goes hand-in-hand with a zest for the out-of-doors. Here is the marriage of city and wilderness, of futuristic progress and primordial protectiveness, of suave urbanity and rugged rusticity.

A typical British Columbian will fight fiercely for wilderness conservation while struggling to keep up with the Joneses (or Wongs, as the case may be). For residents of this province, a day spent in the mountains is as likely as a night at the opera; often both are enjoyed in the same day. And talk about cosmopolitanism: It wouldn't be surprising to find a Greek Canadian employed by a Hong Kong multinational firm taking a German colleague for an after-work ale at a British pub, for dinner at an East Indian restaurant, then to a Japanese nightclub.

Vancouver, a city of half a million people in a metropolitan area of 1.5 million, is surrounded and deeply indented by water on three sides, and set against a backdrop of evergreen-cloaked mountains. Some call it the most beautiful city in the world, ranking it ahead of San Francisco, Hong Kong, and Rio de Janeiro. Many Americans paid it little attention prior to Expo 86, the resoundingly successful world's fair that provoked a tourism boom. But the business world, especially that of the Pacific Rim, discovered Vancouver long before that—so much so that, because of foreign investment here, Asian business interests often refer to the city as "Hongkouver." Indeed, Canada's window to the west finds itself increasingly important in the economic life of the continent as the 21st century approaches.

Victoria, some say, is "more English than the English." A former trading post built on a superb natural harbor, it has evolved over a century and a half into a peaceful garden city. Its 250,000 inhabitants have two main economic focuses: government (British Columbia's provincial functions are based here) and tourism. Visitors strolling the streets find a proliferation of shops dealing in Waterford crystal and Victorian antiques, tartans, and fish and chips. And no one would consider leaving town without taking high tea at the venerable Empress Hotel.

Outside the cities, British Columbia lives up to its publicity as "Super, Natural." Most of Vancouver Island, 280 miles long and 50 to 75 miles wide, is a spectacular wilderness. Eagles and elk wander its 7,000-foot mountains, and sea lions and whales frolic in its seaward fjords. Vancouver, by the way, is *not* on Vancouver Island. Victoria *is*. That relative isolation, despite streamlined ferry and air connections, has contributed much to Victoria's smaller-city character.

The Whistler/Blackcomb resort area, 75 road miles north of Vancouver, has been acclaimed by *Ski* magazine readers as North America's second most popular ski resort (after Vail, Colorado). Along the Sunshine Coast, north of Vancouver, and throughout the islands of the Strait of Georgia, life revolves around small fishing villages and tiny farm communities. Even the heavily populated Lower Mainland region, which extends east from Vancouver nearly 100 miles along the Fraser River lowlands and south to the U.S. border, is speckled by wetland sanctuaries and hot springs, all beneath the gaze of towering mountain sentinels on its northern edge.

---

1. History, Geography, and People

HISTORY

For centuries before the arrival of white settlers, Canada's Pacific coastline was dominated by various native tribes, including Coast Salish (in the Fraser Delta), Nootkas, Kwakiutls, Bella Coolas, Tsimshians, and Haidas. These tribes are believed to have been descendants of a Fraser River culture that thrived around the time of Christ. Archeologists have found stone carvings, utensils, and fishing tackle showing supreme artistry and skill.

The British Columbian coastal tribes were blessed with an abundance of food and natural resources. Excellent hunters and trappers, they hunted deer, bear, ducks, and geese with bow and arrow, and harvested the wealth of the sea. They snared salmon, black cod, and herring, harpooned seals and sea lions, and stalked the sea otter for its warm fur. Children gathered berries from the forest undergrowth, dug clams, and plucked crabs from tidal flats. The seemingly endless forests, especially the easily split cedar, provided the raw material for houses, clothing, and utensils. The abundant resources enjoyed by the coastal tribes enabled them to conduct a steady trade with the people of the interior, especially up the Fraser River.

Coastal native society was complex and sophisticated. The people saw their lives as interwoven with the natural world around them, and a religion evolved based on kinship and communication with all living things, in which differences between animate beings were seen as superficial. Clans were named for legendary creatures —Raven, Eagle, and Whale, for example—who, it was said, could appear in human form as teachers, perhaps, or heroes.

Totemic symbols identified these real or imaginary animals. They appeared most notably on the famous totem poles, which were carved to honor the dead, to document social events, and to record history and oral tradition. Masks and houseposts also gave wood-carvers opportunities to demonstrate their art.

Wealth and lines of descent, both patrilineal and matrilineal, led to a hierarchy within clans. It became increasingly important to maintain the prestige of one's social position, and to improve it by obtaining greater wealth or performing heroic deeds. One of the primary vehicles for doing so was the potlatch: The chief or clan leader would invite neighboring leaders of equal or greater wealth, feed, house, and entertain them for weeks on end, and give away much of his wealth, thereby climbing in social rank. Protocol then demanded that his humbled guests invite him to future potlatches where he would be honored with even more riches than he had doled out.

An estimated 80,000 Native Canadians lived along British Columbia's Pacific Coast when the first white explorers arrived. Spanish ships skirted the coast in 1774, and the ubiquitous English navigator Capt. James Cook charted parts of Vancouver Island's coastline in 1778. Their glowing reports of the area's wealth of sea otter, beaver, and other furs excited the interest of British and American traders. Capt. George Vancouver—who had been a 21-year-old lieutenant on Cook's earlier voyage of discovery—took possession of the area for Great Britain in 1792. (It is said that young Lt. Peter Puget exclaimed to Captain Vancouver, "This is the most beautiful place I've ever seen!" The captain's alleged reply: "Yes, but you should have seen it 14 years ago.")

By this time, the westward movement of European settlers was already beginning. In July 1793, Alexander Mackenzie completed a cross-Canada journey by water and on foot. In 1808, Simon Fraser reached the Pacific near modern Vancouver after traveling down the river later named in his honor. His expedition opened the way for a series of fur-trading posts to be established on the Fraser River by the Hudson's Bay Company. Among them was Fort Langley, established in 1827 as the first settlement in the Lower Mainland. Located about 28 miles upstream from the Fraser River's mouth, it is today a national historic park.

Continual conflict between Great Britain and the United States was essentially resolved when the Oregon Treaty of 1846 established the boundary between the U.S. and Canada at the 49th Parallel "to the middle of the channel which separates the continent from Vancouver's Island; and thence southerly through the middle of the said channel, and of Fuca's Straits to the Pacific Ocean."

Fort Victoria, founded as Fort Camosun in 1843, became the western headquarters of the Hudson's Bay Company. When Vancouver Island was designated a Crown Colony in 1849, Victoria became its administrative center. The island colony was united with

British Columbia in 1866, and when, in 1871, British Columbia became the fifth province of the Dominion of Canada, Victoria was declared the provincial capital.

The fur industry waned in the early part of the 19th century, and gold, not sea otters, became the base upon which British Columbia grew and prospered. Alluvial gold was discovered in the lower Fraser River valley in 1858, and four years later in that part of the upper Fraser known as Cariboo country. By 1865, some $25 million in gold dust later, the rush was over. But that was long enough for thousands of new settlers to discover a home here. Victoria mushroomed on the strength of gold income, as steamships plied the lower Fraser and a coach road connected the navigable portion of the river with the Cariboo.

The first settlement on the Burrard Inlet sprang up in the early 1860s after the discovery of coal. But timber quickly emerged as more important commercially, and the Hastings Sawmill became the center of the young community. Liquor was not permitted on company land, so in 1867 an opportunist named John Deighton, nicknamed "Gassy Jack" after his gift for gab, opened a saloon in nearby Maple Tree Square. Business was so successful that a community known as Gastown grew around Deighton's saloon. The Gastown settlement was approved as a town site by the provincial government in 1870, and was officially named Granville.

The town's future was more or less assured in 1884 when the Canadian Pacific Railroad chose it as the western terminus to the first transcontinental railway. On April 6, 1886, on completion of the track, Granville was incorporated as the city of Vancouver. But barely two months later, on June 13, the city of 1,000 was obliterated by fire, a forest slash burn that ran out of control. The number of buildings that survived could be counted on one hand. (The only one standing today is St. James Anglican Church, at the corner of Cordova and Gore streets.)

City founders wasted no time in rebuilding their city. By Christmas 1886, in fact, the number of buildings had grown to 800—a construction rate of more than four a day. Hotel Vancouver opened in 1887, the 1,000-acre Stanley Park in 1888, the Granville Street Bridge in 1889, the Orpheum Theatre in 1890, and the Hudson's Bay Company department store in 1893. A steamship line connected Vancouver to Asia in 1891, and a century of transpacific trade began.

When the opening of the Panama Canal in 1915 made the export of grain and lumber to Europe economically practical, British Columbia experienced a boom the likes of which it hadn't seen since the gold rushes of the mid-19th century. Investors laid out thousands of dollars for timberland and mining territory. When settlement of Canada's barren inland prairies got underway, the call for lumber and other supplies went out to British Columbia. B.C.'s population more than doubled to 400,000 in the decade before 1911, and Vancouver's population climbed to well over 100,000.

Victoria, meanwhile, was also booming. Manufacturing and timber money helped the city earn a reputation as one of beautiful homes (notably the spectacular Craigdarroch Castle, built in 1889) and spectacular gardens (like the remarkable Butchart Gardens, created in 1904 from a worked-out limestone quarry). The government city didn't suffer a disastrous fire like Vancouver's, but it endured something potentially worse—a smallpox epidemic in 1892, carried by a ship that had arrived from Asia. Had it not been for the availability of the cowpox vaccine, the city of 16,000 people might have been decimated.

As Vancouver grew around the railroad, Victoria resigned itself to its role as British Columbia's "second city." With a sunnier, milder climate than either Vancouver or Seattle, Victoria was becoming a tourist draw for refugees from both cities, who traveled to Victoria by steamer. Most visitors stayed in the posh new Empress Hotel, built in 1908. It was adjoined by an extensive rose garden and by the Crystal Gardens, a glass-roofed, indoor, saltwater swimming pool that became the social center of Victoria.

Hard times plagued both cities during the years of the First World War and the subsequent Great Depression. The onset of the Second World War, however, created new opportunities in timber, mining, and shipbuilding.

Today, wood processing remains a major industry for both cities. Sufficient power for sawmills, plywood, and paper production comes from hydroelectric developments in the hinterland. Vancouver and Victoria support thriving fishing fleets, and their ice-free harbors greet vessels from all over the world. The Port of Vancouver, with its extensive docks and its mineral and grain-elevator facilities, is the third most active port in North America in terms of foreign tonnage.

In 1986 Vancouver celebrated its 100th birthday with the most publicized event in its history, the five-month-long Expo 86. The main theme of the world's fair was transportation, and it was no coincidence that the most ambitious public transport project in the city's history, the SkyTrain light-rail rapid-transit system, had opened earlier the same year. Victoria hopes to make a similar splash when the British Commonwealth Games, a mini-Olympics, are held in the garden city in 1994.

GEOGRAPHY

British Columbia's mountains were formed millions of years ago, about the same time as the Rocky Mountains, by a great geologic uplift and folding. Glaciers followed, carving the troughs for the Strait of Georgia and for inland waterways that were fed by melting ice waters and torrential rains.

It's easiest to think of southwestern British Columbia as a mountainous land punctuated by waterways. The largest of those bodies of water is the Strait of Georgia, which separates Vancouver Island from the Canadian mainland. Averaging about 20 miles across, it is the dominating physical feature between the Vancouver Island Ranges and the Fraser Plateau.

The Fraser River, which cuts an 850-mile-long swath through the British Columbian mountains from its source in Jasper National Park, broadens over its last 100 miles into a gentle valley before dumping into the Strait of Georgia. The Fraser Valley supports most of the population of the province of British Columbia, including Vancouver, which lies on the northern edge of its delta. Another deep indentation, the Burrard Inlet, marks the boundary between Vancouver and the ruggedly mountainous North Shore.

Victoria lies 60 miles from Vancouver, almost due south, at the southeastern edge of Vancouver Island. The Juan de Fuca Strait divides it from Washington State's Olympic Peninsula, 20 miles distant. The Haro Strait, cutting an 8-mile-wide path between Vancouver Island and Washington's San Juan Islands, acts as a capillary linking the Strait of Georgia with the Juan de Fuca Strait, Canada's artery to the Pacific Ocean.

The region's geography is responsible not only for its beauty. It is the cause of the mild but often rainy climate.

Most weather systems move into southwestern British Columbia off the jet streams that follow the moderate Japan Current, which curls past the west coast of Vancouver Island after leaving the Gulf of Alaska. That coastline is bathed by rain clouds that get hung up on the island's mountainous 7,000-foot-high spine. Fronts that find their way around Vancouver Island, often passing by sheltered Victoria, can't get beyond the wall of peaks behind Vancouver and the Lower Mainland. Downtown Vancouver receives 57 inches of rain a year, most of it between October and March; the average high temperature ranges from 74°F (23°C) in July to 41°F (5°C) in January. Victoria gets half as much rainfall as Vancouver—26 inches—to go with average temperatures varying from 72°F (22°C) in July to 43°F (6°C) in January. The average length of winter snow cover is 11 days in Vancouver, a mere 3 days in Victoria.

PEOPLE

Three-quarters of all British Columbia citizens live in the province's southwestern corner. Individuals of British descent (English, Scots, Irish, and Welsh) comprise the largest percentage (about 40%) of Vancouverites and Victorians, but they are by no means the only significant group.

In fact, it is now estimated that 25% of Vancouverites, and perhaps 200,000 British Columbians, are Chinese or of Chinese descent. Tens of thousands of them are recent immigrants from Hong Kong, who have moved their families and considerable financial assets out of Asia because of the impending turnover of the British Crown Colony to mainland China. Previous waves of Chinese migrants to Canada's west coast came in 1858 for the Fraser Valley gold rush and in the 1880s to help build the trans-Canada railway.

Life for the Chinese in British Columbia has not always been easy: From their earliest arrival, and through much of the 20th century, they were treated as second-class citizens; they did not achieve the right to vote until the late 1940s. Today, however, they are perhaps the wealthiest ethnic group in the province. Vancouver's Chinatown, several square blocks around the intersection of Main and Pender streets east of downtown, is the second largest in North America, after San Francisco's. Victoria's Chinatown is not so large, but it is no less significant.

Another highly visible ethnic group is Indo-Pakistani, of whom more than 50,000 live in greater Vancouver. Most Indian nationals who immigrate to Canada are devotees of the monotheistic Sikh religion, a minority religion in their ancestral country. Baptized Sikh men wear colorful turbans to cover the tightly coiled hair they must never cut. Influential merchants, the Sikhs' principal ethnic

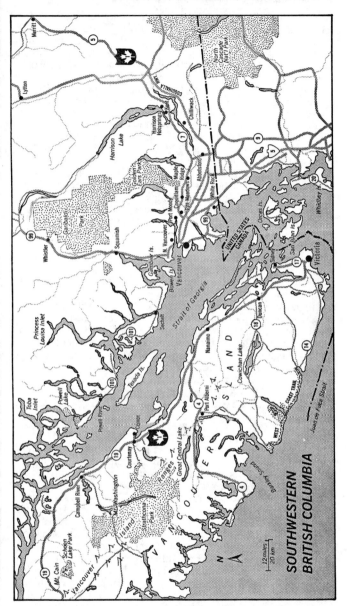

SOUTHWESTERN BRITISH COLUMBIA

center is the Punjabi Market on Main Street between 49th and 51st avenues.

Though French-speakers are on even footing with English in

bicultural Canada, French Canadians are a scattered minority of about 80,000 citizens in British Columbia. They have their own newspaper, radio and television station, and a sizable community, Maillardville, in Coquitlam, east of Vancouver in the Fraser Valley. In fact, Coquitlam has the only bilingual school system in the province.

South European immigrants—Italians (about 30,000) and Greeks (8,000)—have distinct communities in both Vancouver and Victoria, as well as a proliferation of popular restaurants. In Vancouver, the principal Italian district is along Commercial Drive north and south of Broadway; the Greek community is centered near the University of British Columbia, along Broadway between McDonald and Alma streets.

An estimated 60,000 Germans, 25,000 Dutch, and 23,000 Ukrainians make their homes in British Columbia. Many emigrated from their native European lands following the Second World War, settling into farming life-styles in the Fraser Valley or the lowlands of Vancouver Island. Other European immigrants, especially Scandinavians, found livelihoods in lumbering or fishing, much as they had done in their homelands. Japanese, Vietnamese, and Filipinos also have sizable ethnic communities in southwestern British Columbia.

The Native Canadian population of 47,000, about one-third of whom live in southwestern B.C., have a far lower average income and higher mortality rate than the white population. Three bands of Coast Salish live on two large reserves in Greater Vancouver—one located beneath the north end of the Lion's Gate Bridge in North Vancouver, the other on the Burrard Inlet near the foot of Mt. Seymour. A half-dozen more reserves are located in metropolitan Victoria and the adjacent Saanich Peninsula.

2. Art and Architecture

Truly British Columbian art is that of the indigenous coastal tribes. Today, contemporary native and non-native artists have adapted their totemic designs to silver jewelry, wood and jade carving, paintings and drawings, ceramics, and more traditional basketry. Galleries specializing in native art are found throughout the province, including Water Street in Vancouver's Gastown and Government Street in downtown Victoria. Don't miss Haida artist Bill Reid's classic cedar sculpture, *Raven and the First Men,* in the University of British Columbia's Museum of Anthropology.

Emily Carr, a native of Victoria, is B.C.'s single most famous artist. Especially well known for her sketches and almost mystical paintings of coastal rain forests and native culture, Carr turned to writing later in life. By the time of her death in Victoria in 1945 at the age of 74, she had produced six incisive autobiographical books. The Emily Carr Room in the Vancouver Art Gallery houses 157 paintings and drawings she bequeathed to the people of British Columbia. The Emily Carr College of Art and Design on Vancouver's Granville Island carries on the work she began as a teacher. In Victoria more of her art is on display at her longtime home and at the Emily Carr Gallery.

Today's B.C. artists are as likely to be working in fabrics or ceramics as on canvas. A large concentration of artists have studios on Granville Island; many more are scattered widely through both communities.

Two names stand out in British Columbia architecture, one from the past and one from the present. Francis Mawson Rattenbury designed Victoria's landmark Empress Hotel and Parliament Buildings, as well as famous hotels in Banff and Lake Louise and courthouses and banks in several B.C. cities between 1893 and 1930. Arthur Erickson is Canada's greatest living architect, a genius who seems able to make buildings disappear into their environments. Among his creations are the Museum of Anthropology at the University of British Columbia and, in downtown Vancouver, the law courts at Robson and Howe streets and the MacMillan Bloedel tower on West Georgia Street. Although they never met, the two men collaborated on one project: Erickson converted the courtrooms and corridors of Rattenbury's Robson Square Courthouse into the Vancouver Art Gallery.

3. Suggested Reading

A large writers' community thrives in southwestern British Columbia, though few of its inhabitants have achieved the fame of Canadian writers Margaret Atwood and Mordecai Richler. Events like the Vancouver Writers Festival in late October seem certain to help the community prosper.

British Columbia's most successful commercial writer in the late 1980s has been W. P. Kinsella, a resident of White Rock on the U.S. border. Author of 17 books, Kinsella gained recognition so slowly that at first he had to support himself by running a pizza parlor and driving a taxi in Victoria. But in 1988 his baseball novel, *Shoeless Joe,* was turned into the successful movie *Field of Dreams* starring Kevin Costner. Perhaps now the world will discover his fine collections of Native Canadian stories, such as *The Miss Hobbema Pageant* (Harper & Collins).

Southwestern British Columbia is home to an energetic poetry movement. Some of the poets are native sons and daughters. Works by Robin Skelton, P. K. Page, Susan Musgrave, Robert Bringhurst, Joe Rosenblatt, and Marilyn Bowering are among the best.

On British Columbia's native population, a good source is *A Guide to B.C. Indian Myth and Legend* by Ralph Maud (Talonbooks). Any of a dozen books on history tell the region's history well, but Terry Reksten's *Rattenbury* (Sono Nis) stands alone as a fascinating profile of B.C.'s most famous architect and his times. Readers fascinated with politics might pick up Stan Persky's incisive *Fantasy Government* (New Star), on the administration of B.C. Premier Bill Vander Zalm and his Social Credit party. (Vander Zalm owns, and lives in, Richmond's Fantasy Gardens development: hence the title.)

There are a great many guidebooks of different types available on southwestern British Columbia. While I hope this is the best, it can't cover everything. Jurgen Gothe's *First Rate* (Brighouse) is one of the most entertaining volumes of restaurant critiques I've ever read. Shoppers can bank on Anne Garber's *The Vancouver Shopper* (Johnston Associates), now in its third edition. Visitors with children should look for *Kids! Kids! Kids! in Vancouver* by Daniel Wood and Betty Campbell (Douglas & McIntyre), which tells everything families need to know. Hikers can consider the trail guides published by Gordon Soules of North Vancouver or by The Mountaineers of Seattle. As for coffee-table volumes, it would be hard to do better than the ambitious Bob Herger–Rosemary Neering project, *The Coast of British Columbia* (Whitecap).

BEFORE YOU LEAVE HOME

Don't wait until you're on your way to read this chapter. It contains information that will help you plan your trip, and is designed to save you time, money, luggage space, and perhaps aggravation.

In the following pages, you'll get a crash course in the nuts and bolts of travel in British Columbia. I've tried to answer each of the following questions: (1) Where can I get basic tourist information on Vancouver and Victoria? (2) What travel documents must I carry? (3) What is the currency system like? Is my American money good? What about my credit cards? (4) What are the best times to go? (5) How shall I pack? (6) What health precautions should I take? (7) What about insurance? (8) Where can I get medical or legal aid, should I need it?

Finally, I will discuss the metric measurement system and postal services, and make suggestions for disabled travelers, senior citizens, single travelers, and families.

1. Sources of Information in the U.S.

Your first contact should be **Tourism British Columbia.** The provincial government tourist agency has detailed information on all the varied tourism regions of B.C. This book deals with only two of them. There's a toll-free number you can call from anywhere in North America: 800/663-6000.

Tourism B.C. has three offices in the United States, all of them on the West Coast. In the Los Angeles area, see them at 2600 Michelson St., Suite 1050, Irvine, CA 90010 (tel. 714/852-1054; fax 714/852-0168); in the Bay Area at 100 Bush St., Suite 400, San Francisco, CA 94104 (tel. 415/981-4780; fax 415/981-0223); in the Pacific Northwest at 720 Olive Way, Suite 930, Seattle, WA 99801 (tel. 206/623-5937; fax 206/447-9004).

The agency's head office is in the Parliament Buildings, Victoria, BC V8V 1X4 (tel. 604/387-1642; fax 604/387-1590). Most tourist requests are handled at 865 Hornby St., 8th Floor, Vancouver, BC V6Z 2G3 (tel. 604/660-2861; fax 604/660-3383).

Your next sources are the visitors' bureaus for the respective cities. For **Tourism Vancouver,** write or call the Vancouver Travel InfoCentre, P.O. Box 49296, Vancouver, BC V7X 1L3 (tel. 604/683-2000; toll free 800/663-8555; fax 604/682-1717). For **Tourism Victoria,** write or call 612 View St., 6th floor, Victoria, BC V8W 1J5 (tel. 604/382-2127; toll free 800/663-3883; fax 604/361-9733).

If you're planning to spend time outside the cities, get in touch with these folks as well: For mainland B.C., the **Tourism Association of Southwestern British Columbia,** Box 48610, Bentall P.O., Vancouver, BC V7X 1A3 (tel. 604/688-3677; fax 604/688-1817). For Vancouver Island, the **Tourism Association of Vancouver Island,** 405 Bastion Square, Suite 302, Victoria, BC V8W 1J1 (tel. 604/382-3551; fax 604/382-3523).

Canadian government tourism offices are often found in association with consulates in major American cities. These deal with the country as a whole, and are not likely to have voluminous detailed information on Vancouver and Victoria.

2. Passport and Other Documents

Citizens and legal, permanent residents of the United States do not require passports or visas to cross the U.S. border into Canada. It's a good idea, however, to carry identification papers (a birth certificate will do) in case any questions arise. Naturalized citizens should be able to produce a naturalization certificate; permanent residents are advised to carry their alien registration (green) card. Visitors 18 and under, if traveling without a parent or guardian, should carry a letter of authorization stating their name and the length of their trip.

Citizens of countries other than the United States require a valid passport to enter Canada, whether directly or via the U.S. Many also require visas. Inquiries should be directed to the Canadian embassy, high commission, or consulate in their home countries before departure for North America.

American citizens wishing to study or work in Canada must be authorized to do so prior to arrival. Work permits are granted only if no Canadian citizen or permanent resident is deemed qualified for the job; the government is quite sticky about this. Interested persons should check with a Canadian embassy or consulate for details.

Customs regulations are discussed in Chapter IV, "Getting to Know Vancouver," under "Orientation: Arriving."

The nearest U.S. immigration and customs checkpoint to Vancouver, and one of the busiest in North America, is the Peace Arch station north of Seattle, P.O. Box 280, Blaine, WA 98230 (tel. 206/332-6318). A full staff is on duty 24 hours a day. Canadian immigration officials can be reached by calling 604/273-4113.

Clearing customs going either direction is normally a fast, painless procedure. The typical northbound rap (entering Canada) is: "Where do you live? Where are you going? How long do you plan to be gone? What's the purpose of your trip? Are you carrying any fruit, vegetables, or firearms? Okay, fine, go ahead." Southbound, you'll hear similar questions: "What is your citizenship? Where do you live? How long have you been gone? Did you buy anything in Canada that you are returning home with? (What?) Are you carrying any fresh produce?" Unless you give a "wrong" answer, act suspicious, or are overly reluctant to answer, you're home free.

---

3. Credit/Currency

There's little difference between the United States and Canada in terms of currency systems. Both are decimal based, and both figure in dollars and cents. But the American dollar is worth about 15% more, at least at the time this is being written. What that means is that every Canadian dollar you spend actually costs you only about 86 cents in U.S. money. To put it another way, if you budget $1,000 U.S. for your trip, you can spend $1,160 Canadian.

Greenbacks are widely accepted in Canada. Banks and other financial institutions offer a standard rate of exchange that may vary slightly day by day. Commercial establishments, most of whom welcome U.S. dollars, may offer a lower rate of exchange—or a higher one. The Canadian government urges visitors to use Canadian money to avoid exchange problems when traveling in the country; but I've never experienced exchange problems with U.S. dollars beyond the occasional unfavorable rates.

You can bring into or take out of Canada any amount of money, but if you are importing or exporting sums of $5,000 or more, you must file a report of the transaction with U.S. Customs.

Traveler's checks, in U.S. or Canadian funds, are the safest way to carry money and they are universally accepted by banks (which sometimes charge a small fee to cash them) and by larger merchants. Normal banking hours in Canada are 10am to 3pm Monday through Friday.

Major credit cards are widely accepted in British Columbia, especially American Express, MasterCard, and VISA, and, to a lesser extent, Diners Club, Carte Blanche, and EnRoute. The amounts spent in Canadian dollars will be automatically converted by your company to U.S. dollars when you are billed.

Note: The following abbreviations are used in accommodation and dining listings:

AE	American Express
CB	Carte Blanche
DC	Diners Club
DISC	Discover
ER	EnRoute
MC	MasterCard
V	VISA

A final monetary note: Unless noted otherwise, all prices quoted in this book are in Canadian dollars.

---

4. When to Go

Any time of the year can be a good time to visit, depending upon your interests. The Vancouver-Victoria climate is Canada's balmiest, with warm summers and mild, rainy winters.

The six-month tourist season runs April through September. Hotels often raise their prices 20% to 30% during this period, and they are still fully booked. On the other hand, the weather is nicer (with rainfall sporadic, not continual), special events are far more numerous, and many seasonal attractions are open only during tourist season. Days are long in these northern climes (16 hours of daylight in mid-June), lending themselves to a variety of outdoor sports and activities.

The off-season is less expensive, less crowded, easier to get reservations in, and more conducive to indoor activities. Remember to bring an umbrella! Winter sports-lovers don't have far to travel to some of the continent's best-loved and most challenging ski resorts.

CLIMATE

The month-by-month temperature range in Vancouver and Victoria is almost identical. The difference is in precipitation: Victoria, protected from southerly chinook breezes by Washington's Olympic Range, gets far less than Vancouver, which lies against mountains that draw the wet stuff. Average annual rainfall in Vancouver is 57 inches; in Victoria, just 26 inches.

Average Temperatures and Number of Days of Rain

VANCOUVER	Jan	Feb	Mar	Apr	May	June	July	Aug	Sept	Oct	Nov	Dec
Avg. Temp (°F)	36	39	43	49	55	60	64	63	57	50	43	39
Avg. Temp (°C)	2.5	4	6.5	9	13	16	17.5	17.5	13.5	10.5	6.5	4
Rainy Days	20	17	17	14	12	11	7	8	9	16	19	22

VICTORIA	Jan	Feb	Mar	Apr	May	June	July	Aug	Sept	Oct	Nov	Dec
Avg. Temp (°F)	37.5	40	43	47	54	57	62	61	57	50	42.5	39.5
Avg. Temp (°C)	3	4.5	6	8.5	12	14	16.5	16	14	10	6	4
Rainy Days	16	14	13	10	8	7	5	6	8	13	16	18

SPECIAL EVENTS AND FESTIVALS

There's no shortage of special events and festivals in any month, though they certainly proliferate during the brilliant days of summer.

In Vancouver the biggest events are the Sea Festival in July, featuring a week of concerts, parades, and fireworks over English Bay, and concluding with a bathtub race across the Strait of Georgia from Nanaimo; and the Pacific National Exhibition, the fifth-largest fair in North America, which runs from the third weekend of August through Labor Day.

Vancouver also has an annual Chinese New Year parade in late January or early February; a jazz festival in late June; a folk fest in mid-July; a comedy fest in early August; a film festival in early October; and a writers' festival in late October.

Victoria prides itself on being a town of refined musical tastes, especially jazz. It turns it on in April with the TerrifVic Dixieland Jazz Festival, and in late June, there's Jazz Fest International. For six weeks in July and August, the Victoria International Festival spotlights almost nightly classical performances.

Both cities go outré in September with annual "fringe festivals," emphasizing counterculture (or, at least, out-of-the-mainstream) art forms. On New Year's Eve, each has a First Night, a merchant-sponsored, alcohol-free party in the downtown streets that has proven immensely popular.

Outside the cities, two fine events in the Lower Mainland attract fine and performing artists from around the world: the B.C. Festival of the Arts in Chilliwack in late May and the Harrison Festival of the Arts at Harrison Hot Springs in early July.

Following is a list of some of the leading annual events throughout the region, with 1990 dates listed. Most will move ahead one day in 1991, though some may move back a week.

JANUARY: **Vancouver:** 1, Polar Bear Swim, English Bay; 27, Chinese New Year parade, Chinatown; **Victoria:** 18–21, Pacific Cup Oldtimers Hockey Tournament.

FEBRUARY: **Victoria:** 23, Flower Count.

MARCH: **Victoria:** 1–3, Classic Boat Festival; **Vancouver Island:** 31–April 7, Pacific Rim Whale Festival, Tofino and Ucluelet.

APRIL: **Vancouver:** 1–7, Festival of Fools, Granville Island; **Lower Mainland:** 15, Antique Car Easter Parade, New Westminster; **Victoria:** 18–22, TerrifVic Dixieland Jazz Party; **Vancouver Island:** 22, Snow-to-Surf Race, Courtenay.

MAY: **Vancouver:** first week, MayWorks Festival; 9, North Shore Waiters Race, Capilano Suspension Bridge, North Vancouver; 14–21, Vancouver Children's Festival; 20, Queen Victoria Day Celebration, Burnaby Village Museum; **Lower Mainland:** 12–13, Fraser Valley International Arts Festival, Abbotsford; 18–21, Cloverdale Rodeo, Cloverdale; 20–21, Hyack Festival, New Westminster; 20–21, May Day Celebration, Fort Langley; 22–27, B.C. Festival of the Arts, Chilliwack; 26–27, Delta Pioneer Days, Delta; 26–June 3, Dogwood Days, Coquitlam; **Victoria:** 19–21, Victoria Day Celebration; 25–27, Swiftsure Race Weekend; 23–27, Victoria Exhibition; **Vancouver Island:** 14–21, Empire Days, Cumberland; 18–20, Empire Days, Nanaimo; 25–27, Country Music Fair & Jamboree, Mill Bay; 25–July 7, Nanaimo Theatre Festival, Nanaimo.

JUNE: **Vancouver:** 2–3 or 9–10, International Dragon Boat Festival, False Creek; 22–July 1, DuMaurier International Jazz Festival; 23–25, North Vancouver Folkfest; **Lower Mainland;** 16–17, Langley Days, Langley; 29–July 3, Golden Spike Days, Port Moody; 29–July 8, Harrison Festival of the Arts, Harrison Hot Springs; **Sunshine Coast–Whistler:** 17, Horseshoe Bay Days, Horseshoe Bay; 25–August 31, Summer Street Scene, Whistler; **Victoria:** 2–3, Oak Bay Tea Party; 9–10, Wind Festival; 22–July 1, Jazz Fest International; 24–July 1, Folkfest '89; 16–17, Victoria International Boat Race; **Vancouver Island:** 8–10, Lake Days Celebration, Lake Cowichan; 16, B.C. Highland Games, Courtenay; 29–July 1, Dixieland Jazz Festival, Sidney.

JULY: **Vancouver:** 1, Canada Day; 9–15, Vancouver Sea Festival (concluding July 15 with a bathtub race across the Strait of Georgia from Nanaimo); 13–15, Vancouver Folk Music Festival; mid-July–mid August, Early Music Festival, University of British Columbia; 30–August 10, Vancouver Chamber Music Festival; **Lower Mainland:** 1, Canada Day; 29–August 5, Fort Festival Days, Fort Langley; **Victoria:** 1, Canada Day; 1–August 31, International Festival; **Vancouver Island:** 1, Canada Day; 1–30, Summer Festival of the Arts, Ganges, Saltspring Island; 6–August 18, Summer Music Festival Comax; 7–8, Sea Dog Days, Port Alberni; 7–15, Bathtub Week, Nanaimo; 19, All Sooke Day; 19–22, Duncan-Cowichan Summer Festival, Duncan; 31–August 2, Coombs Bluegrass Festival, Parksville.

AUGUST: **Vancouver:** 3–12, Vancouver International Comedy Festival; 4–5, Powell Street (Japanese) Festival; 18–September 3,

Pacific National Exhibition; **Lower Mainland:** 4–6, Antique Threshing Bee, Chilliwack; 11–12, Abbotsford International Airshow, Abbotsford; 31–September 3, Bluegrass Festival, Chilliwack; **Sunshine Coast–Whistler:** 4–5, Squamish Days loggers festival, Squamish; 10–12, Festival of the Written Arts, Sechelt; 25–26, Summer Music Festival, Squamish; **Victoria:** 3–11, Fine Arts '90; 17–19, SunFest; 30–September 3, Classic Boat Festival; **Vancouver Island:** 3–6, Nautical Days, Comox; 10–12, Filomi Days Celebration, Port Hardy; 17–19, Vancouver Island Exhibition, Nanaimo; 31–September 3, Salmon Festival, Port Alberni.

SEPTEMBER: **Vancouver:** 7–16, Annual Vancouver Fringe Festival; 28–October 14, Vancouver International Film Festival; 24–28, Vancouver Writers Festival; **Victoria:** 1–3, Classic Boat Festival; 19–30, Annual Victoria Fringe Festival; **Vancouver Island:** 7–9, Cowichan Exhibition, Duncan.

OCTOBER: **Vancouver:** various weekends, Oktoberfest; **Victoria:** 19– November 4, British Fortnight.

NOVEMBER: **Vancouver:** 11, Remembrance Day parade; **Victoria:** 3–4, Historical Arms and Militaria Show; 11, Remembrance Day parade.

DECEMBER: **Vancouver:** 1–24, Christmas Craft Market, Granville Island; mid-month to 24, Christmas carol ships, English Bay and Burrard Inlet; 17–January 1, Vancouver Children's Winterfest; 31, First Night. **Victoria:** 1–January 1, Christmas Lighting Competitions; 1–January 6, Christmas lights display, Butchart Gardens; 16, Christmas Lighted Boat Parade, Inner Harbour; 31, First Night.

Holidays

The official public holidays in the province of British Columbia are: New Year's Day (Jan 1); Good Friday, Easter, Easter Monday (Apr 13–16, 1990); Victoria Day (May 21, 1990); Canada Day (July 1); B.C. Day (Aug 6, 1990); Labour Day (Sept 3, 1990); Thanksgiving (Oct 8, 1990); Remembrance Day (Nov 11); Christmas (Dec 25); and Boxing Day (Dec 26).

---

5. What to Pack

My first rule of thumb is this: *Travel as light as possible.* Never carry more than you can handle yourself without assistance. Ideally you shouldn't have more than one suitcase, and a handbag that fits neatly under your seat on the airplane or in the overhead rack on the bus or train. If you're driving you can afford to carry a little more.

The clothing you bring will depend on the time of year you come and whether you're out to ski or to swim. In summer, casual lightweight clothing will suffice most of the time, but always carry a sweater for cool nights. Men should have a jacket and tie, and women an evening dress if formal dining is on the agenda. In winter, you'll want a heavy jacket or coat, preferably waterproof. Gloves and a rain hat are a good idea, too.

Any time of year, a pair of sturdy and comfortable walking shoes is imperative. An umbrella is a wise accessory in all months, and it becomes essential from mid-September to mid-April.

There are a few items you may not have considered that could prove priceless during your stay: (1) a travel alarm clock, so as not to leave yourself at the mercy of your hotel for wake-up calls; (2) a Swiss army knife, which has a multitude of uses from bottle opener to screwdriver; (3) a small flashlight, especially in winter when it gets dark early; (4) a washcloth in a plastic bag, on the outside chance your budget hotel doesn't have one; (5) a pair of light wooden (not plastic) shoe trees to air out your footwear after you put in a hard day on your feet; and (6) a magnifying glass for reading the small print on maps.

There's one more thing you must *never, ever* travel anywhere without—your sense of humor.

HEALTH/MEDICINES

If you're taking a prescription medication, it's wise to bring a copy of the prescription in case it needs to be renewed in Canada. It's wise, also, to bring your visual prescription in case your glasses or lenses are broken or lost and require replacement. For minor emergencies, I always carry a small first-aid kit containing an antibiotic ointment, bandages, aspirin, soap, a thermometer, and motion-sickness pills.

ELECTRICAL APPLIANCES

Canada's electricity is alternating current, just as in the United States, and it uses the same kind of outlets. You can bring and use any appliance without requiring an adapter. Just remember what I said about traveling light.

---

6. Insurance

American travelers should review their health-insurance plans to determine whether they are adequately covered when traveling outside the United States. For those who are not, travelers' health insurance is recommended and widely available. Check with any travel agent or insurance company.

Auto insurance is compulsory in B.C. through the Insurance Corporation of British Columbia (ICBC). Basic coverage consists of "no-fault" accident benefits and third-party legal liability coverage of a minimum of $200,000. Before you leave the States, if you plan to drive, confirm with your insurance company that your policy meets this same requirement. Your company should issue a financial responsibility card, which you must present along with your vehicle registration and driver's license if you have an accident. To report accidents to ICBC, call 520-8222 in Vancouver, 383-1111 in Victoria, or toll free 800/663-3051 anywhere in the province.

---

7. Medical and Legal Aid

Canadian hospital and medical services are comparable to those of the United States, except that medicine is socialized in Canada. Daily hospitalization rates vary; in-patient care can start at $900. Again, be sure you have insurance coverage.

Major hotels have doctors and dentists on call. If you need a referral, call the **College of Physicians and Surgeons of British Columbia** in Vancouver (tel. 773-7758) or the **College of Dental Surgeons of British Columbia,** also in Vancouver, (tel. 736-3621) weekdays between 8am and 4pm. In case of emergency, dial 911 or 0 for an operator anywhere in the province.

The B.C. branch of the **Canadian Bar Association** provides free general legal information on its aid lines: 687-4680 in Vancouver, 388-0416 in Victoria. Lawyer referrals can be obtained by calling 687-3221 in Vancouver or 382-1415 in Victoria.

---

8. Metric Measurements

Canada employs the metric system of measurement. Distances are in kilometers (1km = approx. ⅝ mile); speeds are in km/hour (100kmph = about 65 m.p.h.). One meter is equal to about 3 feet, 3 inches; and there are about 30 centimeters in an inch.

When it comes to liquid measures, things get more complicated. There are 4.6 liters in the imperial gallon, which is about 20% larger than the U.S. gallon. There is 0.94 liter in one U.S. quart. In figuring the cost of gasoline, you must make several conversions to learn that a price of 50¢ a liter is the same as $1.89 (U.S.) per U.S. gallon. (By the way, that's a pretty typical price in the Vancouver area.)

A metric measurement chart can be found in this book's appendix.

---

9. Postal Services

Everything you mail from Canada must bear a Canadian stamp. Postal rates vary; as I write this, it costs 45¢ to send a letter or postcard from Canada to the United States.

Canadian postal codes, you may have noticed, alternate letters and numerals; it's important to put them on all your correspondence.

10. Tips for the Disabled

Virtually every higher-priced accommodation and most in the moderate range have special rooms for the physically handicapped. Some budget hotels may also have appropriate facilities. In all cases, it's important to book well ahead of time to reserve space.

Wheelchair travelers can obtain specific information about traveling in British Columbia by contacting the **Canadian Paraplegic Association,** 780 SW Marine Drive, Vancouver, BC V6P 5Y7 (tel. 604/324-3611).

Services for the hearing impaired are available at the **Western Institute for the Deaf,** 2125 W. 7th Ave., Vancouver, BC V6K 1X9 (tel. 604/736-7391; TDD phone 604/736-2527). The institute has a branch on Vancouver Island at 835 Humboldt St., Suite 302, Victoria, BC V8V 4W8 (tel. 604/384-8088; TDD phone 604/384-3105). There is also a 24-hour Message Relay Centre: voice phone 604/738-1213 in Vancouver, toll free 800/972-6503 outside Vancouver; TDD phone 604/738-3332 within Vancouver, toll free 800/972-6509 outside the city.

Vancouver has a Handicapped Resource Centre (tel. 604/873-3371) and also assists disabled persons with transportation needs (tel. 873-5247).

11. Tips for Senior Citizens

Travelers over the age of 65—in many cases 60, sometimes even 55—may qualify for discounts not available to the younger adult traveler. Some hotels offer rates 10% to 20% less than the officially quoted rate; inquire at the time you make reservations. Public transportation systems and many privately owned attractions give seniors discounts of up to half the regular adult fare or admission price. Get in the habit of asking for your discount.

Vancouver has a program that assists senior citizens with transportation needs (tel. 873-5247).

If you are retired and are not already a member of the American Association of Retired Persons, consider joining. The AARP card is valuable throughout North America in your search for travel bargains.

12. Tips for Single Travelers

Traveling alone in Vancouver or Victoria won't present any more difficulties than in any U.S. city. In many cases, there will be fewer problems. Both cities are safe and clean, with low crime rates and modern transportation systems.

Young budget travelers know that the best places to meet others of similar values are youth hostels and universities. If you're a bit older and more sophisticated, you'll find it easy to start a conversation in the cafés of Vancouver's Robsonstrasse and the tearooms near Victoria's Inner Harbour.

Organized tours are a wonderful place to meet fellow singles looking for no-strings-attached companionship while sight-seeing and dining.

---

13. Tips for Families

Children often get discounts that adults, even seniors, never dream of. For instance, many hotels allow children to stay free with their parents in the same room. The upper age limit of what defines a "child" may vary from 12 to 18, so be sure to check in advance.

Youngsters are almost always entitled to discounts on public transportation and admission to attractions. Though every entrance requirement is different, you'll often find that kids 5 and under are free, those elementary-school age are half-price, and older students (through high school) get significant discounts.

You should also keep your eyes open for family rates at various attractions. These allow the whole clan admission for little more than the tab for just mom and dad.

If you happen to be in the area in May, don't miss the **Vancouver Children's Festival** at Vanier Park: it's the biggest performing-arts celebration for and by kids in North America. Other not-to-be-missed Vancouver events are the **Pacific National Exhibition** in late August and the **Children's Winterfest** over the two weeks surrounding Christmas. French-speaking children enjoy **La Fête Colombienne des Enfants** at Crescent Beach, near White Rock just north of the U.S. border, in late May and early June.

Parents know all too well that whereas it's hard to take the young ones into a classy restaurant, it may be unpleasant to take them into a "greasy spoon." Have no fear: Both Vancouver and Victoria have a wide range of family-oriented restaurants. I've included several in Chapter VI, "Vancouver Dining."

Every family planning a vacation in southwestern British Columbia should obtain a copy of *Kids! Kids! Kids! in Vancouver*. It's available by mail from the publisher, Douglas & McIntyre, 1615 Venables St., Vancouver, BC V5L 2H1, for $6.99 (U.S. $6.08) plus shipping and handling. First published in 1978, and frequently revised and expanded since, this book by teacher-broadcaster Daniel Wood includes over 1,000 ideas for places to go and things to do in Vancouver and the Lower Mainland. A companion volume, *Kids! Kids! Kids! and Vancouver Island,* includes Victoria.

GETTING THERE

Getting to Canada's southwestern corner is no longer the arduous journey it was in the days of George Vancouver, Alexander Mackenzie, and Simon Fraser. Many West Coast Americans find it easier than traveling to New York; and Easterners can find themselves on the Pacific faster than they could be in Europe. Air, rail, bus, private car, and even ship are all viable means of transportation to Vancouver.

1. By Air

Vancouver International Airport is Canada's second busiest (next to Toronto's) with flights continually arriving from and departing for airports throughout North and South America, Europe, Asia, and the Pacific. Victoria has a small international airport for regional flights from Vancouver and Seattle, as well as a number of smaller cities and towns. Visitors flying to southwestern British Columbia from outside the region, therefore, always arrive in Vancouver first.

Special excursion fares may offer savings of up to 40% over regular economy fares. They may have stay requirements—you may have to travel both ways on a Monday through Thursday, and stay over a weekend, for instance—and tickets often must be purchased a minimum number of days (usually 30) before your trip. Consult with a travel agent or call the various individual airlines to ask about taking advantage of these special discount opportunities.

2. By Train

The national **VIA Rail Canada** service, sadly, has announced cutbacks, which will inevitably put as-yet-undetermined glitches in long-distance rail travel to Vancouver and Victoria from the east. The trans-Canada journey is one of the world's spectacular train trips—especially the portion between Calgary and Vancouver, where the track winds through the Canadian Rockies. Travelers from the American Midwest can use Amtrak to connect with VIA Rail in Winnipeg; from the East, in Montréal or Toronto. A ferry link continues rail travel on to Victoria from Vancouver.

Travelers can call VIA Rail for fares and reservations (tel. toll free 800/665-8630).

From the south, Amtrak has a direct San Diego–Los Angeles–San Francisco–Portland–Seattle–Vancouver route; connections to Victoria are made by boat in Seattle.

3. By Bus

This is the most budgetwise method of traveling virtually anywhere in North America. **Greyhound Bus Lines,** the only company that crosses the border into Canada from the United States, has such an extensive network that with perhaps only a couple of transfers, you'll find yourself on British Columbia's west coast.

Greyhound doesn't continue on to Victoria, but **Pacific Coach Lines** does, with transfers at the Vancouver bus depot at 150 Dunsmuir St. (tel. 662-3222).

Bus travel is usually cheaper and often faster than train, and its routes are more flexible if you want to stop off along the way. On the other hand, buses are more cramped, meals are at rest stops only, and inner-city stops are frequent. What's more, trying to sleep on overnight trips can be an exhausting experience.

Greyhound offers a variety of discount fares and unlimited-travel passes in addition to its regular fares. For fare and schedule information, call any Greyhound station in North America.

West Coast budget travelers might consider the Green Tortoise, a "youth hostel on wheels" with sleeping space on the bus. Twice-weekly trips go year round between Los Angeles, San Francisco, Portland, and Seattle, where transfers can be made to Greyhound (for Vancouver) or ferry (for Victoria). Fares ($79 L.A.–Seattle) are paid in cash to the driver. Contact Green Tortoise at P.O. Box 24459, San Francisco, CA 94124 (tel. toll free 800/227-4766).

4. By Car

There are two principal routes to Vancouver. One, from the south, is via U.S. Interstate 5 through Seattle; it becomes Route 99 as soon as it crosses the British Columbia border. The second, from the east, is Trans-Canada Highway 1.

To reach Victoria by car is somewhat more complicated, simply because you must put your car on a ferry. Direct sea runs to Victoria originate in Seattle (via I-5) and Port Angeles, Washington (via U.S. 101); and car-ferry connections to Vancouver Island (and thus by road to Victoria) begin in Anacortes, Washington (via I-5), and Tsawwassen and Horseshoe Bay, British Columbia (both via Route 99).

---

5. By Ship

It's possible to take a cruise ship from California to Vancouver or Victoria, but only during the summer season. The Cunard, Princess, Royal Viking, and Sitmar lines sail from San Francisco to Alaska with stopovers in either or both cities to load new passengers. Several other cruise lines begin the Alaska run at Canada Place in Vancouver. Consult *Frommer's Alaska,* by this same author, for details.

Several daily year-round services connect cities in the state of Washington with Victoria and Vancouver Island. **Washington State Ferries** (tel. 604/464-6400) makes a run twice daily in summer, once in winter, between Anacortes, Wash., and Sidney, north of Victoria, via the San Juan Islands. **Black Ball Transport** (tel. 206/457-4491) runs between Port Angeles, Wash., and Victoria. Two private lines—**Clipper Navigation** (tel. toll free 800/888-2535) and the **B.C. Stena Line** (tel. 604/288-7397)—have daily direct service from Seattle to Victoria's Inner Harbour. Within British Columbia, B.C. Ferries (tel. 604/386-3431) have several routes from the mainland to towns on Vancouver Island. Details on all routes are in Chapter XI, "Getting to Know Victoria."

GETTING TO KNOW VANCOUVER

1. ORIENTATION

2. GETTING AROUND

3. VANCOUVER FAST FACTS

Welcome to Vancouver! The journey is over, and you're ready to explore. But you feel a little lost, and wouldn't mind a helping hand to show you the ins and outs of the city.

That's what this chapter is designed to do. First I'll tell you how to get into town and find things once you're there. Then I'll give you the scoop on getting around the city by public or private transportation. Finally, I've presented what we call the Fast Facts of the place—a miscellany of essential facts that you might have been afraid to ask about, but that might play a big part in how much you enjoy your stay.

1. Orientation

ARRIVING

Located just 19 miles north of the U.S. border, Vancouver is readily accessible by air, train or road.

By Air

More than 7 million air passengers pass through **Vancouver International Airport** each year, arriving from (or heading for) over 250 destinations in 40 countries aboard some 20 major carriers. Among them are Air Canada, Air New Zealand, British Air, Cathay Pacific, CP Air, Continental, Japan Air Lines, KLM Royal Dutch, Lufthansa, Qantas, and United.

The airport is located 8 miles south of downtown Vancouver on Sea Island, in the Fraser River delta adjacent to suburban Richmond.

An $18 million program is underway to improve its facilities at its two terminals. The Main Terminal building serves incoming and

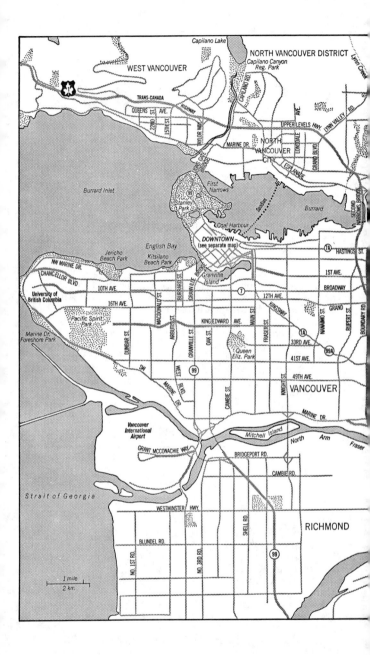

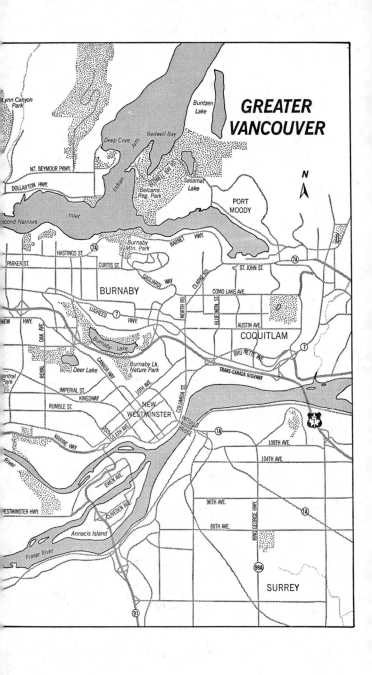

outgoing foreign and domestic flights. The South Terminal is the base for smaller scheduled or charter airlines serving British Columbia, including Air B.C., Air Caledonia, Aquila Air Taxi, Burrard Air, Bute Air, Chilliwack Aviation, Harbour Air, Pacific Rim Airlines, Waglisla Air, and Wilderness Airlines.

The international arrivals lounge is on Level 1 of the Main Terminal; the domestic arrivals lounge is on Level 2. The ticket and check-in area is on Level 3; Transport Canada administrative offices are on Level 4. Within the terminal building, travelers will find restaurants and cocktail bars, bookstores and newsstands, florists and chocolate shops, duty-free shops, and a seafood specialty shop. Services include banks and currency exchange, a post office, a barbershop, hotel reservation telephones, and public phones. Transport Canada information counters on Levels 1 and 3 (tel. 276-6101) are staffed daily from 6:30am to 3am. Tourism B.C. also staffs an information desk (tel. 273-1648).

There's parking at the airport for more than 3,600 vehicles, one-third of them in a long-term lot. The lots close only between 1 and 5am. Call 276-6106 for parking information and charges.

In most instances, clearing **Customs** at Vancouver Airport is a breeze for U.S. citizens and residents. These are the basic regulations:

Each American resident entering Canada for a visit of at least 24 hours may import duty free for consumption in Canada: 40 ounces (1.1 liter) of liquor or 24 cans or bottles of beer; one carton of (200) cigarettes; 50 cigars; 2.2 pounds (1kg) of pipe tobacco; and perfume. (You must be 16 years old to purchase tobacco. Remember, too, that although the drinking age in British Columbia is 19, you can't buy alcoholic beverages in Washington state if you're under 21). Gifts to be left in Canada must not exceed a total value of $400 (Cdn.). Canadian residents returning to Canada after a 48-hour absence have the same limits on liquor, tobacco, and perfume, but their purchases must have a total value of $100 or less. Once a year, they may also import $300 of merchandise after a seven-day absence.

You can bring in *almost* anything you want, but there are strict regulations regarding the import of plants, meats, and firearms. Hunters with valid licenses can bring in some gear, but handguns and fully automatic firearms are prohibited. If you want to fish you must show a nonresident license to import your tackle. Pet animals *may* be admitted with proper vaccination records, but you should inquire in advance about necessary procedures. Don't forget to talk to U.S. Customs as well, about bringing your pet back home!

Canada's Pacific Customs Office, responsible for British Columbia and the Yukon Territory to the north, is headquartered at 1001 W. Pender St., Vancouver, BC V6E 2M8 (tel. 604/666-3586). The airport bureau phone number is 604/276-5552.

Americans returning to the United States after being in Canada at least 48 hours and not more than once a month, may bring back duty free 1 liter of liquor, 100 cigars, one carton of cigarettes, and other items totaling not more than $400 (U.S.). Canadians going to the U.S. may bring in 1 liter of liquor, one carton of cigarettes, 50 cigars or 2 kilograms of tobacco, and other merchandise. Inquiries may go to the U.S. Customs Service, P.O. Box 7407, Washington,

DC 20229; in Vancouver, U.S. Customs can be reached by phoning 604/278-1825.

The airport is easily accessible by three bridges. Travelers **heading into Vancouver** will take the Arthur Laing Bridge, which feeds directly into Granville Street (Highway 99), a straight shot to downtown.

Airport Express bus service to downtown Vancouver is provided by **Perimeter Transportation** (tel. 273-9023). A bus leaves from Level 2 every 15 minutes daily from 6:15am to 10:30pm, then every 30 minutes until 12:30am. It leaves various downtown sites half-hourly between 5:35am and 10:55pm; check at your hotel for the nearest pickup point. Fare is $6.75 one way, $11.50 round-trip. The trip takes 30 minutes.

Public buses also stop at both terminals. Visitors seeking a $1.25 trip to downtown should board the no. 100 Port Coquitlam bus at the terminal, and request a transfer to the no. 20 or no. 17 bus at Marine Drive.

Courtesy buses serve hotels in the immediate airport vicinity, and a shuttle bus links the Main Terminal to the South Terminal.

Nearly 400 taxis serve the airport. Typical fare to downtown Vancouver is $17.

AirLimo (tel. 273-1331), the city's only flat-rate limousine service, operates between the airport and downtown Vancouver with one-way fares of $26—per limo, not per person. It operates 24 hours a day and accepts major credit cards.

Numerous auto rental firms have desks at the airport with vehicles ready for drivers. They include **Avis** (tel. 273-4577), **Budget** (tel. 278-3994), **Dollar** (tel. 278-2528), **Dominion** (tel. 278-7196), **Hertz** (tel. 278-4001), and **Tilden** (tel. 273-3121). It's best to make reservations well ahead of time, especially during busy periods.

By Train

The main Vancouver railway station is at 1150 Station St. (tel. 669-3050), just south of Chinatown and adjacent to the old Expo 86 site near Main Street and Terminal Avenue. It's an ideal location for getting to downtown—just walk off the rail quay and a short block to SkyTrain's Main Station and zip two stops to the Granville Station (or four stops to the Waterfront Station).

By Bus

The bus terminal for both **Greyhound Bus Lines** and **Pacific Coach Lines** is at 150 Dunsmuir St. (tel. 662-3222), near B.C. Place Stadium. Downtown hotels are easy walking distance from here; and SkyTrain's Stadium Station is adjacent.

Bus transfer to Vancouver from Seattle-Tacoma International Airport is available through **Quick Coach Lines** (tel. 604/591-3571). The bus makes stops at the Delta Airport Inn in Richmond, at Vancouver airport, and the Sandman Inn, 180 W. Georgia St., in downtown Vancouver. The 3-hour trip costs $32 one way, $60 round-trip.

By Car

If you're driving, you'll probably be entering the city by one of two routes.

Highway 99 from the Washington border passes under the South Arm of the Fraser River through the George Massey Tunnel, then goes over the North Arm on the Oak Street Bridge—by which time it's no longer a freeway, but a busy city street. To find a bridge across False Street into downtown, you'll have to get off Oak Street. Either turn west to Granville Street (preferred) or east to Cambie Street, then turn north again. Both routes lead directly into the downtown core.

Trans-Canada Highway 1 remains a limited-access freeway all the way into Vancouver's eastern boundary. You'll be routed straight onto Cassiar Street. Take a left at Hastings Street (the first light), adjacent to the Pacific National Exhibition grounds. Follow Hastings (Highway 7A) about 4 miles into the heart of downtown. (If you stay on Cassiar and cross the Second Narrows Bridge into North Vancouver, you'll be on the most direct route to Whistler.)

Canada accepts all valid U.S. driver's licenses, and vice versa. Proof of insurance is required in the event of an accident (see "Insurance" in Chapter II). Make sure you have your vehicle registration with you. Seat belts are mandatory in British Columbia.

By Ship

Vancouver's cruise-ship terminal (tel. 666-3226) is at Canada Place, the multi-sailed architectural wonder jutting into Burrard Inlet. Two hundred sailings (up to four at once) arrive and depart from here annually between May and October. Buses and taxis greet arrivals, but it's just a short walk from Canada Place to the central business district.

B.C. Ferries (tel. 669-1211) arrivals from Vancouver Island land either at Tsawwassen (from Sidney) or Horseshoe Bay (from Nanaimo). Highway 17 from Tsawwassen joins Highway 99 just before the Massey Tunnel; the driving instructions given above take over at that point. From Horseshoe Bay, Highways 1 and 99 head back toward North Vancouver, with connections to downtown Vancouver on Highway 99 across the Lion's Gate Bridge.

INFORMATION

The **Vancouver Travel InfoCentre,** Pavilion Plaza, 4 Bentall Centre, 1055 Dunsmuir St. near Burrard Street (P.O. Box 49296), Vancouver, BC V7X 1L3 (tel. 683-2000, reservation line 683-2772), is your single best source of tourist information. Operated in the heart of the business and shopping districts by Tourism Vancouver, it has a large staff to handle any and all tourist inquiries, and also sells bus passes and tickets to sports and entertainment events. There's even a currency exchange outlet. Open daily from 8:30am to 5:30pm, May 1 through Labor Day; Monday to Saturday from 9am to 5pm the rest of the year.

Another InfoCentre is open during the summer season only outside Eaton's department store at Georgia and Granville streets, Saturday to Wednesday from 9:30am to 5:30pm, Thursday and Friday (shopping nights) from 9:30am to 9pm.

Tourism B.C. has information centers at three locations outside of the Vancouver city limits—in Richmond on Highway 99 just

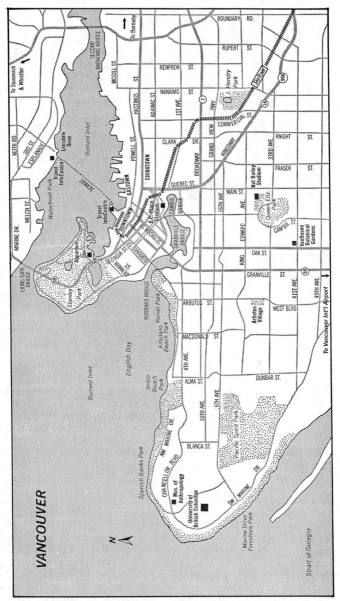

north of the Massey Tunnel, open daily year round; in White Rock at 1224 King George Highway, open daily in summer, weekdays in winter; and in North Vancouver at 131 E. Second St. near Lonsdale Quay, open daily May to September only.

CITY LAYOUT

Central Vancouver extends like a tongue into Burrard Inlet. Defined on three sides by water, the peninsula is crowned by stunning Stanley Park, which takes up its seaward half. Its southern portion, in direct contrast to the park's green serenity, is the most intensively built-up area in North America north of San Francisco and west of Chicago. Beyond this downtown core, the city sprawls for many miles east to the city of Burnaby, south to the Fraser River, and west to the Strait of Georgia.

To get your bearings, it may be helpful to start at Robson Square, the focal point of downtown. This three-block complex of terraces, gardens, waterfalls, restaurants, exhibition halls, skating rink, theaters, and government buildings is an ideal place to orient yourself.

If you stand on the square's top terrace and look toward the Vancouver Art Gallery, built in the early 20th century as a courthouse, you are facing west. (It's actually northwest, but everyone thinks of it as west, due to the diagonal grid layout of the downtown streets.) This is the direction the sun sets, the direction of the Strait of Georgia and Vancouver Island, Stanley Park, English Bay, and the West End.

North across the Burrard Inlet are suburban West and North Vancouver, reached by the Lion's Gate and Second Narrows bridges. Behind them, farther north, is the North Shore Range, among whose peaks are Grouse Mountain and two other developed ski areas.

East are B.C. Place Stadium, Chinatown, and Exhibition Park, and beyond them, the Trans-Canada Highway, traversing the country from coast to coast.

South lies False Creek, spanned by three bridges. Within the narrow inlet, beneath the Granville Bridge, is Granville Island. Vanier Park, location of the Vancouver Museum and other important sights, is at the inlet's mouth. The spacious campus of the University of British Columbia is about 4 miles west. The North Arm of the Fraser River, demarcating Vancouver's southern boundary, is 5 miles south, and beyond that is Vancouver International Airport (and, eventually, the U.S. border). In between lies most of residential Vancouver.

Main Arteries and Streets

Downtown Vancouver is laid out on a grid, with streets running north-south (from Burrard Inlet to False Creek) and east-west (from Chinatown to Stanley Park). From your perch in Robson Square, you are on Robson Street, the city's number-one shopping and dining strip. (In fact, the stretch west of you for five or six blocks is called Robsonstrasse, a label no doubt bestowed for its European appeal.) It runs all the way from B.C. Place Stadium to Stanley Park, and also marks the approximate southern border of the central business district, which extends north about four blocks to West Hastings Street, west about two blocks to Burrard Street, and east about two blocks to Seymour Street.

Georgia Street, which parallels Robson one long block to the north, leads directly into Stanley Park and the Lion's Gate Bridge on the west, and across a viaduct to Main Street on the east. Many upscale hotels and stores, as well as the post office and bus station, are on or adjacent to this street. Two and three blocks farther north, Pender and Hastings streets extend east through Chinatown; Hastings skirts the southern edge of the historic Gastown district and continues all the way east to the Trans-Canada Highway and well into Burnaby.

The most important north-south streets are Burrard, which connects at its south end with the Burrard Bridge; Howe, one-way southbound onto the Granville Bridge; and Seymour, one-way northbound off that same bridge. Granville Street, which runs between them, is a pedestrian mall (with bus and taxi access only) for several blocks of its length. The SkyTrain terminal, SeaBus terminal, and Canada Place are at its north end.

Across the Granville Bridge, Granville Street becomes Highway 99 to the airport; at 70th Avenue, Route 99 staggers east to Oak Street for its run to the border. Broadway, which intersects both Granville and Oak about six blocks south of the Granville Bridge, is a major east west highway (Route 7) that becomes the Lougheed Highway as it enters Burnaby. Main Street, the north-south artery through Chinatown, turns to the southeast as it crosses Broadway and becomes Kingsway, Vancouver's major cheap-motel strip; it leads to New Westminster.

Neighborhoods

The **West End**—that section of downtown west of Thurlow Street, as far as Stanley Park—is said to have the highest population density of any urban area in North America except Manhattan. It tends to be upscale and sophisticated. **Old Gastown,** at the southeast fringe of downtown, was Vancouver's first urban renewal project in the sixties and seventies; today it retains a bohemian ambience. Vancouver **Chinatown** is the second largest in North America; focused around the intersection of Main and East Pender streets, it even has its own cultural center. The Punjabi Market, built along Main Street between 49th and 51st avenues, is the primary shopping area for the **East Indian** community. **Little Italy** runs along Commercial Street near Broadway; the largest concentration of **Greek** Canadians is also on Broadway, but near UBC around McDonald Street. **Kerrisdale,** around 41st Avenue and West Boulevard (west of Granville), is a quaint and charming community without a particular ethnic identification. **Shaughnessy,** between Arbutus and Cambie streets, 16th and 33rd avenues, is an elegant older neighborhood of posh mansions on tree-lined streets.

Finding an Address

Downtown, numbering on north-south streets starts at Powell Street (or, for all practical purposes, Burrard Inlet); on east-west streets at Carrall Street. In fact, little Carrall Street (and, south of False Creek, Ontario Street) is the byway according to which streets are designated "east" or "west." Powell and Dundas streets make the line between "north" and "south." South of False Creek, it's easy to get around because all of the east-west streets are numbered

—except Broadway (9th Avenue) and King Edward Avenue (25th Avenue).

Maps
Tourist InfoCentres give away free maps, showing downtown in detail and main routes through the rest of the city. If you need a better map—and it's certainly helpful for any stay longer than a few days—check bookstores or service stations.

---

2. Getting Around

BY PUBLIC TRANSPORTATION
Vancouver Regional Transit System (BC Transit) operates virtually around the clock, with regular service on the busiest routes from 5am to 2am, and late-night "Owl" service on several downtown-suburban routes until 4:20am. The system covers more than 1,500 square miles of the Lower Mainland. Information is available by calling 261-5100 between 6:30am and 11:30pm. Schedules are widely available, including at InfoCentres.

The system includes SkyTrain, SeaBus, and the well-established fleet of buses and trolleys.

The pride of the system is **SkyTrain**, a fully computerized, magnetically propelled train that runs 16 miles (26km) from downtown to Surrey via Burnaby and New Westminster. It takes 32 minutes to cover the 17 stations, 13 of which are elevated; the four downtown stations are underground. A new leg will extend to Coquitlam; another line to Richmond is in the planning stages.

SeaBus crosses the Burrard Inlet from Waterfront Station (SkyTrain's terminus) to Lonsdale Quay in North Vancouver. The S.S. *Beaver* and S.S. *Otter* carry more than 400,000 passengers a year; neither has ever been stopped by weather. Boats leave Monday through Friday every 15 minutes from 6:15am to 7:15pm, then half-hourly until 1am; Saturday half-hourly 6:30am until 10:15am, then every 15 minutes until 7:15pm, then half-hourly until 1am; Sunday and holidays half-hourly 8:30am until 11:30pm.

Among the most popular **bus** routes is the hourly "Around the Park" service (no. 52) through Stanley Park from late April to late October. Other buses to keep in mind: no. 1 (Gastown–English Bay loop), no. 3 and 8 (English Bay/Downtown–Marine Drive), no. 4 and 10 (UBC–Exhibition Park via Downtown), no. 50 (Gastown–Broadway/False Creek), no. 51 (Granville Island), no. 100 (Port Coquitlam–Vancouver Airport via Marine Drive; from downtown, transfer from no. 20 or 17), no. 120 (Burnaby–New Westminster), no. 246 (North Vancouver), no. 250 (West Vancouver–Horseshoe Bay), no. 406 (Richmond–Steveston), no. 601 (Tsawwassen–Vancouver Island ferry). Many routes to Surrey, Langley, and other communities begin at the New Westminster SkyTrain station.

Fares are the same for train, boat, or bus. You can travel within

the City of Vancouver any time of day or night for the same $1.25
fare (65¢ ages 5 to 13 and 65 and over). Books of 10 "FareSaver"
tickets cost $11.25.

Visitors can buy a DayPass, good for one day's unlimited travel
on buses, SeaBus, and SkyTrain, after 9:30am Monday through Friday or all day Saturday, Sunday, and holidays. Priced at $3.50 for
adults, $1.75 for ages 5 to 13 and 65 and over, it may be purchased
in advance or on the day of use. Tickets and passes are sold at
InfoCentres, convenience stores, drugstores, credit unions, and
other outlets with a "FareDealer" symbol in the window.

During rush hours (Monday to Friday before 9:30am and from
3 to 6:30pm), fares climb to $1.75 (90¢ ages 5 to 13 and 65 and
over) for travel from Vancouver to North Vancouver, West Vancouver, Richmond, Burnaby, or New Westminster, and to $2.50
($1.25 ages 5 to 13 and 65 and over) to Delta, Surrey, Coquitlam,
and points beyond.

Bus fares must be paid in exact change (no bills accepted).
Single-fare tickets are sold at machines in SeaBus terminals and
SkyTrain stations. Transfers, issued on request when you board a
bus, are valid for 90 minutes for travel in one direction only.

BY TAXI

Taxi fares are reasonable unless you're traveling in the wee
hours, when you'll pay drivers double time. Within downtown, you
can expect to travel for under $3, except during rush-hour traffic.
Typical fare to the airport, 8 miles distant, is $17. It's appropriate to
suggest the driver "keep the change" as a tip.

It may be hard to find a taxi to hail anywhere but downtown;
your best bet is to call for pickup. Taxi companies include **Black Top**
(tel. 681-2181), **Checker Taxi** (tel. 681-3535), and **MacLure's** (tel.
731-9211).

BY CAR

The convenience of having a car at one's disposal is a luxury
one does not dismiss lightly. Although rush-hour traffic can be
heavy in Vancouver and gas expensive, and although the city has its
share of inattentive drivers, it's easy to find your way around and you
may find it worth a little aggravation not to be dependent on the
routes and schedules of public transportation.

A great many visitors drive to Vancouver. Those who don't can
rent a vehicle from one of the following firms: **ABC,** 255 W. Broadway (tel. 873-6622); **Avis,** 757 Hornby St. (tel. 682-1621);
Budget, 450 W. Georgia St. (tel. 685-0536) and 1225 Robson St.
(tel. 685-8403); **Hertz,** 666 Seymour St. (tel. 688-2411); **Rent-a-
Wreck,** 225 Kingsway (tel. 876-7155); **Thrifty,** 1400 Robson St.
(tel. 688-2207) or **Tilden,** 1140 Alberni St. (tel. 685-6111). For
long-term travelers, there's also **Canada Camper R.V. Rentals,**
1080 Millcarch St., Mitchell Island, Richmond (tel. 327-3003).
Seasonal motorcycle and moped rentals can be had at **Scooter
Shooter Rentals,** 29 Alexander St., in Gastown (tel. 687-2668).

All major downtown hotels have parking lots for guests, with varying daily charges. There is parking at Robson Square (enter at Smythe and Howe streets), the Pacific Centre (Howe and Dunsmuir), and The Bay (Richards near Dunsmuir). You'll find parking lots at Thurlow and Georgia streets, Thurlow and Alberni, and Robson and Seymour. Metered street parking is in high demand downtown, and it is strictly enforced. (This is why you should carry a pocketful of Canadian coins.) Unmetered parking on side streets may be a long trek from where you're headed. Read signs carefully: If you park in a designated rush-hour lane, expect to be towed.

Driving rules in British Columbia are very similar to those in the United States. (Canadians gave up driving on the left side of the street early in the 20th century.) The biggest difference is that you'll have to deal with the metric system: Speeds and distances are in kilometers and gas is sold by the liter. It is legal to turn right on a red light after you've come to a full stop. Seat belts are mandatory; children under five must be in kids' car seats; helmets are compulsory for motorcyclists.

Members of the American Automobile Association (AAA) can get assistance from the **B.C. Automobile Association** at 999 W. Broadway, Vancouver (tel. 604/732-3911). The association's special road service number is 293-2222.

ON FOOT

I'm a strong advocate of walking whenever possible. Not only do you get exercise; you also see a lot more, experience the ambience of a place, and orient yourself much more quickly. In dry weather, Vancouver is a good walking city, with much scenic beauty and many points of interest. And there could be few excursions more pleasant than a brisk early-morning stroll around Stanley Park. Don't worry: It's completely safe. No muggers.

BY BICYCLE

Even though bike paths are limited in number, cycling is extremely popular in Vancouver. The 5½-mile paved seawall path around Stanley Park and the circuit around the University of British Columbia are two favored recreational excursions, but even the busiest city streets can be easily negotiated by cautious riders. Riding on sidewalks is illegal.

Bicycles can be rented in many locations, including **Bayshore/ West Point Cycles,** 1876 W. Georgia St. (tel. 688-2453); **Reckless Rider Cyclery,** 1840 Fir St. (tel. 736-7325); **Robson Cycles,** 1463 Robson St. (tel. 687-2777); **Sports Rent,** 2560 Arbutus St. (tel. 733-1605); and **Stanley Park Rentals,** 676 Chilco St. (tel. 681-5581). Ask for "The Vancouver Bicycle Map," which points out potential trouble spots like busy streets, dangerous intersections, and steep hills to help riders select their routes.

Bicycles are allowed on the SeaBus on weekends and holidays, but require payment of an extra fare. Bicycles are not allowed in Route 99's George Massey Tunnel beneath the South Arm of the Fraser River, but a shuttle service operates from May to September (tel. 277-2115 for times and details). For other information, call the Bicycling Association of B.C.'s hotline (tel. 731-7433).

---

3. Vancouver Fast Facts

AIRPORT: Vancouver International Airport, 8 miles south of the city center, is the second busiest in Canada. See "Arriving," above in this chapter, for details.

AREA CODE: 604.

AUTO RENTALS: Numerous car-rental agencies serve Vancouver, both at the airport and downtown. See "Arriving" and "Getting Around," above in this chapter, for details.

BABY-SITTERS: Major hotels usually can arrange baby-sitting service on short notice, though a day's advance is preferred. **Ruby's Babysitting Bureau** (tel. 433-7621) will send a baby-sitter to you with 24 hours' notice.

BANKS: Most banks are open 10am to 3pm Monday to Friday. Some may open on Saturday too.

BUSES: City buses will take you virtually anywhere you want to go. Call 261-5100 for information. The bus depot for Greyhound and other long-distance service is at 150 Dunsmuir St., at the corner of Beatty Street near B.C. Place Stadium. See "Arriving" and "Getting Around," above in this chapter, for details.

BUSINESS HOURS: Typical business hours are 8am to 5pm Monday to Friday, with lunch break from noon to 1pm.

BUSINESS SERVICES: Most major hotels offer secretarial, fax, and other services for a fee.

CLIMATE: Vancouver's climate is mild and rainy much of the year, with average highs of 64°F (17.5°C) in July and average lows of 36°F (2.5°C) in January. The highest temperature ever recorded was 89°F (31°C), the lowest, 0°F (−18°C). Most of the prolific rainfall occurs during the winter months. See Chapter II, "Before You Leave Home" for details. For special information, contact the **Van-**

couver **Weather Station,** 4160 Cowley Crescent, Vancouver, BC
V7B 1B8 (tel. 604/276-5409).

CONSULATES: The U.S. consulate is at 1075 W. Georgia St.
(tel. 685-4311). Thirty-five other countries, mainly Pacific Rim and
European nations, have consulates in Vancouver as well. Check the
Yellow Pages for a listing.

CURRENCY: As this was being written, $1 U.S. was equal to
$1.15 Canadian; inversely, 87¢ U.S. equalled $1 Canadian.
    American dollars are widely accepted as payment at most ho-
tels, restaurants, and shops throughout the Vancouver area. But not
every outlet gives the same exchange rate as banks—some offer better, others worse. It's been my experience that banks at the border
charge a higher commission than banks in Vancouver itself for
changing American dollars into Canadian. I've also found exchange
rates to be 1 or 2¢ better per dollar at small exchange banks than at
major banks.
    Typically, a Canadian bank sells notes for a couple of percent
less than the declared exchange value (e.g., $1.15 Cdn. to $1 U.S. at
this writing) and buys at a couple of percent higher (e.g., $1.17).
This, of course, is where it makes its money in the deal. Merchants
may offer an exchange rate of anywhere from 10% to 20%.
    International Securities Exchange has three downtown offices
for exchange at 1036 Robson St. near Burrard (683-4686), 1169
Robson St. near Bute (tel. 683-9666), and 734 Granville St. near
Georgia (tel. 683-4879).
    See Chapter II, "Before You Leave Home," for more informa-
tion.

DENTIST: Some major hotels have a dentist on call. Otherwise,
you can get referrals from the College of Dental Surgeons of B.C.
(tel. 736-3621) Monday to Friday between 8am and 4pm.

DOCTOR: Hotels typically have a doctor on call. The College of
Physicians and Surgeons of B.C. (tel. 733-7758) will provide the
names of three doctors if you call Monday to Friday between 8am
and 4pm.

DOCUMENTS REQUIRED: See Chapter II, "Before You Leave
Home," for details.

DRUGSTORES: The **Shopper's Drug Mart,** 1125 Davie St. (tel.
685-6445) is open from 9am to midnight Monday to Saturday,
9am to 9pm Sunday. It has the longest hours of any downtown
pharmacy. In the suburbs, several Safeway stores have late-night
pharmacies.

ELECTRICITY: As in the U.S., 110 volts, alternating current.

EMERGENCIES: Dial 911 for fire, police, ambulance, and poison control.

EYEGLASSES: Try **London Drugs,** 1187 Robson St. (tel. 669-7374) and in the Pacific Centre (tel. 685-5292); or **Tru-Valu Optical,** 835 W. Broadway (tel. 873-3941). If you wear contact lenses, contact **Image Contact Lens Centre** at 815 W. Hastings St. (tel. 681-9488) or 1189 Robson St. (tel. 685-3937).

HAIRDRESSERS: There's no shortage of these in this style-conscious city. Many major hotels have their own salons, and there are others along Robsonstrasse and in shopping arcades.

HOLIDAYS: See listing in Chapter II, "Before You Leave Home."

HOSPITALS: **St. Paul's Hospital** is right downtown at 1081 Burrard St. (tel. 682-2344). **Vancouver General Hospital** is just south of Broadway at 855 W. 12th Ave. (tel. 875-4411). Other major hospitals include **Shaughnessy Hospital,** 4500 Oak St. at 29th Avenue (tel. 875-2222); its neighbors, **Children's Hospital,** 4480 Oak St. (tel. 875-2345) and **Grace Hospital** (obstetrics), 4490 Oak St. (tel. 875-2424); and in North Vancouver, **Lions Gate Hospital,** 230 E. 13th St. (tel. 988-3131).

INFORMATION: See "Orientation," above in this chapter.

LANGUAGE: English and French are the official languages of Canada. In British Columbia, English is the predominant language.

LAUNDRY/DRY CLEANING: You'll get a better price than your hotel valet service by dropping your clothing off at **Scotty's One Hour Cleaners,** 834 Thurlow St. (tel. 685-7732). There are also numerous Laundromats around the city.

LIQUOR LAWS: You must be 19 years old to buy or drink alcoholic beverages in British Columbia. Spirits are sold only in government liquor stores; beer and wine can also be purchased from some specially licensed private stores and pubs.

LOST PROPERTY: Try the Vancouver Police property room

(tel. 665-2232) or, if you think you may have lost something on public transportation, B.C. Transit (tel. 682-7887).

MAIL: The main post office takes up a full city block at West Georgia and Homer streets. It's open Monday through Friday from 8am to 5:30pm and it has an excellent philatelic center for collectors. There are smaller post office counters in Eaton's and The Bay, Vancouver's two big downtown department stores; some drugstores—those with the Canada Post symbol in their windows—also offer basic services Monday through Saturday. Letters and postcards to the U.S. cost 45¢; within Canada, 39¢.

MAPS: You can get good city and regional maps from tourist information centers, bookshops, automobile clubs, service stations, and even hotel desks.

MONEY: Canadian dollars come in the same denominations as U.S. dollars, but they're easier to tell apart—they come in different colors. What's more, a $1 coin (called a "Loonie") is beginning to supplant the $1 bill. See "Currency," above in this chapter.

NEWSPAPERS: The *Vancouver Sun,* a broadsheet, is published afternoons and evenings, Monday through Saturday. *The Province,* a tabloid, appears Sunday through Friday mornings. Both are sold on newsstands and in many hotel lobbies. *The Georgia Straight,* a weekly entertainment paper, comes out on Thursday.

PHOTOGRAPHIC NEEDS: Your best bet may be **London Drugs,** 1187 Robson St. (tel. 669-7374), located in the Pacific Centre downtown (tel. 685-5292) and at numerous other locations in the Greater Vancouver area. Also: **Lens & Shutter Cameras,** 2912 W. Broadway (tel. 736-3461).

POLICE: Dial 911 in emergency; property crime can be reported at 665-3321.

RADIO AND TELEVISION: AM radio stations include 600 CHRW (classic rock), 690 CBU (classical, no commercials), 730 CKLG (top 40), 980 CKNW (talk and sports), 1130 CKWX (country), and 1320 CHQM (easy listening). FM stations include 96.1 CKO (news only), 99.3 CFOX (progressive rock), 102.0 CITR (alternative music), 102.7 CFRO (community radio), and 105.7 CBC (classical, no commercials).

Among television stations, CBUT (channel 2) and BCTV (channel 8) are Canadian network affiliates, and CKVU (channel 10) is independent. All three major American networks as well as the Public Broadcasting System are received from Seattle.

RELIGIOUS SERVICES: Downtown churches include **Christ Church Cathedral** (Anglican), 690 Burrard St. (tel. 682-3848); **First Baptist Church,** 969 Burrard St. (tel. 683-8441); **Holy Rosary Cathedral** (Catholic), 646 Richards St. (tel. 682-6774); **First Church of Christ Scientist,** 1160 W. Georgia St. (tel. 685-7544);

Central Presbyterian Church, 1155 Thurlow St. (tel. 683-1913); and **St. Andrew's Wesley United Church,** 1012 Nelson St. (tel. 683-4574).

Major non-Christian places of worship near downtown include the **Universal Buddhist Temple,** 525 E. 49th Ave. (tel. 325-6912); the **Akali Singh Sikh Temple,** 1890 Skeena St. (tel. 254-2117); the **Beth Israel Synagogue,** 4350 Oak St. (tel. 731-4161); and many others, including Hindu and Muslim.

RESTROOMS: Look in the same places you would in the U.S., including hotels, restaurants, shopping malls, and other public places.

SAFETY: Whenever you're traveling in an unfamiliar city or country, stay alert. Be aware of your immediate surroundings. Wear a moneybelt and don't sling your camera or purse over your shoulder; wear the strap diagonally across your body. This will minimize the possibility of your becoming a victim of crime. Every society has its criminals. It's your responsibility to be aware and alert even in the most heavily touristed areas.

SHOE REPAIRS: Try **Robson Shoe Renew,** 1108 Robson St., or a major department store.

TAXES: Hotel rooms are subject to a 10% provincial tax. The sales tax is 6% on other goods and services, with food, restaurant meals, and children's clothing exempted. Direct questions to the B.C. Consumer Taxation Branch (tel. 660-4500).

TAXIS: See "Getting Around," above in this chapter.

TELEPHONES: They work just like those south of the border, with local calls normally 25¢. Yes, your telephone credit card is good here. The area code for all of British Columbia is 604.

TIME: Pacific Standard Time—the same as Seattle, San Francisco, and Los Angeles. Daylight savings time is in effect from April to October.

TIPPING: It's appropriate to tip 15% for restaurant meals, 50¢ per bag for porters, and $1 a day for the housekeeper if you're staying more than a couple nights in your hotel. You may tell taxi drivers to "keep the change."

TRANSIT INFO: See "Getting Around," above in this chapter.

USEFUL TELEPHONE NUMBERS: RCMP Tourist Alert (urgent messages), 264-3111 . . . Distress Line Crisis Centre, 733-4111 . . . Rape Crisis Centre, 872-8212 . . . Victims of Violence, 576-8778 . . . Poison Control Centre, 682-5050 . . . SPCA animal emergency, 879-7343 . . . B.C. Highway Report, 277-0112.

WATER: You can drink tap water everywhere.

WEATHER: See "Climate," above, and "When to Go" in Chapter II. For current forecasts, call 273-8331 or 666-1087; for a marine forecast, dial 270-7411.

V

VANCOUVER ACCOMMODATIONS

1. VERY EXPENSIVE HOTELS
2. EXPENSIVE HOTELS
3. MODERATELY PRICED HOTELS
4. BUDGET ACCOMMODATIONS

Vancouver has a wide choice of fine accommodations in all price ranges. The average tourist will find the same high standards as in any Western city.

In this listing, I have organized accommodations first by price and then by the area of the city in which they're located. I have acknowledged four different price categories, according to summer rates for two persons: **very expensive** ($150 and up a night), **expensive** ($100 to $150), **moderate** ($50 to $100), and **budget** (under $50). Prices are quoted in Canadian dollars and do not include the 10% provincial sales tax.

The listed rates are the officially quoted, or "rack rates," and don't take into account any individual or group discounts. Even in the upper price brackets, there are many ways to pay much less. One hotel sales director (who will remain unidentified to protect his job) told me that wise travelers seek reduced rates wherever they stay. Ask for corporate rates, he said. If you don't work for a corporation, identify a big firm (a bank, for instance) and you'll save 20% to 35% off listed rack rates. Family emergencies warrant a medical rate. There are union rates and university rates. Travel-industry rates are 25% off in summer, half-price in winter. Weekend rates are often 50% lower than midweek business travelers' rates, especially in the low season. Speak up to save—if you don't ask the desk, they won't ask you!

Within price categories, accommodations are divided into the following areas of the city: West End, the area between Downtown and Stanley Park, west of Thurlow Street; East of Downtown, east of Main Street, a heavily residential area with a handful of commercial thoroughfares, such as Hastings Street (Route 7A), Kingsway (Route 1A/99A), and the Trans-Canada Highway (Route 1) through Burnaby; South of Downtown, the area extending from Main Street west of the University of British Columbia and south from False Creek to the Fraser River; the Airport, which includes establishments within easy shuttle distance of Vancouver International Airport, especially in the suburb of Richmond; North Shore, the twin suburbs of North Vancouver and West Vancouver, lying on the north shore of the Burrard Inlet; and Gastown/Chinatown, Gastown extending roughly from the waterfront to Pender Street east of Richard Street, Chinatown adjoining it to the east with its core along Hastings, Pender, and Keefer streets down Columbia, Main, and Gore.

Reservations are important at any time, but they are absolutely essential during the June-to-September summer season and other holiday periods. If you arrive without a reservation and have trouble finding a room, Tourism Vancouver (tel. 682-2222) will try to help —but you may have to settle for something several miles from downtown.

A possible solution when times are tight is to get in touch with a bed-and-breakfast agency. Each of the following tries to match visitors and hosts with similar interests:

A Home Away From Home Bed & Breakfast Agency, 1441 Howard Ave., Burnaby, BC V5B 3S2 (tel. 604/873-4888).

Born Free Bed & Breakfast of B.C., 4390 Frances St., Vancouver, BC V5C 2R3 (tel. 604/298-8815).

Canada-West Accommodations Bed & Breakfast Registry, P.O. Box 86607, North Vancouver, BC V7L 4L2 (tel. 604/987-9338).

Copes' Choice Bed & Breakfast Accommodations, 864 E. 14th St., North Vancouver, BC V7L 2P6 (tel. 604/987-8988 or 988-7264).

Old English Bed & Breakfast Registry, P.O. Box 86818, North Vancouver, BC V7L 4L3 (tel. 604/986-5069).

Town & Country Bed & Breakfast in B.C., P.O. Box 46544, Station G, Vancouver, BC V6R 4G6 (tel. 604/731-5942).

Vancouver Bed & Breakfast Ltd., 1685 Ingleton Ave., Burnaby, BC V5C 4L8 (tel. 604/291-6147).

WestWay Accommodation Registry, P.O. Box 48950, Bentall Centre, Vancouver, BC V7X 1A8 (tel. 604/273-8293).

All of the above are members of the **British Columbia Bed & Breakfast Association,** P.O. Box 593, 810 W. Broadway, Vancouver, BC V5Z 4E2, an umbrella agency formed at the request of Tourism British Columbia for promotion and quality control. Each member home is inspected with regard to cleanliness, comfort, courtesy, and service to ensure high standards.

Rates vary widely, but begin as low as $30 single, $40 double, and may range to about $100 for special suites. Indicate your preferred price range when making reservations. Fireplaces, Jacuzzi baths, and heated swimming pools may be available in the higher-price categories. Credit cards usually are accepted.

Note: In the listings below, items that are in boxes denote amenities that appear in every room. Amenities include the following:

A/C	air conditioning
FRIDGE	refrigerator in room
MINI-BAR	small refrigerator stocked with beverages and snacks
TEL	telephone
TV	television

---

1. Very Expensive Hotels

DOWNTOWN

- **Delta Place Hotel,** 645 Howe St., V6C 2Y9 (tel. 604/687-1122; toll free 800/268-1133; fax 604/689-7044). 191 rooms, 6 suites. A/C MINI-BAR TV TEL

This luxurious modern hotel is small enough to give individual service but large enough to provide every possible amenity. Formerly the Mandarin Hotel, it's in the midst of the downtown business and shopping district. Businesspersons love it, because *every* room has executive service with upscale amenities.

The first hint that your room is special is that it has a doorbell. Within, you'll find solid oak cabinets and furnishings, including a custom-built leather-topped desk and a TV hidden in an armoire and controlled (along with the lights) by a bedside console. There are three telephones, including one in the Italian marble bathroom, which has separate shower and oversize bathtub. Most rooms also have private balconies. Other touches include terry-cloth bathrobes, umbrellas, shoeshine service, and a free morning newspaper. There are no-smoking floors and rooms accessible to the disabled.

Dining/Entertainment: Le Café, on the second floor, is the fine dining room, with entrées reasonably priced from $9.95 to $17.95. The West Coast cuisine features local seafood and produce. It's also open for breakfast and lunch, and features a children's menu. The Clipper Lounge has a daily curry buffet and lunch entrées.

Services: 24-hour room service, concierge, valet cleaning.

Facilities: Indoor swimming pool, squash and racquetball courts, weight/exercise room, whirlpool, sauna (with TV), massage room, steam room, business center, and meeting/banquet space for 100.

RATES: May–Sept $184 single, $204 double, $135–$160 weekends; Oct–Apr $162 single, $182 double, $95 weekends; suites to $850. AE, CB, DC, ER, MC, V. Underground parking: $11. *SkyTrain:* Granville.

- **Four Seasons Hotel,** 791 W. Georgia St., V6C 2T4 (tel. 604/689-9333; toll free 800/332-3442 in U.S., 800/268-6282 in Canada; fax 604/684-4555). 364 rooms, 21 suites. A/C MINI-BAR TV TEL

From the Rolling Stones to Prime Minister Brian Mulroney, a wide range of visitors opt for this 28-story hotel. It's easy to miss its Howe Street entrance, but not the stunning greenhouselike atrium that connects it to the 300-store Pacific Centre shopping mall. Built

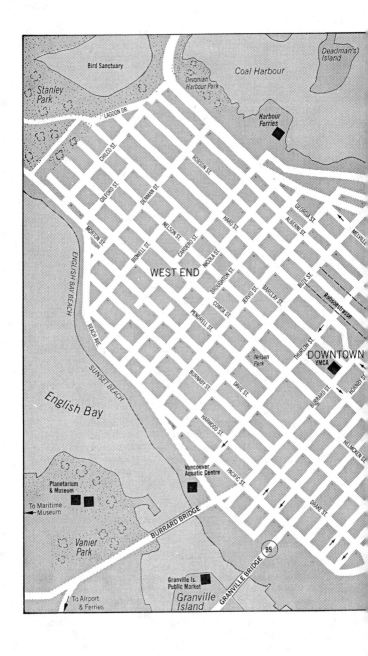

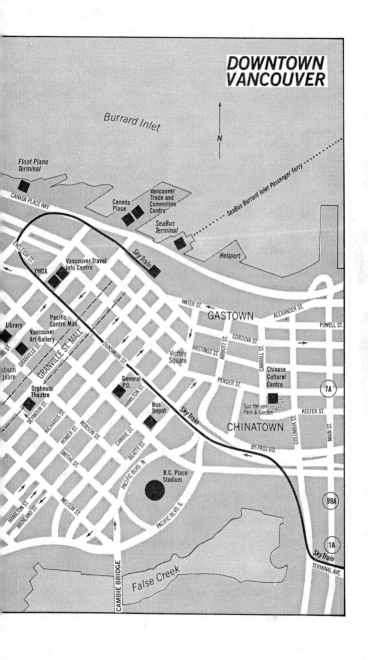

DOWNTOWN VANCOUVER

Burrard Inlet

N

Float Plane Terminal

CANADA PLACE WAY

Canada Place

Vancouver Trade and Convention Centre

SeaBus Terminal

SeaBus Burrard Inlet Passenger Ferry

Heliport

Sky Train

EVELEIGH ST.

YWCA

Vancouver Travel Info Centre

Library

Pacific Centre Mall

Vancouver Art Gallery

GRANVILLE ST.

GRANVILLE ST. MALL

DUNSMUIR ST.

WATER ST.

GASTOWN

ALEXANDER ST.

POWELL ST.

CORDOVA ST.

ABBOTT ST.

CARRALL ST.

HASTINGS ST.

Victory Square

Chinese Cultural Centre

obson Square

SEYMOUR ST.

Orpheum Theatre

General P.O.

HAMILTON ST.

PENDER ST.

COLUMBIA ST.

MAIN ST.

Sun Yat-sen Park & Garden

KEEFER ST.

7A

RICHARDS ST.

HOMER ST.

ROBSON ST.

CAMBIE ST.

BEATTY ST.

Bus Depot

Sky Train

CHINATOWN

BY-PASS RD.

SMITHE ST.

HAMILTON ST.

MAINLAND ST.

NELSON ST.

PACIFIC BLVD. N.

B.C. Place Stadium

PACIFIC BLVD. S.

99A

1A

Sky Train

TERMINAL AVE.

CAMBIE BRIDGE

False Creek

in 1976, it has a subtly Asian decor, starting with the lotus-seated Buddha that greets guests.

The rooms, scheduled for a $4.5 million renovation this year, continue the Asian theme in their art and bonsai plants. Rich wood furnishings include a glass-top desk and an armoire containing the remote-control television. Rooms have two phones, clock radios, hairdryers, terry-cloth bathrobes, and marble-topped vanities. Deluxe rooms have French doors, separating a king-size bedroom from the living area, and two baths. Half the rooms are no-smoking.

Dining/Entertainment: Chartwell, which has hosted such celebrities as Queen Elizabeth II, the late Malcolm Forbes, and Mick Jagger, is considered one of Canada's elite restaurants. The moderately priced Seasons Café, open early to late, extends to the atrium overlooking Pacific Centre. A $25 brunch is served Sunday around the fountain in the Garden Lounge; on Friday and Saturday nights, a dessert buffet is offered to patrons of the lounge's piano bar.

Services: 24-hour room service, concierge, limousine, laundry and valet service, and twice-daily housekeeping. Children get cookies and milk in the evening, room-service menus, and their own robes.

Facilities: Indoor/outdoor pool, fitness center, weight/exercise room, hot tub, whirlpool, saunas; tennis courts in new adjoining office tower. Banquet/meeting space for 600.

RATES: Year round $170–$215 single, $190–$235 double, $245–$665 suites. AE, CB, DC, ER, MC, V. Parking: $12. *SkyTrain:* Burrard.

• **Hotel Vancouver,** 900 W. Georgia St., V6C 2W6 (tel. 604/684-3131; toll free 800/828-7447 in U.S., 800/268-9411 most of Canada, 800/268-9420 Ontario and Québec; fax 604/662-1937). 464 rooms, 42 suites. A/C MINI-BAR TV TEL

The grande dame of the city's hospitality industry, the Hotel Vancouver has hosted royalty and celebrity since King George VI stayed here four days after the hotel opened in May 1939. The hotel's steeply pitched green copper roof is characteristic of a 16th-century French château; artisans from 10 countries spent 12 months carving its classical facades. The lobby, a page out of an Edwardian novel with its antique armchairs and sofas, is equally remarkable for its huge crystal chandeliers and marble pillars. No less than 166 tons of marble, of 25 different types, went into the interior design.

The spacious, soundproofed rooms have pastel color schemes and standard furnishings. Business-class rooms have colonial antique furnishings, separate check-in, working desks, and conference phones. The rosewood-paneled Entree Gold executive floor offers direct check-in with a concierge on the floor, a private lounge, and free local telephone calls. Both upgraded categories include breakfasts. No-smoking rooms and rooms for the disabled are available.

Dining/Entertainment: There's 15th-floor dining and dancing with a spectacular city view at the Roof Restaurant and Lounge. The highbrow Timber Club specializes in West Coast cuisine. Griffin's Bistro serves breakfast, lunch, tea, and dinner in a garden atmosphere. The Lobby Lounge offers a luncheon menu as well as piano music each evening.

Services: 24-hour room service, complimentary morning coffee and newspaper, twice-daily housekeeping, overnight pressing and shoeshine, valet laundry, baby-sitting, secretarial service.

Facilities: Indoor pool, health club with kinesiologist and masseuse, weight room, whirlpool, saunas, tanning bed. Banquet/meeting space for 1,500. Car rental, bank, beauty salon, barbershop, shoeshine stand, shopping arcade.

RATES: Nov–early Apr, $98–$120, business class $140–$175, executive class $175–$195 (all rates plus $20 for two people); early Apr–Oct, $30–$40 more. Suites priced to $1,520. AE, CB, DC, ER, MC, V. Parking: $9. *SkyTrain:* Burrard.

• **Hyatt Regency Vancouver,** 655 Burrard St., V6C 2R7 (tel. 604/687-6543; toll free 800/233-1234; fax 604/689-3707). 612 rooms, 34 suites. A/C MINI-BAR TV TEL

From the spacious street-level lobby to the huge view windows of the 34th floor meeting and banquet rooms, Vancouver's largest hotel is also one of its finest. And it's perfectly situated, adjoining the Royal Centre mall and movie complex.

Guest rooms, done in subtle shades of purple, show an Asian influence in furnishings and decor—lacquered tables, brass lamps, oversized closets, and baths. Many have security vaults. Corner rooms have balconies at no extra charge. Several floors of executive rooms and walnut-furnished suites offer a concierge and private lounge, complimentary breakfasts, and special amenities. No-smoking rooms are available.

Dining/Entertainment: Fish & Co. has, as you might guess, seafood specialties. It's recognized as one of the best in town for lunch, dinner . . . and its 85-foot-long Sunday-brunch buffet. The Café, open daily for all meals, has a salad and pasta bar. Weekday lunch buffets are also offered in the intimate Peacocks Lounge (seafood) and the lively Gallery Bar (roast beef). Both feature nightly piano music, preempted in the Gallery by big-screen sports.

Services: 24-hour room service, concierge, laundry and valet service, doctor and dentist on call, summer program for children. Staff members collectively speak 32 languages.

Facilities: Outdoor pool, health club, weight and exercise machines, saunas, access to racquetball and squash courts, business center, banquet/meeting space for 1,650.

RATES: Apr 16–Oct, $185–$210 single, $205–$230 double, $330–$650 suite, weekend discounts from $130 single; winter, $140–$170 single, $160–$190 double, weekend discounts from $85 single. AE, CB, DC, ER, MC, V. Parking: $7. *SkyTrain:* Burrard.

• **Le Meridien,** 845 Burrard St., V6Z 2K6 (tel. 604/682-5511; toll free 800/543-4300; fax 604/682-5513). 350 rooms, 50 suites. A/C MINI-BAR TV TEL

Classical elegance in the European style is the hallmark of this hotel owned by Air France. You'll feel as if you're walking into an 18th-century mansion. Rather than a vast lobby, you enter a serene series of rooms with marble floors and antique furnishings on oriental carpets, and chandelier-bedecked hallways hung with oil paintings. Soothing classical music provides the final touch.

The guest rooms are equally elegant, with silk bedspreads, TVs hidden in armoires, impressively large desks, and botanical prints on beige walls. Each bathroom has a telephone, marble-topped vanity, scale, hairdryer, and bathrobe. Each room also is stocked with an umbrella for Vancouver's rain. Six floors are reserved for nonsmokers, and rooms accessible to the disabled are available.

Next door is La Grande Résidence, with 162 suites for those who plan to stay in Vancouver at least 30 days. Hollywood production companies often make their home base here.

Dining/Entertainment: Restaurant Gerard is among the city's finest. Café Fleuri serves breakfast and lunch daily in an informal French provincial decor; the café also offers a popular Sunday brunch, and on Friday and Saturday evenings, a seafood buffet and Chocoholic Bar for dessert lovers. La Promenade lounge and Gerard Lounge offer light snacks and piano bars.

Services: 24-hour room service and concierge, twice-daily housekeeping, laundry/valet service with 24-hour pressing, shoeshine, baby-sitting.

Facilities: Glass-covered indoor pool, outdoor deck, weight/exercise room, tennis and squash courts, whirlpool, women's sauna, men's steam room, tanning, massage, hairstylist, business center, meeting/banquet space for 350, gift shop, florist, car rental.

RATES: Apr 16–Oct, $170–$225 single, $190–$245 double; winter, $130–$160 single, $150–$180 double. AE, CB, DC, ER, MC, V. Parking: $10. *SkyTrain:* Burrard.

- **New World Harbourside**, 1133 W. Hastings St., V6E 3T3 (tel. 604/689-9211; toll free 800/663-8882; fax 604/689-4358). 413 rooms, 19 suites. A/C TV TEL

The New World has an enviable location: It's in the heart of the financial district, but overlooks the waterfront. Guests enter a lower lobby lined with 18-foot ficus trees. A black granite staircase leads to the reception area and pillared upper lobby, where a multicolored carpet sets off an area of abstract artworks.

Two color schemes are at work in the guest rooms—warm rose on the north-facing harborfront rooms, cooler sage on the south-facing city-side rooms. All rooms are nicely furnished, with the added luxury of heated tile bathroom floors and hairdryers. Elegant Dynasty Floor rooms feature posher furniture, in-room check-in and check-out, and added amenities. No-smoking rooms are available. Harborfront rooms overlook a railroad yard scheduled to be transformed in the 1990s into a residential and business park.

Dining/Entertainment: The Dynasty is widely regarded as Vancouver's outstanding Chinese restaurant. It's hard to top the view from Vistas on the Bay, a 20th-floor revolving restaurant open for three meals daily. The Lobby Lounge serves breakfast and buffet lunch daily, with piano music evenings. The Channel Bar is packed at night with *karaoke* (Japanese-style sing-along) enthusiasts rocking to the pulse of its high-tech laser-disc sound system.

Services: Room service 6:30am–2am daily, valet laundry, and dry cleaning. Dynasty Floor guests get a Continental breakfast, tea service, newspaper, shoeshine, and turndown service.

Facilities: Indoor pool, weight/exercise room, sauna, meeting/banquet for 800, gift shop.

RATES: May–Oct, $125–$145 standard single (higher rates for views), $145–$165 superior single, $170–$190 deluxe single,

$15 more double, $275–$750 suite; Nov–Apr, $75–$90 standard, $85–$105 superior. AE, DC, ER, MC, V. Parking: $7. *Bus:* 19.

- **Pan-Pacific Hotel Vancouver,** 300–999 Canada Place, V6C 3B5 (tel. 604/662-8111, toll free 800/937-1515 U.S., 800/663-1515 Canada, fax 604/662-3815). 468 rooms, 39 suites. A/C MINI-BAR TV TEL

Apart from Vancouver's natural surroundings, the city's most distinctive landmark is Canada Place, its five soaring white teflon sails reminiscent of a giant vessel leaving port. It houses the Vancouver Trade & Convention Centre and the Alaska cruise ship terminal. Adjoining it is this $100 million hotel, the most expensive ever built in Canada. Guests ride an escalator to the fifth-floor lobby, an open eight-story atrium with its own fountain and 20-foot waterfall. Fine art on the maple walls complements the rose granite floor to complete a look of opulence.

All rooms are superior or deluxe, and all have a feeling of simple luxury. More than 70% have king-size beds. Decor shows an Asian influence. Look for beige tones, textured walls, and large marble bathrooms with telephones. Some suites have Jacuzzis, steam rooms, even baby grand pianos! There are three no-smoking floors and 13 rooms for the disabled.

Dining/Entertainment: The Five Sails offers seafood dinners, accompanied by terrific views across the Burrard Inlet to the mountains. The Suntory Restaurant is justly famous for Japanese cuisine. Cafe Pacifica offers Canadian specialties; it also has a Chinese dim sum bar and a Friday-night Italian buffet featuring the talents of Chef Enrico Balestra, a former opera tenor. The Cascades Lounge has luncheon buffets and a seasonal outdoor patio bar. The hotel has its own bakery and butcher.

Services: 24-hour room service, concierge, valet laundry.

Facilities: Outdoor pool, squash and racquetball courts, indoor track, whirlpool, sauna, tanning, massage, business center, hair salon, barber, shopping arcade, art galleries, florist, gift shop, exchange bank, car rental, meeting/banquet space for 500.

RATES: Mid-Apr to Oct, $169–$209 single, $189–$229 double, $300–$1,250 suite; Nov to mid-Apr, $119–$139 single, $139–$159 double, $200–$900 suite. Children under 18 free with parent. AE, DC, ER, MC, V. Parking: $11. *SkyTrain:* Waterfront.

WEST END

- **Westin Bayshore,** 1601 W. Georgia St., V6G 2V4 (tel. 604/682-3377; toll free 800/228-3000; fax 604/687-3102). 481 rooms, 38 suites. A/C MINI-BAR TV TEL

Beautifully landscaped grounds surround the Westin, which rests on the shore of Coal Harbour like an extension of adjacent Stanley Park. The gardens and a private marina are the trademark of the hotel, a pioneer in the modern hospitality industry when it was built in 1961, and still going strong.

The rooms are classified by their location and view: Tower rooms are largest, with the best views, and therefore cost more. While standard units have two phones, Tower rooms do them one better by adding a bathroom extension. Corner rooms also have balconies. Deluxe amenities are placed in the junior suites, equivalent to executive-level rooms elsewhere. No-smoking and rooms for the disabled are also available. Small pets are permitted.

Dining/Entertainment: Trader Vic's, with its trademark South Seas decor, has Chinese and Continental cuisine with seafood specialties. Its Harbour Bar has nightly entertainment. The Garden Restaurant offers three meals daily and a Sunday-brunch buffet; its Garden Lounge serves lunches by day and entertains with light jazz by night.

Services: 24-hour room service, concierge, valet laundry, courtesy bus, doctor and dentist on call, secretarial services, baby-sitting, fishing trips, and sightseeing cruises chartered through Westin Marina.

Facilities: Indoor and outdoor pools, weight room, fitness trail, bicycle rentals, whirlpool, saunas, massage, meeting/banquet space for 1,000, clothing stores, jeweler, hair salon, barber, florist, gift shop, newsstand, marina with seaplane dock.

RATES: Mid-Apr to Oct, $143–$199 single, $163–$219 double, $293 junior suite, $432–$1,325 larger suites; Nov to mid-Apr, $90–$141 single, $105–$156 double. Children 18 or under free with parent. AE, CB, DC, ER, MC, V. Parking: $7. *Bus:* 242.

- **The Coast Plaza at Stanley Park,** 1733 Comox St. (at Denman St.), V6G 1P6 (tel. 604/688-7711; toll free 800/663-1144; fax 604/685-7210). 85 rooms and 182 suites. A/C MINI-BAR TV TEL

If this 35-story luxury hotel were renamed "Squirrel Plaza," some folks might chuckle, but few could object. After all, Lucy, Cindy, Boom Boom, and the other tree-climbing rodents who venture into the pink marble lobby are treated royally—so much so, in fact, that doormen and bellhops carry hazelnuts in their pockets.

The guest rooms are off-limits to the little guys, however. Every one of the very spacious rooms has a balcony, clock radio, and the sort of furnishings one expects in a fine hotel. Limited Edition floors have special touches. Most suites—which comprise two-thirds of the units—have full kitchen facilities. No-smoking floors and rooms for the disabled are available.

Dining/Entertainment: Humphrey's rooftop restaurant serves fine dinners of West Coast cuisine high above English Bay and Stanley Park. The modern Brasserie has an open kitchen that prepares three meals daily. Shampers is a popular lobby-level disco with a pasta bar.

Services: 24-hour room service, concierge, valet laundry, downtown limousine service. Limited Edition clients get a complimentary breakfast, free morning paper, and other services.

Facilities: Indoor pool, weight room, racquetball courts, saunas, games, piano, gift shop, meeting/banquet space for 450. The 30-store Denman Mall adjoins.

RATES: May to mid-Oct, $170–$220 single, $185–$235 double, $200–$235 larger suites; mid-Oct to Apr, $140–$190 single, $155–$205 double, $195–$225 larger suites. AE, DC, ER, MC, V. Parking: $4. *Bus:* 8.

2. Expensive Hotels

DOWNTOWN

- **The Georgian Court Hotel,** 773 Beatty St., V6B 2M4 (tel. 604/682-5555; toll free 800/663-1155; fax 604/682-8830). 160 rooms, 20 suites. A/C MINI-BAR TV TEL

Many of the standing ovations delivered across the street in B.C. Place Stadium, or a block away at the Queen Elizabeth Theatre, should go to the Georgian Court. This hotel is a class act, an intimate European-style hostelry with faultless service. The lobby is a veritable work of antique art with its mahogany, brass, and beveled glass. Rich handcrafted furnishings grace the restaurant and guest rooms.

Flowers, fresh-cut daily, grace each of those spacious rooms. The vanity and dressing table have marble tops, and the closet is larger than any traveler will normally use. Each room has three phones—bedside, desktop, and bathroom. Executive-floor guests get complimentary breakfasts and other special touches. The hotel has four no-smoking floors; rooms for the disabled are available.

Dining/Entertainment: The William Tell Restaurant and its Swiss chef, Erwin Doebeli, are among Canada's finest. Rigney's Bar & Grill has a sports bar atmosphere; it was named for a former B.C. Lions football player. A baby grand piano and mahogany-paneled bar are earmarks of the posh Club Lounge, where guests can get a Continental breakfast and return for evening entertainment.

Services: Room service, concierge, complimentary morning newspaper, rooms designated for women travelers.

Facilities: Health club with Universal gym, whirlpool, and sauna. Small meetings and banquets accommodated. Gift and sundry shop open mornings and evenings.

RATES: May–Sept, $130–$150 single, $150–$170 double; Oct–Apr, $99–$119 single, $115–$135 double. AE, DC, ER, MC, V. Parking: $6. *SkyTrain:* Stadium.

- **Wedgewood Hotel,** 845 Hornby St., V6Z 1V1 (tel. 604/689-7777; toll free 800/663-0666; fax 604/688-3074). 60 rooms, 33 suites. A/C MINI-BAR TV TEL

In 1983, Greek immigrant Eleni Skalbania bought a dilapidated apartment building for $4.5 million, threw another $3 million into renovations, and transformed an ugly duckling into a swan as elegant and sophisticated as yourself. That swan is the Wedgewood, where European and Middle English styles mingle in a delightfully arty atmosphere. Skalbania's personal touch—she may greet you herself in the warm, cozy lobby, or drop by your table in the dining room—is everywhere, from the antique furnishings to the one-of-a-kind oil paintings.

The rooms are as tastefully decorated as the rest of the hotel, with light wood furnishings, fine-art prints, potted plants, and private flower beds on the balconies. All but 10 are upgraded executive-class rooms with appropriate extras. Some suites even have fireplaces. No-smoking rooms are available. Small pets are permitted here.

Dining/Entertainment: The Wedgewood Dining Room serves fine French cuisine weekdays and Saturday nights. Bacchus Ristorante offers breakfast and Italian cuisine daily. The piano lounge has live entertainment nightly except Sunday beneath an imposing oil painting of Bacchus himself, the Roman god of wine.

Services: 24-hour room service, twice-daily housekeeping, limousine service, morning newspaper, box of chocolates for every new guest, secretarial services, baby-sitting.

Facilities: Squash courts, weight room, aerobics, sauna, whirlpool, massage, hair salon.

RATES (INCLUDING CONTINENTAL BREAKFAST): Low season, $120 regular, $160 executive, $200–$270 suite; $20 more double. AE, CB, DC, ER, MC, V. Parking: $8. *SkyTrain:* Burrard.

- **Hotel Georgia,** 801 W. Georgia St. (at Howe St.), V6C 1P7 (tel. 604/682-5566; toll free 800/663-1111; fax 604/682-8192). 314 rooms and suites. A/C TV TEL

This huge brick relic from the Georgian era has an impressive lobby with gold-touched woodwork, beautiful brass chandeliers, a big fireplace, and heavy carpeting.

Wide, low-lit corridors lead to comfortable gray-carpeted rooms with standard furnishings and basic amenities.

Dining/Entertainment: The Cavalier Grill, off the main lobby, retains a feeling of British royalty with red upholstery and wood decor. It serves continental cuisine. George V Pub, in the dungeonlike basement, offers traditional English pub fare and evening singalong entertainment. The Night Court Lounge has light meals, dancing, and a sports-and-trivia hookup; the Patio Lounge serves business lunches and light dinners.

Services: Room service, valet laundry.

Facilities: Meeting/banquet space for 300, men's and women's clothing stores, jeweler, gift shops, hair salon, barber, shoeshine.

RATES: May–mid-Oct, $111–$131 single, $126–$146 double; mid-Oct–Apr, $103–$123 single, $113–$133 double, $225–$450 suite. Children under 16 free with parent. AE, CB, DC, ER, MC, V. Parking: $6. *SkyTrain:* Granville.

- **Quality Inn,** 1335 Howe St. (at Davie St.), V6Z 1R7 (tel. 604/682-0229; toll free 800/228-5151; fax 604/662-7566). 142 rooms and junior suites, 14 one-bedroom suites. A/C TV TEL

The red facade of this clean, modern accommodation is hard to miss beside the Granville Street Bridge on-ramp.

Rooms have a country charm with knotty-pine furnishings, an imitation quilt bedspread, and a brick wall behind the bed. They're great for families, especially the one-bedroom suites with fully equipped kitchens. It's not well set up for business travelers, however, lacking a desk phone and appropriate services.

Dining/Entertainment: The bright, arty Creekside Café is open daily for breakfast and dinner. Lunch is served in the Creekside Lounge.

Services: Valet laundry.

Facilities: Outdoor pool. Complimentary use of facilities at nearby fitness club.

RATES: May–Sept, $89 single, $99 double, suites $98 to $115; Oct–Mar, $64–$69 single or double, $78–$85 suite; Apr, $69–$

74 single or double, $83–$90 suite. Children under 18 free with parent. AE, CB, DC, ER, MC, V. Parking: free. *Bus:* 4, 7, 8, 10, or 20.

WEST END

- **Ming Court Hotel,** 1160 Davie St., V6E 1N1 (tel. 604/685-1311, toll free 800/663-1525, fax 604/681-0208). 192 rooms. A/C TV TEL

The Chinese Ming dynasty left a legacy of great artistic accomplishment in the 14th to 17th centuries. The appeal of this Malaysian-owned hotel lies largely in its dedication to artistic presentation, not only in its tasteful interior design (including Ming porcelains) but in the artistry of its staff.

The handsome rooms are all very large—450 square feet. All have balconies with views of the downtown skyline or English Bay. Superior and deluxe rooms on the upper floors have minibars and hairdryers; deluxe rooms also have two phones, clock radios, and coffeemakers.

Dining/Entertainment: The Chez Bidou Dining Room features Asian specialties, Continental favorites, and new West Coast taste tempters for three meals daily. The Ming Court Bistro has a popular Asian buffet lunch, while the Garden Court Lounge features evening *karaoke* (sing-along) entertainment.

Services: 24-hour room service, concierge, valet laundry, chauffeur service to business district, doctor and dentist on call.

Facilities: Outdoor pool, sauna, exercise room, business center, gift shop, meeting/banquet space for 280.

RATES: May–Sept, $120–$145 single, $130–$165 double, $250 suite; Oct–Apr, $70–$90 single or double. AE, DC, ER, MC, V. Parking: free. *Bus:* 8.

- **O'Doul's Hotel,** 1300 Robson St., V6E 1C5 (tel. 604/684-8461, toll free 800/663-5491, fax 604/684-8326). 119 rooms, 11 suites. A/C MINI-BAR TV TEL

Recent works by British Columbia artists provide a unifying theme at this Best Western property, located at the west end of the Robsonstrasse shopping strip. When it was rebuilt from scratch in 1986, numerous paintings, sculptures, stained and beveled glass works, tapestries, and murals were commissioned. The result is a museum-quality contemporary art exhibit. A subtle use of colors—from soft pink to burgundy, from mint to rainforest green—is accented with brass and other art-deco touches.

Every room in the six-story hotel is of deluxe quality, with three phones, working desks, clock radios, and hairdryers. Each guest gets special attention, right down to the individually programmed electronic door locks. There are two no-smoking floors and rooms specially equipped for the disabled.

Dining/Entertainment: O'Doul's Restaurant is open for three meals daily with the emphasis on West Coast specialties. The art-deco theme reaches its climax here, accented by a tongue-in-cheek jungle theme (complete with ceramic animals). The adjoining lounge has nightly piano entertainment.

Services: 24-hour room service, concierge, valet laundry, secretarial services.

Facilities: Indoor pool, exercise room, whirlpool, steam room, meeting/banquet space for 150.

RATES: Summer, $125–$165 single, $140–$180 double, $150–$190 twin, $250–$295 suite; winter, $89–$109 single, $99–$119 double or twin, $195–$240 suite. AE, DC, ER, MC, V. Underground parking: free. *Bus:* 8.

- **The Pacific Palisades Hotel,** 1277 Robson St., V6E 1C4 (tel. 604/688-0461, toll free 800/663-1815, fax 604/688-4374). 18 rooms, 206 suites. A/C FRIDGE TV TEL

Constructed as residential apartments and renovated in early 1990, this hotel consists of two towers divided by a lovely outdoor courtyard. A plaque in the lobby, entered off Jervis Street, names hundreds of celebrities who have stayed in this property, a member of the Shangri-La group.

Rooms are mainly spacious one-bedroom suites, with a handful of studios and several larger suites. Most have private balconies. All have full kitchen facilities, the use of which is available for a few extra dollars in standard suites, complimentary in deluxe units. Those deluxe suites also have microwave ovens, coffeemakers, china and crystal table settings, complimentary tea service, two telephones, and better views. No-smoking floors are available.

Dining/Entertainment: Puffin's Dining Room serves country French-style cuisine in a light mirrored setting. The Palisades Coffee Garden facing Robson Street serves three meals daily. Mel Zee's Piano Lounge has nightly entertainment at its glass-topped piano. In summer, the Courtyard Cafe offers outdoor dining.

Services: 24-hour room service, limousine service, valet laundry, guest Laundromat, daily newspaper, secretarial services.

Facilities: Indoor pool, weight/exercise room, racquetball courts, whirlpool, sauna, massage, tanning, bicycle rentals, shopping arcade, gift shop, meeting/banquet space for 200.

RATES: Mid-Apr–Oct, $130–$170 single, $150–$200 double; Nov–mid-Apr, $105–$135 single, $125–$155 double. AE, CB, DC, ER, MC, V. Parking: $6. *Bus:* 8.

- **Sheraton-Landmark Hotel,** 1400 Robson St., V6G 1B9 (tel. 604/687-0511, toll free 800/325-3535, fax 604/687-2801). 353 rooms, 7 suites. A/C TV TEL

If you're looking for a view, look no further than Vancouver's tallest hotel, the West End's most prominent building. Rising like a sentinel over Robson Street, the 42-story structure has a simple, unpretentious lobby but fine facilities within.

Every room has a private balcony with an unobstructed view. Furnishings are comfortable while not posh; deluxe rooms have minibars. There are four no-smoking floors and several rooms for the disabled.

Dining/Entertainment: Cloud 9, a 42nd-floor revolving restaurant and lounge, provides gourmet dining. The Lobby Cafe and Lounge offers casual all-day dining. The Landmark Jazz Bar has pub fare and live entertainment.

Services: Room service, valet laundry, seasonal tour desk.

Facilities: Exercise room, saunas, whirlpool, gift shop, car rental, meeting/banquet space for 600.

RATES: Summer $108–$150 single, $123–$165 double, $200–$400 suite; winter discounts from $85 single or double. AE, DC, ER, MC, V. Parking: $4. *Bus:* 8.

SOUTH OF DOWNTOWN

- **Granville Island Hotel,** 1253 Johnston St., V6H 3R9 (tel. 604/683-7373; toll free 800/663-1840; fax 604/682-3061). 49 rooms, 5 suites. A/C TV TEL

Located at the east end of Granville Island, on False Creek, this hotel is unique in Vancouver for its water location. Constructed like a warehouse, one side is corrugated metal, the other Mediterranean-pink concrete. A green-and-white-striped canopy connects the wings. The lobby boasts a beautiful antique sideboard with a collection of fine porcelain. Downtown is just 6 minutes away by $1 ferry across False Creek.

The rooms are geared for vacationers rather than business-persons. Careful attention has been paid to installing stereo cassette systems with AM/FM clock radios, yet the desk is so small as to be impractical for anything but writing postcards. Wooden louvers cover the windows, and framed serigraphs hang on the walls. The highlight is the huge bathroom with an oversize tub, hairdryer, and bidet. If you want quiet, ask for a room away from the galleria so you won't be disturbed by the music from the nightclub.

Dining/Entertainment: Beneath a three-story galleria, complete with a kinetic calliope machine that actually flies kites by pumping air from a bellows, are the Pelican Bay Restaurant and Night Club. The restaurant serves three meals daily at moderate prices, including a classic oyster stew. Late at night, it turns into a Top 40 disco with a marble dance floor overlooking the marina. Balboa's Pub and Bistro serves on the patio in summer.

Services: Room service, valet laundry.

Facilities: Tennis courts, whirlpool, sauna, fishing and diving charters, meeting/banquet space for 200.

RATES: Summer, $130–$140 single or double, $150 twin, $170–$270 suite; winter rates $20 less. AE, DC, ER, MC, V. Parking: $7. *Aquabus or Granville Island ferry.*

- **Holiday Inn Broadway,** 711 W. Broadway, V5Z 3Y2 (tel. 604/879-0511). 193 rooms and suites. A/C TV TEL

If "Holiday Inn" means something less than elegant to you, you'll think again as you enter the marble-floored lobby of this handsome 16-story hotel.

The rooms aren't flashy, but they're tastefully furnished and decorated with Gretchen Dow Simpson lithographs. Corner rooms have balconies; those on the west side have great views over the False Creek Marina and Granville Island. Executive-floor rooms have minibars, hairdryers, pants pressers, terry-cloth robes, and Continental breakfasts included. Small pets are permitted.

Dining/Entertainment: Stages on Broadway, open for three meals daily, specializes in light California-Continental cuisine. Life-size mannequins keep an eye on diners in the green-purple decor. Stages Lounge is a favorite hangout of lounge potatoes for its big-screen satellite system, sports, and trivia games. Broadway Casino,

Vancouver's largest casino, is also on premises; bets of from 50¢ to $25 may be placed on roulette, blackjack, and sic bo.

Services: Room service, valet laundry. Housekeeping staff performs ironing, sewing, and other services gratis.

Facilities: Indoor pool, weight/exercise room, sauna, tanning, video games. Public tennis courts five minutes' walk away.

RATES: May–Sept, $115–$134 single, $125–$154 double; Oct–Apr, $90–$126 single, $100–$136 double. AE, DC, ER, MC, V. Covered parking: free. *Bus:* 9.

- **Sheraton Inn Plaza 500,** 500 W. 12th Ave. (at Cambie St.), V5Z 1M2 (tel. 604/873-1811; toll free 800/325-3535; fax 604/873-5103). 148 rooms and 5 suites. A/C MINI-BAR TV TEL

Perhaps the most centrally located of any Vancouver hotel, the 17-story Plaza 500 is catty-corner from City Hall, opposite the new $3 million City Square shopping center, and in the middle of the medical district. Built in 1963 and completely renovated in 1988, it features a small but tasteful lobby with an extending sun roof, marble floors and pillars, and a philodendron-bedecked staircase to the second-floor ballroom.

Rooms are spacious, well-lit, and brightly decorated. Most have private balconies, and those on the upper floors have views of the mountains, the water, and/or the downtown skyline. Standard fixtures include walk-in closets, full-length mirrors, six-drawer dressers, easy chairs, and clock radios.

Dining/Entertainment: Remington's is a California-style café serving three moderately priced meals daily in an indoor/outdoor vineyard setting. Adjacent is the Lobby Lounge, which features a piano bar and complimentary hors d'oeuvres from 5 to 7pm daily. In the hotel basement is the Jolly Alderman English pub, a local favorite for lunch and light meals.

Services: Room service, valet laundry, complimentary breakfast for corporate clients.

Facilities: Hair salon, jeweler, skin-care center, meeting/banquet space for 500. Guests use Fitness World health club in City Square (no pool).

RATES: Year round $86.95–$116 single, $86.95–$131 double, $160 suite. AE, CB, DC, ER, MC, V. Parking: $3. *Bus:* 15.

AIRPORT

- **Delta Airport Inn Resort,** 10251 St. Edwards Drive, Richmond V6X 2M9 (tel. 604/278-9611, toll free 800/268-1133, fax 604/270-2317). 460 rooms, 4 suites. A/C MINI-BAR TV TEL

Set amid 14 acres of landscaped gardens, this impressive property is virtually a destination resort. Its pride is its recreation center, which comprises three swimming pools (one indoor and two outdoor), four indoor tennis courts, two squash courts, volleyball court, weight/exercise room, quarter-mile jogging track, golf driving range, pro shop, and mountain bike rental.

Rooms are in two towers and a renovated Terrace wing. Those in the new South Tower are especially large, with refinished wood furnishings and private balconies. Decor features a fishing or game-bird theme. North Tower and Terrace rooms are smaller but equally nice, with wildlife prints and other attractive touches. Small pets are permitted.

Dining/Entertainment: The exquisite Suehiro Steakhouse, located on a tranquil island in a Japanese garden and filled with medieval Asian sculptures, offers teppan-style lunches and dinners of beef, chicken, and seafood, with sushi, sashimi, and sake consommé also on the menu. The Coffee Garden has breakfast buffets, light lunches, and moderately priced dinner entrées; adjoining is The Palm for formal dining. Off the lobby is The Landing piano lounge.

Services: Room service, valet laundry, luggage storage, shuttle service to airport, the Delta River Inn and Lansdowne Shopping Centre. Signature Service offers corporate travelers complimentary breakfasts and upgraded amenities.

Facilities: Recreation center, including Jacuzzi and sauna. Children's creative center for 3- to 8-year olds (including swimming lessons and outdoor playground). Business center, gift shop, hair salon, outdoor barbecue area with cabanas, car rental, Canadian Pacific Air Lines ticket counter, meeting/banquet space for 300.

RATES: May–Sept $115–$130 single, $130–$145 double; Oct–Apr, $10 less. Children 18 or under free with parent. AE, CB, DC, ER, MC, V. Parking: free *Bus:* 401, 403, or 406.

■ **The Delta River Inn,** 3500 Cessna Drive, Richmond V7B 1C7 (tel. 604/278-1241, toll free 800/387-1255, fax 604/278-0969). 407 rooms and 9 suites. A/C MINI-BAR TV TEL

Fishing charters and river cruises begin from this hotel's marina on the Fraser River, just east of the airport. The 11-story Y-shaped structure caters to corporate business clients with a major business center, cellular phone rental, and rooms structured for the working traveler. Asian art blends with English decor to give an international feel.

Rooms are in brown tones with pastel bedspreads and drapes. Furnishings include large dressers, full-length mirrors, and clock radios. Many rooms have private balconies. There are 96 no-smoking rooms; rooms are also available for the disabled.

Small pets are permitted.

Dining/Entertainment: The Pier restaurant is a gourmet venue for West Coast cuisine, with entrées in the moderate-to-expensive range. The Deckhouse Cafe is a three-meal coffee shop with nautical decor. The adjacent Jetty Lounge has an English pub theme. The snazzy Lookout nightclub features disco dancing with a panoramic view over the Fraser from the 11th-floor penthouse. There's also seasonal poolside dining, and private dining in The Sandbar.

Services: Late-hour room service, morning coffee in lobby, valet laundry, airport shuttle, courtesy bus to Lansdowne Shopping Centre and Delta Airport Inn Resort.

Facilities: Outdoor pool with barbecue area, saunas, exercise bike, bicycle rentals, jogging route, children's center, gift shop, car rental, meeting/banquet space for 650. Indoor tennis, squash, and recreational facilities at Airport Inn Resort.

RATES: May–Sept $190 single, $205 double; Oct–Apr $20 less. Children under 18 free with parent. AE, CB, DC, ER, MC, V. Parking: free. *Bus:* 404 or 405.

NORTH SHORE

• **Lonsdale Quay Hotel,** 123 Carrie Cates Court, North Vancouver V7M 3K7 (tel. 604/986-6111; fax 604/986-8782). 57 rooms. A/C MINI-BAR TV TEL

Located on the upper floors of the colorful Lonsdale Quay Market adjacent to the SeaBus Terminal, this delightful small hotel is 12 minutes and an entire world away from downtown Vancouver. Extending into the inlet, it has a view nonpareil of the city skyline, but the flavor of a fishing port, thanks to atmospheric blasts from the Cates Tugboat terminal next door.

There are twin rooms on the third floor of this two-tier inn, spacious double queens are located on the fourth floor. The decor is extremely pleasant and the furnishings are standard, with added niceties like a coffeemaker in every room. No-smoking rooms and rooms for the disabled are available. Ask for a west-side room for the best view.

Dining/Entertainment: Loops Restaurant serves three meals daily from a truly international menu—Japanese and Indonesian items share the spotlight with seafood, pastas, Continental, and West Coast cuisine, all for moderate prices. The open kitchen lends an ambience of welcome; a piano player performs in the evenings, and there's patio dining in summer. The Waterfront Bistro is a favorite meeting and dancing spot for the single crowd in their thirties and forties; it also offers light lunches and snacks. Tugs Pub has a big-screen TV, rock 'n' roll for guests aged 19 to 25, and a burger menu.

Services: Room service, valet laundry, complimentary morning newspaper.

Facilities: Fitness center with weights, exercise room, whirlpool, and sauna. Meetings and banquets for 120.

RATES: Year round $97.50–$105 single, $105–$125 double, $110–$135 twin, $145–$390 suite. AE, DC, ER, MC, V. Parking: $6. *SeaBus.*

• **Park Royal Hotel,** 440 Clyde Ave., West Vancouver V7T 2JT (tel. 604/926-5511). 30 rooms. TV TEL

A lovely ivy-covered Tudor-style mansion set in beautifully manicured English country gardens beside the Capilano River, the Park Royal is just off the north end of the Lion's Gate Bridge. The Park Royal Shopping Centre is a short stroll away, and a riverside path outside the front door leads to Ambleside Beach.

The rooms are elegant, with king-size beds in brass frames, bay windows, plush carpets, and rich wood furnishings including love seats.

Dining/Entertainment: The ambience of an English country inn is evident in the large stone fireplaces and wooden beams of the fine dining room and intimate pub. Both are open seven days, with large windows facing out on the beautiful gardens.

RATES: May–Sept, $90–$145 single, $99–$155 double; Oct–Apr, $60–$80 single, $70–$90 double. Reservations essential. AE, DC, ER, MC, V. Parking: free. *Bus:* 250, 251, 252, or 253.

3. Moderately Priced Hotels

DOWNTOWN

- **Sandman Inn,** 180 W. Georgia St. (at Homer St.), V6B 4P4 (tel. 604/681-2211; toll free 800/663-6900). 216 rooms. A/C TV TEL

The flagship of this popular Western Canada motel chain has an outstanding location opposite the Queen Elizabeth Theatre and the Airporter bus terminal. The rooms are adequate at best, with standard furnishings. Decor varies from beige to dusty rose, with floral or paisley bedspreads and drapes. Local phone calls are free; some rooms have minibars.

Dining/Entertainment: The Georgia Seafood Co. on the third floor specializes in the bounty of the sea; it's open Thursday through Saturday nights only. The adjoining Heartland Coffee Shop serves three meals daily. The JR Country Club is downtown Vancouver's number-one country-and-western bar. The Sportsline Lounge has a big-screen TV, pool table, and darts.

Services: Take-out service from restaurant, valet laundry.

Facilities: Indoor pool, whirlpool, saunas, meeting/banquet space for 250, gift shop, car rental.

RATES: May–Sept, $86 single, $92 double, $98 twin; Oct–Apr, $60 single or double, $64 twin. AE, CB, DC, ER, MC, V. Parking: free. *SkyTrain:* Stadium.

- **Abbotsford Hotel,** 921 W. Pender St., V6C 1M2 (tel. 604/681-4335; toll free 800/663-1700). 83 rooms and suites. TV TEL

A Vancouver classic discreetly located in the heart of the financial district, this seven-story stone building has twice undergone major renovations to enhance its beauty. Its elegant lobby makes liberal use of art deco–style brass. The individually decorated rooms are likewise bright, with striped coverlets and red upholstery.

Dining/Entertainment: The Bombay Bicycle Club is popular for lunches and after-work drinks. There's also a café and a pub on the premises. All are snug and cozy, with "gaslight" illumination, dark-wood paneling, and evocative old prints.

Services: Room service, valet laundry.

RATES: Summer $70 single, $80 double; winter $49 single or double. AE, DC, ER, MC, V. Parking: free 6pm–9am. *SkyTrain:* Burrard.

- **Burrard Motor Inn,** 1100 Burrard St. (at Helmcken St.), V6Z 1Y7 (tel. 604/681-2331; toll free 800/663-0366). 70 rooms. A/C TV TEL

This in-city motel pursues a garden image, and succeeds. All rooms face an inner garden courtyard that cloaks a parking garage; behind closed doors, even the carpets are garden green. You'll find basic amenities and standard furnishings, including a working desk. Kitchenettes and no-smoking rooms are available. Small pets are permitted.

Dining/Entertainment: The Greenhouse restaurant is open for three meals daily. There's an adjoining lounge.

RATES: May–Oct, $58 single, $66 double, $74 twin; Nov–

Apr, $46 single, $56 double, $62 twin. Kitchenettes $6 extra. AE, DC, ER, MC, V. Parking: free. *Bus:* 22.

WEST END

- **Sylvia Hotel,** 1154 Gilford St., V6G 2P6 (tel. 604/681-9321). 90 rooms, 25 suites. TV TEL

A longtime favorite among families and regular Vancouver visitors, the Sylvia is a heritage building constructed as a state-of-the-art apartment house on English Bay in 1912. The imposing stone edifice, now covered with ivy, stays cool in summer, warm in winter, and is very friendly throughout the year. Every room in the original hotel is a little different in size, shape, and decor; try to get a corner unit for the view. Some fully equipped kitchens with gas stoves are available. Sixteen rooms in a 1986 annex have individual heating and air conditioning, but they're also less interesting.

Dining/Entertainment: Sylvia's Restaurant serves fine meats and seafoods with a continental touch for three meals daily. Big windows face the bay or a courtyard lily pond. The adjacent casual bistro is open all day, every day, for light snacks. A glassed-in bar serves a cozy lounge.

Services: Room service, valet laundry.

RATES: Year round $42–$65 single, $50–$73 double or twin, $74–$90 suite, $8 kitchen or additional person. AE, DC, MC, V. Parking: $3. *Bus:* 1 or 8.

- **Barclay Hotel,** 1348 Robson St., V6E 1C5 (tel. 604/688-8850, fax 604/688-2534). 89 rooms. A/C MINI-BAR TV TEL

A French provincial ambience pervades this cozy, recently renovated hotel, one of Vancouver's best bargains. Snowy white inside and out, it has brass chandeliers, polished wood, and an otherwise Old World flavor from the antiques in its marble foyer to the tastefully decorated guest rooms. No-smoking rooms available.

Dining/Entertainment: The Barclay Restaurant, with French specialties, serves three meals daily. The Bistro Lounge has live music nightly and outdoor seating in summer.

Services: Room service, valet laundry.

RATES: Summer $59–$75 single, $85–$95 double; winter $49–$69 single, $59–$79 double. AE, DC, MC, V. Parking: free. *Bus:* 8.

- **Riviera Motor Inn,** 1431 Robson St., V6G 1C1 (tel. 604/685-1301). 40 suites. FRIDGE TV TEL

One of several converted apartment blocks at the west end of Robsonstrasse, the 10-story Riviera has a tiny lobby but very large studio and one-bedroom suites. Every one has a fully equipped kitchen (with four-burner stove and all cooking utensils). The furnishings are far from flashy—a Formica table, vinyl-covered chairs, etc.—but the views from the upper floors are impressive. A penthouse suite even has an Astroturf deck with lawn furniture and a view across Stanley Park.

RATES: Summer $88 single, $98 double; winter $78 single, $88 double. AE, DC, ER, MC, V. Parking: free. *Bus:* 8.

- **Robsonstrasse City Motor Inn,** 1394 Robson St., V6E 1C5 (tel. 604/687-1674). 41 suites. FRIDGE TV TEL

Huge, comfortable rooms are the earmark of this hostelry. The kitchens (all utensils are provided on request for a deposit) have dining nooks attached; there's also a large, nicely furnished living room (with a hideaway sofa for additional guests) and a big bedroom with a walk-in closet and nine-drawer dresser.

RATES: Summer $70–$100 "depending on demand"; winter $50 single or double. AE, MC, V. Parking: free. *Bus:* 8.

- **Shato Inn Apartment Hotel,** 1825 Comox St., V6G 1P9 (tel. 604/681-8920). 22 rooms and suites. TV TEL

A modern three-story cedar structure fewer than three blocks from Stanley Park, the inn has spacious, attractive rooms, some with kitchens and/or balconies. This is a friendly, family-run operation in a quiet neighborhood off Denman Street.

RATES: Summer $70 single, $80 double, $95 twin; winter $55 single, $65 double, $75 twin; kitchens $10 more. MC, V. Parking: free. *Bus:* 8.

- **West End Guest House,** 1362 Haro St., V6E 1G2 (tel. 604/681-2889). 7 rooms.

You'll have to book well in advance to get a room in this quaint bed-and-breakfast inn, barely a block from frenetic Robson Street. This turn-of-the-century Victorian home is in the pink, the same color as its exterior walls. Each room has a different theme and decor, but all have private baths. There's a guest lounge with a piano, and a breakfast room for starting the day gourmet. Smoking is not permitted in the bedrooms or dining area.

RATES (FULL BREAKFAST INCLUDED): $60–$75 single, $65–$80 double. MC, V. *Bus:* 8.

EAST OF DOWNTOWN

- **Exhibition Park Travelodge,** 3475 E. Hastings St. (at Highway 401, Cassiar St.), V5K 2A5 (tel. 604/294-4751; toll free 800/255-3050). 58 rooms and suites. A/C TV TEL

This is what travelers expect from Travelodge: Clean and comfortable, without frills. Rooms here are newly renovated, with full baths and complimentary coffee. One- and two-bedroom suites are available, as are no-smoking and rooms for the disabled. Small pets are permitted.

Dining/Entertainment: 24-hour restaurant is adjacent to the motel.

Facilities: Sauna, whirlpool, coin-op Laundromat.

RATES: $50–$70 single, $55–$75 double, $65–$85 twin, additional persons $6–$8. AE, MC, V. covered parking: free. *Bus:* 14.

SOUTH OF DOWNTOWN

- **City Centre Motor Inn,** 2111 Main St. (at Sixth Ave.), V5T 3C6 (tel. 604/876-7166). A/C TV TEL

A cozy modern motel near Science World on the old Expo 86 site, the City Centre provides complimentary coffee and morning pastries for guests in its lobby. Rooms are standard motel fare; kitchenettes and rooms for the disabled are available.

RATES: $39.50 single, $45 double, tax included. Children under 16 free with parent. AE, MC, V. Parking: free. *Bus:* 3 or 8.

- **Kenya Court Guest House,** 2230 Cornwall Ave., V6K 1B5 (tel. 604/738-7085). 3 rooms. TV TEL

Situated on English Bay at Kitsilano Beach, this three-story heritage apartment building features a handful of large self-contained suites with private entrances. The largest sleeps six. All are clean and attractively decorated, right down to the window boxes. Some two-bedroom suites have ocean views. No smoking is permitted in the building.

Dining/Entertainment: A full breakfast, from coffee and juice, to fruits and croissants, to bacon and eggs, is served daily in a rooftop solarium with a view of the mountains across English Bay. The Kenya Court also has a music room with a piano available to guests.

Facilities: Park across street has large heated outdoor saltwater pool, tennis courts, and jogging trails.

RATES (INCLUDING BREAKFAST): Mar–Sept $65–$85, Oct–Feb less. No credit cards; checks accepted. Parking: limited (on street). *Bus:* 22.

AIRPORT

- **Executive Inn,** 7211 Westminster Hwy., Richmond V6X 1A3 (tel. 604/278-5555; toll free 800/663-2878 in British Columbia and Washington State). 18 rooms, 62 suites. A/C FRIDGE TV TEL

A spacious modern property in central Richmond south of the Dinsmore Bridge at Gilbert Road, this inn offers visitors an immediate feeling of warmth with its glassed-in lobby full of greenery. Rooms have a subdued decor; all suites have complete cooking facilities.

Dining/Entertainment: Tivoli's Too Restaurant specializes in continental cuisine with fresh seafood.

Services: Room service, valet laundry, free airport shuttle.

Facilities: Jacuzzi, massage, jogging trail, health-club affiliation, meeting/banquet space for 120.

RATES: $52–$65 standard single, $62–$75 double; $79–$89 deluxe suite single, $89–$99 double; executive suite with Jacuzzi to $119 double. Additional persons $10. Children under 12 free with parent. 30% discount for seniors in standard rooms. AE, CB, DC, ER, MC, V. Parking: free. *Bus:* 401 or 407.

- **Stay 'n Save Motor Inn,** 10551 St. Edwards Drive, Richmond V6X 3L8 (tel. 604/273-3311; toll free 800/663-0298). 153 units. A/C TV TEL

It's hard to miss the distinctive blue roof, just off Highway 99 North at Cambie Road. Rooms are comfortable without being flashy, with standard furnishings. Kitchen units and rooms for the disabled are available.

Dining/Entertainment: O'Donal's Family Restaurant adjoins.

Services: Free local calls, complimentary airport shuttle service.

Facilities: Spa and exercise room, guest Laundromat.

RATES: May–Sept $79 single or double, Oct–Apr $64 single or double, $8 additional person or kitchen. Weekly rates available off season. AE, DC, MC, V. Parking: free. *Bus:* 401, 403, or 406.

- **Abercorn Inn,** 9260 Bridgeport Rd., Richmond V6X 1S1 (tel. 604/270-7576, toll free 800/663-0085, fax 604/270-0001). 80 rooms. A/C TV TEL

A Best Western property with a Tudor-style exterior, the Abercorn has comfortable rooms and a friendly staff. Some rooms have double Jacuzzi baths or oversized tubs. There's a licensed restaurant and lounge, and complimentary airport shuttle service.

RATES: June–Sept $85 single, $95 double; Oct–May $10 less; suites to $130. AE, DC, ER, MC, V. Parking: free. *Bus:* 420.

NORTH SHORE

- **Grouse Inn,** 1633 Capilano Rd. at Marine Drive, North Vancouver V7P 3B3 (tel. 604/988-7101). 75 rooms. A/C TV TEL

Located at the foot of the road to Grouse Mountain, this motel offers numerous family suites with kitchenettes. It has a restaurant and lots of activities for the children—an outdoor heated pool with a water slide and recreational facilities including a children's play area.

RATES: $45–$75 standard, $65–$95 1-bedroom suite, $85–$130 2-bedroom suite. AE, DC, ER, MC, V. Parking: free. *Bus:* 246.

- **Capilano Motor Inn,** 1634 Capilano Rd., North Vancouver V7P 3B4 (tel. 604/987-8185). 65 rooms. TV TEL

Another entry on the "motel strip" heading toward Capilano Canyon Regional Park, this lodging features a variety of spacious rooms, including standard units, kitchen and family units, and one- and two-bedroom executive suites. It has a heated outdoor swimming pool, sauna, and guest Laundromat. The Capilano Cafe serves breakfast and lunch daily.

RATES: June–Sept $65–$75 single or double; Oct–May $50–$65; suites $95–$155 summer, $65–$125 winter. AE, DC, ER, MC, V. Parking: free. *Bus:* 246.

- **Canyon Court Motel,** 1748 Capilano Rd., North Vancouver V7P 3B4 (tel. 604/988-3181; toll free 800/663-4059 in western Canada). 89 rooms. A/C TV TEL

A clean, friendly, family-run hostelry, the Canyon Court has spacious units with standard furnishings, plus family rooms with kitchenettes, and one- and two-bedroom suites. There's a guest Laundromat, a heated outdoor swimming pool, courtesy coffee, and a restaurant next door.

RATES: June–Sept $55–$65 single, $65–$75 double; $10 less Oct–May. AE, DC, ER, MC, V. Parking: free. *Bus:* 246.

4. Budget Accommodations

DOWNTOWN

- **Hotel California,** 1176 Granville St., V6Z 1L8 (tel. 604/688-8701). 130 rooms. TV TEL

Completely renovated to keep the guest rooms cushioned from the live rock 'n' roll in the downstairs lounge, this hotel is nicer than its exterior might suggest. All but 30 of the spacious bedrooms have full bathrooms (with a tub or shower); the others share facilities. Furnishings are basic but satisfactory. In addition to the lounge, the hotel has a coffee shop and pub.

RATES: Summer $35 single, $40 double; winter $5 less. AE, MC, V. *Bus:* 4, 7, 8, 10, or 20.

- **Kingston Hotel,** 757 Richards St., V6B 3A6 (tel. 604/684-9024). 60 rooms. TEL

This clean, modern bed-and-breakfast inn may not be luxurious, but it makes the most of what it has to offer. The rooms are small but nicely furnished; about half have private baths and color TVs, the others have handbasins and shared facilities. Continental breakfast is served in a small lounge; desserts are available from room service. Intrepid travelers are glad to find a sauna and guest Laundromat. But be aware: This three-story hotel has no elevator.

RATES (INCLUDING CONTINENTAL BREAKFAST): May–Oct, $30–$45 single, $35–$60 double, $50–$65 twin, lower rates for shared bath; off-season $5 less. Student discounts. AE, MC, V. Parking: free. *Bus:* 15.

- **Nelson Place Hotel,** 1006 Granville St., V6Z 1LS (tel. 604/681-6341). 100 rooms. TV

An older but adequately maintained property, the Nelson Place has a small but homey lobby and cozy bedrooms hung with historic map prints. The restaurant serves breakfast and lunch daily. The lounge has live music Wednesday through Saturday nights and adjoining Champagne Charlie's basement pub features exotic dancers (i.e., strippers).

RATES: Summer $45 single, $50 double and twin; winter $5 less. Children under 12 free with parent. AE, MC, V. Parking: free. *Bus:* 4, 7, 8, 10, or 20.

- **St. Regis Hotel,** 602 Dunsmuir St. (at Seymour St.), V6B 1Y3 (tel. 604/681-1135). 84 rooms. TV TEL

An older hotel located right downtown, the St. Regis has a large if spare lobby and spacious guest rooms that sleep four. All rooms have full modern baths, comfortable furnishings, and lots of closet space. The Cottage Gardens coffee shop serves three meals weekdays, breakfast and lunch on the weekend. There's a lounge with big-screen TV and a pub featuring exotic dancers. The desk will handle laundry. Small pets are permitted.

RATES: Summer $45 single, $50 double, $55 twin; winter rates $5 less. Children under 12 free with parent. AE, DC, ER, MC, V. *SkyTrain:* Granville.

- **YMCA,** 955 Burrard St. (at Barclay St.), V6Z 1Y2 (tel. 604/681-0221). 120 rooms. A/C

Rooms, for both men and women, lack size and character, but they're spotlessly clean. There's a single bed, a table, a desk with a lamp, a walk-in closet—and that's it. Washrooms and showers are shared, along with pay phones and a coin-op laundry. TVs can be rented from the desk. Guests may use the Y's athletic facilities, including indoor pool, gymnasium, weight room, and racquetball courts. Jonathan J's, a small café, is open six days for low-cost breakfasts and lunches. No liquor is allowed.

RATES: May–Sept, single $27 nightly, $140 weekly, $400 monthly; double $46 nightly. Oct–Apr, single $23 nightly, $125 weekly, $360 monthly; double $36 nightly. MC, V. Parking: $3.75. *Bus:* 22.

- **The Hotel at the YWCA,** 580 Burrard St., V6C 2K9 (tel. 604/662-8188; toll free 800/663-1424 in northwest U.S. and western Canada; fax 604/684-9171). 166 rooms. A/C TEL

A modern 13-story residence, this Y welcomes women, couples, families, and groups—but no single men. The rooms are larger, with armchairs part of the furnishings; some even have private baths, though most share facilities. There's a TV lounge and a communal kitchen; women may use the swimming pool, sauna, and weight room. The neon-lit cafeteria sells meals for about $4. A YWCA-licensed child-care center is just two blocks away.

RATES: $34–$39 single, $44–$53 twin or double, $54–$59 families, seventh night free for weekly stays. MC, V. Parking: none available. *SkyTrain:* Burrard.

GASTOWN/CHINATOWN

- **Patricia Hotel,** 403 E. Hastings St., V6A 1P6 (tel. 604/255-4301). 195 rooms. TV TEL

Most rooms in this six-story hotel east of Chinatown offer fine views of the downtown skyline. They're simply furnished but well kept. All rooms have ceiling fans and private baths with showers or tubs. A pub on the premises serves three home-cooked meals a day.

RATES: $29–$39 single, $36–$49 double. MC, V. Parking: free. *Bus:* 14 or 21.

- **Dominion Hotel,** 210 Abbott St. (at Water St.), V6B 2K8 (tel. 604/681-6666). 74 rooms. TV

A restored 1899 heritage property in the heart of Gastown, this red-and-white brick palace is a museum of Vancouver nostalgia with a lobby full of fascinating antiques. There are no elevators; an impressive staircase leads to the neatly furnished rooms. Half have private baths; the others share facilities. A complimentary breakfast is served until 11am. Orlando's Fresh Pasta Bar is open 24 hours, and there's live music in the Lamplighter Pub—the first public bar in Vancouver to serve women, early in this century.

RATES (INCLUDING CONTINENTAL BREAKFAST): Summer $39.95–$44.95 single, $49.95–$54.95 double; winter $29.95–$39.95 single, $34.95–$44.95 double, with higher rates for private bath. AE, MC, V. Parking: none available. *Bus:* 14 or 21.

- **Niagara Hotel,** 435 W. Pender St., V6B 1V2 (tel. 604/688-7574). 99 rooms. TV

The handsome hewn-stone facade welcomes guests to this old hotel at the edge of Gastown. The rooms are small and somewhat sparse, but they're clean and adequate for the budget-watcher. Forty have private baths; there's a bathroom on each floor for other guests. The hotel pub serves cafeteria lunches Monday through Saturday.

RATES: $25–$37 single, $30–$42 double, with higher rates for private bath. Children free with parent. AE, MC, V. *Bus:* 19.

- **Backpackers Youth Hostel,** 929 Main St., V6A 2V8 (tel. 604/682-2441). 33 rooms.

More a boardinghouse than a traditional hostel, this former guest house on the edge of Chinatown has 18 three-bed dormitory rooms and 15 private rooms with single or double beds. Bathroom and shower facilities are shared, along with a community kitchen, dining room, library, TV room, pay phone, and coin-op laundry. Bicycle rentals are popular in summer. There's no day or night curfew; everybody gets a front-door key.

RATES: $8 dorm bed, $16 single, $20 double. Cash only. Parking: limited. *SkyTrain:* Main.

EAST OF DOWNTOWN

- **Cariboo Motel and Trailer Park,** 2555 Kingsway, V5R 5H3 (tel. 604/435-2251). 33 rooms, 34 trailer/RV sites. TV TEL

More like a residential community than a motel, the Cariboo has individual cabins with private garages surrounded by lawns, trees, and shrubbery. It's great for families, with a playground nearby. The trailer park is at the rear of the motel units.

RATES: $44–$54 single, $48–$58 double, $10 additional person. Price includes kitchen. Pets $4 on acceptance. $20 for RV hookups, including shower. MC, V. *Bus:* 19.

- **2400 Motel,** 2400 Kingsway, V5R 5G9 (tel. 604/434-2464). 65 rooms. TV TEL

An everyday two-story motel and a not-so-ordinary cluster of a dozen white bungalows comprise this hostelry. The cabins are special; positioned on lovely landscaped grounds, they have kitchens and separate front and back doors.

RATES: $35–$52 single or double. MC, V. Parking: free. Pets $2. *Bus:* 19.

RV Park

- **Burnaby Cariboo R.V. Park,** 8765 Cariboo Place, Burnaby V3N 4T2 (tel. 604/420-1722). 217 full-hookup sites.

Surrounded by 400-acre Burnaby Lake Regional Park, this lovely spot is reached by Gagliardi Way, just north of Highway 1 near Port Moody. Most sites have 30-amp electrical, cable TV, and telephone hookups. Heated washrooms have free hot showers and are disabled accessible.

Facilities include an indoor pool, whirlpool, sunbathing deck, adult lounge, games arcade, coin-op laundry, and a market. There's also a sanitary dump station and a shuttle bus service.

RATES: $16 for full hookups. MC, V.

SOUTH OF DOWNTOWN

- **Walter Gage Residence,** 5961 Student Union Blvd. (at Westbrook Mall), University of British Columbia, V6T 2C9 (tel. 604/228-2963). 3,600 rooms. A/C TV TEL

This is a likely option during the summer months, when most

students are off campus; limited rooms may be available (by reservation) at other times. Three separate towers have self-contained clusters of six single bedrooms around a central kitchen, bathroom, and living room. There are also some self-contained studios and one-bedroom suites for couples. The UBC Student Union across the street has a cafeteria for meals; guests may use UBC's indoor pool, sauna, whirlpool, tennis courts, and fitness center.

RATES: $28–$45 single, $45–$60 double or twin; special family rates on request. MC, V. Parking: free May–Sept, $5/day rest of year. *Bus:* 10, 41, or 42.

• **Vancouver Hostel,** 1515 Discovery St., V6R 4K5 (tel. 604/224-3208 or 224-7111). 300 beds.

The largest youth hostel in Canada is a former air force barracks, a big white building on English Bay's beautiful Jericho Beach at Point Grey. A member of the International Youth Hostel Federation, it has separate dormitories and washroom facilities for men and women, common activity and meeting rooms, and personal lockers. Like most youth hostels, it has fully equipped kitchens for guest use; unlike most, it also has a full-service cafeteria. The lounge has large-screen satellite TV; laundry facilities are available. The building is closed from 10am to 4pm; doors are locked at midnight. Tennis courts and a sailing club are nearby. Downtown Vancouver is a half-hour bus ride distant.

RATES: $8 for IYHA members, $10 for nonmembers, plus linen/blanket rental; annual adult Canadian Hostelling Association membership is $18. Maximum stay three nights during busy periods; reservations suggested. Family rooms by advance booking; no children under 5 or pets accepted. Parking: free, but limited. *Bus:* 4 or 42.

NORTH SHORE

• **Globetrotter's Inn,** 170 W. Esplanade, North Vancouver V7N 1A3 (tel. 604/988-5141). 7 private rooms, 8 dorms with 46 beds.

Formerly the Montrose Hotel, this is now a backpackers' hostel. Travelers will find it less rigid than a formal youth hostel: There's no curfew, and everyone has a front-door key. There are men's and women's dorms, toilets and shower rooms, and a handful of shabbily furnished private rooms for couples traveling together. Guests share a kitchen (with utensils provided), a coin-op laundry, and a livingroom—the only room in which smoking is permitted.

RATES: $12 per bed, $25 single room, $30 double, $35 double with private bath. Seventh night free. Blankets and sheets for $5 deposit. No credit cards. Parking: on street. *Bus:* 236, 239, or 246. *SeaBus:* Lonsdale Quay.

RV Park

• **Capilano R.V. Park,** 295 Tomahawk Ave., North Vancouver V7P 1C5 (tel. 604/987-4722). 250 sites.

These year-round sites at the north end of Lion's Gate Bridge are the nearest to downtown Vancouver. They have 30-amp electrical hookups with lines for cable TV, telephone, water, and sewer,

plus picnic tables. The park offers new washrooms with free showers, a swimming pool, 10-person whirlpool, coin-op laundry,
children's play area, video games, and a lounge.

RATES: Summer $20–$25, winter $15–$20. Reservations
must be made with a deposit for June–Aug. MC, V. *Bus:* 250, 251,
252, 253, or 254.

VI

VANCOUVER DINING

1. VERY EXPENSIVE RESTAURANTS
2. EXPENSIVE RESTAURANTS
3. MODERATELY PRICED RESTAURANTS
4. BUDGET RESTAURANTS

There are as many varieties of fine food in Vancouver as there are ethnic groups represented—and that's a lot.

From hamburgers to poached salmon, Chinese to Italian, Greek to Indian, Hungarian to Ethiopian, you can get whatever your taste buds desire in this city.

The cuisine comes in all price ranges, and in all settings—from seafood eateries overlooking marinas to revolving restaurants atop high rises, from intimately styled French restaurants in quaint residential neighborhoods to overcrowded holes-in-the-wall in Chinatown.

It's hard to keep track of the exact number, but there are well over 1,500 restaurants in Vancouver alone, putting it in serious competition with San Francisco for the most dining establishments per capita of any city in North America. The listings in this book, while substantial, can only scratch the surface.

In an effort to make this section easy to follow, I've broken it down first by price. I have four categories: very expensive, with entrées averaging more than $20; expensive, $15 to $20; moderately priced, $10 to $15; and budget, less than $10. Remember that prices quoted are in Canadian dollars.

Next, consider the part of town where you'd like to eat. If you're staying in a downtown hotel, you can also walk to the West End (west of Thurlow Street), Gastown, or Chinatown. If you're willing to travel farther, you'll find marvelous restaurants in east Vancouver (east of Main Street, all the way to Burnaby); south Vancouver (west of Main Street and south of False Creek, all the way to the Fraser River); the airport area (Richmond and Delta); and North and West Vancouver (north of the Burrard Inlet).

You'll find one of the following types of cuisine noted at the end of each listing: West Coast, nouvelle (Californian), Southwestern, Cajun, steaks, seafood; Continental, French, German, Swiss, Dutch, Scandinavian, British, Italian, Spanish, Portuguese, Hungarian; Chinese, Japanese, Korean, Thai, Vietnamese, Cambodian, Indian, Ethiopian, or Caribbean. If you look, you can find others in Vancouver as well.

West Coast cuisine may be the most intriguing. Essentially an adaptation of nouvelle cuisine to incorporate ingredients readily found in British Columbia and the Pacific Northwest states, it is heavy in seafood, game, and wild herbs. Your entrée may be fresh Dungeness crab or orange mussels from the Queen Charlotte Islands, served with kelp fettuccine, steamed fern shoots, wild chanterelle mushrooms, and acorn squash, in a sauce of peppercress cream, hazelnut butter, or loganberry liqueur. Every chef has his or her own style, so sit back and enjoy.

British Columbia also has its own wines, grown mainly in the Okanagan Valley, 170 miles (as the crow flies) east of Vancouver in southern B.C.'s dry plateau country. In the hills surrounding the serpentine, 75-mile-long Lake Okanagan and the Okanagan River are over a dozen estate wineries, among them Mission Hill, Cedar Creek, and Sumac Ridge. British Columbians are very proud of their wines, and, while most of them lack the character and finish of California wines or even a good Washington State label, they are considerably less costly (thanks to stiff Canadian import duties). Your best bet for a good B.C. vintage is a medium-dry white, such as a chenin blanc, semillon, or riesling.

Restaurant hours vary. Lunch hour is typically noon to 1pm; in the evening, British Columbians rarely dine before 7pm, later in summer.

Reservations are recommended at most restaurants, essential at the most popular. They may not be accepted, however, at some budget establishments and even some moderately priced restaurants; in a worst-case scenario, you'll have to join the crowd in line.

A positive word: There's no tax on restaurant meals in British Columbia.

---

1. Very Expensive Restaurants

DOWNTOWN

- **Chartwell,** Four Seasons Hotel, 791 W. Georgia St. (tel. 689-9333). *Prices:* Appetizers $5.50–$12; entrées $19–$35 dinner, $13.50–$19.50 lunch. AE, CB, DC, ER, MC, V.

Chartwell was the name of Winston Churchill's family manse in the English countryside, and he would have been proud to call this exquisite restaurant his own. Chartwell re-creates some of the atmosphere with rich walnut paneling, parquet floors, a roaring fireplace, piped classical music that seems to come from the drawing room, and even bucolic oil paintings in wall niches that look like windows into turn-of-the-century Oxfordshire.

The food is no less inspiring. The cuisine is West Coast, yes, but with continental touches: Chef Kerry Sear offers innovative starters like smoked rabbit and rosemary pâté with a frozen berry sauce, followed by main dishes like shrimp and monkfish pie with grilled squid, or a West Coast pot-au-feu of veal, duck, chicken, and prawns. The celebrated dessert menu includes the likes of rose-petal soufflé. Service is what you'd expect—impeccable.

Open: Lunch Mon–Fri noon–2pm; dinner daily 5–10:30pm. *Reservations:* Recommended. *Parking:* $6 (valet). *SkyTrain:* Burrard. WEST COAST CONTINENTAL

- **William Tell Restaurant,** Georgian Court Hotel, 756 Beatty St. (tel. 688-3504). *Prices:* Appetizers $4.75–$49.50, entrées $21.75–$25.50 dinner, $8.85–$10.75 lunch. AE, DC, ER, MC, V.

More than a quarter of a century has passed since Swiss-born Erwin Doebeli first opened the William Tell. He started by specializing in the French/German cuisine of Switzerland—appropriately so, for a restaurant named after that country's national hero—and almost immediately received the highest accolades of Vancouver food critics. The praise has continued to grow (though it waned briefly after the William Tell moved into its new hotel quarters a few years back), as the menu has evolved into one that emphasizes continental dishes with West Coast influence.

The ambience is of classical elegance and perfection. Doebeli chose the highest-quality linen, china, and crystal for his table settings, and the framed historical prints on the walls are from his personal collection. His food, most of it locally grown on a 15-acre organic farm, is likewise superb. Diners can begin with blueberry champagne soup or Buendnerfleisch (rump roast), then savor a Campbell's pheasant or éminçé of veal zurichois. The wine list is astounding, but no more so than Doebeli himself, who will likely stop by your table to chat for a while.

Open: Breakfast daily 7–10:30am, lunch daily 11am–2pm, dinner daily 6–9:30pm. *Reservations:* Recommended at dinner. *Parking:* $3. *SkyTrain:* Stadium. SWISS/CONTINENTAL

- **Gerard,** Le Meridien Hotel, 845 Burrard St. (tel. 682-5511). *Prices:* Appetizers $8.50–$16; entrées $22–$27. AE, CB, DC, ER, MC, V.

Just as the Le Meridien hotel chain is consummately French, so too is Gerard, the restaurant. Original oils hang on padded silk walls; fresh flowers are perfectly centered on rich wood sideboards. Everywhere there's an air of refinement. The light-green-and-peach color scheme lends itself to conversation rather than to stifled whispers—and the food is worthy of conversation.

Imagine a meal that starts with a pot-au-feu de St. Jacques et crevettes (scallops and prawns in a rockfish and lobster stock), continues with mignon de veau (medallions of veal in a tomato butter, sweetbread, and caper ragout), and finishes with a passion fruit Charlotte in a sweet-and-sour citrus-and-black-pepper sauce. That sort of treatment is de rigueur here. Diners also have the option of leaving the meal in the hands of chef Olivier Chaleil, who offers a nightly menu dégustation, all-inclusive, for $49. It's an adventure in dining with no risk attached.

Open: Dinner Mon–Sat 6–10:30pm. *Reservations:* Recommended. *Parking:* $5 (valet). *SkyTrain:* Burrard. FRENCH

- **Restaurant Suntory,** Pan-Pacific Hotel, 999 Canada Place (tel. 683-8201). *Prices:* Appetizers $3–$7; à la carte $2.50–$40; complete dinner $19.50–$65; lunch $6.95–$35. AE, DC, ER, MC, V.

Some Japanese restaurants offer the casual ambience of a sushi bar. Some please with teppanyaki, the staccato slicing and frying of meat and vegetables on a tabletop grill. Not as common in North America are restaurants that specialize in sukiyaki and shabu-shabu, beef and vegetable dishes cooked in a broth at your table. The Suntory is unique: It's all three restaurants in one, and it also has private *tatami* rooms on request.

Business travelers from Tokyo and Osaka, and Canadian executives trying to win them over, find they just can't go wrong at the Suntory. (What's more, prices are much lower than in the Land of the Rising Yen.) Sukiyaki and teppanyaki are suggested to first-time Japanese diners, but more creative palates can try a wide variety of delicacies, such as broiled eel or squid cooked in sake and mixed with marinated sea urchin. For special occasions, the 10-course *kaiseki* dinner ($65) will fulfill every dream.

Open: Lunch Mon–Sat 11:30am–2:30pm, dinner daily 5:30–10:30pm. *Reservations:* Recommended. *Parking:* $5 (valet). *SkyTrain:* Waterfront. JAPANESE

WEST END

- **Cloud 9,** Sheraton-Landmark Hotel, 1400 Robson St. (tel. 687-0511). *Prices:* Appetizers $3.95–$8.95; entrées $19.50–$32.50 dinner, $8.45–$15.95 lunch. AE, DC, ER, MC, V.

Vancouver's highest restaurant, revolving at the 42nd floor of the Sheraton, provides dining and dancing with a spectacular view. Rotating once every 85 minutes, Cloud 9 affords bird's-eye outlooks on the Burrard Inlet and North Shore Mountains, on south Vancouver across English Bay and False Creek, and on Vancouver Island across the Strait of Georgia. The seating is structured to allow maximum visual advantage through the spacious windows.

Too often, view restaurants offer less-than-appetizing meals. Such is not the case at Cloud 9, where the food is equal to the setting. Diners might start with oysters Rockefeller ultima (with pernod-flavored spinach and fresh crabmeat) or smoked breast of goose with mushrooms (served over fresh endive with tangy garlic vinaigrette). Popular main courses include fresh salmon en papillote, wrapped and baked with prawns and scallops; and Alberta roast prime rib of beef, garnished with horseradish Spätzle.

Open: Daily breakfast 6:30am–11am, lunch 11am–2:30pm, dinner 5:30–10:30pm. Lounge open to 1am Mon–Sat. *Reservations:* Suggested. *Parking:* $1. *Bus:* 8. WEST COAST

- **Le Gavroche,** 1616 Alberni St. at Cardero (tel. 685-3924). *Prices:* Appetizers $5–$9, entrées $16.50–$26 dinner, $9–$15 lunch. AE, DC, MC, V.

There are many who say this is Vancouver's finest French restaurant, and, although that's saying a mouthful, I'm not one to disagree. After all, wasn't London's Le Gavroche the first three-star Michelin restaurant outside France? This establishment, owned and operated by Jean-Luc Bertrand since the mid-1970s, is not related —but the quality is such that it could easily be a cousin. Located in an elegant old house a few steps from the Westin Bayshore, it offers a perfect cozy setting for a candlelit dinner.

Diners can start with a smoked quail salad in a ginger-and-hazelnut dressing, rabbit pâté with quince purée, or a lobster velouté with Armagnac. Entrées include monkfish in pistachio cream sauce, skate and abalone in lemon butter with blackberries, poached oysters in a seaweed-and-apple-cider sauce, and breast of duck with figs and white porto sauce. Get the idea? It's a house policy, incidentally, to avoid excessively rich foods by using cream and butter sparingly. The wines, especially the Bordeaux, are superb, and in all (and I mean *all*) price ranges; and the service is attentive but unobtrusive.

Open: Lunch Mon–Fri noon–2pm, dinner Mon–Sat 5:30–10:30pm. *Reservations:* Recommended. *Bus:* 242. FRENCH

---

2. Expensive Restaurants

DOWNTOWN

- **The Prow Restaurant,** 100-999 Canada Place (tel. 684-1339). *Prices:* Appetizers $3.75–$8.95; entrées $14.25–$29.75. AE, DC, ER, MC, V.

The five white sails of Canada Place are open to the breezes, seeming to propel the nose of a ship into the waters of Burrard Inlet. Right at the tip of the quay, tucked into what might be (you guessed it) the prow of the ship, is the Prow Restaurant. Huge picture windows open on the inlet and cruise-ship terminal, truly a spectacular setting.

Equally impressive is the cuisine. You can start with smoked Arctic char in shallot dressing or a leek-and-goat-cheese flan; then move on to grilled tuna in a hot anchovy vinaigrette or grilled lamb chops stuffed with currants and pine nuts. Be sure to leave room for dessert.

Open: Lunch daily 11:30am–2:30pm, dinner daily 5:30–10:30pm. *Reservations:* Suggested at dinner. *Parking:* $5 (valet). *SkyTrain:* Waterfront. WEST COAST

- **Vistas on the Bay,** New World Harbourside Hotel, 1133 W. Hastings St. (tel. 689-9211). *Prices:* Appetizers $3.75–$8; entrées $12–$28 dinner, $9–$16 lunch. AE, DC, ER, MC, V.

Chef Peter Buche, who headed up the Canadian team at the 1988 World Culinary Olympics, has a wonderful place to work: 20 stories high, overlooking Burrard Inlet, with a view toward the high peaks of the North Shore Mountains. His cuisine raises eyebrows as well.

There are so many good things on the menu that I hardly know where to begin. I might be tempted to start with the Sable Island roe scallops in roasted-pepper-and-parsley butter, followed by a wild herb salad with glazed St. Maure goat cheese. Then I'd opt for the papillote of Pacific sole with leeks, shiitake mushrooms, white wine, and cream, or perhaps the pork tenderloin dressed with Dungeness crab and macadamia nuts.

Open: Daily lunch 11:30am–2:30pm, light menu 2:30–5:30pm, dinner Sun–Thurs 5:30–10pm, Fri–Sat 5:30–11pm. *Reservations:* Recommended at dinner. *Parking:* Validated. *Bus:* 19. WEST COAST

- **Umberto's Fish House,** 1376 Hornby St. near Pacific (tel. 687-6621). *Prices:* Appetizers $5–$10; entrées $15–$20. AE, DC, MC, V.

The style here is Mediterranean—indeed, it used to be known as La Cantina until owner Umberto Menghi got tired of correcting Expo 86 visitors who thought his restaurant must be Mexican instead of Italian. Virtually everything served here comes from the depths of the sea, not from its shores. There are pastas stuffed with crab meat, a hearty cioppino stew, a blackened catfish with lime papaya relish . . . you get the idea. There's also an outdoor patio for summer dining, when fish is grilled over apple wood.

Open: Dinner Tues–Thurs 6–10pm, Fri–Sat 6–11pm. *Reservations:* Recommended. *Parking:* $4 (valet). *Bus:* 22 (then one block east on Pacific) or 401 (one block west on Pacific). MEDITERRANEAN/SEAFOOD

- **Jean-Pierre's Restaurant,** Plaza Level, 4 Bentall Centre, 1055 Dunsmuir St. (tel. 669-0360). *Prices:* Appetizers $3.95–$9.95; entrées $15–$22.50 dinner, $10.50–$15.25 lunch. AE, DC, ER, MC, V.

Under the summer sun, you might see the colorful umbrellas of a sidewalk café amid the fountains and greenery beneath the Bentall Centre's towers. At other times, you may have to search to find this elegant little restaurant—but it's worth it! Owner Jean-Pierre Bachellerie has employed all the tricks he once learned as food and beverage manager at the Four Seasons Hotel to bring good cuisine and hospitality to a greater share of the Vancouver public.

Menus are handwritten, and change often. Spit-roasted rack of lamb, chateaubriand (straight from the rotisserie), supreme of chicken with crab à l'armoricaine, and poached filet of salmon aux salsifis et concombre are among the popular dishes. Jean-Pierre also offers a pre-theater table d'hôte before 6pm for $16.25, and special French provincial menus on Thursday night for $19.50.

Open: Breakfast Mon–Sat 7:30am–11am, lunch Mon–Sat 11am–4pm, dinner Mon–Fri 4pm–10pm, Sat 4pm–midnight. *Reservations:* Recommended, especially at lunch. *SkyTrain:* Burrard. TRADITIONAL FRENCH

- **Le Mistral Restaurant,** 1025 Robson St. (tel. 687-1105). *Prices:* Appetizers $3.50–$6.95; entrées $9.75–$18.75 dinner, $7.50–$13.50 lunch. AE, DC, ER, MC, V.

Maryse and Jean-Michel Pouget's cozy restaurant in the Robson Galleria is the next best thing to a romantic café on the Riviera. Seafood, prepared in a delightful Marseillaise style, is the house specialty; and it's offered with exquisite white-linen service that extends to an outdoor patio during the summer months.

Hors d'oeuvres include minced frog legs in a seafood mousse, and a duck terrine with pistachio nuts and cognac. Entrées include a monkfish tail crépinette with mustard-seed sauce, and sweetbreads and veal kidneys in puff pastry with rosemary sauce. Reserve at least one full day ahead for the gastronomic menu, a seven-course dinner that changes monthly and highlights the particular talents of chef André Bernier.

Open: Lunch Mon–Fri noon–2pm, dinner Mon–Sat 6–10pm. *Reservations:* Recommended. *Bus:* 8. PROVENCALE.

- **Piccolo Mondo,** 850 Thurlow St. (tel. 688-1633). *Prices:* Appetizers $5–$12, entrées $13–$19. AE, MC, V.

In a too-small beige-and-brown room at the corner of Smythe Street is an establishment many consider to be the best Italian restaurant in Vancouver. Noted food critic Jurgen Gothe, in fact, has declared it *the* best restaurant in the city. Why? Because Piccolo Mondo has succeeded in being many things to many people—trendy and traditional, generous and refined, with Canada's best Italian wine list and a pared-down menu of innovative specials.

Diners are asked to choose from among 30 or more pastas; a half-portion makes a dandy starter. Consider the nido di Lumache, angel-hair pasta with escargots, garlic, walnuts, and pernod. Fish and meat main dishes vary greatly, from mahimahi alla livornese to quail alla Borghese to tripe and beef tongue. The insalata Piccolo Mondo is indeed special: It includes ham, mushrooms, and papaya.

Open: Lunch Mon–Fri 11:30am–2:30pm; dinner Mon–Fri 5:30–10:30pm, Sat 5:30–11pm. *Reservations:* Essential. *Parking:* no charge (valet). *Bus:* 8 (then one block north from Robson). TRADITIONAL ITALIAN

- **Il Giardino di Umberto,** 1382 Hornby St. (tel. 669-2422). *Prices:* Appetizers $5–$10; entrées $15–$20 dinner, $10–$15 lunch. AE, DC, ER, MC, V.

Of five major restaurants owned and operated by Vancouver's famed Italian chef, Umberto Menghi, this is the one where the in crowd congregates. Local celebrities hand the keys to their Ferraris and BMWs to natty valets, then rush into "Umberto's Garden" to gawk at visiting screen stars. The ambience is of a romantic seaside villa, with leather chairs on tile floors beneath high ceilings. When the weather cooperates, there's outdoor patio seating beside a vine-draped terrace.

The menu emphasizes pasta and game. In the former category, capelletti stuffed with squash, and tortellini mascarpone are an interesting change from linguine and fetuccine. Game dishes include pheasant with polenta, quail in grappa, and reindeer prepared in a variety of fashions. Most popular of all, perhaps, are the veals.

Open: Lunch Mon–Fri noon–2:30pm, dinner Mon–Sat 6–11pm. *Reservations:* Essential. *Parking:* $4 (valet). *Bus:* 22 or 401. TUSCAN

- **Bandi's,** 1427 Howe St. near Pacific (tel. 685-3391). *Prices:* Appetizers $5–$10, entrées $13–$22. AE, MC, V.

Chef-owner Bandi Rinky's establishment may be the best thing to greet Eastern European eyes this side of Budapest. Enter the warm, folksy restaurant, and you'll be treated to piquant palate-pleasers you'd never before associated with Hungary.

Start, for instance, with chilled cherry soup, then move on to paraszt sonka (smoked ham with fresh horseradish and scallions). For a main course, try the duck braised in Tokaj, or borjuszelet bankar modra (slices of veal in ragout of sweetbreads, truffles, olives, and foie gras). Accompany your meal with longos (unleavened bread served with fresh chopped garlic), and leave some room for a sweet crêpe dessert. Wow!

Open: Lunch Mon–Fri 11:30am–2pm, dinner Sun–Thurs 6–10pm, Fri–Sat 5:30–11pm. *Reservations:* Recommended. *Bus:* 401, 403, or 406. HUNGARIAN

- **Dynasty Restaurant,** New World Harbourside Hotel, 1133 W. Hastings St. (tel. 689-9211). *Prices:* Appetizers $8–$18; three dishes with rice (for two) $30–$60. AE, DC, ER, MC, V.

Vancouver's most exotic Chinese dining can be experienced behind the sign of the flying *devi,* etched in glass at the entrance to the Dynasty. An ancient Buddhist symbol that represents the highest ideals, the colorful goddess has her likeness reproduced on the specially commissioned Narumi bone china, the menu cover, and elsewhere in the restaurant. Everything here is heavenly, from the imported rosewood furniture to the fine ceramics mounted in niches in the walls.

The menu is 15 pages long and packed with items like sautéed octopus with bamboo pith, boneless pig knuckle with vinegar, deep-fried whole crispy pigeon, and goose webs and vermicelli casserole. Don't let it scare you off: Western diners will also find sliced chicken with enoke mushrooms and red dates, barbecued duck with plum sauce, and grilled Szechuan prawns. Whatever you choose, you'll find it to be *devi*-lishly good.

Open: Lunch Mon–Fri 11:30am–2pm, Sat–Sun 10am–2pm; dinner daily 5–10pm. *Reservations:* Suggested. *Parking:* Validated at dinner. *Bus:* 19. CANTONESE

- **Regent Restaurant,** 888 Nelson St. (tel. 687-8898). *Prices:* Appetizers $4–$15.50; three dishes with rice (for two) $26–$110. AE, MC, V.

Simple and elegant, the art-deco Regent is a little hard to find at first, set back from Nelson Street behind a fountain courtyard. Once you're inside, the dim sum lunches and seafood-specialty dinners will make you think you're in Hong Kong.

Western diners enjoy such dishes as fresh shrimp with cashew nuts, chicken with black-bean sauce, and sliced beef with oyster sauce. But look over your shoulder: There's no doubt a fellow obviously loving every bite of his shredded duck and dried-fish-maw soup.

Open: Daily lunch 11am–2:30pm, dinner 5–10:30pm. *Reservations:* Requested. *Parking:* $2 (validated). *Bus:* 401, 403, or 406. CANTONESE

- **Naniwa-ya Seafood Restaurant,** 745 Thurlow St. at Alberni (tel. 681-6177). *Prices:* A la carte $2.35–$18.50; complete dinner $15.70–$25.95; lunch $5.25–$12.95. AE, MC, V.

This delightful country-style restaurant, specially designed by a Japanese architect, was the first of its kind in Canada to allow diners to choose their own live seafood from seawater tanks on the premises. Named for owner Akio Higashio's native city, "the Osaka place" serves all food on fine Arita-yaki pottery and re-creates an atmosphere of traditional Japan.

Crabs, lobsters, shrimp, scallops, oysters, geoduck ("gooeyduck") and butter clams, and abalone can be prepared on diners' request in a variety of fashions, such as with ginger or ponzu sauce. A special 10-course dinner includes sashimi, tempura, and green-tea ice cream.

Open: Lunch Mon–Fri 11:30am–2:30pm; dinner Mon–Thurs 5–11pm, Fri–Sat 5pm–midnight, Sun 4–10pm. *Reservations:* Suggested. *Bus:* 8. JAPANESE SEAFOOD

- **Kamei Sushi Restaurant,** 811 Thurlow St. at Robson (tel. 684-5767). *Prices:* A la carte $4.75–$15; complete dinner $16–$22.50; lunch $5.25–$7.25. AE, DC, MC, V.

Frenetic Robsonstrasse is the perfect location for this modern restaurant, which could be a transplant from Tokyo's Roppongi or Akasaka districts. Chic diners of all ages and ethnicities flock to the counter to watch the sushi makers hand-roll the vinegared rice-and-raw-fish delicacies that Kamei Sushi first made popular in western Canada.

Sushi isn't the only thing on the menu, of course. Tempura and teriyaki combinations, nabemonos (noodle soups and casseroles), and special shabu-shabu and sukiyaki dinners are also available. Reserve ahead to dine in a tatami room, complete with matted floor and shoji screens. If you're staying outside downtown, you can find other Kamei Sushis at 601 and 1414 W. Broadway in Vancouver, and in Burnaby and Richmond.

Open: Lunch; dinner. *Reservations:* Recommended, especially at lunch. *Bus:* 8. CASUAL JAPANESE

WEST END

- **The Raintree,** 1630 Alberni St. near Cardero (tel. 688-5570). *Prices:* Appetizers $3.95–$9.95; entrées $10.50–$19.50 dinner, $8.50–$10.50 lunch. AE, DC, MC, V.

In this wet climate, it makes sense that the foremost purveyor of West Coast cuisine calls itself the Raintree. This is culinary theater at its best. The decor is simple and elegant, with touches of flamboyance, like the huge papier-mâché irises and tulips framed against the etched-glass dividers and pastel walls. Oversize windows stare out across Burrard Inlet at Grouse Mountain. The service is personal and attentive. On Thursday, Friday, and Saturday nights, the lounge (famous for its vodka drinks) features jazz and blues singers. Says owner Janice Lotzkar: "A restaurant to me is like a magic show, with a stage and props. People come in with an expectation—and we overwhelm them!"

The food is presented with equal artistry. Acclaimed chef Rebecca Dawson buys only fresh local seafood, hormone-free meats, and organic farm produce. And does she produce! Starters include sourdough clam fritters and cold smoked salmon with peppercress cream. The house salad is an unusual collection of local edible greens, including arugula, anise, and radish greens, with a dandelion honey-mustard dressing. Dinner entrées include rockfish steamed in nori, grilled lamb in a loganberry-liqueur-pepper sauce, and kelp fettuccine with sweet peppers and mushrooms. Eat all you want (free refills) of a half-dozen colorful vegetables and three homemade breads. Desserts, baked daily, include the outstanding Nanaimo bar—a layered chocolate treat filled with vanilla custard.

Open: Lunch Mon–Fri 11:30am–2:30pm; Sun 11am–3pm; dinner daily 5:30pm–closing. *Reservations:* Essential. *Parking:* Free lot in evening. *Bus:* 242. WEST COAST

- **The Beach House Restaurant,** 2099 Beach Ave., Stanley Park (tel. 681-7275). *Prices:* Appetizers $5.25–$6.95, entrées $14.95–$18.95 dinner, $8.50–$11.95 lunch. AE, DC, MC, V.

A longtime local favorite, the Beach House is surrounded by the trees and lawns of Stanley Park. A heritage building, it went through several changes of ownership until it was purchased in 1988 and fully renovated inside by Audrey Skalbania. Today the formal dining rooms feel like Grandma's house—a roaring fireplace, bay windows, and classical oil paintings on the walls. The adjoining bistro is more casual, with a tile floor, marble-top tables, and Ecuadorian art. Here area residents play chess and backgammon and watch the action on the tennis courts, a mere backhand lob away.

Most interest focuses on the kitchen, however, as it rightly should. Diners can start with a Caesar salad prepared at the table, a pheasant or veal pâté, steamed mussels, or grilled chorizo sausage with artichoke hearts and feta cheese. The delectable entrées include a unique scallop mousse with shrimp, wrapped in nori seaweed and topped with white wine sauce; pork tenderloin with wild-boar bacon; breast of duckling in raspberry sauce; and tournedos of beef in pepper sauce.

Open: Daily lunch 11:30am–3pm, dinner 5:30–11pm. Adjoining bistro daily 11:30am–11pm (light meals). *Closed:* Mon (Oct–Apr 1). *Reservations:* Recommended in summer and Sunday. *Parking:* Free with validation in evening, $1 at lunch. *Bus:* 19. WEST COAST

- **English Bay Café,** 1795 Beach Ave. at Denman (tel. 669-2225). *Prices:* Appetizers $3.95–$34.95; entrées $11.25–$21.95 dinner, $8.65–$12.95 lunch. AE, MC, V.

The "café" is really three restaurants in one: an elegant dining room upstairs, the Sea Level Bistro downstairs (see budget restaurants), and an outside deck with a barbecue menu, (summers only). The view from any of the three is magnificent, especially at sunset, when all manner of seaworthy craft, from sailboats to freighters, are outlined against the sun setting on the bay. But the skylit fine dining establishment sets a high standard all day long with its rosewood furniture, exotic flower arrangements, and abstract watercolors.

A meal in the second-floor café is guaranteed to be an adventure. Many launch it with a jalapeño martini. The everyday menu offers starters like salmon tartare and Russian caviar, and entrées like seafood Wellington and the English Bay filet steak, smothered with Dungeness crab and béarnaise. Daily specials may include alligator steaks. Passion-fruit flan and white chocolate–amaretto cheesecake are among the more sinful desserts.

Open: Lunch Mon–Fri 11:30am–2:30pm, Sun 10am–2:30pm; dinner daily 5–11pm summer, 6–11pm winter. *Reserva-*

tions: Recommended. *Parking:* $3 (valet). *Bus:* 8. WEST COAST CONTINENTAL

- **The Teahouse Restaurant,** Ferguson Point, Stanley Park (tel. 669-3281). *Prices:* Appetizers $2.95–$5.95, entrées $12.95–$17.95. AE, MC, V.

Like a Victorian country home, this garden mansion is set in the middle of Stanley Park, surrounded by shrubbery against a backdrop of large fir trees. Once a wartime officer's home, it was later an actual teahouse before evolving into this fine dining establishment. Both the drawing room, with its soft pastel decor, and the conservatory, a newer glassed-in wing, present panoramic views of mountainous Howe Sound and toward Vancouver Island across the Strait of Georgia.

The cuisine is as haute as the view. A diner might start with oysters Florentine, hearts of palm Côte d'Azur, or duck-and-veal pâté. Among the outstanding seafood entrées are gratinée de St. Jacques au vermouth, scallops and squid Acapulco, and sea bass with fennel sauce. Heartier eaters might opt for the steak tartare, the chicken Andalusia, or the pheasant aux senteurs aux bois—fileted, marinated in red wine with berries, and served in an oyster-and-mushroom sauce.

Open: Lunch Mon–Sat 11:30am–2:30pm, brunch Sun 10:30am–2:30pm, dinner daily 5:30–10pm. *Reservations:* Essential. *Parking:* Free. *Bus:* 19. CONTINENTAL.

- **Hy's Mansion,** 1523 Davie St. near Nicola (tel. 689-1111). *Prices:* Appetizers $4–$7, entrées $15–$25. AE, DC, ER, MC, V.

Sugar baron B. T. Rogers had this magnificent graystone built for him in 1900. Surrounded by deftly tended grounds, it's now a heritage property with hand-carved terra-cotta fireplaces, oak-paneled halls and staircase, elaborate stained-glass window, and impressive downstairs bar. Vancouver's best steaks are prepared in its kitchen and served in its dining rooms with a flair that would have made old B. T. proud.

Folks with a preference for seafood and poultry will find them on the menu, but those in the know opt for the beef. All steaks are of the highest quality and come in generous portions. "The Only," served only at Hy's, consists of 12 prime ounces marinated in the mansion's unique steak sauce. The standard classics are also here: steak Diane, steak au poivre, filet mignon, French Canadian rib steak, and so forth. Don't forget to ask the maître d' for a tour of the mansion when you're done.

Open: Dinner Mon–Thurs 6–10pm, Fri–Sat 6–11pm, Sun 5–9pm. *Reservations:* Recommended. *Parking:* Valet. *Bus:* 8. CONTINENTAL/STEAKS

- **Chez Thierry,** 1674 Robson St. near Bidwell (tel. 688-0919). *Prices:* Appetizers $5–$10, entrées $15–$20. AE, DC, MC, V.

One thing you can say about Thierry Damilano: He's a good sport. Whether he's coaching the Canadian national windsurfing team (a daytime pursuit) or practicing fencing, the friendly Frenchman always finds time to greet and entertain his guests. Many diners, in fact, order champagne (the real stuff, not a California imitation) just to watch Damilano open it for them—with his saber, in a single lightning slash. That's the sort of trick that keeps this little (16 tables) neighborhood restaurant packed, especially on weekends.

Chef François Launay prefers traditional country recipes to nouvelle cuisine, and he prepares them with a modern touch. The duck terrine and the watercress-and-smoked-salmon salad are fine starters. Outstanding entrées include red snapper poached with sweet red peppers in a saffron sauce, and pork roast with walnuts and honey. The grillades are superb, the desserts delectable.

Open: Dinner daily 5:30–10:30pm. *Reservations:* Recommended; essential on weekend nights. *Bus:* 8. COUNTRY-STYLE FRENCH

EAST OF DOWNTOWN

- **The Hart House,** 6664 Deer Lake Ave., Burnaby (tel. 298-4278). *Prices:* Appetizers $2.95–$8.25; entrées $9.95–$18.95 dinner, $6.95–$11.95 lunch. AE, DC, MC, V.

There's an old English country charm about this 1910 Tudor Revival–style mansion on the shores of Deer Lake in suburban Burnaby. An elegant residence until 1979, its 3½ acres of grounds were once known as Rosedale Gardens, and were visited by flower lovers from across Canada. (They're now a popular venue for weddings: There's one scheduled every Saturday a year in advance.) Local government offered it to Hollywood for the filming of several movies until it was turned into this fine restaurant in 1988. The house is characterized by a flat-roofed central square tower, step gables, and leaded glass windows. Inside, the walls display historical photos of the families who once lived here. Ask for a tour of the three-story house after (or before) dinner.

The menu, heavy on wild game and local seafood, changes seasonally. Look for appetizers like steamed clams and homemade pâté. Outstanding entrées include halibut steak, grilled and topped with baby shrimp and lemon cream sauce; quail stuffed and roasted with fresh herbs; and Alberta prime rib of beef with Yorkshire pudding. For dessert, consider bread pudding with warm whisky sauce, or honeydew melon in ginger-lemon syrup with meringue.

Open: Lunch/brunch Sun–Fri 11:30am–2:30pm, Sat noon–2:30pm; dinner daily 5:30–10pm. *Reservations:* Essential. *Parking:* Free. *Bus:* 131, 132, or 144 to Sperling Avenue. *Directions:* Take Kensington South exit off Trans Canada Highway 1, left on Canada Way, right on Sperling Ave., almost immediate right on Deer Lake Ave. WEST COAST CONTINENTAL

SOUTH OF DOWNTOWN

- **Bishop's,** 2183 W. 4th Ave. at Yew (tel. 738-2025). *Prices:* Appetizers $4.50–$6.95; entrées $9.95–$21.95 dinner, $9.95–$12.95 lunch. AE, DC, MC, V.

Many Vancouverites regard John Bishop as the ultimate host. He personally greets all diners with a warm and gracious welcome, escorts them to their table in his small but elegant restaurant, and introduces them to a catalog of fine wines and what he describes as "contemporary home cooking." Bright, stunning Jack Shadbolt abstracts dot the walls and menu covers, and taped light jazz provides the background sounds, giving the establishment a distinctively arty feel. The decor is candlelight and white linen, the service impeccable.

The menu changes from time to time, but certain time-honored items stay. A popular starter is the Belgian endive salad with goat cheese in crushed almonds and sherry; followed, perhaps, by the black pepper fettuccine with mixed forest mushrooms. Entrées may include steamed mussels with champagne and chervil; grilled oysters with tamarind sauce; Dungeness crabcakes with curried corn relish; sautéed prawn tails with tequila and lime; marinated loin of lamb with ginger and sesame; and char-grilled fillet of beef with horseradish and Dijon mustard. Desserts? Try the papaya flan in macadamia crust, or the sweet that this city raves about: Death by Chocolate. With port, of course.

Open: Lunch Mon–Fri 11:30am–2:30pm, dinner Mon–Sat 5:30–11pm, Sun 5:30–10pm. *Reservations:* Essential. *Bus:* 4 or 7. NOUVELLE

- **Angelica,** 2611 W. 4th Ave. at Trafalgar (tel. 737-2611). *Prices:* Appetizers $3.95–$7.50, entrées $14.95–$18.95 dinner, $5.95–$9.95 lunch. AE, MC, V.

At first you might feel a twinge of conscience, going to a restaurant that's next door to a powerlifting gym and across the street from a fitness center. But Angelica can quickly erase those feelings of guilt. There's a Southern California atmosphere—a blue neon glow across geometric pastels, ceramic fish, and pleated white drapery—that lets you feel you're on Venice Beach with all those sweat-suited joggers zipping past the fishbowl windows.

Owner-chef Mark Potovsky's menu changes daily, governed in part by what he's able to buy fresh locally. For an appetizer, consider salmon tartare with garlic-miso toasts, marinated golden tomato salad, or tuna tempura wrapped in nori. Then salivate over quail filled with veal and chanterelles, mahimahi in black-and-white sesame seeds, smoked duck-and-veal sausage with poached onions, beef with roasted elephant garlic, and so forth. The desserts are equally irresistible.

Open: Lunch/brunch Tues–Sun 11am–2:30, dinner daily 5:30–10:30pm. *Reservations:* Essential. *Bus:* 4 or 7. NOUVELLE

- **Monk McQueen's,** 601 Stamps Landing (upstairs), False Creek (tel. 877-1351). *Prices:* Appetizers $3.95–$12.95; entrées $11.50–$21.25; set menus $24.50–$33 dinner, $14.75–$20.25 lunch. AE, DC, MC, V.

I visited Monk McQueen's the night the Rolling Stones performed at B.C. Place stadium. From the restaurant's outside terrace, I could see the arena's billowy dome directly across False Creek, framed by the downtown Vancouver skyline. I could feel the pulsing rhythms; I could clearly hear each word Mick Jagger sang, which (I later learned) was more than most concert attendees could say. What's more, I did so in a spacious, relaxed atmosphere. Monk McQueen's—built on pilings on False Creek—is actually two restaurants: McQueen's, the fine-dining establishment, and Monk's Oyster Bar, a ground-floor bistro (see "Moderately Priced

Restaurants"). McQueen's has a peaked, skylit roof and wraparound windows to take full advantage of the view. There's live jazz and blues (a far cry from the Stones) during the dinner hours Tuesday through Saturday.

The fare is mainly Continental-style seafood, with starters such as ceviche, scallops jardinière, and oysters Fredy. The choice of entrées includes Atlanta lobster, grilled swordfish, shrimp Corfu, and poached salmon Balmoral (with red wine sauce and prawns); carnivores will also find steaks and other meats, and a nightly fresh fowl or game special. Full four-course dinner menus are good value for big eaters.

Open: Dinner Sun–Thurs 5:30–10:30pm, Fri–Sat 5:30–11:30pm. *Reservations:* Recommended. *Parking:* Valet. *Bus:* 50. *Directions:* Turn north onto Moberly Road in the 900 block of W. 6th Ave.; remain on Moberly until it ends at Stamps Landing. SEAFOOD/CONTINENTAL

- **Papillote Fish & Game House,** 195 W. Broadway at Columbia (tel. 876-9256). *Prices:* Appetizers $4.50–$7.95, entrées $14.95–$22.95 dinner. AE, DC, MC, V.

There's a beautiful view of the city and mountains; romantic piano music plays every night; and diners can sit either in a cozy fireplace-warmed room or a skylit sunroom. In either place, you'll always find a fresh rose on the table. But that's not why folks keep coming back to the Papillote. It's the menu that attracts them.

Nowhere else in Vancouver can diners find the incredible selection of fish and game offered here. In the seafood category, you'll find all the standards—salmon and snapper, scallops and clams—as well as dishes from other regions: John Dory from New Zealand, Arctic char from the Northwest Territories, goldeye from Lake Manitoba, barracuda, cabrilla, Hawaiian ono, and another three dozen-odd finny fellows (subject to availability, of course). And in the game category . . . how about Florida alligator? Colorado wild boar? Alberta buffalo? Yukon reindeer? B.C. pheasant?

Open: Lunch Mon–Fri 11:30am–2pm, dinner daily 5–10pm. *Reservations:* Highly recommended. *Bus:* 9. SEAFOOD/GAME

- **Mulvaney's,** 1535 Johnston St., Granville Island (tel. 685-6571). *Prices:* Appetizers $3.95–$6.95; entrées $9.95–$19.25. AE, DC, ER, MC, V.

This turn-of-the-century New Orleans–style restaurant was already flourishing when Granville Island was still an industrial wasteland. Mulvaney's was an act of courage that paid off, based on the idea that quality will prevail regardless of surroundings. Now that the "island" has blossomed into a popular attraction, this Cajun-Creole cantina can claim pioneer status. It is beautifully situated, overlooking a tranquil waterway, the decor a smart melange of swathed fabrics and rampant greenery. Adjacent to Granville Island's five-theater complex, Mulvaney's offers special dinner theater packages and dancing Thursday through Saturday nights.

The menu is pure Bourbon Street. Oysters Bienville, wild-game pâtés, and marinated salmon tartare are among the appetizers; there are outstanding soups like curried Cajun chowder with scallops and clams, and lemon-caraway sausage-and-corn gumbo. The entrées, which guarantee a bit of tang for the tongue, include pasta jambalaya, rack of lamb Lafayette, and yellowfin tuna filet in phyllo pastry. Mulvaney's courtyard is open for lunch under the name Cafe Creole.

Open: Lunch Mon–Fri 11:30am–3:30pm, dinner Sun–Thurs 5:30–10pm, Fri–Sat 5:30–11pm. *Reservations:* Recommended. *Parking:* Valet Fri–Sat only. *Bus:* 51. CAJUN/CREOLE

- **Tojo's Restaurant,** 777 W. Broadway at Willow, (tel. 872-8050). *Prices:* Full dinners $10.50–$99.50/person. AE, MC, V.

This stylish and ultramodern upstairs establishment might be thought of as Vancouver's ultimate sushi bar. Its owner and chef, Hidekazu Tojo (call him "Tojo-san"), is renowned in local culinary circles for his inventiveness in sushi-making. He keeps his sushi bar small, no more than 10 seats, which enables him to banter with guests while molding fresh seafood and vegetables into memorable morsels.

There's more to Tojo's than the sushi bar. Whether you sit at a table or in a tatami room, you can choose to dine on robata (grilled) specialties, tempura, teriyaki, or his own version of nouvelle Japanese. Many dishes are seasonal. How much you pay depends on what kind of delicacies you choose: Omakase dinners, the chef's specialty, start around $25 per person, but the sky's the limit.

Open: Dinner Mon–Sat 5–11pm. *Reservations:* Highly recommended; essential for sushi bar. *Bus:* 9. JAPANESE

AIRPORT

- **La Belle Auberge,** 4856 48th Ave., Ladner (tel. 946-7717). *Prices:* Appetizers $4.75–$45.50; entrées $13.95–$38.50; menu gastronomique $45. AE, MC, V.

A French country inn deserves to be in the country. So chef *sans pareil* Bruno Marti established his kitchen in Ladner, a sleepy bedroom suburb 40 minutes' drive from downtown Vancouver. The Swiss German could be successful anywhere he wants: Twice, in 1984 and 1988, he led Canadian teams to gold-medal performances in the international culinary Olympics, and he's received nearly every accolade available to a chef, including the B.C. Chef of the Year award in 1989. Here, in this Fraser River Delta fishing community, he's taken over a historic home and made it a point of pilgrimage for gourmets on either side of the border. It's an ideal stop for folks heading for (or arriving from) Victoria or Vancouver Island on the Tsawwassen ferry.

If you insist, you can stick with the traditional menu. You can start with escargots de Bourgogne or lobster bisque à l'Armagnac; proceed to a half-duckling in quince sauce, or milk-fed veal with crab legs Oscar, or entrecôte au poivre flambéed with brandy. But if you really want to know why Marti is regarded as a culinary master, go with the menu gastronomique. In other words, leave your meal entirely in his hands. "People who come to dine, not just to eat, deserve the best I have," Marti says. After your eight-course meal is done, your only regret will be that you can't savor just one more bite.

Open: Dinner daily 6pm–midnight. *Reservations:* Essential. *Bus:* 601. *Directions:* From Vancouver, drive south on Highway 99 to Highway 17, the first exit past the George Massey Tunnel. Proceed south on Highway 17, toward the Tsawwassen ferry terminal, but turn left (west) on 48th Avenue. When you reach the fork in downtown Ladner, stagger right on Elliott Street for one short block, then turn left again onto 48th Avenue. La Belle Auberge is about two blocks ahead, on the left. FRENCH

NORTH SHORE

- **Salmon House on the Hill,** 2229 Folkestone Way, West Vancouver (tel. 926-3212). *Prices:* Appetizers $3.95–$7.95; entrées $13.95–$19.95. AE, MC, V.

This famous Native Canadian–style seafood establishment, high on a hill overlooking West Vancouver, is high on the list of places where locals like to take out-of-town guests. Every table in the multilevel room has a spectacular panoramic view, looking directly across Burrard Inlet and Stanley Park to the downtown skyline. Rough cedar paneling and a variety of Native Canadian artifacts, such as masks and totems, give the restaurant a look of authenticity.

Fresh salmon, barbecued over green alderwood to give it a subtle smoky flavor, is the house specialty. B.C. prawns, Alaska black cod, and salmon wonton are other items of note; carnivores can satisfy their palates here as well.

Open: Lunch Mon–Sat 11am–2:30pm, brunch Sun 11am–2:30pm, dinner daily 5–10pm. *Reservations:* Not accepted. *Parking:* Free. *Directions:* Take 21st Street exit off Highway 1 West, then turn right (toward mountains) and follow signs to Folkestone Way. WEST COAST

---

3. Moderately Priced Restaurants

DOWNTOWN

- **1066 Hastings,** 1066 W. Hastings St. (tel. 689-1066). *Prices:* Appetizers $3.25–$5.95; entrées $9.95–$16.95 dinner, $5.95–$7.75 lunch. AE, DC, ER, MC, V.

Hard by the financial district, less than a block from the New World Harbourside, is this friendly family-owned spot. Look behind the shrubs and ivy, and you'll see the umbrellas on the patio, well patronized on sunny days. Inside is a restaurant that combines a casual daytime atmosphere with an intimate evening mood, sufficiently romantic to inspire Saturday-night dinner dancing.

All ingredients are local; they're prepared with Continental and occasional Asian culinary touches. Dishes include a Northwest bouillabaisse featuring prawns, scallops, and whitefish; prawn-and-black-bean stir fry; loin of lamb wrapped in phyllo pastry; and a grilled paillard of veal with an artichoke-and-garlic sauté. Leave room for dessert, such as strawberry-rhubarb custard pie.

Open: Breakfast Mon–Fri 7–10:30am; lunch Mon–Fri 11:30am–3pm; light meals Mon–Fri 3–5pm; dinner Mon–Sat 5–11pm. *Reservations:* Recommended. *Parking:* Free in evening. *Bus:* 19. *SkyTrain:* Burrard. WEST COAST CONTINENTAL

- **Gary Taylor's Office,** 530 Burrard St. (tel. 682-8252). *Prices:* Appetizers $4.25–$8.25; entrées $7.25–$13.25. AE, DC, MC, V.

Gary Taylor has been a fixture in the Vancouver food and entertainment scene since the 1950s. A jazz musician who has performed with everyone from the Vancouver Symphony Orchestra to D.O.A. of punk-rock fame, he has owned and operated numerous clubs over the past three decades, and is sometimes credited with having "rescued" exotic dancing from the turpitude of lower-income suburbs and establishing it in downtown Vancouver in the seventies.

Today, Taylor is catching up on lost sleep. His current restaurant aims at the business crowd with its early dinner hours. A jazz pianist plays throughout the late afternoon and early evening, and there's a changing menu featuring such beef dishes as prime rib and Madagascar steak, and including specialties like shark in chestnut-and-Frangelico sauce. Budget diners are always pleased by the daily special: baron of beef and a glass of beer or wine for just $5.

Open: Mon–Fri lunch 11:30am–2pm; dinner 3–8pm. *Reservations:* Recommended. *SkyTrain:* Burrard. AMERICAN

- **A Kettle of Fish,** 900 Pacific St. at Hornby (tel. 682-6853). *Prices:* Appetizers $2.95–$25; entrées $9.95–$19.95 dinner, $6.95–$7.95 lunch. AE, DC, MC, V.

Housed in a turn-of-the-century building that once served heavy industry, near the foot of the Granville Street Bridge, is this elegant courtyard restaurant. It's now a lush greenhouse of such warm-weather plants as rubber trees, Norfolk pines, and pandanus. On the window is a big sign: EAT LOTSA FISH. And that's what everyone does.

A laminated, fish-shaped menu declares the appetizers, but the fresh offerings are scrawled on blackboards where they can be changed daily according to availability. Seafood can be grilled, barbecued, blackened, or cooked in natural butter and squeezed lemon: your choice. The fish chowder, a tomato-based bouillabaisse, is superb with a squeeze of lime; an ample portion of fresh wok-cooked vegetables is served with entrées.

Open: Lunch Mon–Fri 11:30am–2:30pm; dinner Sun–Thurs 5:30–9:30pm, Fri–Sat 5:30–10:30pm. *Reservations:* Recommended. *Parking:* Adjacent pay lots. *Bus:* 22, 401, 403, or 406 (walk one block to Pacific and Hornby, then south one block). SEAFOOD

- **Joe Fortes Seafood House,** 777 Thurlow St. near Robson (tel. 669-1940). *Prices:* Appetizers $3.95–$5.95; entrées $9.95–$15.95 dinner, $5.95–$9.95 lunch. AE, DC, ER, MC, V.

Few cities perpetuate a hero-worship for a man like Seraphim "Joe" Fortes. A Barbados-born seaman of African-Spanish extraction, he arrived in Vancouver in 1885 and quickly became a fixture in the city. For three decades, he lived in a squatter's shack on English Bay, where he was a combination lifeguard, constable, chaperone, counselor, teacher, and friend to thousands of children. His funeral cortège in 1923 was the longest in the city's history.

Today, the bar and grill bearing Joe's name is a gathering place for many of Vancouver's upwardly mobile young adults. An oyster bar shucks a dozen varieties to order. Menu selections include cultured mussels steamed in tarragon cream sauce, and grilled Pacific red snapper with shrimp, leeks, and jalapeño hollandaise; there's an extensive daily fresh-fish list; and meat-lovers can choose from steaks and mixed grills.

Open: Lunch daily 11:30am–4pm, light meals daily 4–5:30pm, dinner Sun–Thurs 5:30–11pm, Fri–Sat 5:30pm–midnight. *Reservations:* Recommended. *Parking:* $2 (valet). *Bus:* 8. SEAFOOD

- **Cafe Il Nido,** 780 Thurlow St. at Robson (tel. 685-6436). *Prices:* Appetizers $4.25–$6.25; entrées $11.50–$16.75 dinner, $7.75–$12.75 lunch. AE, ER, MC, V.

Tucked away in the courtyard of Manhattan Square, "The Nest" offers a charming respite from the bustle of downtown Vancouver. Surrounded by shops, offices, and apartments, it's not hard to imagine it in any city—Florence or Milan, for example.

The food certainly underscores the Romanesque flavor: prosciutto and melanzana appetizers, fusilli and capelletti ginger pastas, and main dishes like gamberoni e canastrelle (prawns and scallops in a vol au vent) and pollo diable (chicken breast in a sauce of Dijon mustard, shallots, and peppercorns). The chef's specialty is carello d'agnello: rack of lamb.

Open: Lunch Mon–Fri 11:30am–3:30pm, dinner Mon–Sat 5:30–10:30pm. *Reservations:* Recommended. *Bus:* 8. ITALIAN

- **Chateau Madrid,** 1277 Howe St. near Drake (tel. 684-8814). *Prices:* Appetizers $2.95–$6.95; entrées $11.75–$15.95. AE, DC, ER, MC, V.

Entering this original Spanish restaurant is like walking into an Iberian hacienda. Seating is intimate, handsome waiters attend your every request, and taped flamenco guitar music completes the ambience. It's almost like a more refined chapter out of the tale of Don Quixote, whose likeness graces the restaurant's logo.

You'll get such well-known Spanish dishes here as paella and pollo Asturias (chicken finished with cider), as well as lesser-known delights like pato a la Sevillana (duckling in orange brandy sauce) and pincho marinero (skewered seafood in a sherry and cream sauce). Starters include alcachofas Don Carlos (sautéed artichoke hearts with dry cured chorizo sausage).

Open: Tues–Sat 6–11pm. *Reservations:* Required. *Bus:* 401, 403, or 406. SPANISH

- **Tsui Hang Village,** 615 Davie St. near Seymour (tel. 683-6868). *Prices:* Appetizers $1.50–$7; three dishes with rice (for two) $19–$46. MC, V.

The best way to pick an Asian restaurant is to peek inside and see how many Asians are dining there. If there aren't many, you might wonder what's wrong with the food. At the Tsui Hang, there's no such worry. Gaze through the live seafood tanks at the entrance, and you'll see whole families of Chinese feasting together. Established by immigrants from Hong Kong during the electric days preceding Expo 86, Tsui Hang is rated by some as Vancouver's finest Chinese seafood restaurant.

Crab is the house specialty, prepared in the shell in a choice of sauces such as garlic-black-bean and ginger-butter-cream. The scallop dishes and whole rock cod are equally wonderful. Hot-and-sour soup is a great starter, and the almond jello (a sweet beancurd dish) is a perfect dessert. Late night/early morning diners rave about the rice porridge.

Open: Daily 5pm–3:30am. *Reservations:* Recommended in early evening. *Parking:* Free. *Bus:* 8, 10, 20, 14, or 21. CHINESE SEAFOOD

- **Tai Chi Hin,** 888 Burrard St. at Smythe (tel. 682-1888). *Prices:* Appetizers $2–$7.50; three dishes with rice (for two) $23–$57. AE, MC, V.

The decor of this restaurant feels more like Los Angeles than Beijing. It's open and airy, with chrome, brass, and glass blocks, and liberal use of pastel shades—indeed, very much a reflection of the New Age or new wave music that wafts from the sound system.

But the food is very much gourmet Northern Chinese. The fried smoked duck with coriander and dumplings is on everyone's list of favorites. The crab and asparagus soup is a delicious, hearty starter; the garlic eel is an unusual entrée. Squeamish diners are sometimes put off by the rock cod: Before it is prepared with ginger and scallions, it is presented to the table . . . live, in a plastic case, for inspection.

Open: Daily lunch 11am–2:30pm, dinner 5:30–10:30pm. *Reservations:* Recommended. *Parking:* $2 (valet). *Bus:* 22. MANDARIN/SHANGHAI

WEST END

- **Quilicum Native Indian Restaurant,** 1724 Davie St. near Denman (tel. 681-7044). *Prices:* Appetizers $4.95–$6.95, entrées $10.95–$19.95. AE, MC, V.

Imagine it's the mid-19th century, and whites have yet to establish a settlement at the site of modern Vancouver. You descend a flight of stairs to what could be a Northwest native longhouse. It's a simple room, furnished with wooden benches and tables, and a blazing fire keeps you warm. The pillars are family totems, the masks are carved masterpieces; and the rhythm of chants can be heard in the background. This is the Quilicum—the only restaurant where diners can still feast like the original B.C. coastal residents.

The only major adjustments have been the modernization of cooking technology and the addition of seasonings to make foods more appealing to modern palates. Smoked oolichans (small fish), herring roe on kelp, alder-barbecued oysters, and bannock bread serve as appetizers for what follows: barbecued caribou, rabbit, or goat ribs; baked juniper duck with cabbage and wild rice; smoked salmon with fiddleheads, sweet potato, and hazelnuts. For dessert, try whipped sopalallie berries or cold raspberry soup. The artworks around you are also for sale.

Open: Lunch 11:30–2:30pm, dinner 5–9:30pm. *Reservations:* Recommended. *Parking:* Small free lot. *Bus:* 8. NATIVE CANADIAN

- **Robson Grill,** 1675 Robson St. near Bidwell (tel. 681-8030). *Prices:* Appetizers $2.50–$6.95, entrées $6.95–$16.95. AE, MC, V.

"RG's," as it's called, wants to be known as a restaurant that combines creative cuisine with an entertaining atmosphere. Like the turn-of-the-century railroad station it resembles, it's on the right track. Around the huge beams that support black wooden arches and wrought-iron lighting fixtures, there's seating for 290 guests. In the center of the room, near the entrance, is a large bar island; behind is a dance floor and bandstand where local groups perform sixties and seventies rock nightly from 8:30.

Homemade soups and sandwiches are a hit at lunchtime, while eggs Haida (with smoked salmon) highlight weekend brunches. Everyday dinner entrées include salmon Wellington and chicken stuffed with pistachio and brie. New York cheesecake is the number-one dessert. RG's even has a kids' menu (burgers, pasta, fish and chips) that comes with crayons.

Open: 11:30am–12:30am Mon–Wed, 11:30am–1:30am Thurs–Fri, 11am–1:30am Sat, 11am–midnight Sun. *Parking:* Free. *Bus:* 8. STEAKS/SEAFOOD

- **Delilah's,** Buchan Hotel, 1906 Haro St. at Gilford (tel. 687-3424). *Prices:* Meals $15–$22. MC, V.

A toast to the martini, please. A block west of Denman Street, in the basement of an aging hotel on a quiet residential street, is this campy and crowded spot. You won't find many out-of-town visitors here; it seems that only locals are willing to arrive early and still wait hours for a table. Their first order of business is to sidle up to the bar and order a martini. There are 18 kinds, all of them too big, all of them exceptional. As you wait for your table, you can study the North Beach decor and hand-painted Florentine ceiling, or you can order another martini. Wait: Isn't that tall, flamboyant figure Delilah herself, I mean, himself? Barkeep, another martini!

Finally, you'll be seated, and offered a checklist instead of a menu. You can choose either a three-course or a five-course meal, the latter including soup, salad, appetizer, entrée, and dessert. Gourmet selections change every few months, but you can count on fine seafood and steaks, plus original adaptations of traditional favorites. And after dessert? Well, you can always have a martini.

Open: Dinner daily 5:30pm–midnight; Sun brunch. *Reservations:* Only for six or more. *Parking:* $4 valet (street parking is exceedingly limited). *Bus:* 8 at Denman Street. CONTINENTAL

- **The Chef and the Carpenter,** 1745 Robson St. between Bidwell and Denman (tel. 687-2700). *Prices:* Appetizers $3.25–$5.95; entrées $12.95–$17.95. AE, DC, ER, MC, V.

There hasn't been a carpenter in the business for several years, but the chef is still attracting a regular crowd. Folks keep coming back to this cozy establishment like they might to a close friend's living room. Oil paintings and family portraits adorn the old-fashioned blue wallpaper; lace curtains hang on the windows, and fresh flowers are a cheery addition to each table.

Diners might start with clams Bourgogne or a cognac pâté with veal and chicken livers, then devour a Caesar salad prepared tableside. Popular entrées include sweetbreads Lisbonne in a Madeira sauce, rack of lamb in shallots, and scallops Bombay with a curry-and-pear sauce. Every plate is piled high with five vegetables, and there's always a tempting dessert selection, including flambés. The predominantly French wine list starts at around $15, but climbs to around $170.

Open: Lunch daily 11:30am–2pm, dinner daily 5:30–11pm.
Reservations: Essential on weekend. *Bus:* 8. FRENCH

- **Café de Paris,** 751 Denman St. near Robson (tel. 687-1418).
Prices: Appetizers $5–$8, entrées $14–$17. AE, MC, V.

Ask almost anyone: This is the closest thing in western Canada
to a Left Bank bistro. Crowded and smoky, its walls lined with etch-
ings and the menu scrawled on a blackboard, this place will make
you feel welcome, even if service may sometimes be a little icy—but
then, that's Paris. Locals come back again and again: Why? For the
Bohemian ambience? To read *Le Monde* and listen to Piaf and
Aznavour? If truth be known, it's for the pommes frites.

Chef Patrice Suhner's steak au poivre is superb. That could also
be said about his onion soup, calf brains, kidneys in cream and mustard, coq au vin, mussels baked with garlic, and other traditional
preparations. Every plate gets a generous serving of vegetables, and
the wine cellar is excellent. But still they flock back for the finger
food: the French fries. Even the highbrow food critics rave.

Open: Lunch Tues–Sat 11:30am–2pm, dinner Mon–Sat 5:30–
10pm. *Reservations:* Essential. *Bus:* 8. TRADITIONAL FRENCH

- **Kirin Mandarin Restaurant,** 1166 Alberni St. near Bute (tel.
682-8833). *Prices:* Appetizers $1.50–$28; three main dishes (for
two) $21–$115. AE, MC, V.

As modern and showy as the downtown office tower whose
ground floor it occupies, this is one upscale Chinese eatery that
might be out of place in Hong Kong. It has high skylit ceilings, live-
seafood tanks set into its sage-green walls, pink tablecloths, and lots
of black lacquer trim. So successful has it been that a second Kirin
opened in 1989 at City Square, opposite City Hall and the Sheraton
Plaza 500 at 12th and Cambie.

This is a restaurant for connoisseurs who can enjoy shark's fin
and bird's nest soups at premium prices. Everyone, barring aller-
gies, should have a live lobster or crab: They're prepared in 11
different ways, notably Shanghai-style with ginger, onion, and egg.
Other favorites on the 185-item menu include Szechuan hot-and-
spicy fresh scallops, Peking duck, and various hot pots and chow
meins. If you insist, you can get braised fish maw with sea cucumber
or shrimp eggs or fish snouts. If you're here at lunchtime, there's a
tasty dim sum selection.

Open: Lunch daily 11am–2:30pm, dinner daily 5–10:30pm.
Reservations: Recommended. *Parking:* Free (valet). *Bus:* 8 (1 block
south at Robson Street). MANDARIN

- **Ichibankan,** 770 Thurlow near Robson (tel. 682-6262). *Prices:*
$9–$15. MC, V.

In Tokyo, the name would mean "Number One Place."
There's not much question that this was the first locale in Vancouver to introduce conveyor-belt sushi. That's right: In the basement
of an antique-looking brick building, you can belly up to a big sushi
bar, watch the maki-makers, and choose your own California roll
from the options that make the circuit in front of your eyes.

You'll note four colors of plates, red, white, black, and green;
each designates a different price. When you've had enough, you'll be

charged for each plate in front of you. For those who don't like sushi, there's a slim selection of tempura and teriyaki dishes.

Open: Lunch Mon–Fri 11:45am–2:15pm, dinner Mon–Sat 5–11pm. *Bus:* 8. SUSHI

- **Pepita's,** 1170 Robson St. near Bute (tel. 669-4736). *Prices:* Appetizers $2.95–$8.95; entrées $8.95–$16.95 dinner, $5.95–$7.95 lunch. MC, V.

Across one wall of this lively establishment are written the words: "Viva la Luna! Viva el Sol!" In English, we'd say, "Long Live the Moon! Long Live the Sun!" And indeed, Pepita's is hopping both night and day. This is a little piece of Mexico in the middle of Robsonstrasse—red tile floor, piñatas hanging from the ceiling around the bar, muchos terra-cotta flowerpots and other south-of-the-border ceramics, and mariachi or Latin salsa music on tape. Weekend evenings, a line forms outside to graze on tapas and listen to the live Spanish guitar. It's equally busy at Pepito's in the Kitsilano district: 2043 W. 4th Ave. (tel. 732-8884).

All meals start with a free basket of chips and salsa. You can choose standard Cal-Mex fare like tacos, burritos, and enchiladas, or dive into a house special such as carnero al horno (roast lamb in tequila sauce) or huachinango à la veracruzana (red snapper in tomato and caper sauce). Every plate comes with black beans and a healthy helping of guacamole.

Open: Daily 11:30am–11pm; in summer, Mon–Fri 11:30am–11pm, Fri–Sat 11:30am–1am. *Bus:* 8. MEXICAN

GASTOWN/CHINATOWN

- **Canvas Grill,** 52 Powell St. between Carrall and Columbia (tel. 688-5758). *Prices:* Appetizers $3.25–$8.25; entrées $5.95–$17.25 dinner, $5.95–$9.50 lunch. AE, MC, V.

The canvas in the name stands for the local artists whose changing exhibits make this a combination restaurant/gallery. Their paintings hung on brick walls, the light jazz piped through the establishment, and the energetic wine bar help create an atmosphere of modern bohemianism.

Seafood and poultry predominate on the menu. Starters include escargots with garlic, roasted almonds, sweet pepper, and white wine; and warm scallop salad with three greens and raspberry vinaigrette. There's a selection of pastas, including spinach fettuccine with smoked salmon, fresh dill, and roasted red peppers. Among the outstanding entrées are escalope of salmon on squid linguine with basil cream; grilled monkfish with fresh peach salsa; and medallions of veal with green grapes, mushroom duxelle, and Madeira.

Open: Lunch Mon–Fri 11:30am–2:30pm, dinner Mon–Sat 5:30–10pm. *Reservations:* Recommended. *Bus:* 1 or 50. WEST COAST

- **Le Railcar,** 106 Carrall St. (north of Water St.) (tel. 669-5422). *Prices:* Appetizers $4.50 range; entrées $13.95–$16.95 dinner, $6.95–$12.95 lunch. AE, MC, V.

A retired Canadian Pacific rail car rests unobtrusively beside the tracks a half-block south of Water Street. The ancient Pullman conceals an elegant restaurant with inch-thick mahogany walls, brass fittings, rosewood furniture, tiffany wine cabinets, and the sort of fine porcelain one would get on the Orient Express. In its kitchen is chef Pierre Dubrulle, a French culinary master, universally recognized as one of Canada's finest.

Dubrulle's menu changes frequently, at least seasonally, and usually after he has time-tested his creations at his famous culinary academy in Vancouver's Kitsilano district. If you've got something special in mind, call ahead, and he'll try to accommodate you. Depending upon what's on, I'd be tempted to start with a vichyssoise or a salmon-and-scallop mousse, follow it with a salade niçoise, then dive into a filet of beef Richelieu, a stuffed roast pheasant St. Nicholas, or a filet de rascasse (red snapper) à la basquaise. Dessert could be crêpes Suzettes or peach Melba. Portions are uniformly generous, and the sauces are something special.

Open: Lunch Mon–Fri 11:30am–2pm, dinner daily 5:30–10pm. *Closed:* Sun (winter). *Reservations:* Recommended. *Bus:* 1 or 50. FRENCH

- **Umberto Al Porto,** 321 Water St. (tel. 683-8376). *Prices:* Appetizers $3.25–$8.95; entrées $8.50–$16.95. AE, DC, MC, V.

Many people seek out a good Italian restaurant for the scaloppines and parmigianas. In Vancouver, they come to Al Porto for the pasta and the wine. Located in the basement of a touristy mall on the west side of Gastown, this bright, colorful restaurant boasts what may well be the city's largest wine cellar. Amateur and professional oenologists are invited to visit the cavernous cellar and select a vintage from voluminous listings, divided regionally.

As for the pastas—well, there's agnolotti, cannelloni, lasagne, linguine, penne, rigatoni, spaghetti, tortellini, and my favorite, fettuccine con salmon affumicato (smoked salmon). You can get your scaloppine, if you prefer; try it ai carciofi (with an artichoke lemon sauce). There's good seafood, and other main courses as well.

Open: Lunch Mon–Fri 11:30am–4pm, dinner Mon–Sat 4–11pm. *Reservations:* Recommended. *SkyTrain:* Waterfront. *Bus:* 1 or 50. ITALIAN

- **Noodle Makers,** 122 Powell St. (tel. 683-9196). *Prices:* Appetizers $3.75–$12.95; entrées $8.95–$27.95. AE, DC, MC, V.

Vancouver's Chinatown at the turn of the century was considerably different than it is today. For one thing, the gods and spirits were taken much more seriously. Buildings were constructed according to laws of geomancy, fierce-looking guardians were painted on merchants' doors, and joss sticks (incense) were offered at the family shrine, all as protection against evil forces. Those traditions are maintained at this surprising restaurant, founded in the late 1960s by four very modern noodle makers: an architect, a chemical engineer, a mechanical technologist, and a China-educated historian. Inside, a giant paper lion hovers above four different dining levels. The lowest houses 19th-century artifacts brought by early Chinese immigrants; another level features a waterfall and a pond where carp and goldfish are fed live shrimp by hand twice nightly.

You won't need a fortune teller to let you know how tasty the food is. Modern adaptations of traditional favorites work well here. Try one of these house specials: Noodle Makers Treat, poached salmon with ginger and soya sauce; Ocean Clouds, a scallop, crabmeat, and water chestnut combination; Seagods' Claypot, fish, prawns, oysters, scallops, and abalone in a Chinese claypot; Banana Cornish Hen, braised and smothered in banana sauce; or Emperor's Filet, marinated filet with ginger-green onion or spicy sardare sauce. The restaurant does not add monosodium glutamate (MSG).

Open: Lunch Mon–Fri 11:30am–2pm, dinner daily 5–10pm. *Reservations:* Recommended. *Bus:* 4 or 7. CHINESE

• **Japanese Deli,** 381 E. Powell St. at Dunlevy (tel. 681-6484). *Prices:* Full meals $7.95–$14.95. Cash only.

Japantown isn't what it was before the World War II relocation of Japanese citizens. On their release from internment camps, they scattered to the four winds, and Vancouver no longer has a distinct Japanese community. But this stretch of Powell Street is where the annual festivals take place; where a Buddhist temple and several interesting stores are located; and where you'll find this small and inobtrusive storefront. It seems to appeal mainly to Asian families and young counterculture types: It catered for David Bowie when he serenaded Vancouver, for instance.

The budget beauty of the Japanese Deli is that there's a set price for all you can eat. Most guests dig into the tempura and the nigiri and maki sushi with a vengeance. It's good, and you don't have to stop till you're full. Wash it down with beer or sake.

Open: Tues–Fri 11:30am–8pm, Sat–Sun 11:30am–6pm. *Bus:* 4 or 7. JAPANESE

• **Kilimanjaro,** 332 Water St. (tel. 681-9913). *Prices:* Appetizers $2.95–$8.95; entrées $11.95–$19.95. AE, DC, MC, V.

Anyone who saw the movie *Gandhi* knows that Africa, bordering the Indian Ocean as it does, has a sizable East Indian population. Like any transplanted cuisine, Indian cooking has undergone a few changes in East Africa. Amyn Sunderji's restaurant in Gastown's Le Magasin mall exploits those unique tastes in this Nairobi-style setting, complete with tribal masks and batiks on the walls.

The recipes come from up and down the East African coast: Kenya, Zanzibar, Mozambique, Malagasy, and Zaire; inland to Zimbabwe and Uganda; and well offshore to Mauritius. You can start with mitabaki, spiced crab wrapped in phyllo pastry; or soopu ya samaki unguja, a fish-and-coconut soup with leeks and celery. For a main course, try trout tukutuku, baked with green mangos and tamarind; prawns piripiri, with garlic butter, lime juice, paprika, and Congo peppers; matoke na nyama, plantains steamed in banana leaves, topped with groundnut sauce and served with a beef stew; or chicken moambe, cooked in hot peppers, palm oil, and garlic. The Kilimanjaro is fully licensed; you may need to drink something to put out the fire.

Open: Lunch Mon–Fri 11:30am–4pm, dinner daily 5:30–11pm. *Reservations:* Recommended. *Bus:* 1 or 50. EAST AFRICAN/ INDIAN

EAST OF DOWNTOWN

• **The Cannery,** 2205 Commissioner St. near Victoria Drive (tel. 254-9606). *Prices:* Appetizers $4–$7, entrées $10–$15. AE, DC, MC, V.

Sometimes, fish just tastes better when it's eaten on the docks, within sight of the vessels that hauled it in and carried it to shore. With its panoramic view of industry along Burrard Inlet's south-eastern shore, the Cannery re-creates the mood of canneries that dotted the British Columbia coastline a century ago. The tin roof, rustic beams, and barn-board interior show off a collection of lob-ster pots and other fishing artifacts.

Those in the know order their seafood cooked West Coast-style on the restaurant's 1,000-degree mesquite grill. But if you want your salmon (or whatever else happens to be fresh) baked or poached, pan-fried or barbecued, just ask. Sautéed scallops and prawns, Nova Scotia lobster, Alaskan smoked black cod, king crab legs, and bouillabaisse are other delectable dinners. The Cannery is a four-time B.C. gold medalist for its wine list.

Open: Lunch Mon–Fri 11:30am–2:30pm; dinner daily from 5:30pm; oyster-bar menu from 2:30pm. *Reservations:* Recom-mended. *Parking:* Free. *Bus:* 7 to Victoria Drive. *Directions:* From downtown, head east on Hastings Street, left on Victoria Drive (two blocks past Commercial Drive), right on Commissioner. SEA-FOOD

- **Tommy O's Off Broadway,** 2590 Commercial Drive near Broadway (tel. 874-3445). *Prices:* Appetizers $4–$10, entrées $9–$16.50. AE, DC, MC, V.

This bright trattoria is actually owned by an Irishman, Tommy O'Brien, who long ago discovered he preferred pasta to potatoes. Marble and brass, white tile and carved pine, and fresh flowers on every table create an elegant setting.

It is said that the fettuccine Alfredo is the best in Vancouver, but the other pastas aren't far behind. Made fresh daily in the open kitchen, they are offered in 16 or more different combinations of sauces and noodles. The cioppino is superb, with lobster and other fresh seafood in a clam broth. Or try the rack of lamb, the veal sca-loppine, or the New York steak with crab.

Open: Daily 11am–11pm. *Reservations:* Recommended. *SkyTrain:* Broadway. *Bus:* 9 or 21. NORTHERN ITALIAN

- **The Pink Pearl,** 1132 E. Hastings St. near Clark Drive (tel. 253-4316). Prices: Three main dishes (for two) about $30; dim sum lunch about $10. AE, DC, MC, V.

Vancouver's largest Chinese restaurant has the distinctive air of the dim sum parlors of Hong Kong's Nathan Road. Arrive in the middle of the day at this theater-size 650-seat establishment, and you'll find yourself dodging dozens of cart-pushers shuttling steam-ing bamboo baskets of finger—er—chopstick food from table to table. Despite the huge capacity, you may still have to wait for a table on the weekend. Evenings are somewhat less frenetic, and you may find watching the live seafood tanks near the doors calming.

The fruits of the sea highlight the menu here, and the prepara-tions include the unusual as well as the traditional. Stuffed blue crab shells and filet of sole sautéed with snow peas are two of the best offerings. If you're in the mood for fresh shellfish (abalone, clams, geoducks, oysters, or scallops), crustaceans (shrimp, crab, or lob-ster), or fish (you name it), you'll likely find it here.

Open: Dim sum daily 9am–2:30pm; dinner Sun–Thurs

5–9:30pm, Fri–Sat 5–10:30pm. *Reservations:* Recommended for dinner (not accepted for dim sum). *Parking:* Free. *Bus:* 14, 20, or 21. CANTONESE

- **Szechuan Chongqing Restaurant,** 2495 Victoria Drive at Broadway (tel. 254-7434). *Prices:* Three main dishes (for two) $18–$25. AE, MC, V.

Ensconced in a converted fast-food franchise, this restaurant is a prime example of why you shouldn't judge a book by its cover. The owners have paid minimal attention to the building's exterior and have given a quiet once-over to the interior. What matters, however, is the food: Many esteem this to have the best Szechuan cooking in western Canada. Indeed, the owners are natives of that southwestern Chinese province, and their dishes are hearty and spicy.

Two frequently recommended offerings are Tan Tan noodles, a thick soup with peanuts, cabbage, dried shrimp, garlic, and red chili peppers; and shredded chicken or beef, served with a hot brown sauce on a bed of crispy spinach. For the more adventurous fileted eel and camphor-smoked duck are superb.

Open: Lunch Mon–Thurs 11am–3pm, Fri–Sun 10am–3pm; dinner Mon–Sat 5pm–midnight, Sun 5–10pm. *Reservations:* Highly recommended. *Parking:* Free. *Bus:* 9, 20 or 21. SZECHUAN

- **Rubina Tandoori Restaurant,** 1962 Kingsway at Victoria Drive (tel. 874-3621). *Prices:* Appetizers $2.25–$13.95; entrées $6.25–$14.95, full meals (for two) $29.95–$52.95. AE, MC, V.

Here's another restaurant with a less than attractive exterior but wonderful cuisine. Located on one of the more unsightly stretches of the unsightly Kingsway, the Rubina—like many Indian restaurants—entices diners with its front counter of take-out sweets and snack items. Inside, amid the Asian tapestries and artworks, is an elegant restaurant that runs the gamut of Indian cuisine: tandoori and Moghul dishes from the north, Tamil curries and sambhars from the south, Kerala seafood, Gujerati-style vegetarian, Bombay vindaloos, and Punjabi favorites. There's even belly dancing (where'd that come from?) Friday and Saturday nights.

Many diners opt for the oven-baked tandoori specials, which (as the restaurant's name indicates) are the specialty of the house. Others like the curries (consider fish masala) or vegetarian meals. If you've never tried Indian desserts, here's the place to do it. I personally prefer the sweets made without rosewater.

Open: Lunch Mon–Fri 11:30am–2pm, dinner Sun–Thurs 5–10pm, Fri–Sat 5–11pm. *Reservations:* Recommended. *Bus:* 19, 20, or 21. INDIAN

SOUTH OF DOWNTOWN

- **Alma Street Cafe,** 2505 Alma St. at W. 10th Ave. (tel. 222-2244). *Prices:* Appetizers $3.25–$8.95; entrées $8.95–$13.50. AE, MC, V.

"Eclectic" might be a good word to describe the offerings of this neighborhood restaurant. It combines an interest in natural foods with a blend of Asian and West Coast cuisine in what owner Stephen Huddart describes as "a marriage of East and West." There are changing exhibits of photography or fabric art on the walls, and modern jazz performances every Wednesday through Saturday night from 8 to 11:30pm. Huddart himself is no ordinary man— he is a former broadcast journalist and ethnomusicologist working in Latin America.

The menu changes daily. Some items to look for: Boston blue-fish chowder, black-bean tortilla soup, warm scallop-and-ginger salad, grilled tofu-and-vegetable stir fry, and a shrimp-avocado-artichoke-heart sandwich. Breakfast favorites include chocolate croissants, muesli and granola, and various egg dishes. There's an espresso bar, and the café is fully licensed.

Open: Mon–Thurs 7:30am–11pm, Fri 7:30am–midnight, Sat 8am–midnight, Sun and holidays 8am–11pm. *Reservations:* Recommended. *Bus:* 10 or 22. NOUVELLE AND VEGETARIAN

- **The Amorous Oyster,** 3236 Oak St. near W. 16th Ave. (tel. 732-5916). *Prices:* Appetizers $2.50–$8.95; entrées $8.50–$14.95. AE, MC, V.

Seafood lovers find themselves as happy as clams inside this homey little pearl, the decor of which reminds one of a European chalet. Blue tablecloths and curtains accent a natural wood interior, enhanced by fresh flowers. The chalkboard menu features creative cooking (by Australian chef Sue Adams) in the West Coast, French, and Mediterranean modes.

As the name implies, oysters are a specialty. You can get them prepared at least a half dozen different ways daily, including the an-gels on horseback and green chili pesto. Combination plates are also available, and oyster chowder is a favorite among regulars. Entrées may include salmon dijonnaise, fettuccine and clams, tourtière, and bouillabaisse. There's a short wine list, tailor-made to accompany a dessert of Camembert and pears.

Open: Lunch Mon–Fri 11:30am–2:30pm, dinner Mon–Sat 5:30–11pm, Sun 5–10pm. *Reservations:* Recommended. *Bus:* 17. SEAFOOD

- **Bridges,** 1696 Duranleau St., Granville Island (tel. 687-4400). *Prices:* Entrées $14–$25 upstairs, $5–$12 downstairs. AE, MC, V.

To your left is the Burrard Bridge. To your right, the Granville Bridge. In between, adjacent to the famous Granville Island Public Market on the island's west end, is this immense yellow structure, home of three distinct restaurants. Diners can choose between the formal elegance of the main dining room, the relaxed bistro ambi-ence of the wine bar, or the even more relaxed pub, where fishing enthusiasts regale each other with tales of the one that got away. On the vast garden terrace overlooking False Creek—an extremely popular place on balmy summer evenings and weekend afternoons —diners order from the informal bistro menu.

The food is as fresh and as tasty as market produce—which most of it is. The dining room offers primarily nouvelle prepara-tions of local and imported fish and game; the bistro menu tends to pastas and finger foods.

Open: Upstairs, dinner daily 5:30–10:30pm; downstairs, lunch and dinner daily 11:30am–1am. *Reservations:* Highly recom-mended. *Parking:* Adjacent lot. *Bus:* 51. SEAFOOD

- **Snappers,** 656 Leg-in-Boot Sq., False Creek (tel. 872-1242). *Prices:* Appetizers $4.25–$7.95; entrées $8.50–$18.50 dinner, $6.95–$9.50 lunch. AE, MC, V.

There are many stories, some humorous, some macabre, as to how Leg-in-Boot Square at the False Creek Marina got its name. Modern-day visitors sometimes allude to the lack of parking in the area—that you may have to leg it for several blocks. (Well, Granville Island *is* just 20 minutes by trail through a creekside park!) Diners at Snappers, though, are inevitably happy that they made the effort. Behind the big view windows, beneath the suspended ceiling of reflecting tiles, there's fine seafood and white-linen service offered to the tempo of a tranquil contemporary piano bar.

Start with the roasted bell pepper bisque with assorted fresh seafood, or baby black tiger prawns sautéed with a fruit-and-coconut chutney. Snapper's rich bouillabaisse includes salmon, snapper (of course), prawns, clams, mussels, lobster, and oysters. There are numerous fresh fish preparations, including salmon steamed with a tangerine-and-chive crème fraîche, and scallop fusilli with hearts of palm and artichoke in a garlic cream. Chicken, filet mignon, rack of lamb, and other meats and poultry inspire non-seafood eaters.

Open: Lunch daily 11:30am–5:30pm; dinner daily 5:30–11pm. *Closed:* Sat–Sun lunch in winter. *Reservations:* Recommended. *Bus:* 50. *Directions:* Turn north onto Moberly Road in the 900 block of W. 6th Ave.; remain on Moberly until it ends at Stamps Landing. Then walk about one-half block left past the pub. SEAFOOD

- **Sami's California Cafe,** 2200 Cornwall Ave. at Yew (tel. 737-7777). *Prices:* Appetizers $3.50–$8.95, entrées $3.95–$15.95. AE, MC, V.

Even if California wasn't part of its name, you'd guess the connection right away from the ambience. A rambling, tile-roofed, Spanish-style structure across from Kitsilano Beach is home to Sam Yehia's restaurant; wicker armchairs, ceiling fans, full-size fireplace, terrace dining, curved bar, dance floor, and nightly jazz could as easily place it in Laguna Beach. The only thing that's not Californian here is Yehia himself: Egyptian-born, he arrived in Vancouver by way of São Paulo, Brazil.

The food fits the mood. Appetizers include duck quesadillas (with Chinese plum sauce), Santa Fe crab cakes, Thai mussels, and mesquite-smoked tuna salad. Among the equally international entrées are quack au vin (duck legs braised in red wine with mushrooms and shallots), minestrone ragout (a sausage-and-pasta stew), and ribeye steak Hunan. Several cheesecakes are among the featured desserts.

Open: Mon–Thurs 11:30am–11:30pm, Fri 11:30am–12:30am, Sat 11am–12:30am, Sun 11am–11pm. *Reservations:* Requested. *Bus:* 22. NOUVELLE

- **Santa Fe Cafe,** 1688 W. 4th Ave. at Pine (tel. 738-8777). *Prices:* Appetizers $3.50–$7.95; entrées $9.95–$14.95 dinner, $5.50–$8.50 lunch.

Strictly speaking, the Santa Fe Cafe can't be categorized. Its cuisine goes beyond its New Mexico roots, even though the world-famous restaurants on Chef Edmund Cheung's résumé include Santa Fe's Coyote Cafe. (Others are Berkeley's Chez Panisse and Christopher's—the latter, his brother's establishment.) There's a casual atmosphere here, with changing exhibits of local art on the walls, and paper as well, for budding artists, on the tables.

Southwestern food fanatics can certainly get their fixes here. There's corn crab chowder and chili cheese rellenos for starters, pan-fried linguine with jalapeños, house-made chicken-and-pork Yucatán sausages, and a brilliant seafood chili con queso (with fish, prawns, and scallops). But Cheung's Asian roots are evident as well: a warm wild mushroom salad, Chinese black beans, Oriental spicy lamb, chicken clay pot, and numerous sautés. There's no freezer here, so everything's fresh, and portions are unusually generous.

Open: Lunch Mon–Fri 11:30am–3pm; dinner Sun–Thurs 5:30–10:30pm, Fri–Sat 5:30–11pm. *Reservations:* Highly recommended; essential on weekends. *Bus:* 4. SOUTHWESTERN

- **Monk's Oyster Bar (downstairs)**, 601 Stamps Landing, False Creek (tel. 877-1351). *Prices:* Appetizers $1.50–$7.95; entrées $10.95–$17.95 dinner, $7.50–$12.95 lunch; set menus $16.50–$18.50 dinner, $13.50–$15.50 lunch.

The ground floor of Monk McQueen's (see "Expensive Restaurants") is an informal bistro-style restaurant specializing in Cajun cuisine. Something like a black-marble-and-neon New Orleans warehouse, it has an open grill in the center of the room and two round bars on either side for drinkers.

Most diners start with something from the oyster bar, like an oyster slider with vodka or tequila, then move on to something hot and spicy, like a Szechuan shrimp sauté, seafood Creole, or chicken jambalaya. Monk's also has good blackened New York steaks, and fish are suggested on a daily fresh list.

Open: Mon–Thurs 11:30am–10:30pm, Fri 11:30am–11:30pm, Sat 11am–11:30pm, Sun 11am–10:30pm. *Reservations:* Recommended. *Parking:* Valet. *Bus:* 50. *Directions:* See Monk McQueen's. CAJUN

- **Zeppo's Trattoria**, 1967 W. Broadway near Maple (tel. 737-7444). *Prices:* Appetizers $3.50–$5.95; entrées $5.95–$16.95 dinner, $5.95–$10.95 lunch. AE, MC, V.

A dynamic menu, exceptional food, moderate prices, great service . . . what more could a gourmet ask? How about music? An upbeat piano bar—sometimes jazz, sometimes classical—sets the tone at Zeppo's Wednesday through Saturday nights, creating a near-perfect atmosphere for fine Italian food. The decor is simple, a rose-colored interior with lime trim; and seating is limited to about 60 diners on a raised hardwood dais.

Menus change weekly. A choice of antipasto plates recently offered cold capicolla, bocconcini, olives, squid, eggplant, and prawns; and hot shrimp in phyllo, duck sausage, oysters, snails, scallops, and squid. Stracciatella soup is a favorite of many regulars. Zeppo's features 10 pastas including potato gnocchi in a rich meat sauce, and veal and spinach canneloni. There's fresh seafood, such as grilled Hawaiian mahimahi with ginger and lime; and meat or fowl plates like lamb shank on polenta.

Open: Lunch Mon–Fri 11:30am–2:30pm, dinner Sun–Thurs

5:30–11pm, Fri–Sat 5:30–midnight. *Reservations:* Essential. *Bus:* 10. NOVELLA ITALIAN

- **Orestes' Restaurant,** 3116 W. Broadway at Balaclava (tel. 732-1461). *Prices:* Appetizers $2.95–$8.95; entrées $8.65–$14.95 dinner, $4.95–$9.95 lunch. AE, DC, MC, V.

Melodic Greek music wafts through the rafters as a belly dancer, dripping with coins, glides past the tables. Although this taverna is large (it can seat 225 people), there are turnaway crowds on weekends—and on Thursday night, when scores of boisterous regulars from the surrounding Greek neighborhood drop in. With rooms on several levels, Orestes' decor varies from white plaster with sky-blue trim, to a skylit courtyard with louvered windows, to rooms with hardwood floors and pillows on the benches. There's outdoor dining in summer, when the front doors open out.

Aficionados of Greek food know these appetizers: calamaraki, dolmades, spanakopita, oktapothi, homous. They're all delicious. The avgolemono soup and Greek salad are good starters for less indoctrinated diners. Souvlakia kebabs of lamb, beef, chicken, pork, prawns, and salmon are roasted over an open fire and come with potatoes and vegetables. Moussaka and chicken-okra casseroles are superb, as are the prawns tourkolimano.

Open: Lunch daily 11:30am–4:30pm; dinner Sun–Wed 4:30–10pm, Thurs–Sat 4:30pm–midnight. *Reservations:* Recommended. *Bus:* 10 or 22. GREEK

- **Malinee's,** 2153 W. 4th Ave. between Arbutus and Yew (tel. 737-0097). *Prices:* Appetizers $4.75–$9.75; three main dishes with rice (for two) $18–$31.

Two former *farang* (white foreigners) returned to North America from Bangkok and brought with them a gourmet chef, Kem Thong. Together, they opened Malinee's, a restaurant that is truly a step above others of its ilk, in terms of both menu and service. Amid the greenery, neoclassical Thai paintings, and batik tablecloths are attentive servers in handsome black-and-white outfits. Malinee's is to other Thai eateries as a fine French restaurant is to a bistro. But its gourmet elegance is affordable.

Lovers of spicy Thai food who are used to curries, lemon grass, coconut milk, and chili-peanut sauces will find those here, but much more besides. A meal for four might start with stir-fried clams or steamed mussels, chicken saté, spring rolls, and fried cashews. Follow that with a lemon shrimp soup (tom yum kung), Rayong beef with broccoli (nua hoy), chicken cashew in red curry (kai pad pangali), vegetables, and rice (to cut the heat). Don't miss the special house curry of squid, shrimp, and mussels stir-fried in coconut milk with green and red chilies. Try a tropical fruit—jackfruit or rambutan—with mango or coconut ice cream to finish.

Open: Lunch Mon–Fri 11:30am–2:30pm, dinner Sun–Thurs 5–10pm, Fri–Sat 5–11pm. *Reservations:* Recommended. *Bus:* 4. THAI

- **Picasso Cafe,** 1626 W. Broadway (tel. 732-3290). *Prices:* Appetizers around $4.95; entrées $8.95–$15.95 dinner, $5.25–$10.95 lunch. Cash only.

Here's a worthwhile venture: on-the-job restaurant-management training for 10 street kids, through the auspices of the Option Youth Society. Not only do the kids get paid for learning, but all proceeds benefit the society's efforts. Pablo Picasso himself would have been pleased. Prints of many of his works are framed on the walls of this garden-style café.

The food is surprisingly good, and quite creative. A tasty and filling dinner might start with a seafood vol-au-vent, followed by southwestern chicken (with cornbread and red pepper sauce) or filet de boeuf in red wine sauce. Lunches range from Cajun crab sandwiches, to spinach fettuccine, to tiger prawns sautéed in passion fruit and kiwi with butter-and-lime sauce.

Open: Lunch Tues–Fri 11:30am–2:30pm, dinner Tues–Thurs 5:30–8pm, Fri–Sat 5:30–9pm. *Reservations:* Preferred. *Bus:* 10. INTERNATIONAL

NORTH SHORE

• **Seven Seas Seafood Restaurant,** foot of Lonsdale Ave., North Vancouver (tel. 987-3344). *Prices:* Appetizers $3.50–$7.95, entrées $8.50–$12.25. AE, MC, V.

Until 1958, the Seven Seas plied the waters of the Burrard Inlet, carrying passengers between downtown Vancouver and North Vancouver. A year after its permanent retirement, Diamond Almas and his father purchased the vessel and turned it into a floating seafood restaurant. Almas and his own son, Mathew, now operate the business. It still looks much like it did three decades ago—reminiscent of a white hatbox with a neon sign on top—but the fish is as fresh and good as ever.

Nowhere in greater Vancouver is a greater choice of seafood dishes available. The best way to enjoy them is in the Seven Seas famous 65-dish hot-and-cold seafood buffet. The standard salmon, halibut, and oysters are here, of course, and in several different preparations; but it's the more unusual dishes that make this a delight: octopus in basil, scallops in saffron cream, baked Fraser River sturgeon, Scottish pickled herring, pan-fried squid, smoked eel, curried prawns, shrimp jambalaya, and so forth.

Open: Lunch daily 11am–2pm; dinner Sun–Thurs 5–10:30pm, Fri–Sat 5pm–midnight. *Closed:* Mon holidays and one week (for dry-dock maintenance) every other winter. *Reservations:* Recommended. *Parking:* Free in evening. *SeaBus:* Lonsdale Quay. *Bus:* 246. SEAFOOD

• **Corsi Trattoria,** 1 Lonsdale St., North Vancouver (tel. 987-9910). *Prices:* Appetizers $4.95–$8.95, entrées $10.50–$15.45 dinner, $7.95–$11.95 lunch. AE, DC, MC, V.

Back in Italy, whence the Corsi brothers hail, a trattoria is the place to head for pasta. The Corsi Trattoria—at the foot of Lonsdale Street, across from Lonsdale Quay—is a long way from Rome, but don't let that stop you. The old-country family of Mario (of the Park Royal Hotel) and Antonio (of the Cafe Roma, below) has run several trattorias, so the bros know their stuff.

There are a couple dozen pastas on the Corsi menu, made fresh daily from semolina, flour, and eggs. They include fettuccine (with meat, wild mushrooms, and truffles); rotoli (stuffed with veal, spinach, and ricotta); and trenette (with smoked salmon, cream, olives, and tomatoes). Consider the "For Italians Only" spaghetti trasteverini, with chicken, black beans, garlic, hot peppers, and olive oil; and l'abbuffatta ("the feast"), an enormous meal of four pastas, salad, lamb, veal, prawns, zabaglione, and espresso.

Open: Lunch Mon–Fri noon–2pm, dinner daily 5–10:30pm. *Reservations:* Recommended. *SeaBus:* Lonsdale Quay. *Bus:* 246. ITALIAN PASTA

- **Cafe Roma,** 60 Semisch Ave. at Esplanade, North Vancouver (tel. 984-0274). *Prices:* Entrées $5.95–$15.95. AE, DC, MC, V.

A casual family charmer with the requisite red-checkered tablecloth, Cafe Roma sits on the middle of the fence between pizzeria and upscale dining. It's owned by Antonio Corsi, a well-known name in North Shore restaurant circles (see Corsi Trattoria, above). Decor heavy in the Italian national colors—red, white, and green —lets you know what country you're in as you peruse the lengthy menu.

There are 50 pastas, some of them old-country favorites; a half dozen personally prepared pizzas; calzone; and numerous fish and meat dishes, including excellent halibut and scaloppine. Eight multiple menus allow guests to try a variety of pastas, pizzas, or entrées.

Open: Lunch Mon–Fri noon–2pm; dinner Mon–Thurs 5:30–10:30pm, Fri–Sat 5:30–11pm, Sun 5:30–9:30pm. *Reservations:* Recommended. *SeaBus:* Lonsdale Quay. *Bus:* 246. ITALIAN

---

4. Budget Restaurants

DOWNTOWN

- **Steamers and Stews,** 900 Pacific St. at Hornby (tel. 682-6853). *Prices:* $3.75–$8.95. AE, DC, MC, V.

A casual bistro in the lower floor of A Kettle of Fish (see moderate listing), this little eatery is perfect for the person who wants a meal of angels on horseback or cold, cracked Dungeness crab without the trappings of a big dinner. And the bouillabaisse is just as good as it is upstairs.

Open: Mon–Fri 11am–9:30pm, Sat–Sun 5:30–10pm. *Bus:* 22, 401, 403 or 406 (two blocks from stops). SEAFOOD

- **The Elephant & Castle,** 700 Dunsmuir St., Pacific Centre (tel. 685-4545). *Prices:* $4.95–$13.95. AE, DC, ER, MC, V.

This is the flagship of a nationwide Canadian chain of British pubs, with franchises from Victoria to Ottawa. Its temporary Expo 86 outlet earned international fame when it hosted Prince Charles, Princess Diana, and Prime Minister Margaret Thatcher. Here's where you can get a ploughman's lunch and a pint of Watney's Red Barrel on tap in a modern, folksy atmosphere.

Open: Sun–Wed 11am–7pm, Thurs–Sat 11am–11pm. *Parking:* Pacific Centre. *SkyTrain:* Granville. ENGLISH PUB-STYLE

- **The Unicorn,** Plaza of Nations, 770 Pacific Blvd. S. (tel. 683-4436). *Prices:* $4.95–$11.95. AE, MC, V.

"The loveliest of them all was the unicorn." When the Irish

Rovers first recorded their big hit in the mid-1960s, they weren't planning to become publicans as well as musicians. They've done well, though, with this establishment on the old Expo 86 site adjacent to B.C. Place Stadium. Shepherd's pie, fish and chips, and clam chowder highlight the menu, and there's appropriate folk-oriented entertainment nightly.

Open: Mon–Sat 11:30am–1am; Sun 11:30am–midnight. *Parking:* $5 (adjacent pay lots). *Bus:* 15. *SkyTrain:* Stadium. ENGLISH PUB-STYLE

- **The Scanwich,** 551 Howe St. (tel. 687-2415). *Prices:* $3.50–$7.50. MC, V.

Those of us with Scandinavian forebears, who love those little open-faced sandwiches known as smørrebrød, wish we could make them like our grandmothers could. Here's a place that can. There are no fewer than 35 authentic smørrebrød on the menu, from rullepølse (spiced veal roll) to home-marinated Icelandic herring. You can even get Swedish meatballs—with red cabbage and lingonberry sauce, of course—and wash it down with aquavit and a Frydenlund beer. Breakfasts are good, too, served in an atmosphere of Tivoli Gardens posters and piped Dixieland and big-band tunes.

Open: Mon–Fri 7am–4pm. *SkyTrain:* Granville. DANISH-SWEDISH.

- **Presto Panini Cafe,** 822 Thurlow St. near Robson (tel. 684-4445). *Prices:* $2.75–$6.25. AE, MC, V.

This small storefront offers some of the tastiest and most unusual quick meals you're likely to find anywhere: varieties of panini (a flat bread, served as a hot sandwich) and penne (a quill-shaped pasta). First-timers are drawn to the classical panini (salami, cappicolla, mozzarella, and provolone cheese, served with mustard chutney) and the penne with eggplant or artichoke hearts. The café also offers a vegetable calabeze (ginger-coconut) soup, salads, and antipasti. It has an espresso bar, wine, and beer.

Open: Mon–Thurs noon–10pm, Sat–Sun noon–midnight. *Bus:* 8. ITALIAN FAST-FOOD

- **Las Tapas,** 760 Cambie St. between Georgia and Robson (tel. 669-1624). *Prices:* $1.45–$5.25/dish. AE, MC, V.

Just around the corner from the Queen Elizabeth Theatre is this likely locale for pre- and postconcert nibbles. Tapas, the appetizer-sized Spanish answer to fast food, are served in a big tiled room that looks and feels like somewhere distant. Dishes like eggplant, calamares (squid), garlic shrimp, spicy chorizo sausage, and marinated lamb are available in small, medium, or large portions.

Open: Mon–Thurs 11:30am–10pm, Fri 11:30am–11:30pm, Sat 5–11:30pm, Sun 5–10pm; later hours if concert schedules warrant. *Bus:* 15 or 242. SPANISH TAPAS

- **La Bodega,** 1277 Howe St. near Drake (tel. 684-8815). *Prices:* $1.95–$6.95/dish. AE, DC, MC, V.

This popular bar-restaurant on the ground floor of the Chateau Madrid restaurant (see "Moderately Priced Restaurants") is like a dark, cozy cavern with its brick walls and mounted bull's head. Choose from hot and cold tapas like mejillones (mussels in vinaigrette or a pepper wine sauce), albondigas (Spanish meat balls), besugo en salsa (red snapper), or empanadilla (Spanish pie). Wash it down with fruity sangria.

Open: Mon–Sat 11:30am–1am. *Bus:* 401, 403, or 406. SPANISH TAPAS

- **A Taste of Jamaica,** 941 Davie St. between Hornby and Burrard (tel. 683-3464). *Prices:* $4–$7.75. Cash only.

This tiny rasta diner with just six tables and a solid diet of reggae music is where Jimmy Buffett might come searching for changes in latitude. He'd find ackee and codfish with a fried plantain dumpling on the menu, as well as a variety of vegetable, fish, and meat curries—goat, for instance. The highlight of his meal might be an ice-cold guava or mango juice.

Open: Mon–Sat 11am–11pm, Sun 5–11pm. *Bus:* 8. JAMAICAN

- **Forster's,** Granville Square, 200 Granville St. (tel. 689-8888). *Prices:* $4.95–$18.95. AE, MC, V.

A friendly family operation overlooking Canada Place adjacent to the SeaBus terminal, this restaurant offers an international menu with everything from shirred eggs Lorraine to chicken Beijing, steak Madagascar to Caribbean lobster tails. There's a special children's menu for those 12 and under. Forster's is fully licensed, and has live nightly entertainment.

Open: Mon–Thurs 6:30am–11pm, Fri 6:30am–midnight, Sat 7am–midnight, Sun 10am–10pm. *Parking:* Free. *SkyTrain:* Waterfront. FAMILY-STYLE

- **Leswick's on Georgia,** 418 W. Georgia St. (tel. 688-0939). *Prices:* $2.50–$6.25. Cash only.

Another family restaurant, Leswick's offers clean, simple decor, and cafeteria-style service with posted menu. Breakfasts are cheap, burgers with the works cost just $4.25, and baked ham dinners are at the top of the line.

Open: Mon–Fri 7am–9pm, Sat 7am–8pm. *Bus:* 242. FAMILY-STYLE

- **Monte Cristo Restaurant,** 1098 Robson St. at Thurlow (tel. 682-2131). *Prices:* $3.95–$13.95. AE, MC, V.

A bright corner café with big windows seemingly made for people-watching, the Monte Cristo challenges hungry visitors to walk past its elegant pâtisserie section to the restaurant at the rear. Those who make it find frittatas, croque sandwiches, seafood and poultry dishes, and pastas like orange-tarragon fettuccine. Others are waylaid by almond chocolate croissants with espresso, or perhaps apple crêpes Calvados flambé . . .

Open: Sun–Thurs 9am–9pm, Fri–Sat 9am–10pm. *Bus:* 8. INTERNATIONAL

WEST END

- **Dover Seafood,** 945 Denman St. (tel. 683-1517). *Prices:* $4.95–$8.95. AE, MC, V.

A faithful replica of an English tearoom, this charming little corner eatery exudes both atmosphere and gentility. Horse brasses decorate the walls, and the menu features "sweets" and announces high tea. The focus is on fish and chips; try the Dover sole, accompanied by traditional cockney lager and lime.

Open: Sat–Thurs 11:30am–9:30pm, Fri 11:30am–10pm. *Bus:* 8. FISH AND CHIPS

- **Penny Lane Bistro & Cafe,** 1025 Robson St. (tel. 689-1888). *Prices:* $2.75–$9.95. MC, V.

This isn't really British, but the Beatles certainly were! You'll hear their music before you see the restaurant/lounge: "She Loves You" and "Yellow Submarine," descending from a second-floor balcony over Robsonstrasse. The ambience is dedicated to the Fab Four: Even the menu is shaped like a record jacket and liberally spiced with John Lennon–style humor. There are salads, burgers, and other standard fare; but the specialties of the house are meat or fish schnitzels and a C-food hot pot.

Open: Daily to 1:30am. *Bus:* 8. POTPOORI

- **Heidelberg House,** 1164 Robson St. near Bute (tel. 682-1661). *Prices:* $8–$11 dinner. AE, DC, MC, V.

Like a Bavarian chalet in the middle of Robsonstrasse, the Heidelberg House is a cozy, dimly lit, wood-paneled establishment with alpine murals and stags' heads on the walls. Come for lunch, when there's an all-you-can-eat buffet for just $6.25, or dinner, to try the famous schnitzels and Apfelstrudel.

Open: Daily 10am–midnight. *Reservations:* Suggested weekend evenings. *Bus:* 8. GERMAN

- **Settebello,** 1133 Robson St. near Thurlow (tel. 681-7377). *Prices:* $4–$10. AE, DC, ER, MC, V.

When the sun is out, there may be no more popular place for the Robsonstrasse shopping set to grab a light meal and a glass of Chianti than the roof-deck patio of Umberto Menghi's youngest restaurant. Salads, pasta, and finger food like calamari and breaded zucchini are popular fare, but best are the individual brick-oven pizzas. Tell the server what you want, from seafood to salsiccia (spinach and chile peppers).

Open: Daily 11:30am–midnight. *Bus:* 8. LIGHT ITALIAN

- **Souvlaki Place,** 1807 Morton St. near Denman (tel. 689-3064). *Prices:* $3.95–$7.95. Cash only.

This is where English Bay beachgoers flock for souvlaki, the skewered lamb and vegetable dish with the incredibly inviting aroma. There's a handful of tables inside the unlicensed establishment, but if the weather cooperates, diners often take their meal across Beach Avenue and stretch their legs in the grass or the sand. The diner also serves very tasty felafel.

Open: Daily 11:30am–11pm. *Bus:* 8 (at Denman). GREEK

- **Won More,** 1184 Denman St. near Davie (tel. 688-8856). *Prices:* Main dishes average $8.50. Cash only.

The hot and spicy cuisine of China's Szechuan province holds sway at this small second-floor eatery. This is down-home Chinese hospitality—three-wok kitchen in the front window, steaming plates being rushed to crowded tables. The Kung Pao chicken (with the red chiles) is superb, and the moo shu pork is to die for.

Open: Dinner daily 4–10:45pm. *Bus:* 8. SZECHUAN

- **Nakornthai Restaurant,** 1157 Davie St. (tel. 683-6621). *Prices:* Appetizers $3.50–$6.50; full dinners $7.75–$11.75; full lunches $4.75–$7. AE, DC, MC, V.

If you find Szechuan cooking too hot, you'd be well advised to steer clear of Thai. If, however, your palate craves chiles, lemon grass, and coconut milk, the Nakornthai is for you. In an atmosphere of Thai temple art, you can sup on tom yum goong (hot-and-sour prawn soup), gang kiew-wah gai (chicken and eggplant in a green curry), nuea ob (beef strips in honey, soy sauce, and garlic), and pad Thai (stir-fried rice noodles with tofu, shrimp, eggs, and peanuts). There's a $7.95 luncheon buffet Thursday to Saturday.

Open: Mon–Sat 11:30am–11:30pm; Sun 5:30–10:30pm. *Bus:* 8. THAI

- **Greenhut Vietnamese Cuisine,** 1429 Robson St. near Broughton (tel. 688-3688). *Prices:* Appetizers $2.50–$6.95; entrées $5.50–$14.95 dinner, $4.95–$6.95 lunch. MC, V.

Across the street from the Sheraton-Landmark is this fine little restaurant. Although it uses a mural of Viet fishermen as its logo, fish is not a highlight of its menu. The food is great nevertheless, especially the curries and salad rolls. There are plenty of vegetarian dishes and combination meals, with brochettes—pork, chicken, beef, lamb, and seafood—a big favorite. You may find branches elsewhere in Vancouver: near Granville Island at 1500 W. 2nd Ave, and in Kerrisdale at 41st Avenue and West Boulevard.

Open: Sun–Thurs 11am–midnight, Fri–Sat 11am–2am. *Bus:* 8. VIETNAMESE

- **Saigon,** 1500 Robson St. at Nicola (tel. 682-8020). *Prices:* Entrées $6.95–$16. AE, MC, DC, V.

Large and tastefully plain, the Saigon has no Asian imprint except in the general atmosphere. The only decorations are sprigs of foliage above the low, soft, rattan-shielded lamps. Portions are generous and service is fast and courteous. While all kinds of meat and seafood dishes are on the menu, vegetarians are especially welcome. There's an extensive list of beers, wines, and liqueurs.

Open: Sun–Thurs 11am–11pm, Fri–Sat 11am–midnight. *Bus:* 8. VIETNAMESE

- **Sea Level Bistro,** 1795 Beach Ave. (tel. 669-2225). *Prices:* $2.95–$6.95. AE, MC, V.

The lower level of the English Bay Café (see "Expensive Restaurants") is a popular meeting place for West End sophisticates. Cuisine is upscale but lighter and in somewhat smaller portions than upstairs: finger food, salads, sandwiches, and pastas. They include the lamburgini (a ground-lamb burger), Singapore curried rice noodles, and squid steak marinated in tequila and lime.

Open: Fri–Sat noon–1am, Sun–Thurs noon–midnight. *Reservations:* Suggested. *Parking:* $3 (valet). *Bus:* 8. INTERNATIONAL

- **The Fresgo Inn,** 1126 Davie St. near Thurlow (tel. 689-1332). *Prices:* $2.50–$6.95. Cash only.

As a late-night hangout for all manner of men and women, the Fresgo is rapidly becoming an institution for Vancouver people-watchers. A garden-style buffet/cafeteria, it serves enormous breakfasts, a classy array of hamburgers, and a variety of other tasty dishes.

Davie Street night owls enjoy the taped rock music, which seems to play nonstop.

Open: Mon–Sat 8am–3am, Sun 8am–midnight. *Bus:* 8. CAFE-TERIA

- **Rooster's Quarters,** 836 Denman St. at Haro (tel. 689-8023). *Prices:* $5.75–$8.75. Cash only.

When mealtime rolls around, you only need to look for the lines in the streets to find this French Canadian chicken eatery. Look beyond the golf-oriented decor to discover superb Montreal-style barbecue chicken, crispy on the outside, melt-in-your-mouth tender on the inside. Quarter- and half-chickens are served with french fries, cole slaw, and a soft bun.

Open: Mon–Fri 11am–11pm, Sat–Sun 11am–10pm. *Bus:* 8. CHICKEN

GASTOWN/CHINATOWN

- **The Only (Fish & Oyster Cafe),** 20 E. Hastings St. at Main (tel. 681-6546). *Prices:* $4.95–$8.95. No credit cards.

This skid-row eatery is a Vancouver institution: pan-fried fish so fresh you can almost see its fins still wiggling, savory Manhattan-style clam chowder bubbling in the pot. There's no alcohol served, and there are no public washrooms, but there *are* lines around mealtimes, so be forewarned.

Open: Mon–Sat 11am–10pm. *Bus:* 8, 14, 20, or 21. SEAFOOD

- **Old Spaghetti Factory,** 53 Water St. (tel. 684-1288). *Prices:* Appetizers $2.25–$3.95; entrées $6.75–$11.45 dinner, $5.95–$7.45 lunch. AE, MC, V.

Gastown is one of Vancouver's havens for antique shoppers, so it almost doesn't come as a surprise to see the collection that dominates this old coffee- and tea-packing plant. Every kind of contraption you might imagine seems to be here: including old street lamps, fine tiffany glass, a penny farthing cycle mounted on a wall . . . and a 1910 B.C. Electric trolley car, now a part of the restaurant's seating area. You can sup on New York steak, veal à la parmigiana, green-and-gold fettuccine, or Mama Pulosi's secret lasagne; but most folks come for the spaghetti, prepared in nine different ways.

Open: Mon–Sat 11:30am–10pm, Sun 11:30–9pm. *Reservations:* For 6 or more. *Bus:* 1 or 50. ITALIAN/PASTA

- **Al Forno,** 103 Columbia St. at Water (tel. 684-2838). *Prices:* $7–$14. AE, MC, V.

"The furnace" is indeed the focus of this corner favorite: a huge, wood-burning, brick oven that bakes pizzas and calzones the way you always heard they could be made. The oven keeps the entire place toasty on those rainy winter evenings.

Open: Lunch Sun and Tues–Fri 11:30am–2pm; dinner Sun and Tues–Thurs 5–11pm, Fri–Sat 5pm–12:30am. *Bus:* 1 or 50. ITALIAN/PIZZA

- **New Diamond Restaurant,** 555 Gore Ave. between Keefer and Pender (tel. 685-0727). *Prices:* Three main dishes (for two) $18–$35 dinner; dim sum (for two) about $15 lunch. MC, V.

A longtime favorite among the several dozen restaurants in Chinatown, this large second-floor dim sum parlor is nondescript except for the golden dragon that adorns one full wall. Come for lunch, when dim sum carts carry their exotic selection (ever try stuffed duck's feet, or steamed pig's blood with chives?) from table to table. The fresh-fish list is a good place to look for dinner: The crab preparations—for instance, with white (coconut) sauce—are superb.

Open: Mon–Tues and Thurs–Sun 7:30am–3pm and 5–10pm. *Reservations:* Recommended for dinner. *Bus:* 19 at Main. CANTONESE

- **On On Tea Garden,** 214 Keefer St. (tel. 685-7513). *Prices:* Three dishes (for two) $18–$32. MC, V.

Former Prime Minister Pierre Trudeau made this the most famous of all Chinatown restaurants when he used it as a headquarters of sorts for his secret courtship of Margaret some 20 years ago. In fact, it's pretty ordinary, with Formica furnishings and friendly waiters. The hot-and-sour soup is very good, as are the garlic prawns. This is one of the few Chinatown diners where you can get Americanized victuals like chop suey and egg foo yung.

Open: Tues–Thurs 11am–9pm, Fri–Sat 11am–10pm, Sun 4–9pm. *Reservations:* Recommended. *Bus:* 8 or 19. CANTONESE

- **Phnom Penh Restaurant,** 244 E. Georgia St. near Main (tel. 682-5777). *Prices:* Dishes $5–$6.25. MC, V.

Cambodian cooking strikes a cautious balance between delicate Vietnamese and the more aggressively spicy Thai cuisine. This family restaurant offers Western Canada's best of the genre. Hot-and-sour soup (with fish or prawns) is a perfect start to a meal; chicken with lemon grass and marinated beef on rice could complete it. Adventurous diners might finish with a fruit-and-rice pudding. There's a small list of beers to accompany meals.

Open: Mon and Wed–Sun 10am–9:30pm. *Bus:* 8 or 19. CAMBODIAN

- **India Village,** 308 Water St. (tel. 681-0678). *Prices:* $2.50–$8.95. AE, MC, V.

Across the street from the old Gastown steam clock, up the steps of an old building, is this casual, fully licensed restaurant. South Asian art and peacock feathers adorn the walls, ceiling fans re-create a colonial mood, and ragas play softly in the background. The food—even meat and chicken curries—is mild enough for almost any palate. Start with samosas or mulligatawny soup, then order a tandoori dish (chicken, lamb, or fish), and wash it down with a mango lassi. There are numerous vegetarian specials.

Open: Daily 11am–11pm. *Bus:* 1 or 50. INDIAN

- **Brothers Restaurant,** 1 Water St. at Carrall (tel. 683-9124). *Prices:* Appetizers $2.95–$6.95; entrées $6.95–$10.95 dinner, $4.95–$7.95 lunch. AE, MC, V.

A Franciscan monastery atmosphere, complete with staff in friars' robes, provides a warm ambience that especially appeals to families and older folks. Pastas, burgers, chowder, and light Continental dishes are the fare. Children get balloons and their own menu. A bistro lounge with wine casks caters more to young adults;

the adjoining Punchlines comedy theater is under the same ownership, and you can put together a dinner/show packages easily.

Open: Mon–Thurs 11:30am–10pm, Fri–Sat 11:30am–midnight, Sun 11am–9pm. *Reservations:* Suggested, especially on weekends. *Bus:* 1 or 50. FAMILY-STYLE.

EAST OF DOWNTOWN

• **Vong's Kitchen,** 5989 Fraser St. at E. 45th Ave. (tel. 327-4627). *Prices:* Three dishes (for two) $12–$18. No credit cards.

Tiny and crowded, with simple Formica tables and inevitably steamed-up windows, Vong's is Vancouver's favorite Asian hole-in-the-wall. The facts that it's not licensed to serve alcoholic beverages and demands cash on the barrelhead only seem to attract more disciples to its jade chicken and atomic rice.

Open: Wed–Sat 5–9:30pm, Sun 4:30–9pm. *Reservations:* None (arrive early). *Bus:* 8. NORTHERN CHINESE

• **New Seoul,** 1682 E. Broadway at Commercial Drive (tel. 872-1922). *Prices:* Three dishes (for two) $15–$20. MC, V.

Cook your own dinner on top of your table: That's the premise behind what may be the city's best Korean eatery. Every table has a small gas burner for cooking marinated strips of beef, pork, chicken, or prawns. And as long as you're in Seoul, you won't want to miss Korea's favorite appetizer—kim chee, a cold, intensely spicy pickled cabbage dish.

Open: Mon–Sat 11am–11pm, Sun 3–11pm. *Bus:* 9, 20, or 21. KOREAN

SOUTH OF DOWNTOWN

• **Dutch Pannekoek House,** 520 W. Broadway at Cambie (tel. 876-1913). *Prices:* $3.65–$6.25. MC, V.

This was the first of its breed in North America, introducing the Dutch version of the French crêpe. The pannekoek is a solid meal: In fact, the house offers 36 varieties, from bacon, mushroom, and cheese, to apple, ginger, and strawberry with whipped cream—all of them platter size. You may run into other Dutch Pannekoek Houses in the Vancouver area: It's a growing chain.

Open: Daily 7am–3pm. *Bus:* 9 or 17. DUTCH PANCAKES

• **Athene's,** 3618 W. Broadway at Collinwood (tel. 731-4135). *Prices:* Appetizers $3.95–$6.95; entrées $8.95–$10.95. MC, V.

The atmosphere is pure Mediterranean: tile floors, bright white walls, classic vases set into niches, greenery spilling over the trellises that act as room dividers. Greek music sets the mood for spanakopita (spinach pie), dolmades (stuffed grape leaves), oktapothi (pickled octopus with capers), calamari, moussaka, and other delicacies. Try the arni psito, or lamb shoulder. The full bar features Greek wines, like retsina, and liquors, such as ouzo.

Open: Mon–Thurs 11:30am–10:30pm, Fri–Sat 11:30am–11:30pm. *Reservations:* Recommended. *Bus:* 10 or 22. GREEK

• **Heaven & Earth India Curry House,** 1754 W. 4th Ave. near Burrard (tel. 732-5313). *Prices:* $8.95–$13.50. AE, MC, V.

Curry is not, as many Americans choose to believe, a yellow

powder that comes out of a small tin can. The word may refer to any blend of spices—though cardamom, cumin, and turmeric are common ingredients. This restaurant makes it right, in dozens of different ways (and different heat levels). The name is apt: There's a dark, earthy atmosphere here, but the food is heavenly. There are dishes typical of both south and north India, with about an equal choice of meat or vegetarian plates.

Open: Daily 5–10pm. *Reservations:* Recommended. *Bus:* 4. INDIAN CURRIES

- **Lalibela Ethiopian Cuisine,** 2090 Alma St. at W. 5th Ave. (tel. 732-1454). *Prices:* $7.95–$10.95. MC, V.

Cuisine from this northeastern African land has been called "the ultimate finger food." The title fits—you won't get a spoon, fork, or knife here. Instead, your plate will be dominated by a large millet pancake called injera bread. On and around it will be a smorgasbord of foods like doro (chicken tips) in a sauce of mushrooms, onions, and red peppers; zilzil (beef) with a hearty red berbere sauce; gomen wot (a vegetable stew of cabbage, carrot, potatoes, and hot green peppers); and misir wot (a spicy lentil stew).

Open: Lunch Tues–Sun noon–2pm, dinner Tues–Sun 5–11:30pm. *Reservations:* Recommended. *Bus:* 7. ETHIOPIAN

- **Fogg n' Suds,** 3293 W. 4th Ave. at Blenheim (tel. 73BEERS). *Prices:* Appetizers $2.50–$7.95, entrées $3.95–$9.95. AE, MC, V.

The flagship of a growing chain of restaurants occupies a semi-basement room near Kitsilano. It's named in part for Phileas Fogg (of *Around the World in 80 Days*), but the "Suds" take priority here: Canada's largest beer list has some 250 brews from 36 countries. (Customers get passports stamped for each new beer they consume.) The menu is also worldly: American hamburgers, Mexican nachos, Italian pastas, Japanese yakitori, Greek calamari, German schnitzel . . . There's another Fogg n' Suds in the West End, at 1215 Bidwell St. at Davie (tel. 683-BEER); also on East Broadway near Cambie (tel. 87BEERS); and in Burnaby.

Open: Daily from 11:30am. INTERNATIONAL

- **Earl's,** 1601 W. Broadway at Fir (tel. 736-5663). *Prices:* Appetizers $2.95–$6.95; entrées $4.95–$13.95. AE, MC, V.

There are nine Earl's restaurants in greater Vancouver; this location is one of the more accessible. Chrome-plated chairs, marble-top tables, pop art, and an open kitchen lend a thoroughly modern look. Tragically hip penguins meander through an oversize menu that offers nachos and chicken wings, salads and sandwiches, pastas and stir fries. The bar is big on margaritas and specialty cocktails. Close relations: Broadway Earl's, 901 W. Broadway (tel. 734-5995); Earl's On Top, downtown at 1185 Robson St. (tel. 669-0020); Earl's Tin Palace, 303 Marine Drive, North Vancouver (tel. 984-4341).

Open: Sun–Thurs 11am–11pm, Fri–Sat 11am–12:30am. *Parking:* Free. *Bus:* 9 or 10. INTERNAIONAL

- **The Naam Restaurant,** 2724 W. 4th Ave. near MacDonald (tel. 738-7151). *Prices:* Appetizers $1.50–$5.50, entrées $3.25–$7.95. Cash only.

Vancouver's oldest natural-foods restaurant never closes. Located in the heart of Kitsilano, this small (24 seats), rustic eatery is an institution. The food is not only good for you; it's really good. The salad bar charges per 100 grams (about 3 ounces). Light entrées include spinach enchiladas, pita sandwiches, and tofu burgers; for dinner, spaghetti, vegetable-and-tofu-teriyaki stir fries, and macrobiotic specials. There's a breakfast menu, and lots of spice teas and fruit drinks. Lest you think vegetarians are too pure, there are also pizzas, cakes and pies, beer and wine.

Open: 24 hours daily. *Bus:* 4 or 22. VEGETARIAN

NORTH SHORE

- **The Tomahawk Barbecue,** 1550 Philip Ave. at Marine Drive, North Vancouver (tel. 988-2612). *Prices:* $2.50–$9.95 AE, MC, V.

   There are those who suggest that the touristy Tomahawk, hiding behind its roadside totem poles, is the archetype after which every other kitschy Native American–theme restaurant in North America has modeled itself. Dating from the halcyon days before the Great Depression, it has developed a reputation for more than frivolity. In fact, locals line up here for the huge, low-priced breakfasts. And at least one Canadian magazine rated the hamburgers as the nation's best.

   Open: Sun–Thurs 7am–10pm, Fri–Sat 7am–11pm. *Parking:* Free. *Bus:* 242 or 246. FAMILY-STYLE

- **Frankie's Inn,** 59 Lonsdale Ave. near 1st Street (tel. 987-3811). *Prices:* $1.95–$4.75. Cash only.

   A natural favorite among low-budget travelers, here's a simple café where full roast-beef dinners and steak-and-eggs breakfasts cost less than $5. Japanese dishes, like tempura and sukiyaki, are also on the menu.

   Open: Mon–Fri 9am–8:30pm, Sat 9am–3:30pm. *SeaBus:* Lonsdale Quay. *Bus:* 246. FAMILY-STYLE

VII

WHAT TO SEE AND DO IN VANCOUVER

1. THE TOP ATTRACTIONS
2. MORE ATTRACTIONS
3. KIDS' VANCOUVER
4. ORGANIZED TOURS
5. SPECIAL AND FREE EVENTS
6. SPORTS AND RECREATION

SIGHTSEEING STRATEGIES

Vancouver is a fascinating city with a multitude of major attractions. When your time for sightseeing is limited, it's often difficult to decide how to distribute your time. Here are some proposed strategies:

If You Have One Day

Spend your time getting to know the core area. After breakfast, get a perspective on Vancouver from Harbour Centre or Canada Place, then follow the walking tours of Gastown and downtown, including the Vancouver Art Gallery (see Chapter VIII). Enjoy lunch at a Robsonstrasse café, then a sunny afternoon at Stanley Park; be sure to visit the world-acclaimed Vancouver Aquarium while you're there. If it's rainy, consider the museums suggested in the three-day itinerary.

If You Have Two Days

Vancouver is surrounded by the natural beauty of the Canadian West Coast. Spend day one as described above. Your second morning is a good time to enjoy the great outdoors. Savor the view from Grouse Mountain, above North Vancouver, then dawdle a while at Capilano Canyon Regional Park, with its famous suspension bridge. Return to Vancouver for a late lunch in Chinatown or Granville Island, and spend the afternoon exploring one or both of those communities.

If You Have Three Days

Spend days one and two as described above. On your third day, capture a little culture. In the morning, select from among the Vanier Park museums on the south shore of English Bay: the Vancouver Museum for history, the Gordon Southam Observatory and H. R. MacMillan Planetarium, the Vancouver Maritime Museum, and St. Roch National Historic Site. Lunch at one of the many fine restaurants along West 4th Avenue or Broadway, then head west to the campus of the University of British Columbia, where your afternoon will be divided between the UBC Museum of Anthropology, famous for its West Coast tribal artifacts, and the botanical gardens.

If You Have Five Days or More

One day should be reserved for a ride north to Squamish on the Royal Hudson steam train and a return cruise aboard the M.V. *Britannia* through spectacular Howe Sound. Your itinerary should also include Queen Elizabeth Park and the VanDusen Garden, the Burnaby Village Museum, Science World B.C. at the former Expo 86 site, and the Italian, Greek, and East Indian communities. Dine at least once at a restaurant specializing in West Coast cuisine; enjoy a theatrical or symphonic performance; and take in a seasonal sports event, such as ice hockey or Canadian football. Numerous mountain and seaside parks, the ski resort town of Whistler, and Fraser River Valley attractions such as Fort Langley and Harrison Hot Springs beckon adventurers with time to burn.

---

1. The Top Attractions

STANLEY PARK

One of the world's great urban parks is just a 15-minute walk west of Vancouver's central business district. Named for the Canadian governor-general who dedicated it in 1889 (thanks to the conservationist vision of the Vancouver city council), Stanley Park is a 1,000-acre promontory of forest land that juts like a mushroom into the middle of the Burrard Inlet. Almost completely surrounded by water, it is lush with Douglas fir, red cedar, and hemlock, and is home to myriad birds and small mammals. It's crisscrossed by dozens of trails, some of them long ago trodden by Native Canadians, and surrounded by a 6½-mile seawall that attracts scores of cyclists, joggers, and pedestrians (and their dogs). It also contains two lakes, three major restaurants, numerous beaches, playgrounds, and picnic areas, and many other attractions.

The park is most readily approached via Beach or West Georgia

Street. Drivers must enter via Georgia, as traffic through the park is one-way counterclockwise. Avoid driving during rush hours, however: This is the sole thoroughfare across the Lions Gate Bridge to North and West Vancouver.

The 2-hour walk around the seawall is the best way to get a feel for the park and orient yourself to Vancouver's remarkable geographical setting. Most attractions are on the eastward-pointing finger of the park, closest to downtown and Coal Harbour. Detour to the left at the **Vancouver Rowing Club** to discover a monument to Lord Stanley; **Malkin Bowl,** site of summer "Theater Under the Stars"; and, beyond that, rose gardens. Another path leads to Stanley Park's major internal attractions: the **Vancouver Aquarium** and two **zoos,** one specifically for children. (See "Kids' Vancouver," below.)

The promenade passes the **Royal Vancouver Yacht Club** and the **Deadman's Island** naval reserve training base. On the left, **Brockton Oval,** a cricket pitch and cinder jogging track, has public showers and changing facilities. Near Brockton Point is a cluster of late 19th-century **totem poles** and dugout canoes carved by the Kwakiutl and Haida. Close to the 2-mile mark of the walk, a marine statue of a *Girl in a Wet Suit* looks a lot like Hans Christian Andersen's *Little Mermaid* in Copenhagen. There's a children's water playground, a miniature railway, and pony rides on the left.

From this point, expect more wilderness and fewer human-made points of interest. At 3 miles, **Prospect Point,** the peninsula's northernmost extremity, looks toward West Vancouver across the First Narrows from a 200-foot clifftop; the Prospect Point Cafe here is a popular restaurant. As the view shifts toward Vancouver Island, look for **Siwash Rock,** a legendary site to native tribes. Another restaurant, the Teahouse, is at **Ferguson Point. Second Beach** has a saltwater swimming pool at 5 miles. Then the park opens up near **Lost Lagoon,** a one-time swamp inhabited by Canada geese and rare trumpeter swans. (Tell the kids to bring bread crumbs.) Nearby are a pitch-and-putt golf course, tennis courts, shuffleboard, and lawn bowling.

Vancouver Aquarium, Stanley Park (tel. 682-1118 or 685-3364).

This exhibition of aquatic wildlife is renowned the world over. The third largest aquarium in North America claims to have some 8,000 marine species. In the Max Bell Marine Mammal Centre, visitors can observe the underwater behavior of killer and beluga whales, sea otters, harbor seals, and diving puffins. Whales perform several times daily; current show times are posted on the door.

Elsewhere in the aquarium, two galleries depict local marine life, while two others concern themselves with tropical creatures. The Sandwell North Pacific Gallery re-creates the B.C. coastline with animals like the giant octopus, wolf eel, jellyfish, and anemones. The adjacent Rufe Gibbs Hall shows freshwater life.

Temperatures are kept a little warmer in the H. R. MacMillan Tropical Gallery, with its colorful, beautifully delicate fishes, as well as sea turtles and sharks. The Graham Amazon Gallery transports visitors to the South American jungle with a complete exhibition of flora and fauna, from exotic birds and primates to crocodiles and piranhas.

The Clamshell Gift Shop has handcrafts and books, and is one of Vancouver's best places to buy souvenirs. The aquarium also has a theater and research laboratories.

Open: Daily 10am–5:30pm; July 1–Labor Day daily 9:30am–8pm. *Admission:* $5.75 for adults, $4.75 for seniors and students, $3.25 for children 5 to 12, free for children under 5. *Bus:* 19; "Around the Park" bus April 29–October 29 only.

Stanley Park Zoo, Stanley Park (tel. 681-1141).

The modest zoo has a somewhat limited collection of foreign and native Canadian animals—otters, seals, penguins, polar bears, monkeys, snakes, and tropical birds. If you're looking for an animal "fix" and can't get south to Seattle's Woodland Park Zoo or Tacoma's Point Defiance Zoo, this will have to do. Nearby is a fine **Children's Zoo** where youngsters can cuddle up to domesticated animal babies like goats, rabbits, and llamas. Also in the vicinity is a Kangaroo House of Australian creatures.

Open: Public zoo daily 10am–6pm; Children's Zoo May–Sept daily 10am–6pm, weekends only in winter. *Admission:* Public zoo no charge. Children's Zoo, adults $1.60, children and seniors 80¢, family $3.20. *Bus:* 19; "Around the Park" bus Apr 29–Oct 29 only.

MUSEUMS

Vancouver Art Gallery, 750 Hornby St., Robson Sq. (tel. 682-5621).

The former provincial courthouse is, in a way, a collaboration of British Columbia's two most famous architects. Built in neoclassical style in 1911 by Francis Rattenbury, who also designed Victoria's Empress Hotel and Legislative Buildings, its somber chambers and corridors were transformed into bright exhibit halls in 1983 by Arthur Erickson. Impressive Greek columns and stone lions still greet the visitor, but inside, a new glass-topped dome sprays natural light throughout the spacious rotunda and four floors.

Temporary exhibits feature contemporary Canadian and international painters, sculptors, photographers, and video artists, especially British Columbian and East Asian. The permanent collection includes European and North American masters—among them Pablo Picasso, Marc Chagall, Francisco Goya, Georges Braque, Thomas Gainsborough, and John Constable, plus Canada's Group of Seven, whose landscapes exerted a heavy influence on the nation's art in the 1920s and 1930s.

Don't miss the Emily Carr Gallery, which displays the work of British Columbia's most famous artist. A native of Vancouver Island, Carr captured the mystery and power of the coastal rain forests and their native inhabitants around the turn of the 20th century. Before her death in 1945, Carr bequeathed 157 paintings and drawings to the people of B.C. Private donations have expanded the collection further.

The Children's Gallery, off the main lobby, has changing exhibits (with educational undertones) of interest to youngsters. Hard-core art-lovers may want to visit the research library (in the former law library), with its hundreds of art magazines, thousands of books, catalogs from myriad other museums around the world, and files on contemporary Canadian artists. The Gift Shop, one of Vancouver's best bets for souvenir shopping, carries books on Emily Carr and reproductions of her art. Look for *Vanguard* magazine, a local art publication with an international following. Hungry? Try the Gallery Cafe, overlooking the Sculpture Garden.

Free guided tours are led by museum docents at least twice each weekday. Check the schedule at the gallery's information desk.

Open: Mon–Wed and Fri–Sat 10am–5pm; Thurs 10am–9pm; Sun and holidays noon–5pm. *Closed:* Tues, Oct–May. (Gift shop and restaurant remain open.) *Admission:* $2.75 adults, $1.25 seniors and students, free for children under 12. Free Thurs after 5pm. *Bus:* 3, 8, 15, or 17. *SkyTrain:* Granville, two stops.

Vancouver Museum, 1100 Chestnut St., Vanier Park (tel. 736-4431).

Coastal tribes once had a village on the tip of land that juts into English Bay between the Burrard Street Bridge and Kitsilano Beach. Today, the carefully manicured parkland is the site of this oddly shaped museum, its roof resembling the conical shape of a traditional native woven-cedar-bark hat.

Beneath the roof is the largest civic collection in Canada, one that traces the history of Vancouver and the Lower Mainland from prehistoric to modern times. The same building also contains the H. R. MacMillan Planetarium (see below).

The Vancouver Museum has three wings, all of which combine rotating permanent displays and temporary exhibitions. The A Wing focuses on native prehistory and culture, from 8,000 years ago to the arrival of white settlers. The B Wing looks at the growth of the city from 1750 to the early 20th century; there's usually also a temporary display bridging the gap between the First World War and the 1990s. Highlights include life-size replicas of a Hudson's Bay Company trading post, the steerage portion of an immigrant ship, an 1887-vintage Canadian Pacific rail car, and reconstructed rooms from Victorian and Edwardian homes. The C Wing has the Briggs Collection of Japanese jade and ivory, plus major visiting shows, often Pacific Rim–related. All told, the museum's collection includes more than 300,000 artifacts and memorabilia, but you can't see them all in a single visit!

The Museum Gift Shop sells modern Native Canadian artifacts, jewelry, weavings, and prints, as well as historical books and standard souvenirs. The Museum Restaurant has lunches and snacks with a view of English Bay.

There's a 24-hour information line on programs and exhibits: Call 736-7736.

Next door, the **Vancouver Archives,** 1150 Chestnut St. (tel. 736-8561), has a huge collection of historical documents dating from the city's founding. The building is open Monday through Friday from 9:30am to 5:30pm, and there's no charge for exploration.

Open: Daily 10am–5pm. *Closed:* Mon, Sept–May except holidays. *Admission:* $4 adults, $1.50 students and seniors, free for children under 5, $8 families. Combined admission with Maritime Museum (see "More Attractions," below): $6 adults, $2.75 students and seniors, $12 families. *Bus:* 22, three blocks south on Cornwall Avenue. *Boat:* Granville Island Ferry from Vancouver Aquatic Centre, Beach Avenue at Thurlow Street, Sat–Sun and holidays 10am–5pm, every 15 minutes.

H. R. MacMillan Planetarium, Vanier Park (tel. 736-3656).

Considered one of North America's finest planetariums, this indoor theater on the Vancouver Museum's second floor was a gift to the City of Vancouver from a local industrialist. Viewers recline in comfortable armchairs with plush headrests and gaze at the Milky Way on the dome above them. A Zeiss star projector and hundreds of special-effects devices take you on a dramatic trip through time and space, on a search for other worlds or for an in-depth look at the night sky. Shows are entertaining and educational for all ages.

Teenagers and young adults enjoy the spectacular laser sound-and-light shows at night. Using a combination of planetarium special effects, surround-sound, and laser imagery, the productions feature the music of world-famous rock groups. (In 1989, these included Pink Floyd and an "Aussie Invasion," with the likes of INXS, Midnight Oil, and Crowded House.) Buy your ticket in advance and arrive early for a seat, as no latecomers are admitted.

Art or photography exhibits related to astronomy are displayed in the upper gallery, outside the doors to the planetarium.

Open: Show times Tues–Thurs 2:30 and 7pm, Fri 1, 2:30, and 7pm, Sat–Sun 1, 2:30, 4, and 7pm; daily in summer 1, 2:30, 4, and 7pm. Laser shows Tues–Thurs and Sun 8:30pm, Fri–Sat 8:30 and 9:45pm. *Closed:* Mon, except July–Labor Day. *Admission:* $4 per person; summer rates, $4.25 adults, $3 seniors and children under 18. Laser shows $5.25 per person. *Directions:* See Vancouver Museum, above.

Gordon Southam Observatory, 1100 Chestnut St., Vanier Park (tel. 738-2855).

The only public observatory in Western Canada is housed in a small building beside the museum-planetarium complex. There's no charge to go in and have an astronomer—a volunteer from the British Columbia Space Sciences Society—explain how to operate the Zeiss telescope, with its interchangeable filters, to view the sun, moon, planets, and stars.

Public programs and workshops are held throughout the year for all ages. Probably the most popular are the "Shoot the Moon" photography sessions on full-moon nights, in which patrons with 35-millimeter single-lens reflex cameras can take their own pictures of the Earth's satellite.

Open: Tues–Sun noon–5, 7–11pm July–Labor Day; weekends and holidays only in winter. Occasional unannounced closures; telephone in advance of visit. *Admission:* Free.

Museum of Anthropology, University of British Columbia, 6393 NW Marine Drive (tel. 228-5087, recording 228-3825).

This masterpiece of specialized architecture, designed by Arthur Erickson on the model of a traditional native cedar house, contains the world's finest collection of the artifacts of Canada's West Coast tribes. The Great Hall is an awesome showcase of totem poles, houseposts, bentwood boxes, and other massive works of art, much of it preserved from before the time of white settlement. Windows 45 feet tall look out on the Point Grey cliffs, where a simulated Haida tribal village, containing more totem poles and longhouses, hangs over the Strait of Georgia.

There were many tribes along this coast—Haida, Tsimshian, Kwakiutl, and Salish, to name a few—but their cultures were similar (see Chapter I, "History, Geography, and People"). The totemic designs carved on poles, houseposts, masks, and other media usually depicted their clans or the legendary creatures after which they were named: Raven, Eagle, Bear, Whale, Otter, and Frog, for instance.

Totemic art is very much alive in contemporary Indian art. There is no better example than the prominently displayed yellow-cedar sculpture *Raven and the First Men,* designed and carved by Haida artist Bill Reid, and based on the legends of his own tribe. An enormous stylized raven stands stoically atop a giant clamshell, as perhaps a half-dozen tiny men try to force their way out. The expressions on the men's faces range from fear and confusion to stubborn insistence.

Jewelry and sculpture in gold, silver, bone, and argillite—a jet-black stone mined only in B.C.'s Queen Charlotte Islands—make up the Walter and Marianne Koerner Collection of native arts. There are also fine displays of ceremonial masks and baskets.

There's more to the museum than native culture. The traditions of Asia and the Pacific, along with many parts of Africa and Latin America, are well represented in arts and crafts, notably fine collections of masks and textiles. The entire permanent collection is accessible to visitors in glass-topped storage drawers; information on all objets d'art is available in computer-produced data books.

Guided and self-guided tours are available, the latter either with a rented cassette deck and tape or with the museum's excellent guidebook. There's a small but excellent gift shop, specializing (of course) in native crafts, opposite the ticket booth. Sunday afternoon concerts, evening lectures, youth programs, changing exhibits, and other special events keep the museum a stimulating venue throughout the year.

Open: Tues 11am–9pm, Wed–Sun 11am–5pm. *Closed:* Dec 25–26. *Admission:* $3 adults, $1.50 students and seniors, $1 children, free for children under 6, $7 families. Free Tues. *Bus:* 42 direct; 4 and 10 go from downtown to central campus.

NORTH VANCOUVER

Capilano Canyon Regional Park, 3735 Capilano Rd., North Vancouver (tel. 985-7474).

This 15-acre park may be the nearest place to downtown Vancouver to feel that you're a world away, in the midst of a primeval rain forest. Douglas firs and red cedars tower like skyscrapers over the wild Capilano River as it pours through a deep canyon to the Burrard Inlet. A famous suspension bridge stretches across the river near the south end of the park, and a salmon hatchery near its northern end replenishes the stock of spawning coho and chinook that turn the stream's waters nearly red from July through October.

The **Capilano Suspension Bridge** may be a tourist trap, but it's a spectacular one. Stretching 450 feet across, at 230 feet above the canyon floor, this swinging wood-and-wire rope bridge gives you a phenomenal feel for the beauty of the natural setting. You'll see tiny people on paths weaving through the forest, shrouded by the mists of a 200-foot waterfall; kayakers and canoeists can sometimes be seen battling the rapids below. (Because the bridge is on privately owned property within the park, there's an admission charge. At Lynn Canyon Park on the eastern edge of North Vancouver, there's a similar but less famous suspension bridge that's 10 feet higher—and free.)

Adjacent to the bridge are a restaurant, outdoor barbecue area, native carving display, and the Trading Post, Vancouver's largest souvenir and gift shop. Guided forestry and anthropology tours begin here.

More energetic visitors, however, are delighted to wander the Capilano trails on their own. A series of well-maintained trails, with steps to aid walkers on the more precipitous sections, flank the river on either side. It's 4½ miles down to the Burrard Inlet at the Lions Gate Bridge, but only about a mile upstream to Cleveland Dam, behind which Capilano Lake preserves Vancouver's fresh-water supply.

About one-quarter mile below the dam, on the east side of the river, is the **Capilano Salmon Hatchery.** About two million salmon eggs each year are hatched here. There's no admission; outdoor displays explain the salmon's remarkable life cycle as you watch the fish in various stages of development swimming in glass-fronted tanks.

Open (Suspension Bridge): Daily May–Sept 8:30am–dusk; Oct–April 9am–5pm. *Closed:* Christmas Day. *Admission:* $4.50 adults, $3.75 seniors, $3.50 students, $1 children 5 to 12, free for children under 5. *Bus:* 246 to Ridgewood/Capilano.

Grouse Mountain Resort, 6400 Nancy Greene Way, North Vancouver (tel. 984-0661).

A 100-passenger aerial tramway, known as the Superskyride, whisks visitors in just 8 minutes (4 minutes in ski season) to a 3,700-foot elevation, near the top of Grouse Mountain. The views of the city and harbor are magnificent.

The chalet at the top is a base for walking on paved paths or hiking on well-trodden trails. You can opt for a helicopter tour or a chair-lift ride to the mountain's 4,100-foot peak, a frequent site for major hang-gliding competitions. There are even pony rides and an adventure playground for the kids.

The **Grouse Nest** restaurant (tel. 986-6378) is popular for romantic dinners and Sunday brunches; the cost of the trip up is included with the meal.

See "Sports and Recreation: Skiing," later in this chapter, for details on winter sports activities.

Open: Daily 10am–10pm. *Admission:* $9.95 adults, $7.50 seniors and students, $5 children 6 to 12, free for children 5 and under. *Bus:* 246 to Edgemont/Ridgewood, then transfer to 232.

Royal Hudson Steam Train, B.C. Railways, 1311 W. 1st St. at Pemberton Ave., North Vancouver (tel. 987-5211, 68-TRAIN, or toll free 800/663-1500 in western North America).

The last operating survivor of 65 steam trains that served Canada half a century ago, this beautifully restored iron horse runs daily, mid-May to mid-September, on the B.C. Rail line from North Vancouver to the logging town of Squamish, 40 miles north. En route, it skirts the rugged coastline of Howe Sound, introducing travelers to some of the most dramatic landscape in North America. Wild streams thread their way through lush evergreen forests, then tumble from cliffs into the green waters, themselves speckled with islands and fishing boats.

B.C.'s *Royal Hudson,* Engine 2860, is the only steam locomotive in North America that operates daily scheduled service on the main line of a major railroad. Restored from its heyday and immaculately maintained, the locomotive pulls nine coaches on the two-hour trip to Squamish. Another Hudson steam engine pulled King George VI and Queen Elizabeth more than 7,500 miles across Canada, from Québec City to Vancouver, in 1939, thereby earning the designation "Royal" for all Hudson locomotives.

Royal comfort is part of the experience today: There's full refreshment and bar service, and an on-board gift and souvenir stand. Narration is provided by members of the Royal Hudson Steam Train Society, 744 W. Hastings St., Suite 206, Vancouver V6C 1A5 (tel. 689-9222).

There's a layover of about 1½ hours in Squamish to give travelers time for lunch and sightseeing—the mountains here are spectacular—before the *Royal Hudson* returns to North Vancouver.

Open: Wed–Sun, third week of May to mid–July, and Labor Day through third week of September; daily, mid-July to Labor Day. Train departs North Vancouver 10:30am, returns 4pm. *Round-trip fares:* $24 adults, $20 seniors and students, $14 children 5 to 11, free for children under 5. *Reservations:* Essential, at least 48 hours in advance. *Bus:* Departs Vancouver bus terminal, Cambie and Dunsmuir, at 9:30am; picks up at Georgia and Granville, Georgia and Burrard, and Georgia and Denman, en route to the B.C. Railway terminal. *Directions:* Cross Lions Gate Bridge, turn right on Marine Drive, proceed about 0.6 mile, then turn right on Pemberton Avenue.

M.V. *Britannia,* Harbour Ferries, 1782 W. Georgia St. at Denman St., Coal Harbour (tel. 688-7246, 687-9558, or toll-free 800/663-1500).

Most visitors like to combine the Royal Hudson excursion with a one-way journey to or from Squamish aboard this cruise vessel. Following the coast through Howe Sound, it offers a different perspective on the same magnificent view seen by rail travelers. The boat has two seating levels, both with large viewing windows, and a sundeck on top. (In the spring and fall, in particular, it may be wiser to save the boat for the return, when the temperatures are a little warmer.) It also has a snack bar. Shuttle buses operate between the boat and rail terminals to return travelers to their own vehicles when the day's travels are over.

Open: Same days as train (above). Boat departs terminal at 9:30am, returns at 4:30pm. *Round-trip fares:* Train and boat, $42 adults, $38 seniors and students, $25 children 5 to 11, free for children under 5. *Reservations:* Essential, at least 48 hours in advance. *Bus:* 242, or hotel pickup ($2).

---

2. More Attractions

MUSEUMS

Vancouver Maritime Museum, 1905 Ogden Ave., Vanier Park (tel. 737-2211).

Perched on the banks of English Bay, this museum documents Vancouver's ties to the sea throughout history. Galleries recall the 18th-century European explorers, the city's growth as a port city, and the modern fishing industry. There are numerous naval exhibits, including a full-size replica of a modern tugboat's wheelhouse.

The highlight of the museum is **St. Roch National Historic Site** (tel. 666-3201). This Royal Canadian Mounted Police patrol boat, a two-masted ketch, was the first sailing vessel to navigate the Northwest Passage (from west to east) in 1944. Free guided tours are conducted by Environment Canada, Parks. Admission is included with entrance to the Maritime Museum.

Outside, extending into English Bay, is **Heritage Harbour,** the home of restored heritage vessels, traditional craft of foreign lands, visiting tall ships, and many special maritime events.

Open: Thurs–Tues 10am–5pm, Wed 10am–9pm. *Admission:* $3.50 adults, $2 seniors, $1.50 students and children, no charge Wed after 5pm. *Bus:* 22, four blocks south on Cornwall Avenue. *Boat:* Granville Island Ferry from Vancouver Aquatic Center, Beach Avenue at Thurlow Street, Sat–Sun and holidays 10am–5pm, every 15 minutes.

Science World British Columbia, 1455 Quebec St. at Terminal Ave. (tel. 687-8414 or 687-7832).

Housed in what used to be the World Expo Centre, this fascinating cross between a museum, a laboratory, and a laser light show gives you a series of hands-on experiences. On your way through, you touch a tornado, lose your shadow, blow square bubbles, walk inside a camera, and step on sound waves. You see a zucchini explode when zapped with a charge of 80,000 volts, stroll through the interior of a beaver lodge, compose music on an electric guitar, and run your hands through magnetic liquids. These are just a few of the encounters en route. There's a cafeteria and gift shop, geared to science-lovers, of course.

The complex also houses the **Omnimax Theatre** (tel. 687-OMNI), with the largest screen of its kind in the world. A huge domed auditorium shows special films that seem to make the audience a part of the action. Call for presentation times and current productions. Separate tickets are required.

Open: Daily 10am–5pm. *Admission:* $6 adults, $4.50 seniors and students, $3.50 children, free for children 3 and under. Additional charge for Omnimax film. *Bus:* 3, 8, or 19. *SkyTrain:* Main.

B.C. Sports Hall of Fame, B.C. Pavilion, Exhibition Park, E. Hastings and Renfrew Sts. (tel. 253-5655).

A grand tribute to British Columbia's contributions to sports, this museum showcases 68 different sports in 115 exhibits. It traces the history and development of each sport, sometimes by means of soundtracks dramatizing great moments. The hall boasts one of the greatest collections of trophies and medals assembled anywhere, along with photos, equipment, and personal mementos of the province's most famous athletes. A permanent exhibit features every B.C. athlete who has won an Olympic medal since 1912.

Open: Mon–Fri 9:15am–4:45pm. Extended hours during Pacific National Exhibition, last three weeks of August. *Admission:* By donation. *Bus:* 10 or 14.

B.C. Sugar Museum, B.C. Sugar Refinery, Rogers St., Port of Vancouver (tel. 253-1131).

The growth of the refinery closely parallels the historical growth of Vancouver. This theme is emphasized in old photographs and a 25-minute documentary film. There are also interesting displays of a plantation locomotive and sugar-making equipment dating from 1715.

Open: Mon–Fri, 9am–5pm. *Admission:* Free. *Bus:* 2, 4, 7, or 10; then two blocks north off East Hastings Street.

Hastings Sawmill Store Museum, 1575 Alma St., Jericho Beach Park (tel. 228-1213).

Vancouver's first general store, floated to this site from its original location on Burrard Inlet, is loaded with the sort of artifacts that it might have contained 120 years ago. Nineteenth-century clothing and furniture, native baskets, photographs, and such lesser goods as nails and mustache cups keep it charmingly cluttered.

Open: Daily June–mid-Sept 10am–4pm, year round Sat–Sun 1–4pm. *Admission:* By donation. *Bus:* 4, 7, or 42.

Grocery Hall of Fame, 1241 Homer St. near Davie (tel. 669-2214).

If you enjoy studying the changes through which the Morton Salt girl has gone this century; if you appreciate the differences in Coca-Cola's logo over the decades, and recall the Campbell's Soup kids with affection, then this little storefront museum is for you. There's shelf after shelf of packages, tins, and advertising, plus a projected store shelf in the year 2010.

Open: Sat 9am–noon. *Admission:* Free. *Bus:* 8, 10, 14, 20, or 21; then three blocks east on Davie.

Vancouver Police Museum, 240 E. Cordova St. at Main (tel. 665-3346).

The city police exhibit their century-long history in permanent displays of weapons, counterfeiting equipment, and gambling paraphernalia seized during raids.

Open: Daily 11:30am–4:30pm. *Admission:* Free (donations accepted). *Bus:* 8.

UNIVERSITY OF BRITISH COLUMBIA

One of Canada's largest universities, with 40,000 students, UBC has a breathtaking setting on Point Grey, overlooking the

Strait of Georgia and English Bay, surrounded by beaches and dense forests.

UBC has numerous attractions open to visitors: its Museum of Anthropology (see "Top Attractions," above), botanical gardens (see below), the world's largest nuclear cyclotron, a geological museum, geophysical and astronomical observatories, various research centers open to public tours, and a wide range of cultural and sports facilities.

Free campus tours are offered Monday to Friday at 10am and 1pm from May through September. Specific questions and requests should be directed to the **Community Relations Office,** UBC, Vancouver V6T 1W5 (tel. 228-3131).

TRIUMF, TRI-University Meson Facility, 4004 Wesbrook Mall south of W. 16th Ave. (tel. 222-1047, ext. 435).

This world-class nuclear-physics research laboratory is operated jointly by UBC, the University of Victoria, Simon Fraser University in Burnaby, and the University of Alberta. Its cyclotron, with a maximum energy of 520 million electron volts, operates 24 hours a day at least 80% of the year.

Open: 75-min tours Mon–Fri 11am and 2pm May–Aug; Wed–Fri 1pm only Sept–Apr. *Admission:* Free. *Bus:* 41.

M. Y. Williams Geological Museum, Geological Sciences Centre, Stores Rd., Gate 6 (tel. 228-5586).

About 4.5 billion years of mineral and fossil history are on display, including the skeleton of an 80-million-year-old Lambeosaurus dinosaur.

Open: Mon–Fri 8:30am–4:30pm. *Admission:* Free. *Bus:* 10, 41, or 42.

UBC Astronomical Observatory and UBC Geophysical Observatory, Main Mall, Gate 1 (tel. 228-2802).

These side-by-side facilities welcome public visits. The star-gazing section is open most clear Saturday nights, other nights by appointment. The geophysical section offers tours to explore (among other things) earthquake probability and magnetic storms.

Open: By appointment year round; astronomy section Sat 8pm–midnight. *Admission:* Free. *Bus:* 10, 41, or 42.

Information on the university's farming and forestry research centers can be obtained from the **UBC Community Relations Office** (tel. 228-3131), Old Administration Building, Main Mall and Memorial Road. The **Fine Arts Gallery, Frederic Wood Theatre,** and **UBC School of Music** share student work with the public (see Chapter X, "Vancouver Nights"); and the university's aquatic, tennis, and winter sports centers are open for public use (see "Sports and Recreation" below in this chapter). Miles of hiking trails wind through the University Endowment Lands, which buffer the campus from the rest of the city.

PARKS AND GARDENS

Queen Elizabeth Park and Bloedel Conservatory, Cambie St. at W. 33rd Ave. (tel. 872-5513).

Two former Oak Ridge stone quarries have been converted

into this 133-acre civic arboretum with a domed floral conservatory in its midst. The park's eastern slope is a living museum that contains every major species of tree and shrub native to coastal British Columbia, plus a handful of foreign specimens. A rose garden, 20 tennis courts, and a pitch-and-putt golf course share the grounds.

Bloedel Conservatory is a triodetic Plexiglas dome, 70 feet high and 140 feet in diameter, that harbors a tropical environment. Within are 500 varieties of plants from jungle and desert, more than 100 free-flying tropical birds, and streams and ponds filled with colorful *koi*, Japanese carp. A plaza with lighted fountains and covered walkways surrounds the conservatory, located atop Little Mountain—at 500 feet the highest point within the Vancouver city limits. There are fine views from the café and gift shop.

Open: Daily, 10am–9pm summer, 10am–5pm winter. *Closed:* Christmas Day. *Admission:* $2.30 adults, $1.15 seniors and children, $4.60 families. *Bus:* 15.

VanDusen Botanical Garden, 5251 Oak St. at W. 37th Ave. (tel. 266-7194).

One of the city's largest botanical gardens, with 55½ acres, occupies the site of an abandoned golf course in the well-to-do Shaughnessy district. The garden is unique in that plants are arranged according to their ecological niche or botanical relationship: Pathways and wooden bridges lead visitors through a variety of geographical zones.

The garden contains one of Canada's fullest collections of ornamental plants, including spring bulbs, rhododendrons, summer annuals, and heathers. It also has an Elizabethan-style hedge maze and a children's topiary garden. The Alma VanDusen Garden has colorful perennials around meandering streams and across meadows. Numerous sculptures are placed around the grounds.

There are lovely views of downtown Vancouver and the North Shore mountains from Sprinklers Restaurant. The garden also has a popular gift shop.

Open: Daily, 10am–8pm summer, 10am–4pm winter. *Closed:* Christmas Day. *Admission:* $3.75 adults, $2 seniors and students, $1.75 children, $7.75 families. *Bus:* 17.

Dr. Sun Yat-sen Classical Chinese Garden, 578 Carrall St. near Pender (tel. 689-7133 or 662-3207).

This $5.3 million masterpiece behind the Chinese Cultural Centre opened for Expo 86 as the first full-scale classical garden ever built outside China. Modeled after Ming Dynasty (1368–1644) gardens, it was created by a team of 52 experts from the city of Suzhou, who spent a year in the construction.

Westerners may initially find it sparse in vegetation, but the Chinese consider plants to be just one-fourth of a garden's serene yet ever-changing appeal. They seek a philosophical yin-yang balance of small and large, light and dark, soft and hard, flowing and immovable. This garden's elements, most of them imported from China (in 950 crates), include massive rocks (convoluted limestone, prized as natural sculptures) and numerous buildings—pavilions, terraces, covered walkways, and lookout platforms, each unique in design. Reflecting pools of water and carefully tended plants—pine, bamboo, plum, and flowering shrubs—complete the picture.

The gift shop has an excellent selection of Chinese artifacts, including ceramics and scroll paintings, and books on culture and history.

Open: Daily, 10am–8pm May–Sept, 10am–4:30pm Oct–April. *Admission:* $3 adults, $2 seniors and children, free for children under 5, $6 families. *Bus:* 19.

Nitobe Memorial Garden, 6565 NW Marine Drive, Gate 4, University of British Columbia (tel. 228-4208).

Like a Zen sanctuary, this authentic 2.4-acre garden behind UBC's Asian Centre offers visitors a meditative escape from the surrounding campus bustle. Those who visit often remark on the almost timeless harmony of the changing seasons. The lake waters reflect delicate cherry blossoms in the early spring, the colorful leaves of maples in the fall . . . and numerous bridal gowns in the summer. Arched bridges wind past stone lanterns and through immaculately maintained woods to a traditional teahouse.

Open: Daily 10am–dusk. *Closed:* Sat–Sun Oct. 10–mid-March. *Admission:* $1.25 adults, 50¢ seniors and students, free for children under 6. Free on Wed. *Bus:* 10 or 42.

UBC Botanical Garden, 6250 Stadium Rd. near SW Marine Drive and W. 16th Ave., Gate 8, University of British Columbia (tel. 228-4208).

This garden, established in 1916 as the first university botanical garden in Canada, has numerous components in its 70 acres. They include the B.C. Native Garden, featuring specimens from coastal woodland and peat bog to dry interior; the E. H. Lohbrunner Alpine Garden, displaying mountain flora from around the world; the Food Garden, with fruits, vegetables, and edible plants grown on espaliers; the Physick Garden, a re-created 16th-century garden of medicinal herbs, laid out around a sundial; and the Asian Garden, with an outstanding collection of magnolias, rhododendrons, and blue Himalayan poppies.

Open: Daily 10am–dusk. *Admission:* $2.50 adults, 75¢ seniors and students, free for children under 6. *Bus:* 41.

B.C. Parkway. This 50-acre linear park follows the SkyTrain route 12 miles from Main Street to New Westminster Station. The 7-Eleven Bicycle Path and John Molson Way jogging path are the connecting links between 32 city parks. En route, there are also children's adventure playgrounds, theme gardens, floral displays, heritage plazas, and an International Mile of Flags.

Open: Year round. *Admission:* Free. *SkyTrain:* All stops from Main Street east.

ETHNIC COMMUNITIES

Little Italy, Commercial Drive between Venables St. and E. Broadway.

Since most Italian Canadians came from the poorer southern regions of Italy, Neapolitan and Sicilian styles tend to dominate Vancouver's Italian community. Commercial Drive doesn't have the "grit" of Little Italy in New York, but it does have dozens of charming shops, a wonderfully relaxed atmosphere of large awnings over shaded sidewalks, and plenty of streetcorner gossip.

Italians love to eat and dress well. Restaurants here attract crowds with antipasti, pastas, and homemade gelati (Italian ice creams). The grocery stores sell dozens of varieties of fresh and dried pasta, cheeses, and cured meats; other shops specialize in one of these foods. The cafés, which have the best espresso in town, double as men's social clubs, often to the exclusion of women. Italian tailors and leather importers are well represented on the Commercial Drive strip. Two gift shops—**Ital Records** and **Atlantic Imports**—are side-by-side in Commercial's 1400 block.

The **Italian Cultural Centre**, 3075 Slocan St. (tel. 430-3337), is well east of Little Italy on the Grandview Highway. It provides social services to families and hosts Italian movies and concerts. Its library of art books was donated by the Italian government. Carnevale, the Italian Mardi Gras, is celebrated at the center every year with two days of eating and dancing. During Italian Days in late June or early July, several blocks of Commercial Drive are blocked off for shopping, feasting, and merrymaking.

Greektown, West Broadway between MacDonald and Alma Sts.

To casual visitors, the most notable feature of this part of Vancouver is the proliferation of Greek restaurants, all seeming to boast the Aegean blue and white of their nation's flag. But look again: There are food stores, selling olive oil, phyllo dough, feta cheese, grape leaves, and fresh squid. There are bakeries, with delicious honey-sweet pastries like baklava. There are *kaffenion,* men-only social clubs housed in billiard parlors and coffeehouses. There are jewelers, urging patrons to buy "evil eyes" to ward off misfortune, and "worry beads" to chase away anxiety attacks. And there's **Minerva Greek Imports,** 2856 W. Broadway, Vancouver's best source of woolen sailors' hats, wooden wine gourds, baptismal and wedding candles, coffeemaking *briki,* and cassettes of Greek music, from bouzouki instrumentals to Melina Mercouri.

St. George's Orthodox Church, W. 31st Ave. and Arbutus St., is the focal point for this deeply religious community. Visitors are welcome to drop in and admire the church's art and architecture, particularly its sacred icons. (Women should not wear slacks or shorts.) Sunday services are in Greek, with lots of incense-burning and chanting. The **Greek Community Centre** (tel. 266-7148) is next door to the church.

Easter is the biggest holiday of the year, and it's celebrated with full spiritual devotion. To the general public, Greek Days in late June may be of more interest. West Broadway is blocked to traffic from noon to the following early morning for street dancing and general feasting.

Chinatown, Main and Pender Sts.

See Chapter VIII, "Walking Around Vancouver."

Japan Town, Powell St. and Dunlevy Ave.

Once the focus of a sizable community, this area was more decidedly Japanese prior to the Second World War, when Japanese Canadians were placed in internment camps. Today Vancouver's Japanese are scattered throughout the metropolitan area, although they return en masse to Oppenheimer Park for O-Bon dances in July and the annual Japanese Festival in August.

The **Vancouver Buddhist Church** is on the corner of Jackson Avenue opposite the park. Several small shops, on Powell Street west to Gore, include the Japanese Deli (see dining). Nearby is the **Japanese Food Centre,** 349 E. Hastings St. near Gore.

Punjabi Market (Little India), Main St. between E. 49th and E. 51st Aves.

Greater Vancouver's 60,000 East Indians have their largest community in the city's southeastern quadrant. Here on Main Street is a two-block stretch of shops that sell nearly everything you might find in New Delhi: silk saris, gold bangles, religious icons, Punjabi-language videos and cassette tapes, traditional musical instruments, and so forth. Grocery stores have huge bins of spices and dried vegetables for curries and other dishes; rosewater-sweet *gulab jamun* and other taste-tempters fill the front counters of restaurants like the Himalaya and the Bombay Sweet Shop.

These streets are jammed during traditional Sikh festivals such as Baisakhi, which takes place on a Saturday in mid-April. A cast of thousands parades through the cheering Main Street throngs about midday. Most other Saturdays, there are colorful 11am weddings at the Arthur Erickson–designed **Khalsa Diwan Gurudwara** temple, 8000 Ross St. at SW Marine Drive (tel. 324-2010). Visitors are welcome with advance notice. It's a tremendous cultural experience, one that doesn't end until you share a fiery vegetarian lunch with the wedding party in the temple basement!

BURNABY

Burnaby Village Museum, 6501 Deer Lake Ave., Century Park, Burnaby (tel. 294-1233).

Here's a living, open-air museum that takes history seriously and makes it fun. Spread across this five-acre plot is a typical Lower Mainland community, circa 1890–1925. Its 30-plus buildings have been transplanted from other locations or reconstructed. There's a church, school, general store, residential log cabin, pharmacy, dentist's office, Chinese herbalist, photography studio, barber shop, and more. The steam-powered sawmill, blacksmith shop, and printing press are fully operational. A miniature steam train (for kids) and turn-of-the-century ice-cream parlor are enchanting. Guides in period costume are well informed. The village offers old-time crafts and baking demonstrations throughout the year.

Open: Daily 11am–4:30pm mid-March to mid-Oct and mid-Nov to mid-Dec; Sun only 11am–4:30pm mid-Oct to mid-Nov. *Closed:* Mid-Dec to mid-March. *Admission:* $3.50 adults, $2.50 students and seniors, $2 children 6 to 12, free for children under 6, families $8. *Bus:* 120, 131, or 132. *Directions:* Take Kensington Avenue exit from Highway 1.

Burnaby Art Gallery, 6344 Deer Lake Ave., Century Park, Burnaby (tel. 291-9441).

A heritage building just a short stroll from the Burnaby Village Museum, the gallery specializes in 20th-century art.

Open: Tues–Wed and Fri 9am–5pm, Thurs 9am–9pm, Sat–Sun noon–5pm. *Admission:* Free. *Bus:* 120, 131, or 132.

Simon Fraser University, Gaglardi Way, Burnaby Mountain, Burnaby (tel. 291-3210).

This modern institution atop 1,200-foot Burnaby Mountain has a commanding view of the Lower Mainland. When it opened in 1965, its stunning architecture won acclaim for Vancouverite Arthur Erickson. Among campus attractions, the **Museum of Archeology and Ethnology** (tel. 291-3325) has fine native displays (open Mon–Fri 9am–4pm and Sat–Sun noon–3pm; free). The **University Art Gallery** (tel. 291-4266) has an excellent collection of Inuit art (open Mon noon–6pm, Tues–Fri 10am–4pm; free).

Open: Free campus tours with student guides, July 1 to Labor Day, hourly 10:30am–3:30pm. One-hour tours by appointment at other times of year. *Bus:* 135, 144, or 145. *Directions:* East 7 miles on Hastings Street, right on Sperling Avenue, left on Curtis Street. Curtis becomes Gaglardi Way and climbs mountain to SFU.

RICHMOND/AIRPORT

Fantasy Garden World, 10800 No. 5 Road, Richmond (tel. 271-9325).

There are two parts to this tourist-oriented complex, owned by British Columbia Premier Bill Vander Zalm. The botanical garden features stunning seasonal displays: 200 varieties of tulips and 1,000 rhododendrons in spring; a dazzling show of roses and other annuals in summer. It also has a Biblical garden with Christian scenes, a children's farm with rides and animals, exotic aviaries, a wedding chapel, a carillon, and a gazebo teahouse.

The European Village—unmistakable from the highway, with its profile of Old World facades—has 20 shops and restaurants marketing Scottish tartans, German Bratwurst, French lace, Swiss chocolates, Scandinavian woolens, English pub ales, and so forth. European street entertainment is performed weekends and summer weekdays in the cobblestone plaza. You may even see Vander Zalm, who has a residence in a Dutch-style château on the premises.

Open: Hours vary seasonally. *Admission:* European Village free. Garden, $4 adults, $3.50 seniors, $2 children. *Bus:* 404 or 405. *Directions:* Take Steveston Highway exit from Highway 99 south.

Reifel Bird Sanctuary, 5191 Robertson Road, Westham Island, Delta (tel. 946-6980).

This 850-acre estuary marsh at the mouth of the south fork of the Fraser River is considered by the B.C. Wildlife Society to be a crucial wetland. Countless thousands of migratory birds, traveling the Pacific Flyway, land here to rest and feed. Myriad others spend the winter in this protected habitat, and still other species make this a year-round home, nesting and rearing their young here in late spring and summer. In all, over 230 species have been identified, some of them extremely rare—like the Temminck's stint and the spotted redshank. The sanctuary has an observation tower, picnic tables, washrooms, and two miles of trails. You're likely to find the greatest activity in the fall, the least in midsummer.

Open: Daily 9am–4pm. *Admission:* $2.50 adults, 50¢ children. *Directions:* Take Tsawwassen exit (Highway 17) off Highway 99 south. Turn west on 48 Avenue through Ladner. Route becomes River Road West. Turn right on Westham Island Road across river, and follow to end. Sanctuary is five miles west of Ladner.

Guan Yin Chinese Buddhist Temple, 9160 Steveston Highway, Richmond (tel. 274-2822).

Perhaps the best example of traditional Chinese religious architecture in North America, this rather ostentatious structure has golden porcelain tiles and flying dragons on its rooftop. Climb the granite stairway, past guardian marble lions and an enormous incense burner; remove your shoes, then reverently enter the main worship hall.

Directly ahead are three golden images of the Buddha, to whom chants are delivered in ceremonies at 10:30am each Saturday. To his right is an enormous sculpture of Guan Yin, goddess of mercy, with her thousand arms and heads. Behind are funeral tablets to deceased ancestors and written requests for assistance from beyond. The temple has a bonsai garden, small museum, resource library, gift counter, and a chapel where you shake sticks and have your fortune told (in Chinese). Inquire about lectures and meditation classes.

Open: Daily 10am–5pm. Prayer ceremony 10:30am Sat. *Admission:* Free; donations appreciated. *Bus:* 403. *Directions:* Take Steveston Highway exit off Highway 99 south.

Steveston. Established as a Japanese fishing village around the turn of the century, this quaint harbor community is a great day trip from Vancouver, especially on Saturday or Sunday morning. Arrive soon after dawn, when fishers from all over the Fraser River delta region congregate at **Government Wharf** to sell seafood directly from their boats. It's hectic . . . and fascinating.

Afterward, drop into the tiny **Steveston Museum,** on the top floor above the post office (Moncton St. at 1st Ave.) to see a photographic history of old Steveston and a number of Japanese artifacts. A few blocks east on Moncton is the **Dojo,** or martial arts center, a traditional-style building that draws the province's best masters in judo, kendo, and other pursuits. It's open to visitors on Sunday. There are several Japanese grocery stores and a couple of outstanding fish-and-chips shops—**Dave's** and the **Steveston Seafood House**—on Moncton Street.

Bus: 402. *Directions:* Take Steveston Highway exit west off Highway 99 south, travel 4½ miles west to No. 1 Road, turn left ½ mile, then right onto Moncton Street.

NORTH SHORE

Mt. Seymour Provincial Park, Mt. Seymour Rd., North Vancouver (tel. 986-2261).

Offering a view to match that of Grouse Mountain, Mt. Seymour rises 4,767 feet above the Burrard Inlet's Indian Arm. The road winds through ancient stands of fir, cedar, and hemlock to a cafeteria and gift shop at the peak's 3,300-foot level. From there, a chair lift—heavily used by skiers in winter—climbs to alpine meadows, and a hiking trail goes straight to the mountaintop. On clear days, you can see Washington State's snowcapped Mt. Baker in the southern distance.

Open: Daily 7am–11pm. Chair lift daily 11am–5pm July–Aug, Sat–Sun 11am–5pm Sept–Oct. *Admission:* Park free. Chair lift $3 adults, $1.50 children under 12. *Bus:* 211 or 215. *Directions:* Cross Second Narrows Bridge on Highway 1 west, go east on Mt. Seymour Parkway for 3 miles, then north on Indian River Road, which becomes Mt. Seymour Road.

Lynn Canyon Park, Peters Rd., North Vancouver (tel. 987-5922).

The **Lynn Canyon Suspension Bridge,** originally built in 1912, may be even more thrilling than the one in Capilano Canyon. At 225 feet it's only half as long, but the drop of 240 feet into the Lynn Canyon is 10 feet farther than at Capilano. There's lots of hiking in the heavily wooded 300-acre park and reserve. (Sly Stallone fans take note: Most of *First Blood* was filmed here.) The park's **Ecology Centre** shows films and slide shows on natural history subjects. Staff members lead frequent walking tours.

Open: Daily dawn–dusk. *Admission:* Free. *Bus:* 228 or 229, then walk 5 blocks west on Lynn Valley Road. *Directions:* Take Lynn Valley Road northeast off Highway 1, continue 1½ miles to Peters Road, turn right.

Lynn Headwaters Regional Park, Lynn Valley Rd., North Vancouver (tel. 987-7131).

An inaccessible wilderness until the mid-1980s, this park features a network of hiking trails with some mountain views.

Open: Daily dawn–dusk. *Admission:* Free. *Directions:* Same as for Lynn Canyon Park, but continue up Lynn Valley Road approximately 4 miles.

North Shore Museum and Archives, 209 W. 4th St., North Vancouver (tel. 987-5618).

Exhibits feature North Vancouver history, shipbuilding, and Native Canadian artifacts. Extensive archives contain about 6,000 photographs.

Open: Wed–Sun 1–4pm. *Admission:* By donation. *Bus:* 242. *SeaBus:* Lonsdale Quay.

Presentation House Gallery, 333 Chesterfield Ave., North Vancouver (tel. 986-1351).

This art gallery emphasizes photography by local, national, and international artists.

Open: Wed–Sun noon–5pm, Thurs noon–9pm. *Admission:* $2 adults, $1 seniors and students; free Wed. *Bus:* 242. *SeaBus:* Lonsdale Quay.

Horseshoe Bay. This picturesque cove at the foot of Howe Sound is best known as the staging area for ferries to Nanaimo (on Vancouver Island), Langdale (on the Sunshine Coast), and Bowen Island. But it's a lovely small community in its own right, with numerous shops, waterfront restaurants, and a designer brewery, **The Troller.** Horseshoe Bay is a good place to rent a boat for a day of salmon fishing in Howe Sound.

Bus: 250. *Directions:* Highway 1 west, 8 miles from Lions Gate Bridge.

3. Kids' Vancouver

By now you've already discovered a handful of good ideas for sights the kids will enjoy, but if you're staying more than a few days with the children, you won't want to be without Daniel Wood's *Kids! Kids! Kids! in Vancouver,* published by Douglas & McIntyre (4th edition, 1988).

In **Stanley Park** (see "Top Attractions," above), younger children won't want to miss the Children's Zoo, miniature railway, and playgrounds. The whole pack will like the Vancouver Aquarium, Stanley Park Zoo, Lost Lagoon, and a drive (or a walk) around the Seawall.

In **Vanier Park,** get the family hooked on the stars at the H. R. MacMillan Planetarium in the Vancouver Museum (see "Top Attractions: Museums"), and let them board a real icebreaker, the *St. Roch,* in the Vancouver Maritime Museum (see "More Attractions: Museums," above).

Science World B.C. (see "More Attractions: Museums"), on the old Expo '86 site, is a hands-on experience guaranteed to change their view of the world.

Burnaby Village Museum (see "More Attractions: Burnaby," above) will appeal to even the least scholarly child because of the way it makes history fun (especially in the old-time ice-cream parlor). Some youngsters will enjoy the totem poles and other Native Canadian artifacts in city museums; others may prefer the natural appeal of the botanical gardens.

In **North Vancouver,** kids will love traversing the suspension bridges at Capilano Canyon or Lynn Canyon parks.

A walk through **Chinatown** is an adventure in a different world. The strange sights (like barbecued ducks hanging in shop windows), smells (as in an herbalist's shop), and sounds (such as fireworks during a dragon dance) are immensely exciting to many youngsters, and Chinese toys are thought-provoking.

One of **Granville Island**'s biggest attractions for youngsters is the **Kids Only Market** (1496 Cartwright St., beside the access road to the island; open daily 10am–6pm, closed Mon except in summer). Various fun activities are scattered up and down its two stories. The 27 shops here cater to children (and indirectly to their parents) with toys, books, records, clothes, food, and even computers! Nearby, the **Children's Water Park and Adventure Playground** lets you relax while the kids release some energy. If they get wet or dirty, you can use the changing facilities in Isadora's restaurant.

If your children are sports-oriented, check out the list of sports activities later in this chapter. Here are some other suggestions just for the kids:

Playland, Exhibition Park, Hastings and Cassiar Sts. (tel. 255-5161).

A traditional Midwest-style amusement park, Playland has 40 rides, including Canada's largest wooden roller coaster. You'll find clowns, a midway where you can test your strength or intelligence, and, of course, lots of hot dogs and cotton candy.

Open: Apr–Sept; hours vary seasonally. *Admission:* $2.50. Rides extra: All-day pass $14.95 adults, $10.95 children under 4 feet tall. *Bus:* 10 or 14.

Maplewood Farm, 405 Seymour River Place, North Vancouver (tel. 929-5610).

This 5-acre farm, operated by the North Vancouver Parks Department, has a large number of domestic animals and birds for petting. There are two main visiting areas: "Goathill" and "Rabbitat." If you happen to be in town Memorial Day weekend, don't miss the annual Sheep Fair; the Farm Fair falls in mid-September.

Open: Tues–Sun and holidays, 10am–4pm. *Admission:* $1.35 adults, 85¢ children, $4 families. *Bus:* 211 or 214.

Vancouver Children's Festival, Vanier Park, 1100 Chestnut St. (tel. 280-4444).

If you're in town with kids, *don't,* under any circumstances, miss it! A performing arts celebration for the younger set, it features Canadian and foreign artists in music, dance, theater, mime, and puppetry productions. In past years, the cultures of Japan, China, Spain, and Zimbabwe have shared their work with North American children.

Open: Third week of May. *Admission:* No charge at site; performances $3.85–$5.85. *Bus:* 22, then walk 3 blocks south on Cornwall Ave. *Boat:* Granville Island Ferry from Vancouver Aquatic Centre.

La Fête Colombienne des Enfants, 2916 McBride Ave., Crescent Beach, Surrey (tel. 531-1611).

French-speaking children will enjoy this festival, in a seaside community just north of the U.S. border. There's a Gallic village atmosphere all weekend, with performances and sidewalk entertainment in Canada's "other" language.

Open: Memorial Day weekend, 9:45am–3pm. *Admission:* No charge at site; performances $4. *Bus:* 351.

---

4. Organized Tours

Many travelers prefer the comfort of letting someone else handle their sight-seeing arrangements. Transportation, admissions, timing, and narration are things they'd prefer not to have to worry about. Listed below are a variety of tours.

BUS TOURS

Bell Tours, P.O. Box 35368, Vancouver V6M 4G5 (tel. 604/535-2587).

Vancouver City Tour, 4 hours, $26 adults, $17 children, with lunch; $20 adults, $12 children, without lunch.

Vancouver City Break, 3 days, 2 nights, $340–$485 per person single occupancy, $210–$350 double. Hotel and city sight-seeing included. Meals not included.

1st Tours, Harbour Ferries, 1782 W. Georgia St., Vancouver V6G 2V7 (tel. 604/688-7246 or toll free 800/663-1500).

Vancouver City Tour, 3½ hours, $26 adults, $23 seniors and students, $16 children 5–11, departing 9:30am mid-May to mid-Sept.

Vancouver Mini Tour, 1½ hours, $15 adults, $12 seniors and students, $10 children 5–11, departing 9:30am and 1:30pm mid-May to mid-Sept.

Gray Line of Vancouver, 900 W. Georgia St., Suite 108, Vancouver V6C 2W6 (tel. 604/681-8687; toll free 800/663-0667).

Vancouver, 4 days, 3 nights, $409–$639 per person single occupancy, $279–$399 double. Hotel and city sight-seeing included. Meals not included.

Vancouver city tours, 3½–4 hours, $29.50–$39 adults, $15–$19.50 children, departing 9:30 or 10am and 2pm daily.

Pacific Coast Lines, 150 Dunsmuir St., Vancouver (tel. 604/662-7575).

Introduction to Vancouver, 1¾ hours, $15.50 adults, $7.75 children 5–11, departing 9:30am mid-May to Sept, 1:30pm Oct to mid-May.

Vancouver Grand City Tour, 3 hours, $23.50 adults, $11.75 children 5–11, departing 9:30am and 1:45pm mid-May to Sept.

Majestic North Shore Tour, 4 hours, $32.50 adults, $16.25 children 5–11, departing 1:45pm mid-May to Sept. ($25.50 adults, $12.75 children without Grouse Mountain skyride.)

Combination Tour, 5¾ hours plus 2-hour lunch break, $43 adults, $21.50 children 5–11, departing 9:30am mid-May to Sept. ($36 adults, $18 children without Grouse Mountain Super-skyride.)

BOAT TOURS

1st Tours, Harbour Ferries, 1782 W. Georgia St., Vancouver V6G 2V7 (tel. 688-7246 or toll free 800/663-1500).

Paddlewheel Harbour Tour, 1½ hours, $15 adults, $12 seniors and students, $10 children 5–11, departs 9:30am, 11:30am, 1:30pm and 3:30pm, mid-May to mid-Sept. Aboard M.V.P. *Constitution.*

Fraser River Tours (tel. 250-3458 or 584-5517).

Atria Star Tour, 3½ hours, $18 adults, $15 seniors, $13 children 5–12, departs 10am and 2pm daily in summer from Westminster Quay, noon daily in summer from BridgePoint, Richmond.

Pitt River Tour, 6 hours, $35 adults, $30 seniors, $20 children 5–12, $5 children under 5, departs 10am daily in summer from Westminster Quay. Box lunches $5.50 additional.

Gray Line Water Tours, 900 W. Georgia St., Suite 108, Vancouver V6C 2W6 (tel. 604/681-8687).

Captain's Harbour Tour, 2 hours, $19.50 adults, $9.75 children, departs 10am and 2pm July to mid-Sept.

S.S. Beaver Steamship Company, 554 Cardero St., Barbary Coast Yacht Basin, Vancouver V6G 2W6 (tel. 682-7284).

Indian Arm Adventure Tour, 4½ hours, $12–$25 per person, mid-May to late Sept. Includes lunch.

Sunset Dinner Cruise, 3 hours, $35 per person, departs 6:30pm mid-May to late Sept. Includes buffet meal on English Bay.

AIR TOURS

Great Canadian Seaplane Tours, Harbour Air, Waterfront Street between Canada Place and Westin Bayshore Hotel (tel. 688-1277).

Vancouver Panorama, 30 minutes, $49 per person.

Sunshine Coast Explorer, 75 minutes, $120 per person.

Glaciers and Alpine Lakes, 75 minutes, $120 per person.

Picnic by a Wilderness Waterfall, 3 hours, $210 per person, includes one-hour luncheon.

Vancouver Helicopter Tours, 455 Commissioner St. (tel. 683-HELI).

The Greater Vancouver Scenic, 15–20 minutes, $79 per person.

The North Shore Discoverer, 45–50 minutes, $149 per person.

The Coastal Mountain Odyssey, 1¾ hours, $275 per person. Includes 10-minute stop on glacier.

The Pacific Nighthawk, 20–25 minutes, $150 per person.

---

5. Special and Free Events

Vancouver starts the year with one of its biggest events: **First Night,** a New Year's Eve performing arts festival that closes the streets of downtown. Admission to the shows, held at a variety of venues, is a $5 button. Tens of thousands of revelers are convinced anew each year that they can have a good time without getting drunk: No alcohol is served. The following morning, thousands of hardy folks show up at icy English Bay for a **Polar Bear Swim.** (They probably thereafter resolve never to enter water that cold again.)

In late January or early February, the Chinese community launches its lunar year—be it the year of the Horse, the Dragon, or whatever—with a noisy parade through the streets of Chinatown. This **Chinese New Year** celebration formally lasts two weeks—from new moon to full moon.

Come summer, the **Vancouver Sea Festival** draws throngs to the shores of English Bay during the second full week of July. Highlights include a parade along Beach Avenue, the city's biggest pyrotechnic display, and the finish of the Nanaimo-to-Vancouver bathtub race. There's no charge for the festivities, including numerous open-air concerts.

The **Pacific National Exhibition** (tel. 253-2311), the fifth largest fair in North America, runs for 17 days in late August and early September, concluding on Labor Day. There's something for everyone here, from big-name entertainment to a demolition derby, livestock demonstrations to logging competitions, fashion shows to a frenetic midway. Adults and teenagers pay $6 admission, seniors and children 6 to 12 pay $3, and tots get in free.

A complete list of major annual events in Vancouver and vicinity appears in Chapter II, "When to Go."

---

6. Sports and Recreation

As you might expect of a city sports-crazy enough to have a provincial hall of fame that applauds its heroes in 68 different pursuits, Vancouver has a wide choice of spectator and participant sports.

SPORTS
Tickets for professional sports events can be purchased from Vancouver Ticket Centre outlets (tel. 280-4444). There are branches in major malls and department stores throughout the city, or they can be ordered by phone and charged to a major credit card.

Baseball
The **Vancouver Canadians** (tel. 872-5232), a Milwaukee Brewers farm club, play a 144-game schedule in the AAA Pacific Coast League. Home games are at aging Nat Bailey Stadium, 33rd Avenue at Ontario Street, adjacent to Queen Elizabeth Park. The season begins in April and continues to early September. Games are Monday to Saturday at 7:30pm and 1:30pm on Sunday; ticket prices to see future big-league stars are no more than $7.50 for box seats, $5 for covered grandstand, $3 for kids. The Brewers, Montreal Expos, and Toronto Blue Jays sometimes play preseason major-league exhibition games here in late March or early April.

The University of British Columbia and Simon Fraser University have teams that compete against other major Canadian schools. Secondary schools and younger children also have leagues.

Basketball
The University of British Columbia competes against other Canadian universities in men's and women's basketball with international rules. Burnaby's Simon Fraser University plays in NAIA Division 1 competition against four-year colleges in Washington and Oregon. The SFU women's team has been especially strong in recent years.

Cricket
This slow-moving British sport, which bears the vaguest of resemblances to baseball, is played every weekend from late April to September. Brockton Oval at Stanley Park is the site of regular Saturday and Sunday matches between amateur clubs in the B.C. Cricket Association.

Football
The **B.C. Lions** (tel. 681-5466) play a 20-game schedule in the Canadian Football League. Home games are at B.C. Place Stadium. The season runs from late June into November, with the Grey Cup

title, symbolic of CFL supremacy, in late November. Home games start at 7:30pm—usually Tuesday or Wednesday in July and August, Friday or Saturday beginning in mid-September. Tickets cost $12 (end zone) to $22 (midfield).

Canadian football is a bit different from American. The field is 10 yards longer, for instance, and teams have only a three-down offense.

Both UBC and SFU have teams. SFU plays NAIA ball against small colleges in Washington and Oregon (U.S. rules).

Horse Racing

"The Track" at **Exhibition Park** (tel. 254-1631) is the venue for thoroughbred racing April 10 to October 15. Post times are 6:15pm weekdays, 1:15pm weekends and holidays. There are full clubhouse ($4.50) and covered grandstand ($2.50) facilities, as well as an excellent restaurant.

As soon as the racing season ends in Vancouver, the trotting season gets underway at the **Cloverdale Raceway**, 6050 176 St., in suburban Cloverdale, about 25 miles southeast of Vancouver. There's harness racing here from October to April, with post times 6:55pm Monday, Wednesday, and Friday; 1:05pm Saturday, Sunday, and holidays. The raceway has a 3,300-seat glass-enclosed grandstand, licensed clubhouse, and cafeteria.

Ice Hockey

The **Vancouver Canucks** (tel. 254-5141) play an 80-game schedule in the National Hockey League. Home games are at Pacific Coliseum in Exhibition Park. The regular season runs from October through March, with playoffs for the championship's Stanley Cup extending into May. Home games begin at 7:35pm weekdays, 5:05pm Saturday, 7:05pm Sunday, with a handful of 2:05pm Sunday and holiday games. Tickets cost $13 to $27.

As hockey is Canada's unofficial national sport, there's fierce competition at every level, from the youngest juniors through colleges and semipro leagues.

Lacrosse

Canada's official national sport is played from May through August at various locations, including Renfrew Community Park, West Point Grey Park, and Hastings Community Centre Park. The top local league is the Western Lacrosse Association. Contact the B.C. Lacrosse Association (tel. 324-2114) for information.

Rodeo

The **Cloverdale Rodeo** (tel. 576-9461), one of North America's largest, takes place the third full weekend of May at the Lower Fraser Valley Exhibition Grounds, 6050 176 St., Cloverdale. Competitors from all over the continent vie for prize money in events like bronco and bull riding and calf roping.

Rugby

Another British sport with a strong following in British Columbia, rugby is played from mid-September to April at more than a score of parks in metropolitan Vancouver. Clubs play others in their association, including the Vancouver Rugby Union (tel. 922-8012) and the B.C. Rugby Union (tel. 687-3333). UBC and SFU have teams of their own.

Soccer

The semiprofessional **Vancouver 86ers** (tel. 294-7459) play a full season of games at Swangard Stadium, Kingsway and Patterson Avenue in Burnaby, from June to mid-September. Games are typically 7:30pm Sunday; tickets are $8 adults, $4 students, $3 children under 12.

Both UBC and SFU have teams.

RECREATION

Living close to the outdoors as they do, Vancouver residents are active nearly every weekend. The following listing can touch on only a few of the activities that may be of interest to Vancouver visitors. An umbrella agency for amateur sports—**Sport B.C.,** 1367 W. Broadway at Hemlock (tel. 737-3058)—will be able to put visitors in touch with the sport of their choosing in a matter of minutes. In addition to the sports mentioned above and below, they have connections to archery, badminton, boxing, curling, fencing, field hockey, figure and speed skating, gymnastics, handball, horseshoe pitching, judo, kendo, rowing, shooting, softball, table tennis, track and field, triathlon, volleyball, water polo, waterskiing, weightlifting, wrestling, and more.

Those who lack appropriate equipment for any sport can probably get it from **Sports Rent,** with the following locations: 2560 Arbutus St. at Broadway in Kitsilano (tel. 733-1605); 1192 Marine Drive at Pemberton St., North Vancouver (tel. 986-1605); and 3531 Kingsway, Burnaby (tel. 432-7368).

Ballooning

Fantasy Balloon Charters in surburban Langley (tel. 736-1974) offer silent early-morning flights in the shadow of Washington's imposing Mt. Baker. Trips cost $165 for adults, half-price for kids under 60 pounds, or $135 each for groups of four adults.

Beaches

Perhaps because it rains so much of the year, Vancouverites love to sunbathe. Some escape to Hawaii or Mexico for a few weeks of winter, but even they soak up the hot sun on sandy B.C. beaches in summer. And many people swim, although the water temperature doesn't exceed 65°F (18°C) even in midsummer.

Most accessible to downtown are the beaches at Stanley Park. **Second Beach,** beside the playground at the southwest corner of the park, has a shallow, unheated pool that children enjoy. **Third Beach,** a bit more isolated, is on the west side of the park near the Teahouse Restaurant. There is no First Beach—unless you bestow that honor upon the beautiful sandy **English Bay Beach** along Beach Avenue outside of the park, opposite the English Bay Cafe.

On the south shore of the bay, **Kitsilano Beach** (tel. 731-0011) has a huge, modern saltwater pool heated to 78°F (25°C). Located off Cornwall Avenue opposite Vine Street, it's shallow at one end for kids, deep at the other for advanced swimmers. It's open from

Victoria Day (May 24) to Labor Day, weekdays from 7am to 8:45pm, weekends from 10am to 8:45pm; admission is $1.30 for adults, 65¢ for seniors and children, $2.60 for families.

West of "Kits" Beach is a string of strands extending several miles west, then south around Point Grey and the University of British Columbia. First and largest is **Jericho Beach,** which begins at the end of Alma Street off Point Grey Road. **Locarno Beach** is next, between Discovery and Tolmie streets off NW Marine Drive; then comes **Spanish Banks,** farther along Marine Drive.

Adventurous souls who continue all the way around Point Grey to where the cliffs drop rapidly from the UBC campus will encounter **Wreck Beach,** where college students come au naturel to soak up rays on every square inch of their bodies.

At the north foot of the Lions Gate Bridge, **Ambleside Park** has a ¾-mile sandy beach facing the Burrard Inlet entrance to Vancouver Harbour. It's popular among North Shore residents.

From June through August, lifeguards are on duty at Second Beach, English Bay Beach, Kitsilano Beach, Jericho Beach, Locarno Beach, and Spanish Banks.

Bicycling

Bike paths around Stanley Park, and along the south shore of English Bay at Kitsilano and Jericho beaches, are especially popular with cyclists. In addition, the 7-Eleven Bicycle Path follows B.C. Parkway along the SkyTrain route from Main Street to the New Westminster Station, linking 32 parks en route.

There are about 20 locations in the Vancouver area to rent bikes. Close to the 5.6-mile seawall loop is **Stanley Park Rentals,** 676 Chilco St. (tel. 681-5581), with 12-speeds for $5 per hour and tandem bikes for $8 per hour.

The **Bicycling Association of British Columbia** has a hotline (tel. 731-7433), sharing information on group rides and other upcoming events.

For competitors, the Gastown Grand Prix on July 1 is run through downtown over several cordoned-off streets. And on Labor Day weekend, the Tour de White Rock Cycle Race plies a route near the U.S. border south of Vancouver.

Boating

Numerous operators have vessels for charter rental, bareboat or skippered, for periods from a few hours to several weeks. In central Vancouver, the Coal Harbour area near the Westin Bayshore Hotel and Granville Island are the best places to look. Horseshoe Bay, west of West Vancouver, and Richmond's Fraser River shoreline, near the international airport, also have major docks.

Delta Charters, 3500 Cessna Drive, Richmond (tel. 273-4211), at the Delta River Inn, has bareboat and skippered power boats, 26 to 46 feet. Weekly bareboat rates range from $1,200 to $3,600 during high season (June 11 to September 16), $1,000 to $2,900 off season. The skipper's fee is $130 per day.

Pacific Quest Charters, 1521 Foreshore Walk, Granville Island (tel. 682-2205 or toll free 800/662-1810 mid-February through August), has sailboats 27 to 41 feet and power boats 32 to 36 feet. They sleep four to eight persons. Rental rates during peak season (July 1–September 8) are $165 to $435 daily, $950 to $2,490 weekly; 20% discounts May 20 to June 30 and September 9 to 29, 30% discounts September 30 to May 19. The skipper's fee is $125 per day.

Other operators with full charter services are **Barbary Coast Yacht Basin,** 554 Cardero St., Coal Harbour (tel. 669-0088); and **Sewell's Landing Marina,** 6695 Nelson St., Horseshoe Bay (tel. 921-7461).

Sailors can listen to a taped marine forecast by calling 270-7411. Those unfamiliar with local waters, or unsure of their own skills, can enroll in three- to six-day courses at the **Sinbad School of Seamanship,** 1805 Maritime Mews, Granville Island (tel. 688-1195).

Canoeing/Kayaking

Within the Vancouver city limits, False Creek and the shores of English Bay provide good paddling waters. (Burrard Inlet is not recommended because of heavy harbor traffic and hazardous currents in the First and Second Narrows.) Indian Arm, a 19-mile-long semi-wilderness inlet that defines the eastern boundary of North Vancouver, is a suggested alternative for more adventurous sorts. There are numerous large glacial lakes east of Vancouver. Novices may prefer Deer Lake, a quiet park in central Burnaby.

Rentals are available from **Sports Rent** (see above); **Ecomarine Ocean Kayak,** 1668 Duranleau St., Granville Island (tel. 689-7575) for False Creek and English Bay; **Deep Cove Canoe and Kayak Rentals,** Deep Cove (tel. 929-2268) for Indian Arm; and **Deer Lake Boat Rentals,** 2148 Franklin St., Burnaby (tel. 255-0081) for Deer Lake.

Diving

Because of the long, protected coastline, British Columbia and adjacent Washington State have some of the most accessible and safest scuba diving in the world. In fact, Canada's first undersea park, Telegraph Cove in Howe Sound, is an easy trip from Vancouver. All told, there are more than two dozen recommended dive locations in Howe Sound and Indian Arm. Lighthouse Park, at the northern entrance to Burrard Inlet, is reputed to have the most interesting seascape and widest variety of marine life in the Vancouver area.

Information, equipment, and diving courses are available from **The Diving Locker,** 2745 W. 4th Ave., Vancouver (tel. 736-2681) and 720 Marine Drive, West Vancouver (tel. 921-7800).

Fishing

The Vancouver area offers anglers a choice between world-class freshwater or saltwater fishing. Rainbow and cutthroat trout, char, kokanee, and whitefish are prevalent in southwestern B.C. lakes and rivers, and huge sturgeon have been taken from the Fraser River. Saltwater varieties include all species of salmon (chinook, coho, pink, sockeye, and chum), halibut, ling cod, rockfish, and snapper.

You need a license to fish in British Columbia if you're 15 or older (for tidal waters) or 16 or older (for freshwater or nontidal waters). Regulations change frequently, as dictated by fish conservation studies, so current rules should be checked in the annual B.C.

Fishing Regulations Synopsis. No license is required for catching shellfish, though size restrictions apply.

The B.C. Department of Fisheries (tel. 666-0383 during office hours) has a 24-hour phone line during spring, summer, and fall (tel. 666-2268 or toll free 800/663-9333). It gives recorded information of interest, including openings, closings, and restrictions, where the big ones are hitting, and what lures they're hitting on.

Numerous fishing operators have charters available.

Golf

The "sport of kings" is played year round in Vancouver, except when snow covers the fairways or rain makes the greens too soggy.

There are five public courses in the city. Most accessible to downtown may be the **University Golf Club,** 5185 University Blvd. (tel. 224-1818), a 6,560-yard par-71 course. It has a beautiful new clubhouse with a big pro shop and locker rooms, the Thunderbird Bar and Grill for dining, a sports TV lounge, and 280-car parking.

Leading private clubs, most of which have reciprocal privileges with other North American clubs, include **Capilano Golf and Country Club,** 420 Southborough Drive, West Vancouver (tel. 922-9331); **Marine Drive Golf Club,** West 57th Ave. and SW Marine Drive (tel. 261-8111); **Point Grey Golf and Country Club,** 3350 SW Marine Drive at Blenheim St. (tel. 266-7171); **Seymour Golf and Country Club,** 3723 Mt. Seymour Pkwy., North Vancouver (tel. 929-2611); and **Shaughnessy Golf and Country Club,** 4300 SW Marine Drive at Kullahun Drive (tel. 266-4141).

Hiking

This sport is everywhere: All you need is a good pair of walking shoes. Most visitors start in Stanley Park or at one of the numerous large provincial and regional parks found in the North Shore Mountains—Cypress, Capilano River, Lynn Headwaters, Mt. Seymour, Belcarra, Burke Mountain, and Golden Ears. There are literally hundreds of miles of trails.

If you're looking for trail information or would like to join a group hike, contact the **Alpine Club of Canada** or **Vancouver Natural History Society,** both at 1200 Hornby St. (tel. 687-3333).

Hunting

License fees for non-Canadian residents to carry firearms are steep—$118 to hunt all game, $59 for game birds and small game only. (It's only $19 for residents of Canada.) Species licenses required for the following animals cost nonresidents about six times what they do Canadians: black and grizzly bear, caribou, cougar, mule and white-tailed deer, elk, moose, mountain goat, mountain sheep, and wolf. Specific requirements should be studied in the annual B.C. Hunting and Trapping Regulations Synopsis.

Ice Skating

Right in the middle of downtown Vancouver, **Robson Square** offers free skating from November to early April on its central rink. But there's no skate rental here; you'll have to bring your own. Other rinks that do rent skates: the **West End Community Centre,** 870 Denman St. at Nelson (tel. 689-0571), open evenings and weekends October through March; **Britannia Community Centre,** 1661 Napier St. off Commercial Drive (tel. 253-4391); **Kerrisdale Arena,** 5760 East Blvd. (tel. 261-8144); and the **UBC Thunderbird Winter Sports Centre,** 6066 Thunderbird Blvd. (tel. 228-6121), with public skating Friday night and Sunday afternoon.

Mountaineering

Mountains are one thing there's no shortage of in this corner of British Columbia. Neither is there a lack of mountaineers and rock climbers. Experts know where to go; one of their favorite ascents is The Chief, a stark wall that looms above the town of Squamish at the head of Howe Sound.

Beginning and intermediate climbers can take courses, and experts can bone up on local knowledge, with the assistance of the **Federation of Mountain Clubs of B.C.,** 1200 Hornby St. (tel. 687-3333). Backpacking trips to interior British Columbia are also organized here.

River Rafting

Although a score of streams in British Columbia attract whitewater enthusiasts, two in particular are of interest to short-term Vancouver-area visitors: the Chilliwack River, 65 miles east of the city, and the Thompson River, 160 miles to the northeast. Both have Class II to IV rapids, making them accessible to rafting newcomers but exciting to veterans of the sport. Rates are typically in the $59 to $69 range, per person, for half-day runs, with overnight trips about twice that. Young children (under 10) typically are not accepted. The season may extend from April to October, with most rafting done between June and August.

Action River Expeditions, 5389 SE Marine Drive, Burnaby (tel. 437-6679), runs 20 different B.C. rivers, with trips lasting from 1 to 18 days. **Hyak River Expeditions,** 1958 W. 4th Ave., Vancouver (tel. 734-8622), has Chilliwack and Thompson river runs and full-week journeys. **Kumsheen Raft Adventures,** 281 Main St., Lytton (tel. 455-2296 or toll free 800/482-2269), focuses on the Thompson and Fraser, at whose junction they are based. **R.A.F.T. Ranch,** Chilliwack Lake Road, Chilliwack (tel. 684-RAFT or toll free 800/663-RAFT), has expeditions leaving from its own backyard.

Running

Jog anywhere you like. **Stanley Park** is a particular favorite of locals. For longer trips, consider **John Molson Way,** a gift of Molson Brewery B.C. Ltd. as part of its 200th-anniversary celebration in 1986. This track follows the 12-mile SkyTrain route from Main Street to New Westminster Station, crossing 32 neighborhood parks en route.

Sailboarding

Better known as windsurfing, this new sport—which combines surfboard and sail—has become extremely popular in Vancouver. Beginning, intermediate, and advanced instruction is offered by **Windmaster,** Denman and Pacific Sts. at the English Bay Beach House (tel. 685-7245), and **Windsure Windsurfing School,**

1300 Discovery St. at Jericho Beach (tel. 224-0615). Instruction packages include board rentals and wet suits.

Sailboards are not allowed at the mouth of False Creek near Granville Island, between the Granville and Burrard bridges.

Sailing

Lessons are offered by **Jib Set Sailing School,** 1020 Beach Ave. (tel. 657-4172), and **Sea Wing Sailing School,** 1808 Boatlift Lane (tel. 669-0840). Many boat charter operators also have sailboats available for rent by experienced sailors. The inland waters here are a joy for those with know-how.

Skiing

There are seven major ski areas within easy driving distance of Vancouver. The area everyone talks about is **Whistler/Blackcomb.**

The two mountains flanking the world-class resort village of Whistler, 75 miles north of Vancouver on Highway 99, were rated by *Ski* magazine in 1989 as North America's second most popular ski resort, after only Vail, Colorado. Whistler Mountain, established as a ski area in the mid-1960s, boomed in the 1980s with the opening of Blackcomb—whose one-mile vertical drop is the highest serviced vertical of any ski area on the continent.

There are more than 1,500 hotel and luxury condominium units at the base of the lifts, along with dozens of restaurants and shops. Whistler Village is a year-round resort.

Whistler Mountain has a 5,006-foot vertical and 133 groomed runs, serviced by two gondolas (one high-speed), 11 chairs, and three other lifts and tows. Helicopter skiing makes accessible another 100-plus runs on nearby glaciers.

Blackcomb has a 5,280-foot vertical and 95 groomed runs, serviced by nine chairs, and three other lifts and tows. Year-round skiing is possible on Blackcomb Glacier.

For more information on these areas, contact the Whistler Resort Association, P.O. Box 1400, Whistler VON 1BO (tel. 604/932-3928 or 685-3650; reservations 604/932-4222; toll free in Alaska, Hawaii, and eastern Washington, 800/634-9622; in western Washington, 206/628-0982; snow report: 687-6761 or 932-4191).

Three areas in the North Shore Mountains are readily visible from metropolitan Vancouver—especially after dark, when their lights are on for night skiing. **Grouse Mountain,** 6400 Nancy Greene Way, North Vancouver V7R 4N4 (tel. 984-0661), overlooks the Burrard Inlet from 4,100 feet above sea level. It has a 1,200-foot vertical and 12 groomed runs, serviced by a tramway, four chairs, and five other lifts and tows. Snow report: 986-6262.

Also on the North Shore, **Mt. Seymour,** 1700 Indian River Rd., North Vancouver V7G 1L3 (tel. 986-2261), has a 1,350-foot vertical with 20 groomed runs, serviced by four chairs and one tow. Snow report: 986-3444.

Cypress Bowl, P.O. Box 91252, West Vancouver V7V 3N9 (tel. 926-5612) has a 1,700-foot vertical with 18 groomed runs, serviced by three chairs and one tow. Snow report: 926-6007.

Farther east, a two-hour drive up the Fraser Valley, is **Hemlock Valley,** P.O. Box 7, Site 2, Rural Route 1, Agassiz V0M 1A0 (tel.

604/797-4411 or 524-9741). This family-oriented area has a 1,200-foot vertical, with 30 runs serviced by three chairs and one tow. It also has night skiing. Overnight packages are offered in concert with Harrison Hot Springs (see Chapter "Excursions from Vancouver"). Snow report: 520-6222.

Manning Park Resort, Manning Provincial Park V0X 1R0 (tel. 604/840-8822), is more of a wilderness experience than the other areas, offering equal alpine and nordic opportunities. For downhillers, it has a 1,400-foot vertical, with 20 runs serviced by two chairs and two other lifts and tows. Snow report: 733-3586.

All southwestern B.C. areas have rental packages available.

Cross-country skiers will find 19 miles of track-set trails and 120 miles of wilderness trails at Manning Park. Mt. Seymour has about 50 miles of nordic trails, Hemlock about 20 miles.

Whistler Resort itself had only about 16 miles of trails, but **Mad River Nordic Centre,** south of Whistler, has 38 miles of groomed trails equipped with warming huts and a nordic ski school.

At Cypress Bowl, the **Hollyburn Ridge** nordic center has 16 miles of groomed and set track, including three miles lit for night skiers.

Swimming

There are two great year-round indoor facilities in Vancouver. Both have 50-meter Olympic-size heated pools, with separate teaching pools, diving tanks, saunas, whirlpools, and exercise gyms. The **Vancouver Aquatic Centre,** 1050 Beach Ave. (tel. 665-3424) at the foot of Thurlow Street on False Creek, and the **UBC Aquatic Centre,** University Blvd. (tel. 228-4521) next to the Student Union Building, have varying hours for public swimming and changing charges, so it's best to call ahead. There are also pools downtown in the **YMCA** and **YWCA,** the latter for women only.

Tennis

When the sun is shining, especially in spring and summer, Vancouverites are on the courts in force. There are some 250 public courts around the city, but you may still have to wait in line for playing time on weekends and evenings. After all, they're nearly all free.

Stanley Park has the most courts in the city: 21, including 17 near the Beach Avenue entrance and four more by Lost Lagoon. There are another 20 courts at **Queen Elizabeth Park** and 10 more at **Kitsilano Beach Park.** The **UBC Tennis Centre,** on Thunderbird Boulevard (tel. 228-2505), has 10 outdoor and four indoor courts. After dark, you can use the lit public courts at the **Langara Campus** of Vancouver Community College, on West 49th Avenue between Main and Cambie streets.

Water Sports

There are a slew of family-fun water-sports centers around the Lower Mainland.

Canada Games Pool and Fitness Centre, 65 E. 6th Ave., New Westminster (tel. 526-4281), has a giant waterslide, water games like rope swings and an overhead trolley, an enormous Jacuzzi, and a 5,000-square-foot fitness facility. It's open 6:30am to 10:30pm daily year round.

Newton Wave Pool, 13730 72nd Ave., Surrey (tel. 594-7873), has two waterslides, a 3-foot-wave generator, and various fitness equipment. It's open noon to 4pm and 6:30 to 10pm Monday to Thursday, 11am to 9pm Friday to Sunday; admission is $5 adults, $3.75 students, $2.50 children.

Splashdown Park, 4799 Highway 17, Tsawwassen (tel. 943-2251), is a recreational complex with a half dozen interwoven water slides of the ever-popular twister and tube (and twister-tube) varieties, plus smaller and wider slides for the more timid. There are also picnic tables, hot tubs, mini-golf, a video arcade, concessions, and so forth. It's adjacent to the B.C. Ferry terminal to Vancouver Island.

WALKING AROUND VANCOUVER

1. Downtown

Begin your walking tour of downtown Vancouver at **Harbour Centre** (1), 555 W. Hastings St. between Seymour and Richards (tel. 689-0421). The observation deck, 553 feet above the city streets, offers a breathtaking 360-degree panorama of the entire Vancouver area. Telescopes and explanatory plaques assist viewers, and there's a 1,000-image multimedia show, *Children of the Rainbow,* about the city and its people. It's open June through September from 8:30am to 10pm; admission is $3 for adults, $2.50 for seniors and students. Take the glass "Skylift" elevator. A revolving restaurant, The Top of Vancouver, is one floor above the observation deck.

Exit Harbour Centre by its Cordova Street (north) doors. Across the street, a little bit to the west, is **The Station** (2). Once the Canadian Pacific Railway depot, it's been completely renovated in its original Beaux Arts style, and is now the Waterfront terminal of the SkyTrain light-rail system and the SeaBus to North Vancouver. There are numerous shops and cafés on the ground floor, with three levels of offices above.

Next door to the west is **Granville Square** (3), a 32-story office tower. Beyond, extending into Burrard Inlet, are the unmistakable sails of **Canada Place** (4).

Built as the Canada Pavilion for the Expo '86 world's fair, Canada Place has quickly become as much a trademark of Vancouver as Australia's Sydney Opera House, which it vaguely resembles. Five

80-foot-tall fiberglass sails give the structure the appearance of a clipper ship leaving port. From inside, they create a unique skylight over the impressive **Prow Restaurant** (see Chapter VI, "Expensive Restaurants: Downtown") and an entry hall that boasts a unique collection of native quilts and totem poles. An indoor concourse has several international fast-food outlets and souvenir shops.

Some 43 descriptive plaques along the outdoor **Promenade Into History** encourage visitors to make self-guided tours around Canada Place—and discover Vancouver's history at the same time. Free guided tours are also offered daily from 9am to 5pm from the information booth (tel. 688-TOUR) on the downtown side of the complex. The complex also houses:

The **Vancouver Trade and Convention Centre,** with three levels, 21 meeting rooms, a 16,700-square-foot ballroom, a main exhibition hall of 94,000 square feet, and a capacity of 11,000 guests;

The **World Trade Centre** office complex, including the Asia Pacific Foundation.

The luxurious 505-room **Pan-Pacific Hotel.** (See Chapter V, "Very Expensive Hotels: Downtown.")

The **Cruise Ship Terminal,** which berths up to four ships at a time (200 sailings a year) during the summer season. Nearly all of them ply the Inside Passage route to Alaska.

The **CN Imax Theatre** (tel. 682-IMAX), the home of a giant five-story screen on which travel, nature, and technology-oriented movies are presented. There are daily matinees on the hour from noon to 5pm, and evening double features at 7 and 9pm. Admission is $6 adults, $5 seniors and students, $3.50 children for matinees; $8 adults, $7 seniors and students, $5.50 children at night.

On leaving Canada Place, venture south on Howe Street. At the corner of Hastings is **Sinclair Centre** (5), 757 W. Hastings St. (tel. 666-0140). This unique restoration of four early 20th-century buildings houses a variety of shops, services, and federal government offices. It's best known denizen is **Leone,** an exclusive retailer of imported European clothing (see Chapter IX, "Shopping").

Hastings and West Pender, which parallels it to the south, are the center of Vancouver's **financial district.** Here you'll find a score of national and international banks as well as the **Vancouver Stock Exchange** (6). The VSE's Visitors Centre (tel. 643-6590 or 689-3334) is at Granville and Dunsmuir streets; open Monday through Friday, it offers tours and video presentations from 6am to 5pm.

The **Pacific Centre Mall** (7) (tel. 688-7236) covers three full blocks between Pender and Robson, and Howe and Granville streets. Downtown Vancouver's largest underground shopping mall, it includes 200 stores, numerous fine eating places, banks, and other services. From the glass-domed atrium of the Four Seasons Hotel, a three-story waterfall splashes into a pool surrounded by fountains. **Eaton's,** one of the city's two largest department stores, extends into the mall at Granville and Georgia streets. The other, **The Bay** (The Hudson's Bay Company), is catty-corner; its basement is a part of the **Vancouver Centre** (8) (tel. 684-7537), a smaller mall adjoining the Pacific Centre. (See Chapter IX, "Vancouver Shopping.")

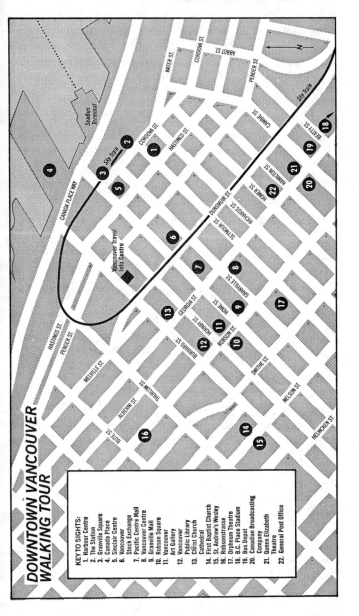

DOWNTOWN VANCOUVER WALKING TOUR

KEY TO SIGHTS:
1. Harbour Centre
2. The Station
3. Granville Square
4. Canada Place
5. Sinclair Centre
6. Vancouver Stock Exchange
7. Pacific Centre Mall
8. Vancouver Centre
9. Granville Mall
10. Robson Square
11. Vancouver Art Gallery
12. Vancouver Public Library
13. Christ Church Cathedral
14. First Baptist Church
15. St. Andrew's Wesley
16. Robsonstrasse
17. Orpheum Theatre
18. B.C. Place Stadium
19. Bus Depot
20. Canadian Broadcasting Company
21. Queen Elizabeth Theatre
22. General Post Office

The six-block stretch of Granville Street from Hastings to Nelson is a pedestrian mall, the only vehicular traffic allowed on the street itself being bus traffic. This northern end of the **Granville Mall**

(9) is heavily devoted to shopping; the southern two blocks, below Robson, are a bit tawdry, with numerous theaters, video arcades, and pawnshops that appeal to a young street-smart set.

Exit Pacific Centre or Granville Mall onto Robson Street. On the south side of the street, between Howe and Hornby, is **Robson Square** (10) (tel. 668-2830), widely considered the town center because it houses B.C. government offices and the law courts, designed by famed architect Arthur Erickson, at its Nelson Street end. This extensive development also has an underground Media Centre for lectures, exhibitions, films, and concerts; an ice-skating rink; a food court (with cheap and tasty fast food); and other facilities. Tourism British Columbia has an office here.

Directly opposite, on Robson Street, are the former courts, now rehabilitated as the splendid **Vancouver Art Gallery** (11) (see Chapter VII, "Top Attractions: Museums"). The main branch of the **Vancouver Public Library** (12) (tel. 665-2287) is a block west on Burrard at Robson; author readings are frequent events here, and historical photos are on display. A three-month library card will cost you $20; $15 is refundable when you turn it in.

Some of the city's most magnificent early 20th-century stone churches are north and south of here on Burrard Street. A full block north, at the corner of Georgia, is **Christ Church Cathedral** (13) of the Anglican Church of Canada. South two blocks, on opposite sides of Nelson Street, are **First Baptist Church** (14) and **St. Andrew's Wesley** (15) (United Church of Canada).

West of Burrard, several blocks of Robson Street have a distinctly European ambience with their high-fashion boutiques, trendy restaurants, and gift and novelty shops. Although the street signs don't say so, this stretch is best known as **Robsonstrasse** (16). This is where you can dine on Bratwurst or coquilles St-Jacques, sip espresso or buy English Breakfast tea, nibble Swiss chocolates or Belgian waffles, buy last weekend's London *Times,* check out the latest sexy lingerie, or have your hair done by a European-trained coiffeuse. (See Chapter IX, "Shopping.")

If you get caught up in the Robsonstrasse whirlwind, you may choose to end your downtown walking tour here. Otherwise, reverse direction and proceed east on Robson Street. One block past Granville, and a half block south on Seymour, is the eclectic but elegant **Orpheum Theatre** (17), built in 1926. Now the home of the Vancouver Symphony Orchestra (see Chapter X, "Vancouver Nights"), the 2,800-seat theater was built for the Chicago-based Orpheum vaudeville circuit. Plan to return for a performance to see the Spanish arches, travertine walls, and remarkable plasterwork ceiling.

Continue east on Robson for another five blocks, until it ends at **B.C. Place Stadium** (18) (tel. 669-2300 or 661-DOME). Some call this $126 million inflated-dome stadium a giant spaceship; a journalist friend of mine refers to it as "the marshmallow in bondage" because of the appearance of its white fiberglass roof, kept aloft by fans and restricted by cables. Opened in 1983, the 60,000-seat stadium is home to the B.C. Lions of the Canadian Football League and the Vancouver Whitecaps of the North American Soccer League (see Chapter VII, "Sports"). Numerous trade shows and one-time sporting events are held here, and it's the primary venue for big-time concerts. Guided one-hour tours are offered daily at

11am and 1 and 3pm when events permit. Admission is $3.50 for adults, $2.75 for seniors and students, $2 for young children.

In front of the stadium is the **Terry Fox Monument,** honoring a modern Canadian hero from suburban Port Coquitlam. As a 19-year-old cancer victim in 1980–81, Fox ran more than halfway across Canada on an artificial leg, raising money for cancer research, until the disease forced him to quit and eventually took his life.

Leave the stadium and walk north on Beatty Street one block to Georgia Street. Turn left. On your right is the downtown **Bus Depot**(19); a block ahead on your left is the western headquarters of the **Canadian Broadcasting Company** (20). Opposite the CBC on Hamilton Street is the **Queen Elizabeth Theatre** (21), a modern venue for theater and operas.

Facing the theater, catty-corner from the CBC, is the **General Post Office** (22), open Monday to Friday from 8am to 5:30pm. Stamp collectors will be attracted to its excellent Philatelic Centre, open from 8am to 5pm.

To return to your starting point, walk one block west, to Richards, then three blocks north to Harbour Centre.

---

2. Gastown

Start at **Harbour Centre** (1), Cross Cordova, turn right (east), and take the left-hand fork onto Water Street, and you'll be in Gastown. Vancouver was founded here in 1867, incorporated and inadvertently razed in 1886, and rebuilt with Victorian dignity. Eight decades later, having fallen derelict, Gastown was scheduled for the wrecking ball. But in 1971 the government of British Columbia designated it a heritage area, launching the renovation that has made it a charming if touristy district of shops, restaurants, nightclubs, and cobbled streets shaded by trees and imitation old-time gaslamps.

As you begin, the first building on your left is **The Landing** (2), 375 Water St. (tel. 687-1144), a restored 1905 Klondike gold-rush warehouse converted to an exclusive shopping and office block with a fine restaurant and an eagerly anticipated European-style hotel. A couple of storefronts farther, duck into the **Inuit Gallery** (3), 345 Water St. (tel. 688-7323), a virtual museum of native Canadian art and artifacts (see Chapter IX, "Shopping").

At the corner of Cambie Street, pause to study the **Gastown Steam Clock** (4), framed in bronze, the only one of its kind in the world. Powered by an underground steam system that also heated surrounding buildings, it has a glass window that enables passersby to observe its works. The clock shrilly whistles the Westminster Chimes theme every 15 minutes, and noisily spews steam on the hour.

There are more interesting shops on the next couple of blocks, including Native Canadian crafts and antique outlets. Check out **The Courtyard** (5) arcade, 131 Water St.; the tiny **fish-head water fountain** (6) at the corner of Abbott Street; and **Gaoler's Mews** (7), 12 Water St., a little shopping center built around winding turn-of-the-century passageways.

Maple Tree Square (8) is the spiritual center of Gastown. This spot, where Water, Carrall, Alexander, and Powell streets converge, was probably the location of Captain John Deighton's original Globe Saloon. Legend says the Yorkshireman disembarked from a canoe in 1866, accompanied by his native mistress, a dog, and a barrel of whisky. The spirits and Deighton's natural gift of gab persuaded local sawmill workers to help him build the first structure of future Vancouver: his saloon. The river pilot's nonstop monologue earned him the nickname "Gassy Jack" and helped attract further development to the area, such as stores and a hotel. The town assumed Jack's nickname. In 1970, a bronze **statue of Gassy Jack** standing on his whisky barrel was erected in Maple Tree Square. It faces **Hotel Europe** (9), 43 Powell St., an early 20th-century flatiron building that was once the city's most luxurious apartment house.

Heading back up Cordova Street from Carrall, you'll pass **Blood Alley Square** (10) about one-half block on the right. This dead-end alley provided a covert location for shady deals during Gastown's wild days, and was a place where many business arrangements were terminally concluded.

3. Chinatown

Vancouver's Chinatown is the largest in Canada and the second-largest in North America, after only San Francisco. (With the recent influx of Hong Kong immigrants boosting the Chinese population in the metropolitan area to nearly a quarter million, it will soon be giving the Bay Area a run for top honors.) This traditional market quarter is focused along Hastings, Pender, Keefer, and Georgia streets from Carrall to Gore.

Start your tour at the **Chinese Cultural Centre** (1), 50 E. Pender St. between Carrall and Columbia (tel. 687-0729). It serves as a center for social services, community programs, and instruction in language, art, and t'ai chi, and sponsors the annual Chinese New Year parade and related events. There are free changing public exhibits of local history and/or traditional culture in the multipurpose hall. A restaurant and museum are planned in the future. The small bookstore will sell you an excellent, detailed walking-tour brochure of Chinatown.

Behind the CCC is the **Dr. Sun Yat-sen Classical Chinese Park and Garden** (2), 578 Carrall St. (tel. 662-3207). (See Chapter VII, "More Attractions: Parks and Gardens.") Admission is charged to the $6 million garden, but the adjacent park is free.

The **Sam Kee Building** (3), 8 W. Pender St. at the southwest corner of Carrall, west of the Cultural Centre, is listed in the *Guinness Book of World Records* as the narrowest building in the world. A two-story steel-framed building constructed in 1913, its ground floor is 5 feet 10 inches wide. Bay windows on its upper floor add another 50% to its width. An architectural firm is the current tenant.

Just west is **Shanghai Alley** (4), rumored to have been the site of the first Chinese settlement in Vancouver in the 1870s or 1880s.

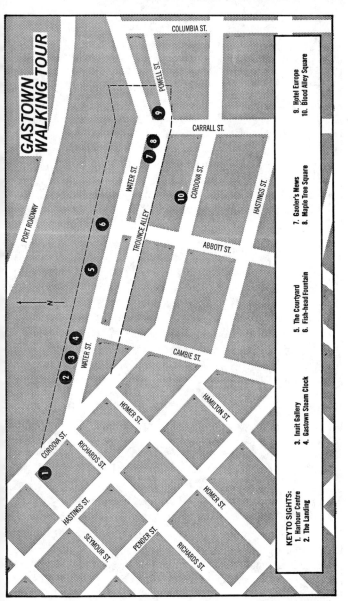

GASTOWN
WALKING TOUR

KEY TO SIGHTS:
1. Harbour Centre
2. The Landing
3. Inuit Gallery
4. Gastown Steam Clock
5. The Courtyard
6. Fish-head Fountain
7. Gaoler's Mews
8. Maple Tree Square
9. Hotel Europe
10. Blood Alley Square

Only three Chinese buildings still stand in this narrow lane, but in its early 20th-century heyday, it was the site of a public bath, theater, restaurants, pawnshops, stores, and residences.

Cross Pender Street, head east, opposite the Cultural Center.

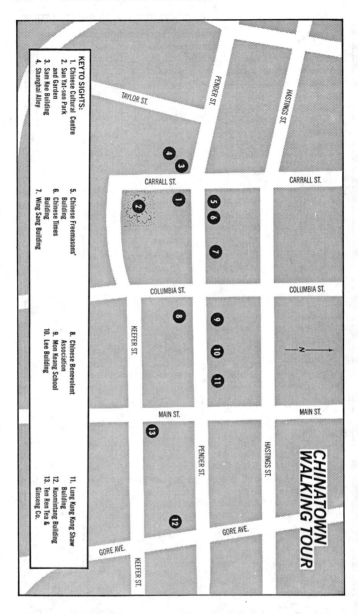

KEY TO SIGHTS:
1. Chinese Cultural Centre
2. Sun Yat-sen Park
   and Garden
3. Sam Kee Building
4. Shanghai Alley

5. Chinese Freemasons'
   Building
6. Chinese Times
   Building
7. Wing Sang Building

8. Chinese Benevolent
   Association
9. Mon Keang School
10. Lee Building

11. Lung Kung Kong Shaw
    Building
12. Kuomintang Building
13. Ten Ren Tea &
    Ginseng Co.

CHINATOWN WALKING TOUR

The **Chinese Freemasons' Building** (5) (1901), 5 W. Pender St.,
housed a society that lent heavy financial support to Sun Yat-sen's
1911 Chinese Revolution. The **Chinese Times Building** (6)
(1902), 1 E. Pender St., was the home of Chinatown's first newspa-

per. The community's first bank was in the **Wing Sang Building** (7), 51-67 E. Pender St.; built in 1889, this is Chinatown's oldest standing building. The shops in this block seem to have the best and lowest-priced selection of traditional crafts and other souvenirs.

Across Columbia Street, the **Chinese Benevolent Association** (8) (1909), 108 E. Pender St., provides welfare services throughout the community. **Mon Keang School** (9) (1921), 123 E. Pender St., was the first in Canada to offer Chinese classes at the high-school level. The **Lee Building** (10) (1907), 127-133 E. Pender, once concealed an opium factory. The **Lung Kung Kong Shaw Building** (11), 135 E. Pender St., is newer but displays traditional Chinese architectural details.

Pender and Main is the commercial heart of modern Chinatown. Throughout the community, you'll see numerous restaurants, from Cantonese dim sum parlors to noodle houses to formal dining rooms. Keep an eye out for bakeries, where you can try moon cakes or *bao,* steamed buns with meat or sweet bean fillings. You can enjoy doing your grocery shopping like the Chinese, especially if you have a kitchen in your hotel room: Buy your fresh vegetables and thousand-year-old eggs from the sidewalk stands at one store, pick out a live eel or a preserved pressed duck from another. Everything is written in Chinese pictograms, so if you don't know what you're buying . . . guess. Life should be an adventure.

It's a different experience to venture into any of Chinatown's several herbalist shops. The dried sea horses, reindeer antlers, snakeskins, buffalo tongues, ginseng root, and other items on sale here are remedies for various ailments. Each shop has at its rear a traditional doctor's office, where herbs and teas are prescribed in appropriate mixtures.

Continue up Pender another block past Main, then turn right at Gore. The **Kuomintang Building** (12), 529 Gore St., was built in 1920 as the western Canadian political headquarters of the Chinese Nationalist Party, which retains power in Taiwan. Overseas politics were once of essential interest to Canadian Chinese.

Turn right at Keefer, stopping into the **Ten Ren Tea & Ginseng Co.** (13) at the corner of Main for a sample of their excellent ginger or jasmine tea. Then proceed north on Main, turn left (west) at Hastings, then left (south) on Columbia to the Cultural Centre, where you began. As you go, study the architecture of Chinatown's traditional buildings. Most of them have recessed balconies, which helped cool the interiors of homes of steamy South China. Look for the use of different colors—red is associated with happiness and prosperity, blue and green with peace and fertility—as well as decorative carvings. The dragon motif, symbolic of royalty and longevity, is common.

4. Granville Island

What, in fact, is Granville Island?

It's an adult entertainment center, with a hotel, eight restaurants and lounges, and three theaters. It's a place for the children, with a water park and Kids Only Market. It's a focus for the arts community, with numerous galleries and guilds as well as the Emily Carr College of Art and Design. It's an industrial center, the seat of two major and several smaller factories. It's a market center, with a huge public market and dozens of independent merchants. It's a social entity, containing a houseboat village, schools, a community center, and ferry terminals. Yet for all practical purposes, it's hardly more than a decade old.

Vancouver likes to think of the 38-acre promontory beneath the Granville Street Bridge as an "urban park." There's a remarkable story behind its development. Once a marshy tidal flat in False Creek, it was reclaimed for heavy industry in 1917, and became an ironworks and shipbuilding center through the years of the Second World War. By the 1960s it was an eyesore, plagued by rats and heaps of garbage.

In 1972, the federal government agreed to sponsor the island's redevelopment to the tune of $19.5 million. The goal was a multiuse facility, with industrial and commercial themes as well as arts and entertainment. Planners maintained the warehouse appearance of the island, its tin and stucco siding, false-fronted buildings, rail tracks, and seawall. They tied it together visually with canopies, streetworks, and bright colors. Much of the most visible work had been accomplished by 1979, but the renovation continues even today under federal management.

Driving on the island today is no real problem, so long as you remember that the traffic flow is one-way counterclockwise. There's 3-hour free parking from 7am to 7pm, and unlimited parking after 7pm—but given the space restrictions, it's always somewhat limited. (If you're driving from downtown on the Granville Street Bridge, keep right on West 4th Avenue, then turn right onto Fir Street, right again onto West 2nd Avenue, and left onto Anderson Street.) Buses no. 50 (Gastown–False Creek) and 51 (Broadway/Granville) do swings around the island.

You can also arrive by water aboard a miniature passenger ferry. **Granville Island Ferries** (1) (tel. 684-7781) leave the Aquatic Center, beneath the Burrard Street Bridge at Beach Avenue, every six minutes daily from 7:30am to 8pm (later in summer); and there's an **Aquabus** (2) (tel. 874-9930) from the Hornby Street Dock on False Creek.

Start your tour at the **Granville Island Information Centre** (3), 1669 Johnston St. opposite the bus stop (tel. 666-5784), near the public market. The info center has an excellent museum-style exhibit and audiovisual presentation to explain Granville Island's evolution. Pick up an island map and special events calendar here.

Granville Island is a great place for wandering. Many of the buildings contain art galleries and craft cooperatives, bookstores and bakeries, custom jewelers, and ship's chandlers. (Most businesses are open daily, 9am to 6pm.) Peek into some of the studios just west of the Info Centre, and you may see artisans throwing potter's clay, weaving cloth, blowing glass, hammering gold, etc. Across Johnston Street is **Mulvaney's** (4) Cajun restaurant (see Chapter VI, "Expensive Restaurants: South of Downtown"), and, next door, the **Arts Club Theatres** (5) (see Chapter X, "Vancouver Nights"). The Aquabus terminal is adjacent to the theater.

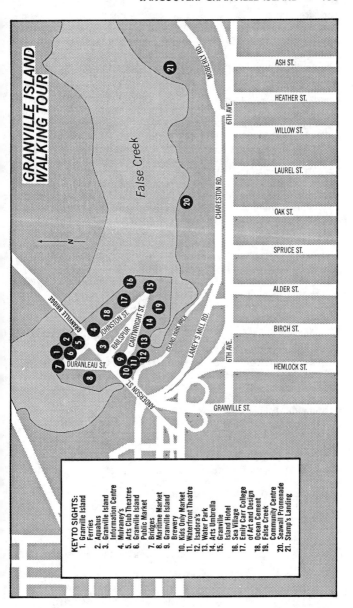

GRANVILLE ISLAND
WALKING TOUR

False Creek

N

KEY TO SIGHTS:
1. Granville Island
   Ferries
2. Aquabus
3. Granville Island
   Information Centre
4. Mulvaney's
5. Arts Club Theatres
6. Granville Island
   Public Market
7. Bridges
8. Maritime Market
9. Granville Island
   Brewery
10. Kids Only Market
11. Waterfront Theatre
12. Isadora's
13. Water Park
14. Arts Umbrella
15. Granville
    Island Hotel
16. Sea Village
17. Emily Carr College
    of Art and Design
18. Ocean Cement
19. False Creek
    Community Centre
20. Seawall Promenade
21. Stamp's Landing

The 50,000-square-foot **Granville Island Public Market** (6) is next. All manner of fruit and vegetable, meat and seafood, wine and cheese, flowers and candy can be purchased here, and there's a seemingly endless series of international fast-food counters. Best of all is the people-watching. Every Wednesday from June through September, there's a Farmers' Truck Market from 9am to 4pm. The market is open year round: 9am to 6pm daily in summer, closed Monday (except public holidays) in winter.

At the end of Johnston Street are the Granville Island Ferry terminal and **Bridges** (7) restaurant (see Chapter VI, "Moderately Priced Restaurants: South of Downtown"). Turn sharply and head south down Duranleau Street. There are more art studios on your left. On your right are the buildings of the **Maritime Market** (8), where you can buy a yacht from a broker or order one custom-made from a boatbuilder, outfit it with help from a chandler and sailmaker, and sign up for sailing lessons to figure out how to get around in it. You can even rent a kayak here from the **Ecomarine Ocean Kayak Centre.**

Cross Anderson Street and point yourself east on Cartwright Street. The first building on your left is the **Granville Island Brewery** (9) (tel. 688-9927), British Columbia's most esteemed cottage brewer. No preservatives or chemicals are used in the production of cold Island Lager (a Bavarian-style pilsner) or sweet, dark Island Bock. Free tasting tours are offered hourly from 1 to 5pm on Saturday, Sunday, and holidays; 2pm only Monday through Friday. You can buy eight-packs of lager or a variety of gifts year round, Monday to Saturday from 10am to 7pm (to 9pm May to September) and Sunday from noon to 6pm.

Opposite the brewery is the **Kids Only Market** (10), 27 shops and services geared completely for the younger set. There are toy stores and clothing shops, rides and games, ice-cream stands, and even a day-care center. Next door is the **Waterfront Theatre** (11) (see Chapter X, "Vancouver Nights"), whose adjunct Carousel Theatre schedules frequent youth-oriented shows; and a few steps down Old Bridge Street is **Isadora's** (12) (tel. 681-3748), a co-op restaurant that will please both children (peanut butter sandwiches, chocolate-coated bananas) and adults (stuffed croissants, light entrées, wine list). There's an indoor play station and an outdoor **Water Park** (13) with movable water cannons to keep the youngsters happy and busy. (Changing facilities are available.)

Farther down Cartwright Street are the studio/galleries of the **Crafts Association of B.C.,** the **Potters' Guild of B.C.,** and **Arts Umbrella** (14), with some 50 classes in all aspects of the performing and fine arts for kids from preschool through high school. Cartwright ends at the **Granville Island Hotel** (15) (see Chapter V, "Expensive Hotels: South of Downtown") at the eastern edge of the island.

Directly north of the hotel is **Sea Village** (16), a neighborhood of elaborate floating homes. Also in the vicinity are architects' and attorneys' offices, and a computer learning center aboard the **Granville Island Barge.**

Two entities dominate Granville Island's north shore. The **Emily Carr College of Art and Design** (17), 1399 Johnston St. (tel. 687-2345), has an open-air mall where you can view students' work in progress. **Ocean Cement** (18), between the college and the public market, is the island's largest still-operating industry. By the time you've passed the cement plant, you're back at the Info Centre.

To extend this tour, head back to the **False Creek Community Center** (19), adjacent to the Arts Umbrella on the southeast side of

Granville Island. There are facilities for all ages and public tennis courts outside. Follow the **seawall promenade** (20) down the south shore of False Creek, which is another award-winning urban redevelopment project. It's a 20-minute stroll through landscaped parkland to **Stamp's Landing** (21), past a mixture of luxury town houses, apartments, and senior-citizen residences. At the east end of the promenade are the **False Creek Marina** and several fine restaurants, including **Monk McQueen's** and **Snappers** (see Chapter VI, "Expensive Restaurants: South of Downtown," and "Moderately Priced Restaurants: South of Downtown").

IX

VANCOUVER SHOPPING

1. BEST BUYS
2. MARKETS
3. SHOPPING A TO Z

Shopping in Vancouver is fun. From trendy Robsonstrasse and Gastown to ethnic neighborhoods like Chinatown, a multitude of fascinating shops beckon, offering everything from the latest in European fashions to ancient Ming ceramics.

The cornerstones of Vancouver shopping are two department stores, **The Bay** (Hudson's Bay Company) and **Eaton's.** Their main outlets are across the street from one another at Granville and Georgia streets, in the heart of downtown. Both are connected to major underground shopping malls, **Pacific Centre Mall** and **Vancouver Centre,** with more than 300 shops between them.

Another "don't miss" shop is **Leone,** an international fashion magnet in **Sinclair Centre** at 757 W. Hastings St. near Canada Place. This two-story shopping center has 31 outlets; it occupies four interconnected heritage buildings, restored in grand fashion.

Some of the most interesting shopping areas were described in Chapter VIII, "Walking Around Vancouver." In downtown Vancouver, **Robsonstrasse**—that portion of Robson Street between Burrard and Jervis streets—carries a vaguely European atmosphere through its high-fashion boutiques, intriguing gift shops, and trendy restaurants. The shops and eating establishments of **Gastown,** the original 19th-century Vancouver, face tree-lined, brick-paved streets. Adjacent **Chinatown's** markets, crafts shops, and restaurants could as easily be on the other shore of the Pacific. **Granville Island's** imaginative mix of galleries, theaters, restaurants, specialty shops, and a public market make it one of the city's most popular destinations.

Thursdays and Fridays are late shopping nights in downtown Vancouver. Normal shopping hours are 9am to 5:30pm Monday,

Tuesday, Wednesday, and Saturday, 9am to 9pm Thursday and Friday, and noon to 5pm on Sunday.

---

1. Best Buys

ANTIQUES: There are three principal areas. Tourists like Gastown, but area residents opt for south Granville Street, where elegant early British and Asian pieces are found, or the lesser-known shops along Main Street south of Chinatown. The best prices can be obtained at antiques auctions—but you have to know what you're bidding on. Try **Love's Auctioneers and Appraisers,** 1635 W. Broadway at Fir St. (tel. 733-1157), on Wednesday at 1 and 7pm; **Appleton Auctioneers,** 1238 Seymour St. between Davie and Drake Sts. (tel. 685-1715), Tuesday at 7pm; or **Tyldesley's Ltd.,** 4428 Main St. at East 29th Ave. (tel. 874-4238), Tuesday at 1 and 7pm (viewing Mon to Fri 9am to 5pm).

ART: There are fine galleries all over the city, but the consensus recommends south Granville (between 6th and 15th) for traditional oils, and the studios of Granville Island for more contemporary works.

BOOKS: **Duthie Books** (downtown and West Point Grey) and **Blackberry Books** (Granville Island and Sinclair Centre) have the most comprehensive collections, but if it's a bargain you're seeking, try **The Book Warehouse,** with outlets on Robsonstrasse and in Kitsilano. For details, see "Shopping A to Z," below.

CRAFTS: Water Street in Gastown is the center for collectors of traditional Northwest Coast Native Canadian arts and crafts. These are always a hit among visitors. Look for woodcarvings (ceremonial masks, miniature totem poles, bentwood boxes, calabash bowls), jewelry (carved silver, gold, jade, and black argillite), weaving (including fine blankets), leatherwork, basketry, and carvings and sculptures of soapstone, whalebone, and walrus-tusk ivory. Always popular are Cowichan sweaters, handspun from undyed raw wool by natives of Vancouver Island. Because they retain the sheep's natural lanolin and oils, they are resistant to rain and snow, and are especially long-wearing.

Two of the finest shops in the Vancouver area are the University of British Columbia Museum of Anthropology gallery and the Capilano Trading Post, at the Capilano Suspension Bridge in North Vancouver. Both are discussed in Chapter VII, "Top Attractions."

FASHIONS: Robsonstrasse has trendy mid-priced North American active wear. South Granville shops are more upscale, specializing in European imports. The department stores and shopping malls, of course, carry a wide variety of styles and price ranges.

Canada's best-known fashion designer is Alfred Sung. Other noted Canadian designers to look for are Simon Chang, Tom D'Auria, Susie Hayward, and Jean-Claude Poitras.

FOOD: Salmon boxes are probably the two biggest sellers among visitors. Smoked or canned Pacific salmon, packed in a cedar box bearing a native motif, makes a wonderful gift for friends back home. Many gourmet specialty shops will even ship frozen fresh salmon to your home, timed for your return. Other good choices are maple syrup (and maple sugar candy), B.C. honey, wild rice, and English teas and biscuits. You'll find all these and more, for the best prices, on the food floors in major department stores.

JEWELRY: The most interesting pieces are those crafted by native artisans of silver, gold, British Columbia jade, or black argillite, a semiprecious stone mined only in the Queen Charlotte Islands.

SOUVENIRS: Shops selling T-shirts and Canada Place keychains are ubiquitous on major shopping streets, like those of Robson-strasse and Gastown. The best prices and selections are found in the major department stores.

TOYS: Handcrafted wooden toys from British Columbia's ever-green forests are handsome remembrances of a visit here. Check the selection at **Kids Only** on Granville Island or **Kids' Alley** at the Lonsdale Quay Market.

WINE: For B.C. wines, including Cedar Creek and Mission Hill, check the wine shops in the department stores and public markets.

---

2. Markets

Three major public markets are easily reached from downtown Vancouver.

Granville Island Public Market, Johnston St., Granville Island (tel. 666-5784).

For details on this 50,000-square-foot market, see Chapter VIII, "Walking Around Vancouver." From 9am to 4pm Wednesdays between June and September, there's a farmers' truck market.

Open: Daily 9am–6pm. *Closed:* Mon in winter, except public holidays. *Bus:* 51. *Ferry:* Granville Island Ferry or Aquabus across False Creek.

Lonsdale Quay Market, 123 Carrie Cates Court, North Vancouver (tel. 985-6261).

This colorful two-tier collection of market vendors, specialty shops, and restaurants on North Vancouver's waterfront even houses a hotel! (See Lonsdale Quay Hotel in Chapter V, "Vancouver Accommodations.") The ground floor is the food floor—fresh produce, seafood, meats, bakery items, gourmet delicacies, wines, and a row of international fast-food outlets offering everything from burritos to pasta, sushi to espresso. The upper story comprises a variety of fashion stores, bookstores, gift shops, houseware outlets, craft shops, as well as Kids' Alley—a number of children's shops offering toys, puppets, kites, clothing, and a special play area.

Open: Sat–Wed 9:30am–6:30pm, Thurs–Fri 9:30am–9pm. *SeaBus:* Lonsdale Quay.

Robson Public Market, 1610 Robson St. at Cardero (tel. 682-2733).

A glass atrium soars over produce sellers and an international food fair in this contemporary market, whose design recalls that of London's Crystal Palace. French, Italian, Greek, Chinese, and Japanese food, plus grilled salmon, bagels, and stuffed pita bread are all found here for the asking. There are also houseware and leather-goods outlets, a video store, a florist, and a newsstand.

Open: Daily 9am–9pm. *Bus:* 8.

---

3. Shopping A to Z

ANTIQUES

Artemis Antiques Ltd., 321 Water St. near Cordova, Gastown (tel. 685-8808).

18th- and 19th-century furniture is the specialty here, along with clocks, paintings, bronzes, art glass, and other objets d'art—including art nouveau and art deco articles.

Open: Mon–Sat 10am–5pm and by appointment. *Bus:* 1 or 50.

Frankie Robinson Oriental Gallery, 3055 Granville St. near W. 16th Ave. (tel. 734-6568).

Bronzes, cloisonné, porcelain, textiles, Buddha images, prints, paintings, furniture, and other "mysteries" of the East are available here, as well as contemporary fine Asian art.

Open: Mon–Sat 10am–5pm and by appointment. *Bus:* 20 or 401.

Granville Antique Gallery, 3025 Granville St. near W. 15th Ave. (tel. 736-7407).

One of the newer antique outlets in the city, this store features English, French, and Dutch furniture of 19th- and early 20th-century vintage, a wide variety of early Canadiana, as well as paintings, tapestries, carpets, bronzes, and ceramics.

Open: Daily 10am–5pm and 6–9pm. *Bus:* 20 or 401.

Hampshire Antiques Ltd., 3149 Granville St. (tel. 733-1326).

British wares are readily available here, including furniture, paintings, ceramics, and marine items such as clocks and barometers. A library of antique collectors' reference books is available for perusal. Hampshire also offers a generous antiques finder service, taking potential clients from their hotels or the airport to galleries of possible interest, and arranging shipment and delivery of any purchases.

Open: Mon–Sat 10:30am–5pm. *Bus:* 20 or 401.

Uno Langmann Ltd., 2117 Granville St. beneath the Granville Bridge (tel. 736-8825).

Old Masters of the 18th and 19th centuries and early 20th-century paintings are the forte of this outstanding gallery. Also on display are furniture, silver, porcelain, Oriental carpets, and West Coast Native Canadian art.

Open: Mon–Fri 9:30am–5pm, Sat 10am–4:30pm. *Bus:* 51.

ART

Bau-Xi Gallery, 3045 Granville St. between W. 15th and 16th aves. (tel. 733-7011).

The gallery is nationally renowned for the important new artists it has introduced over the years. Paul and Xisa Wong present the work of accomplished artists along with that of newcomers.

Open: Mon–Sat 9:30am–5:30pm. *Bus:* 20 or 401.

Cartwright Gallery, 1411 Cartwright St., Granville Island (tel. 687-8266).

A publicly subsidized gallery, the Cartwright presents exhibitions of nationally known artists in a variety of media, from metalsmithing to woodwork to tapestries.

Open: Tues–Sat 10am–5pm, Sun 11am–3pm. *Bus:* 51.

Federation Gallery, 952 Richards St. near Nelson (tel. 681-8534).

This showcase of the Federation of Canadian Artists changes its exhibitions of acrylics, watercolors, oils, drawings, and other media every couple of weeks. Many of Canada's leading painters are represented.

Open: Tues–Fri 10am–4pm, Sat 11am–3pm. *Bus:* 15 two blocks north.

Gallery of B.C. Ceramics, 1359 Cartwright St., Granville Island (tel. 669-5645).

Owned and operated by the Potters' Guild of British Columbia, this spacious facility has continuing shows of clay artists (including sculptors), most of whose designs are remarkably innovative.

Open: Tues–Sun 10:30am–5:30pm. *Bus:* 51.

Gallery Shop, Vancouver Art Gallery, 750 Hornby St. at Robson (tel. 682-2765).

This is the place to come for fine art reproductions and art books, including the works of Emily Carr and other Canadian artists. Also represented are jewelry by B.C. designers and carvings by native artisans.

Open: Mon–Wed and Fri–Sat 9:30am–5:30pm, Thurs 9:30am–9pm, Sun noon–5:30pm. *Bus:* 8.

Alexander Harrison Galleries, 2932 Granville St. between W. 14th and 15th aves. (tel. 732-5217), and at 2022 S. Park Royal Shopping Centre, West Vancouver.

Widely regarded as one of the city's outstanding galleries of traditional Western art, the highly praised collection here includes Canadian classics and local landscapes.

Open: Mon–Sat 9:30am–5:30pm, Sun noon–5pm. *Bus:* 20 or 401.

Kenneth Heffel Fine Art, 2247 Granville St. between W. 7th and 8th aves. (tel. 732-6505).

This gallery has probably the finest private collection of Canada's acclaimed Group of Seven and their contemporaries. Another exhibition hall offers the work of current B.C. artists.

Open: Tues–Sat 10am–6pm. *Bus:* 20 or 401.

Terra Cotta Gallery, 3610 W. 4th Ave. at Dunbar St., Kitsilano (tel. 733-9181).

The use of natural materials is the common thread running through the works presented here. Ceramics, glazed and fired in a variety of ways by different artists, are the mainstay; also shown are blown glass, wood-turned bowls, and handmade paper works.

Open: Tues–Sat 10:30am–6pm, Sun 1–5pm. *Bus:* 4 or 7.

BOOKS

Duthie Books, 919 Robson St. at Hornby (tel. 684-4496), and 4444 W. 10th Ave. near Sasamat St., West Point Grey (tel. 224-7012).

The downtown store is by far the city's largest—with some 20,000 volumes, many of them hardcover, on the main floor alone, and a separate "Paperback Cellar" down a spiral staircase. Whether you're looking for fiction or nonfiction, you'll probably find it here. The UBC off-campus outlet has a more academic emphasis.

Open: Mon–Fri 9am–9pm, Sat 9am–6pm, Sun noon–5pm. *Bus:* 8 or 15.

Blackberry Books, 1663 Duranleau St., Granville Island (tel. 685-4113 or 685-6188). Also in Sinclair Centre, R250, 757 W. Hastings St. at Granville (tel. 685-0833), and at 2206 W. 4th Ave. at Yew St., Kitsilano (tel. 733-1673).

The Granville Island store stocks a broad selection of books on art, architecture, and cuisine. Paperback literature dominates at the downtown and Kitsilano stores.

Open: Daily 9am–9pm (Granville Island and Kitsilano); Mon–Sat 9am–6pm (Sinclair Centre).

The Book Warehouse, 1150 Robson St. near Thurlow (tel. 685-5711). Also at 632 W. Broadway near Heather St., Kitsilano (tel. 872-5711).

Remainders are the mainstay here, but that translates to big savings (usually at least 20%) off the list prices of best-selling hardcovers and paperbacks. The selection is good and current.

Open: Daily 10am–10pm. *Bus:* 8 (Robson St.) or 10 (Kitsilano).

Also in the downtown area, **Voyager Books and Maps,** 722 Smithe St., carries a wide range of travel literature.

Other specialty stores tend to cluster near the University of

British Columbia. They include **Banyen,** 2671 W. Broadway (back-to-nature, metaphysics); **Comicshop,** 2089 W. 4th St. (comics and fantasies); **Graffiti Books,** 3514 W. 4th St. (visual and performing arts); **Pink Peppercorn,** 2686 W. Broadway (cookbooks); **Siliconnections,** 3727 W. 10th St. (business and computer); **Vancouver Kidsbooks,** 3083 W. Broadway (children's); and **White Dwarf Books,** 4374 W. 10th St. (science fiction and astronomy).

CHINA AND CRYSTAL

Millar & Coe, 419 W. Hastings St. near Homer (tel. 685-3322).

This store, established in 1912, offers customers a choice of some 1,200 china patterns, 300 crystal patterns, and 200 flatware styles, making it Canada's largest dealer. Waterford crystal, Wedgwood, Royal Doulton, and other famous names are available. There's also a wide selection of figurines and giftware.

Open: Mon–Thurs and Sat 9:30am–5:30pm, Fri 9:30am–9pm. *Bus:* 8, 10, or 20.

Villeroy & Boch Creation, 1156 Robson St. near Bute (tel. 688-6061).

The Vancouver outlet for the world's largest maker of ceramic products. Dinnerware, crystal, and related items are available. Worldwide shipping can be arranged.

Open: Sat–Wed 10am–6pm, Thurs–Fri 10am–9pm. *Bus:* 8.

CRAFTS

Authentic Cowichan Indian Knits, 424 W. 3rd St., North Vancouver (tel. 988-4735).

Freda Nahanee's home-industry shop, on the North Vancouver Indian Reserve, offers its namesake sweaters from Vancouver Island as well as carved-silver Kwakiutl jewelry, Squamish woodcarvings, beaded leather moccasins, woven baskets, and other crafts.

Open: Mon–Sat 10am–6pm. *Bus:* 242.

Heritage Canada, 356 Water St., Gastown (tel. 669-6375). Also in Vancouver Centre (tel. 669-2447) and at Blackcomb Lodge, Whistler (tel. 932-4667).

Handcrafted silver and gold jewelry, original argillite carvings, Cowichan sweaters, moccasins, woodcarvings, and serigraph prints are among the goods available.

Open: Mon–Sat 10am–6pm. *Bus:* 8 (Cordova St.).

Hill's Indian Crafts, 165 Water St. near Cambie, Gastown (tel. 685-4249).

The second-floor gallery is a treasure trove of one-of-a-kind totem poles, ceremonial masks, bentwood boxes, animal plaques, Salish weavings, and other artifacts. They've all got price tags but they're not cheap. Downstairs, jewelry, moccasins, and other artworks are more within most visitors' budgets. One of Vancouver's longest-established crafts shops, Hill's opened in 1946.

Open: Daily 9am–9pm. *Bus:* 8 (Cordova St.).

Images for a Canadian Heritage, 779 Burrard St. at Robson (tel. 685-7046).

Carvings in stone and wood by native and non-native artists, are the focus of this fascinating gallery at the east end of Robsonstrasse. Inuit sculpture in soapstone, whalebone, ivory, jade, and marble, Northwest Coast tribes' masks and jewelry, modern pottery and basketry, and original paintings and graphics are all included in the collection.

Open: Mon–Sat 10am–6pm, Sun and holidays noon–5pm. *Bus:* 8.

The Indian Gallery, 456 W. Cordova St., Gastown (tel. 684-6290).

Northwest Coast native art and Inuit sculpture, including many works of museum quality, comprise the collection. Look for totem poles, ceremonial masks, animal plaques and paddles, bentwood boxes, and silver and gold jewelry.

Open: Tues–Sat 11am–6pm. *Bus:* 8.

Inuit Gallery of Vancouver, 345 Water St., Gastown (tel. 688-7323).

Considered to have Canada's number-one collection of masterworks of Native Canadian art, this remarkable gallery should be on every visitor's "don't miss" list, whether you buy anything or not. Also displayed are masks and other artifacts from Papua New Guinea. Worldwide shipping is easily arranged.

Open: Mon–Sat 10am–6pm, Sun noon–5pm, and by appointment. *Bus:* 8 (Cordova St.).

DEPARTMENT STORES

The Bay, 674 Granville St. at Georgia (tel. 681-6211).

The Hudson's Bay Company dates back more than three centuries, to a network of trading posts and forts first established in the 1670s. The modern coast-to-coast chain is now more popularly known simply as "The Bay." The main downtown store, an imposing white structure with Greek columns, has seven levels of merchandise of all types. Many visitors buy a woolen Hudson's Bay point blanket, a true piece of Canadiana woven in England; its colorful stripes originally represented the number of beaver pelts taken in trade. English bone china can be found on the fifth floor, and the Okanagan Estate Wine Cellar on the Vancouver Centre mall level.

Open: Mon–Wed 9:30am–6pm, Thurs–Fri 9:30am–9pm, Sat 9:30am–5:30pm, Sun noon–5pm (downtown store). *Bus:* 8, 10, or 20. *SkyTrain:* Granville.

Eaton's, 701 Granville St., Pacific Centre Mall (tel. 685-7112).

Vancouver's "other" huge department store is Eaton's. Its numerous fashion boutiques include styles from traditional to avant garde, among them the classic designs of Canadian Alfred Sung. You'll find fine china and crystal, kitchenware and gourmet foods, books and souvenirs, a Kids' World, three restaurants, as well as a beauty salon, bakery, photo studio, florist, jeweler, optometrist, pharmacy, post office, shoe repair, ticket center, and travel agent. The seventh floor has a bargain annex with great deals on clothes, especially on children's and men's clothing.

Open: Mon–Wed 9:30am–6pm, Thurs–Fri 9:30am–9pm, Sat 9:30am–5:30pm, Sun noon–5pm (downtown). *Bus:* 8, 10, or 20. *SkyTrain:* Granville.

Holt Renfrew, 633 Granville St. at Dunsmuir, Pacific Centre Mall (tel. 681-3121).

If The Bay is Vancouver's Macy's, then Holt Renfrew is its Saks Fifth Avenue. The elegant store has an upper level especially popular among the fashion-conscious for its classic designs, sportswear, and shoes. Naturally, it's got everything else a good department store should have as well.

Open: Mon–Wed 9:30am–6:30pm, Thurs–Fri 9:30am–9pm, Sat 9:30am–5:30pm, Sun noon–5pm. *Bus:* 8, 10, or 20. *SkyTrain:* Granville.

Woodward's, 101 W. Hastings St. at Abbott, Gastown (tel. 684-5231).

This highly respected, family-owned local chain is a charming alternative to its fast-paced competition. Of special interest to consumers are its Woodwynn bargain floors, offering great savings in dry goods, shoes, and other items.

Open: Mon–Wed and Sat 9:30am–5:30pm, Thurs–Fri 9:30am–9pm. *Bus:* 14, 20, or 21.

FASHIONS

Leone, Sinclair Centre, 757 W. Hastings St. at Howe (tel. 683-1133).

Vancouver's trendiest high-fashion outlet is designed like a theater for patrons of the arts. A galleria stages the creations of well-known European designers, with clothing, footwear, leather goods, accessories, and fragrances. A cappuccino bar also has light lunches.

Open: Mon–Fri 9:30am–6pm, Sat 9:30am–5:30pm, Sun noon–5pm. *Bus:* 8, 10, or 20. *SkyTrain:* Waterfront.

Edward Chapman, 833 W. Pender St. between Howe and Hornby (tel. 685-6207). Also in Hotel Georgia, 801 W. Georgia St. at Howe (tel. 684-2833); Westin Bayshore Hotel, 1601 W. Georgia St. (tel. 685-6734); Oakridge Centre, 650 W. 41st Ave. (tel. 261-3223); and "Chappy's," 2135 W. 41st Ave. in Kerrisdale (tel. 261-5128).

This establishment, famous for its traditional British woolens, celebrated its 100th anniversary in 1990. The main store in the financial district has a wide choice of men's and women's clothing and specialty items. The store at the Hotel Georgia is a "boutique shoppe" for women and men. At the Westin Bayshore and Oakridge Centre, men's fashions only are featured, while Chapy's in Kerrisdale is exclusively a women's store.

Open: Mon–Sat 9am–5:30pm (main store). *Bus:* 19.

Alfred Sung of Toronto, 1143 Robson St. near Thurlow (tel. 687-2153).

Canada's most highly regarded fashion designer operates this exclusive shop for women on Robsonstrasse. The lines are clean, simple, and refined.

Open: Mon–Wed and Sat 10am–6pm, Thurs–Fri 9am–9pm, Sun 11am–6pm. *Bus:* 8.

Boboli, 2776 Granville St. at W. 12th Ave. (tel. 736-3458).

This elegant shop in the south Granville shopping district has exclusive designer clothing, shoes, and accessories for men and women. The owners travel to Italy four times a year to stock the latest in European fashions.

Open: Mon–Thurs 9:30am–6pm, Fri 9:30am–9pm, Sat 9:30am–5:30pm. *Bus:* 20 or 401.

Club Monaco, 1153 Robson St. near Thurlow (tel. 687-8618).

Men, women, and children can find more moderately priced Alfred Sung clothing here than at the designer boutique next door. The styles tend toward preppy.

Open: Mon–Wed and Sat 10am–6pm, Thurs–Fri 9am–9pm, Sun 11am–6pm. *Bus:* 8.

E. A. Lee, 466 Howe St. near W. Pender (tel. 683-2457).

The shop was founded in the 1920s, but E. A. Lee has modern European styles for nineties executives, women as well as men. Cottons, cashmeres, leathers, and other fabrics are offered. Private consultations and same-day tailoring are among the many services provided.

Open: Mon–Sat 9am–5:30pm. *Bus:* 401.

Mark James, 2941 W. Broadway at Bayswater St., Kitsilano (tel. 734-2381).

Men's and women's fashions, including many current European imports, at moderate prices. The inventory focuses on linens, silks, and natural cottons in summer, woolens in winter.

Open: Mon–Thurs 10am–6pm, Fri 10am–9pm, Sat 10am–5:30pm. *Bus:* 10 or 22.

Mondo Uomo, 2709 Granville St. at W. 12th Ave. (tel. 734-6555).

A refined European menswear boutique, Mondo Uomo carries classic and progressive styles of clothing, shoes, and accessories. The store itself won a local award for commercial architecture.

Open: Mon–Thurs and Sat 10am–6pm, Fri 10am–8pm. *Bus:* 20 or 401.

Neto, 347 and 359 Water St. at Cordova, Gastown (tel. 682-6424).

Men's and women's fashions of European design are manufactured here in Gastown. The line is noted for its colorful leather and lambskin clothing, but it also features woolens, linens, and silks, as well as matching shoes, handbags, and other accessories. Custom orders are welcomed. Neto ships all over the world.

Open: Mon–Thurs and Sat 10am–6pm, Fri 10am–9pm, Sun noon–6pm. *Bus:* 8. *SkyTrain:* Waterfront.

Savoie Giulini, 2698 Granville St. at W. 12th Ave. (tel. 736-8751).

The stock here comes straight from Milan: men's and women's high-fashion Italian clothing and accessories, including ladies' shoes, leather, lingerie, handbags, perfumes, hosiery, silk scarves, and swimwear.

Open: Mon–Thurs 10am–6pm, Fri 10am–7pm, Sat 10am–6pm. *Bus:* 20 or 401.

Bratz, 2828 Granville St. at W. 13th Ave. (tel. 734-4344).

This is where the rich kids' parents shop—not only are the clothes for newborns to teen-agers imported from Europe; there's even a children's hair salon on the premises.

Open: Mon–Sat 9:30am–5:30pm. *Bus:* 20 or 401.

Peppermintree, 4243 Dunbar St. at W. 27th Ave., Dunbar (tel. 228-9815).

This store has perhaps the largest stock of children's clothing, shoes, and accessories in Vancouver. Domestic and imported styles are moderately priced. There's a play area to occupy the kids while mom or dad shops.

Open: Mon–Sat 9:30am–5:30pm. *Bus:* 22.

Armadillo, 3385 Cambie St. at W. 19th Ave. (tel. 873-2916).

Billing itself as a "designer discount boutique," Armadillo takes 50% to 80% off the suggested retail prices of silks, cottons, woolens, and other fabrics from France, Italy, and Asia.

Open: Tues–Sat 10:30am–5:30pm. *Bus:* 15.

FOOD

Cheena B.C. Ltd., 667 Howe St. near Georgia (tel. 684-5374).

This retail shop for gourmet souvenir gift foods packs smoked salmon for travel. Fish, beef jerky, chocolates, honey, and other items will be delivered to hotels.

Open: Mon–Sat 9am–8pm. *Bus:* 401. *SkyTrain:* Granville.

Murchie's Tea & Coffee, 970 Robson St. (tel. 662-3776). Also 1200 Homer St. at Davie; 850 N. Park Royal Shopping Centre, West Vancouver; and Richmond Centre, Richmond.

This is *the* Vancouver institution for gourmet teas and coffees from around the world. Buy in bulk, if you like. Seminars on tea and coffee can be arranged. Fine bone china, crystal, and giftware are also sold.

Open: Mon–Wed and Sat 9:30am–6pm, Thurs–Fri 9:30am–9pm, Sun noon–5pm (Robson St.); Mon–Fri 9:30am–5pm (Homer St.). *Bus:* 8 (Robson St.).

Pacific Rim Shellfish Corp., 1807 Mast Tower Rd. at Duranleau, Granville Island (tel. 687-4531).

Live lobsters, Dungeness crab, oysters, mussels, clams, geoduck, and scallops are kept in saltwater tanks of more than 15,000 gallons. Lobster or crab is cooked, on request, at no extra charge. Salmon and other fresh catches are sold, and can be packed for travel.

Open: Daily 9am–6pm. *Bus:* 51.

Salmon Village, 779 Thurlow St. near Robson (tel. 685-3378).

Smoked salmon and caviar are the specialties of this gourmet food outlet just off Robsonstrasse. All purchases can be packaged and shipped for travelers.

Open: Daily 9am–10pm. *Bus:* 8.

Ten Ren Tea & Ginseng Co., 550 Main St. at Keefer, Chinatown (tel. 684-1566).

A variety of fine Chinese teas and drinking implements are sold here, with samples offered in a corner tea ceremony. One wall of the shop is dominated by cases of ginseng root, an astringent medicinal herb for which you can pay astronomical prices.

Open: Daily 9:30am–6pm.

JEWELRY

Henry Birks & Sons, 710 Granville St. at Georgia (tel. 669-3333).

This long-established jeweler brings quality and tradition to a wide range of watches, clocks, diamonds, and other stones, gold, silver, pearls, china, crystal, flatware, handbags, and men's and women's gift items. Repairs are done on the premises.

Open: Mon–Wed 9:30am–6pm, Thurs–Fri 9:30am–9pm, Sat 9:30am–5:30pm. *SkyTrain:* Granville.

Georg Jensen (Canada) Ltd., 648 Hornby St. near Georgia (tel. 688-4744).

Sterling-silver jewelry of Scandinavian design, most of it imported from Denmark, is offered in this exclusive shop. Stainless-steel flatware, crystal, glassware, and Danish teak accessories are also displayed.

Open: Mon–Sat 9:30am–5:30pm. *Bus:* 242.

Jade World, 1696 W. 1st Ave. at Pine St. (tel. 733-7212).

Five master carvers conduct free tours of the jade factory and carving studio. Tours conclude in the large gift shop, where a wide variety of jade is sold. Jade World mines the stone itself in northern British Columbia, and keeps 100 *tons* in stock at all times!

Open: Mon–Fri 8am–4:30pm. *Bus:* 22 (1 block west to Burrard, 1 block north at Cornwall).

MALLS AND SHOPPING CENTERS

Pacific Centre Mall, 700 W. Georgia St., between Dunsmuir and Robson, Howe and Granville (tel. 688-7236).

More than 180 shops and service outlets occupy this architectural delight, downtown Vancouver's largest mall. A skylit atrium connects it to the Four Seasons Hotel, and a three-story waterfall lends a playful feeling to the interior decor. Stores include Eaton's and Holt Renfrew department stores, clothiers, jewelers, home furnishings, electronics, bookstores, gift shops, and three dozen family restaurants and fast-food outlets. There are also several banks and a theater complex. The mall is connected underground to Vancouver Centre, and directly linked to SkyTrain.

Open: Mon–Wed and Sat 9:30am–5:30pm, Thurs–Fri 9:30am–9pm, Sun noon–5pm. *SkyTrain:* Granville.

Vancouver Centre, 650 W. Georgia St., between Dunsmuir and Georgia, Granville and Seymour (tel. 684-7537).

The Bay anchors this complex of 120 shops and service outlets, which connects underground to the Pacific Centre at the Granville SkyTrain station.

Open: Mon–Wed and Sat 9:30am–5:30pm, Thurs–Fri 9:30am–9pm, Sun noon–5pm. *SkyTrain:* Granville.

Sinclair Centre, 757 W. Hastings St. at Howe (tel. 666-4483).

Four city landmarks, within a stone's throw of Canada Place and the Waterfront Station, were elegantly restored by a federal grant and linked by a central court to create this upscale shopping center. It comprises the 1910 Post Office, the mosaic-tiled 1911 Winch Building, the 1913 Customs Examining Warehouse, and the art deco Federal Building, constructed in 1937. New Canadian citizens are still sworn in here Monday and Friday. Sophisticated Leone (see "Fashions") is the flagship store of the complex, which contains 18 other shops, 12 food outlets and bistros, and art galleries on the atrium and mezzanine levels.

Open: Mon–Fri 10am–5:30pm, Sat 10am–5pm. *Closed:* Sun and public holidays. *Bus:* 22. *SkyTrain:* Waterfront.

Royal Centre Mall, 1055 W. Georgia St. at Burrard (tel. 689-1711).

After a $10 million face-lift and expansion in 1989, this mall, which adjoins the Hyatt hotel, boasts 30 shops and restaurants, plus a major cinema complex. It connects underground to the Burrard SkyTrain station.

Open: Mon–Thurs and Sat 9:30am–5:30pm, Fri 9:30am–9pm. *SkyTrain:* Burrard.

Harbour Centre, 555 W. Hastings St. at Seymour (tel. 689-7304).

Forty-five specialty shops and a food market are located across the street from Waterfront Station. The Harbour Center Observation Deck affords an outstanding bird's-eye view of the city.

Open: Mon–Wed and Sat 9:30am–5:30pm, Thurs–Fri 9:30am–9pm. *SkyTrain:* Waterfront.

The Landing, 375 Water St. at Cordova, Gastown (tel. 687-1144).

A new multipurpose development overlooking the waterfront, the Landing combines 19 retail outlets, an office complex, and an 84-room European-style hotel scheduled to open by 1991. Fashion boutiques and restaurants predominate. The building was formerly a warehouse, built in 1905 from Klondike gold-rush profits.

Open: Mon–Wed and Sat 9:30am–5:30pm, Thurs–Fri 9:30am–9pm. *SkyTrain:* Waterfront.

Park Royal Shopping Centre, Marine Drive and Taylor Way, West Vancouver (tel. 922-3211).

When Park Royal opened in September 1950, it was a Canadian pioneer: the nation's first shopping center. Today, it consists of two malls on opposite sides of Marine Drive. Within them are 190 stores and services, including three major department stores—The Bay, Eaton's, and Woodward's. There are also fashion stores, jewelers, children's stores, home furnishings and entertainment, sporting goods, a fitness center, 11 restaurants and 23 other food outlets, and numerous services.

Open: Mon–Wed and Sat 9am–5pm, Thurs–Fri 9am–9pm, Sun noon–5pm. *Bus:* 250 or 253.

Eaton Centre Metrotown, 4700 Kingsway near Nelson Ave., Burnaby (tel. 438-4700).

There are some 175 shops and services in this beautiful new development, just a few minutes from downtown Vancouver on the SkyTrain. Eaton's and two other department stores—Bretton's and the Real Canadian Superstore—anchor the mall, which features marble walkways, twin glass domes, and interior landscaping. Among the shops are 59 clothing stores, 17 shoe stores, and 26 food outlets.

Open: Mon–Tues and Sat 9:30am–5:30pm, Wed–Fri 9:30am–9pm, Sun noon–5pm. *Bus:* 19. *SkyTrain:* Metrotown.

Metrotown Centre, Kingsway near Nelson Ave., Burnaby (tel. 438-2444).

An 80-foot atrium covers 150 retail outlets and another 50 professional offices, anchored by Sears and Woodward's stores. A 100-store addition, including The Bay, is under construction.

Open: Mon–Tues and Sat 9:30am–5:30pm, Wed–Fri 9:30am–9pm, Sun noon–5pm. *Bus:* 19. *SkyTrain:* Metrotown.

TOYS

Kaboodles, 4449 W. 10th Ave. at Sasamat Street, West Point Grey (tel. 224-5311), and **Kids Only,** Cartwright and Anderson sts., Granville Island (tel. 684-0066).

There's a little of everything for the children in these shops, from T-shirts to model dinosaurs. The staff is knowledgeable as to what's hot among today's kids.

Open: Mon–Thurs and Sat 9:30am–5:30pm, Fri 9:30am–9pm (West Point Grey); Mon–Sat 9:30am–5:30pm (Granville Island). *Bus:* 10 (West Point Grey); 51 (Granville Island).

Kinderspel, 3039 Granville St. at W. 15th Ave. (tel. 734-0321).

Located on the sophisticated south Granville Street fashion strip, this store naturally carries highbrow imports—European items, fragile Asian dolls, and top-of-the-line North American products. Older kids enjoy the computers and electronic games downstairs.

Open: Mon–Sat 9:30am–5:30pm. *Bus:* 20 or 401.

Toy Warehouse, 6027 Fraser St. between E. 44th and 45th aves. (tel. 324-1274).

This small store is a bargain hunter's delight—brand names such as Fisher-Price and Mattel along with lesser-known toys, at discounts averaging about 30% off other retailers's prices.

Open: Mon–Sat 9:30am–5:30pm.

Windmill Toys, 2387 W. 41st Ave. near Vine St., Kerrisdale (tel. 261-2120).

This may be the city's best toy store, especially in the moderate price range. All the popular items, from Teenage Mutant Ninja Turtles to the latest versions of Barbie, are available, along with outstanding educational toys. A back room entertains the children with a model train and giant stuffed animals.

Open: Mon–Thurs and Sat 9:30am–6pm, Fri 9:30am–9pm. *Bus:* 18 or 41.

X

VANCOUVER NIGHTS

1. THE PERFORMING ARTS
2. THE CLUB AND MUSIC SCENE
3. THE BAR SCENE
4. MORE ENTERTAINMENT

Vancouver is an entertainment-oriented city, offering everything from highbrow culture such as theater, symphony, and dance to the less sedate pleasures of jazz or rock 'n' roll. Shows that closed on Broadway (or off Broadway) a couple of seasons ago may be big hits today in Vancouver. The Canadian West Coast's outstanding opera, symphony, and dance companies share stage time with touring troupes from all over North America and overseas. Jazz and rock music are big attractions; the city is on the touring itinerary of nearly every famous recording artist. In film, Vancouver has become known as "Hollywood North": A half dozen major U.S. network television programs are shot here, and the region is a popular venue for major California studio productions.

Full information on all major cultural events is available from **Arts Hotline,** 884 Granville St. in the Orpheum Theatre (tel. 684-ARTS). The office is open Monday to Friday 9am to 8pm, Saturday 9am to 5pm. Current listings can be found in the two daily newspapers, *The Sun* and *The Province; The Georgia Straight,* a weekly newspaper devoted to arts and entertainment, or the *West Ender,* another weekly; and the monthly *Vancouver* magazine.

The following is a quick-reference list of major performance spaces in Vancouver, with box office telephone numbers. Details are provided in the listings below.

Queen Elizabeth Theatre	(tel. 873-3311)
Vancouver Playhouse	(tel. 873-3311)
Orpheum Theatre	(tel. 684-2787)
Vancouver East Cultural Centre	(tel. 254-9578)
B.C. Place	(tel. 669-2300)
Pacific Coliseum	(tel. 253-2311)

Tickets for nearly all major events can be obtained at **Ticket-Master** (Vancouver Ticket Centre), 1304 Hornby St. (Call 280-3311 for information, or 280-4444 to place credit-card orders on American Express, MasterCard or VISA). TicketMaster has 40 outlets in the greater Vancouver area, including all Eaton's and Woodward's department stores, major shopping malls, and downtown at the Vancouver Travel InfoCentre, 1055 Dunsmuir St.

Discount tickets are often available for midweek and matinee performances. Check with specific theaters or concert halls.

Throughout the summer, there's lots of free entertainment all over this lively city. Wherever people "hang out"—in places like Granville Island, English Bay Beach, Robson Square, and the Plaza of Nations on the former Expo '86 site—street buskers provide free music, mime, juggling, and other diversions. And numerous festivals bring outstanding artists of all pursuits to parks and performing arts centers at little or no charge.

1. The Performing Arts

MAJOR CONCERT/PERFORMANCE HALLS

Queen Elizabeth Theatre, 649 Cambie St. at Dunsmuir (tel. 665-3050 for information, 873-3311 for tickets).

The focal point of Vancouver's performing arts, the Q.E. is a beautiful and expertly designed 2,800-seat theater. Broadway musicals, grand opera, ballet, symphony, drama, rock, recitals, and touring theatrical productions hit the stage here. This huge stage complex also includes the smaller Vancouver Playhouse (see following entry).

Open: Box office, 543 W. 7th Ave. at Cambie St., Mon–Fri 9:30am–4:30pm. *Prices:* Vary according to performance, but may range from $5 to $45. *Bus:* 242. *SkyTrain:* Stadium.

Vancouver Playhouse, 600 Hamilton St. at Dunsmuir (tel. 665-3050 for information, 873-3311 for tickets).

This 650-seat theater is home to the Vancouver Playhouse Company, the city's leading resident company. It presents six major productions in a season that runs from October to May. The 1989–90 roster included classics by Ibsen and Coward, a pair of modern European plays, and two contemporary productions by Canadian playwrights. In winter, the stage hosts the Dance Centre subscription series of classic and contemporary dance.

Open: Box office, 543 W. 7th Ave. at Cambie St., Mon–Fri 9:30am–4:30pm. *Prices:* Adults $10–$19.80 midweek, $21 and $23 weekends; students and seniors $10–$12 midweek, no weekend discounts. *Bus:* 242. *SkyTrain:* Stadium.

Orpheum Theatre, 884 Granville St. at Smithe, stage door entrance on Seymour St. (tel. 684-2787).

Built in 1927 during the age of vaudeville, the Orpheum has hosted a veritable hall of fame of the entertainment world, from

Bob Hope to Marilyn Monroe, Igor Stravinsky to Louis Armstrong. But it took a citizen campaign in the 1970s to save it from the wrecking ball. The City of Vancouver bought the building, restored it to its Roaring Twenties splendor, and made it the home of the Vancouver Symphony Orchestra. Many concerts and musical events are held here. Visitors take note of the ornate theater's gilt ornamental plasterwork, painted domed ceiling, crystal chandeliers, and Wurlitzer organ.

Tours: On designated days, once or twice a week; call for the current schedule and reservations. Tours last 1 hr. and are free.

Open: Office Mon–Fri 9:30am–5:30pm. *Prices:* Symphony $8–$25, discounts for students and seniors; other events vary. *Bus:* 8, 10, or 20. *SkyTrain:* Granville (2 blocks north).

Vancouver East Cultural Centre, 1895 Venables St. at Victoria Drive (tel. 254-9578).

This converted early-20th-century church is probably the most adaptable performing-arts space in Vancouver. On any given night, the VECC may host sophisticated adult or light children's theater, classical music recitals or folk performances, jazz dance or ballet. The acclaimed Tamahnous Theatre makes its home at this 280-seat venue, and internationally known artists frequently perform. A lounge opens 1 hour before shows.

Open: Daily. *Prices:* Vary according to performance. *Reservations:* Recommended; all seats are general admission. *Bus:* 20 or 21.

B.C. Place, 777 Pacific Blvd. S. (tel. 669-2300 or 661-DOME).

Huge rock acts, like the Who and the Rolling Stones, play at this $126 million inflated-dome stadium. Opened in 1983, it has 60,000 seats. It's better known as a sports venue.

Tours: Daily 11am, 1pm, 3pm, when events permit. Tours last 1 hr.; cost is $3.50 for adults, $2.75 seniors and students, $2 young children.

Open: Box office Mon–Fri 9am–4:30pm. *Prices:* Vary according to act. *Bus:* 242. *SkyTrain:* Stadium.

Pacific Coliseum, Renfrew St. at Hastings, Exhibition Park (tel. 253-2311).

Located on the grounds of the Pacific National Exhibition, the old coliseum hosts many big-name concerts when it's not already booked for Vancouver Canucks hockey, pro wrestling, or another big sporting event. You won't find the Stones here, but groups like Chicago, the Judds, and Fine Young Cannibals have drawn sellout crowds.

Open: Box office Mon–Fri 9:30am–4:30pm and before events. *Prices:* Vary according to act; usually in the $25 range. *Bus:* 14 or 21.

Robson Square Media Centre, 800 Robson St. at Howe (tel. 660-2830).

This ultramodern showcase-cum-exhibition area contains two theaters and an outdoor stage, serving for almost everything from pop concerts and dance performances to avant-garde theatricals and ethnic cultural events.

Open: Mon–Fri 9am–5pm; other times based on event's schedule. *Prices:* Vary according to act; often free. *Bus:* 8.

THEATER

Arts Club Theatre, 1585 Johnston St., Granville Island (tel. 687-1644). Also 1181 Seymour St. at Davie (same phone).

Vancouver's most active theater is actually three. The 425-seat Granville Island Mainstage, established in 1979 in a former industrial warehouse on False Creek, presents major dramas, comedies, and musicals from Shakespeare to Neil Simon, *Steel Magnolias* to *Little Shop of Horrors.* (The adjoining Backstage Lounge has live entertainment after weekend stage performances.) The Arts Club Revue Stage, beside the Granville Island Public Market, offers an intimate, cabaret-style showcase for small productions, late-night improvisation, and musical revues like Lanie Robertson's Billie Holiday biography *Lady Day at Emerson's Bar and Grill,* and the punk-rock classic *Angry Housewives.* The original (1965) theater on Seymour Street, in a former gospel hall, highlights avant-garde plays and works by Canadian authors. The 210-seat "walk-up" stage stimulates audience involvement; it was the launching pad for many fine local talents, including Hollywood star Michael J. Fox.

Open: Box office Mon–Sat 9:30am–7pm. *Prices:* $14 to $19, with discounts for students and seniors. *Bus:* 51 (Granville Island); 8, 10, or 20 (1 block west of Seymour at Davie Street).

Back Alley Theatre, 715 Thurlow St. at Georgia (tel. 688-7013).

The raison d'être of this intimate downtown theater is "theater sports"—a unique form of improvisational theater performed weekend nights by the Vancouver Theatresports League. Quirky, satiric, and often hilariously funny, it features two opposing teams of five actors wrestling without scripts over theatrical themes. A referee, three judges who award points, and fanatical audiences complete the picture.

Open: Improvisational comedy Mon and Thurs 8pm, Theatresports Fri 8 and 11pm, Sat 7, 9, and 11pm. *Prices:* $8 adults, $6 students; seating is first-come, first-served. *Bus:* 242.

Firehall Arts Centre, 280 E. Cordova St., Gastown (tel. 689-0926).

This 125-seat theater, occupying (since 1975) Vancouver's original No. 1 Firehouse, is the home of three innovative companies—the Firehall Theatre Co., the Touchstone Theatre, and Axis Mime. All are noted for their experimentation and originality. Dance events and concerts are also staged at the theater.

Open: Box office opens 5pm on days of performances. *Prices:* Adults $10 and $12, students $8; 2-for-1 prices for previews and weekend matinees. *Bus:* 8.

Frederic Wood Theatre, Gate 6, University of British Columbia (tel. 228-2678).

UBC student performances include five or six productions from September to November and January to March. During the 1989–90 season, plays by Chekhov, Brecht, Howard Brenton, and Oliver Goldsmith were presented, along with a Stephen Sondheim musical. There's also a summer season of lighter material. The Dorothy Somerset Studio offers a venue for more intimate plays.

Open: Box office Mon–Fri 8:30am–4:30pm. *Prices:* Adults $10, students $7. Summer season, all seats $7. *Bus:* 10.

Theatre Under the Stars, Malkin Bowl, Stanley Park (tel. 687-0174).

From June to August, on nights without rain, professional-amateur productions of popular musicals are performed at Stanley Park's Malkin Bowl bandshell. This is a picnic-on-the-grass event—don't forget your blanket.

Open: Curtain time Mon–Sat 8:30pm, June–Aug, weather permitting. *Prices:* Adults $12, seniors and children $8. *Bus:* 8.

Vancouver Little Theatre, Heritage Hall, 3102 Main St. at E. 16th Ave. (tel. 876-4165).

Serious dramas by new Canadian playwrights, as presented by Pink Ink Productions, share the stage with controversial classics, such as *Screwtape* (based on C. S. Lewis's novel) and Caryl Churchill's *Vinegar Tom.*

Open: Show times Tues–Sat 8:30pm; box office 30 min. earlier. *Prices:* Adults $10, seniors and students $8. *Bus:* 3.

Waterfront Theatre, 1405 Anderson St., Granville Island (tel. 685-6217).

The island's "other" major theater complex, the Waterfront is the home of: (1) the New Play Centre, which sponsors hit-or-miss original works by B. C. playwrights; (2) the Carousel Theatre, which offers family entertainment; and (3) the Green Thumb Children's Theatre. Sometimes shows that are successful at the Arts Club or Vancouver Playhouse theaters may move here if they are preempted by other scheduled productions. Script-development workshops, readings, and new play festivals are often held at the Waterfront.

Open: Box office Mon–Fri 9am–5pm. Shows Tues–Sat 8pm, matinees Wed and Sun 2pm. *Prices:* Adults $12, seniors and students $10. *Bus:* 51.

OPERA

Vancouver Opera, 1132 Hamilton St. (tel. 682-2871).

Four lavish productions are presented between late October and early May each year at the Queen Elizabeth Theatre, with English subtitles projected above the stage so viewers can follow the foreign-language arias. Works—which often feature international stars—range from traditional classics (Bizet's *Carmen,* Verdi's *La Traviata*) to 20th-century standards (Lehar's *The Merry Widow,* Stravinsky's *The Rake's Progress*) to esoteric modern productions. The Vancouver Opera Association is celebrating its 31st season in 1990–91.

Prices: Adults $19–$55, students and seniors from $11.

ORCHESTRAL AND CHORAL MUSIC

Vancouver Symphony Orchestra, 400 E. Broadway (tel. 684-9100; ticket information 876-3434).

The city's acclaimed, extremely active orchestra presents as many as a dozen concerts a month, in a wide variety of series and recitals. There's the Masterworks series of great classical works; Air Canada Classics, with theme presentations, such as a program of

Russian composers; Tea & Trumpets, with more modern classics and ethnic music; Seagram Pops, often including show tunes and other contemporary favorites; and Sun Family Pops, a children's series. If that's not enough, a summer concert series takes the orchestra all over the Lower Mainland, from White Rock and Cloverdale on the U.S. border to Blackcomb Mountain at Whistler. Its usual venue is the ornate Orpheum Theatre, an ideal orchestra stage.

Prices: Adults $9.50–$35; reduced rates for students and seniors.

Festival Concert Society, 3737 Oak St. (tel. 736-3737).

This association sponsors a Coffee Concert series every Sunday at 11am, September through May, at the Queen Elizabeth Theatre. The one-hour concert may be classical, jazz, folk, dance, theatre, or opera, but it's always pleasant and relaxing. Baby-sitting is provided for a nominal charge.

Open: Box office open Sun 10am for tickets. *Prices:* $4.

Vancouver Chamber Choir, 1254 W. 7th Ave. (tel. 738-6822).

Western Canada's only professional choral ensemble, the Chamber Choir presents a six-concert main series annually at the Orpheum Theatre. When it is not touring internationally or recording, the group also performs a chamber music series at Ryerson United Church, 2195 W. 45th. Ave. at Yew Street.

Prices: Adults $12–$24, students and seniors $10–$15 (Orpheum series).

The Vancouver Bach Choir, 5730 Seaview St., West Vancouver (tel. 921-8012).

This 150-voice ensemble, generally considered Vancouver's top amateur choir, presents three major concerts a year at the Orpheum Theatre, one of them a Christmas season sing-along performance of Handel's *Messiah*. The group has won several international competitions.

Prices: Vary according to performance and venue.

Vancouver New Music Society, 207 W. Hastings St. (tel. 874-6200).

Seven annual concerts, featuring the work of contemporary composers, are given at the Vancouver East Cultural Centre between September and April. The society presents innovative groups, sometimes in conjunction with such other media as dance or film, and avant-garde foreign composers.

Prices: Adults $12, students $8.50.

Vancouver Society for Early Music, 1254 W. 7th. Ave. (tel. 732-1610).

The music of the medieval, Renaissance, and baroque eras is perpetuated by this group, using instruments of the time. Concerts are held at locations all over the city, including the UBC Recital Hall and St. Andrew's Wesley Church, 1012 Nelson St. The society's annual highlight is the Festival of Early Music, which draws musicians from all over North America to UBC in July and August.

Prices: Adults $12, seniors and students $7 (UBC); informal concerts, adults $4, seniors and students $3.

University of British Columbia School of Music, Recital Hall, Gate 4, 6361 Memorial Road (tel. 228-3113).

UBC presents eight faculty and guest-artist concerts between September and November, January and March, often featuring renowned performers.

Open: Box office Mon–Fri 8:30am–4:30pm. *Prices:* Adults $10, students and seniors $5.

DANCE

Vancouver has a surprising number of new, relatively unknown contemporary dance companies. Watch the media for performance dates, or check with the **Dance Centre** (tel. 872-0432), a nonprofit group providing information on dance in the city. Many local troupes are featured in the Discover Dance series at the Vancouver Playhouse, or in the free Summerdance Series at Robson Square Plaza and Granville Island Courtyard.

Ballet British Columbia, 502-68 Water St. (tel. 669-5954).

This major troupe, founded in 1986, performs at the Queen Elizabeth Theatre. It's repertoire ranges from classical ballet to contemporary works. Ballet B.C. also hosts visits by the National Ballet of Canada, the Royal Winnipeg Ballet, the Pacific Northwest Ballet of Seattle, Les Ballets Jazz de Montréal, and other touring groups.

Prices: Adults $12–$24, students and seniors $10–$22.

Anna Wyman Dance Theatre, 1705 Marine Drive, West Vancouver (tel. 662-8846).

Vancouver's best-known professional contemporary dance troupe is bold, colorful, and aggressively theatrical, with a worldwide following: It sold out an entire tour in China. Try to catch a free outdoor appearance in late summer at Granville Island or Robson Square. The indoor and touring season concludes in March.

Prices: $9–$12 for indoor theater appearances.

---

2. The Club and Music Scene

NIGHTCLUBS AND CABARETS

Commodore Ballroom, 870 Granville St. at Smithe (tel. 681-7838).

After a $1 million facelift, this longtime institution (built in 1929) is probably Vancouver's number-one cabaret. Major rock, jazz, blues, reggae, and other performers are booked here in a never-ending stream. Deborah Harry, SkaBoom, Judy Mowatt, Taj Mahal, Youssou n'Dour, and Albert Collins were among the lineup in one recent four-week stretch. Up to 1,000 guests can squeeze into the Commodore, which has four bars, six video screens, and a suspended wooden dance floor sprung with railway car springs, rubber tires, and horsehair.

Open: Most nights from 7:30pm. *Prices:* Drinks $3. *Admission:* Varies according to act. *Bus:* 8, 10, or 20.

86 Street Music Hall, Plaza of Nations, 750 Pacific Blvd. S. at Cambie Street (tel. 683-8687).

A high-tech cabaret on the old Expo site, this club consistently draws outstanding local, national, and international acts—including, for instance, Vancouver's own Bryan Ferry, Toronto's Tragically Hip, Australia's Hoodoo Gurus, and American jazz innovators Hiroshima. 86 Street seats 850.

Open: Wed–Sat 7pm–2am, Sun 6pm–midnight. *Prices:* Drinks $3.50. *Admission:* Fri–Sat $5, more for major artists; advance tickets may be purchased from TicketMaster. *SkyTrain:* Stadium.

Soft Rock Cafe, 1925 W. 4th Ave. at Cypress St., Kitsilano (tel. 736-8480).

Dinner theater in a comfortable, upscale atmosphere. Diners can sup on steaks, seafood, or pasta while listening to top local or North American rock acts (no heavy metal here!), then work off their meal on the dance floor beneath the stage. Sunday is jazz night. Nondiners appreciate the café's elaborate sushi bar.

Open: Dinner 6–11pm, shows start Tues–Sun 7:30pm. *Prices:* Drinks $3.25, dinner $8.95–$17.95. *Admission:* Varies according to act. *Bus:* 4.

COMEDY CLUBS

Punchlines Comedy Theatre, 15 Water St. at Carrall, Gastown (tel. 684-3015).

Jay Leno, Howie Mandel, and other famous comedians have performed at this club—albeit before they became truly "big." Monday is Amateur Night. Tuesday through Thursday there are comedy "jams," featuring improvisational troupes such as the No Name Players. Standup comics take the stage on weekends.

Open: Box office Mon–Fri noon–6pm. Doors open 8pm. Show time in summer (May–Sept), Mon–Thurs 9:30pm, Fri–Sat 9:30 and 11:30pm. Winter shows 30 min. earlier. *Prices:* Drinks $3. *Admission:* Mon $2, Tues $2.50, Wed–Thurs $5 and $6, Fri–Sat $7.50 and up (depending upon act). Dinner-show packages at adjacent Brothers Restaurant. *Bus:* 8.

Yuk Yuk's Komedy Kabaret, Plaza of Nations, 750 Pacific Blvd. S. at Cambie St. (tel. 683-8687).

Leading Canadian and American stand-up comics perform at this club on the Expo '86 site. Amateurs take the stage on Wednesday nights.

Open: Show time Wed–Thurs 9pm, Fri–Sat 9 and 11:30pm. *Prices:* Drinks $3.50. *Admission:* Wed $3, Thurs $5, Fri–Sat $7.50. *SkyTrain:* Stadium.

JAZZ, BLUES, FOLK

Jazz is big in Vancouver—in fact, it has its own "hotline." The **Coastal Jazz and Blues Society** (tel. 682-0706) offers full information on all current and upcoming jazz events, including dates, times, and ticket prices.

Every June, the **du Maurier International Jazz Festival** is held at venues all over Vancouver. The following month, the **Vancouver Folk Festival** is held. Both feature free performances in addition to paid-admission events.

Alma Street Cafe, 2505 Alma St. at W. 10th Ave. (tel. 222-2244).

Ethnomusicologist Stephen Huddart's eclectic neighborhood eatery (see Chapter VI, "Vancouver Dining") is one of the best places in the city to catch modern jazz performers—including many of the best from eastern Canada or south of the border.

Open: Mon–Thurs 7:30am–11pm, Fri 7:30am–midnight, Sat 8am–midnight, Sun and holidays 8am–11pm; music Wed–Sat 8–11:30pm. *Prices:* Drinks $2.75, entrees $8.95–$13.50. *Admission:* No cover. Reservations suggested. *Bus:* 10 or 22.

Blarney Stone, 216 Carrall St. between Powell and Cordova, Gastown (tel. 687-4322).

This Irish pub-cum-nightspot has a relaxed and rollicking atmosphere for those who like St. Patrick's Day every day—the irreverent, full-throated ballads of a traditional Dublin band, for instance. You don't have to know the steps to join the lively crowd on the dance floor.

Open: Tues–Sat 5pm–2am; music starts 9pm. *Prices:* Drinks $3, meals $10–$16. *Admission:* Tues–Thurs $3, Fri–Sat $4. No cover for diners. *Bus:* 8.

Carnegie's, 1619 W. Broadway near Fir St. (tel. 733-4141).

Top local and touring artists in both traditional and modern jazz perform at this popular bar and grill nightly from 9pm to 1am. The atmosphere is that of an upscale English pub, with rich wood furnishings and fine upholstery.

Open: Mon–Fri 11am–1am, Sat 4:30pm–1am. *Prices:* $6 minimum; dinner entrées $7.95-$13.95. *Admission:* No cover. *Bus:* 10.

Glass Slipper, 185 E. 11th Ave. at Main St. (tel. 682-0706).

This showcase for the Coastal Jazz and Blues Society and the New Orchestra Workshop offers contemporary and improvised jazz in an intimate, informal, inexpensive setting. Look for it downstairs from the Cinderella Ballroom.

Open: Fri–Sat 8pm–2am, Sun 8pm–midnight. *Admission:* $5 cover, more for special acts. *Bus:* 3.

Hot Jazz Club, 2120 Main St. at E. 5th Ave. (tel. 873-4131).

Dixieland, swing, and big band sounds blast from the instruments of local and visiting musicians at this casual club. Wednesday is "jam night" when performers get together and improvise. There's a good-sized floor for free-form dancers, and a full bar offering light snacks.

Open: Tues–Sat 8pm–1am. *Prices:* Drinks $3. *Admission:* Tues–Thurs $3, Fri–Sat $5, more for special acts. *Bus:* 8 or 19.

Landmark Jazz Bar, Sheraton Landmark Hotel, 1400 Robson St. at Nicola (tel. 687-9312).

Bavarian mottos on the wall notwithstanding, there's no oompah-pah in this rambling beer cellar. Instead, jazz, rhythm and blues, or jazz-influenced rock holds forth four nights a week. Meals are solid fare; there's a big dance floor to help you work off the calories.

Open: Mon–Sat 11:30am–1:30am, Sun noon–midnight; music Wed–Sat 10pm. *Prices:* Drinks $2.50, meals $3.95–$9.85, $2 buffet Mon–Fri 5–7pm. *Admission:* $5 Wed–Sat after 9pm. *Bus:* 8.

Yale Hotel, 1300 Granville St. at Drake (tel. 681-YALE or 681-9253).

When it comes to seeing and hearing gritty-voiced blues greats like Clarence "Gatemouth" Brown, John Hammond, or Charlie Musslewhite, it's somehow appropriate that the venue should be in a somewhat seedy neighborhood. This late-19th-century hotel fits the bill. It's a spot for hard-core blues-lovers: "We don't like to vary too much from the real stuff," says owner Jim Tortyna.

Open: Mon–Sat 5pm–1:30am, Sun 5pm–midnight. Music Mon–Sat 9pm–1:30am, boogie-woogie piano Thurs–Fri 5–7pm, jam sessions Sat 3–8pm and Sun 7pm–midnight. *Prices:* Drinks $2. *Admission:* Varies according to act; often free. *Bus:* 8, 10 or 20.

ROCK MUSIC

Like most major cities, Vancouver has no shortage of places to listen and dance to live rock bands. These are a few of the most popular.

Club Soda, 1055 Homer St. near Helmcken (tel. 681-8202).

A large nightclub big with the twenties set, Soda showcases big-name local Top 40 bands and lesser-known touring groups from Tuesday to Saturday. Monday is heavy-metal night; Sunday is turned over to local innovators. Seating is theater-style; the club has a large dance floor and state-of-the-art video.

Open: Mon–Sat 8pm–2am, Sun 8pm–midnight. *Prices:* Drinks $3. *Admission:* Thurs men $4, women free; Fri–Sat $4 everyone. *Bus:* 8, 10, or 20 (3 blocks west on Granville St.).

Metro, 1136 W. Georgia St. between Thurlow and Bute (tel. 687-5566).

"Raucous" may be the best word to describe this huge club, devoted to rock in all its forms. Local and touring bands play behind an enormous dance floor, populated by a relatively young crowd. On Ladies Night (Wednesday), the Mr. Nude Rock 'n' Roll competition draws throngs of young women to watch glistening muscles.

Open: Mon–Sat 8pm–2am. *Prices:* Drinks $3.50. *Admission:* Mon–Thurs men $1, women free; Fri–Sat $5. *Bus:* 242.

Railway Club, 579 Dunsmuir St. at Seymour (tel. 681-1625).

. Attracting a nonyuppie, nonhippie, nonheavy-metal, generally proletarian clientele, here's a place where you can enjoy a pub-style weekday lunch, sip a quiet afternoon drink, or boogie to outstanding bands at night. Rustic in atmosphere, this upstairs establishment has a quieter conversation lounge separated from the dance floor and stage by a long wooden bar. Bands like the Secular Atavists, the Cranium Miners, and Bob's Your Uncle, all with strong local followings, perform nightly. There's jazz Saturday from 3 to 7pm.

Open: Mon–Fri noon–2am, Sat 2pm–2am, Sun 4pm–midnight. *Prices:* Drinks $3. *Admission:* Members $1, guests $3; $10 membership requires a member's endorsement. *SkyTrain:* Granville.

Richard's on Richards, 1036 Richards St. between Nelson and Helmcken (tel. 687-6794).

If there's any one club that can be considered Vancouver's "in" place, it's Richard's. Drawing a well-dressed young professional crowd that likes to "network" in the festive atmosphere, it features four bars, a laser-lighting system, and live soft-rock bands nightly beginning at 9:30. A semicircular mezzanine balcony overlooks the main dance floor.

Open: Mon–Sat 7pm–2am, Sun 7pm–midnight. *Prices:* Drinks $3.50. *Admission:* Sun–Tues $3, Wed–Thurs $4, Fri–Sat $5. *Bus:* 8, 10, or 20 (2 blocks west on Granville).

Roxy, 932 Granville St. between Smithe and Nelson (tel. 684-ROXY).

The emphasis here is on "classic rock" of the fifties, sixties, and seventies, presented by live bands. The atmosphere is casual and fun —Tom Cruise–clone bartenders straight out of *Cocktail,* weekly theme parties (often with vacation giveaways), old-time movies, stand-up comedy, and a Wednesday "Student Night."

Open: Mon–Sat 8pm–2am, Sun 8pm–midnight. *Prices:* Drinks $3.25. *Admission:* Mon–Wed $2, Thurs $3, Fri–Sat $4, Sun free. *Bus:* 8, 10, or 20.

Town Pump, 66 Water St. near Abbot, Gastown (tel. 683-6695).

One of Vancouver's favorite mingling grounds, this Gastown club draws top local and national acts to a casual, antique-filled atmosphere. It offers a full menu restaurant and piano lounge (open 5–9pm) before the loud music and dancing take over. The drink menu features a large number of imported beers.

Open: Mon–Thurs 5pm–1am, Fri–Sat 5pm–2am, Sun 5pm–midnight. *Prices:* Drinks $3. *Admission:* Varies according to act. *Bus:* 8 (Cordova St.).

COUNTRY AND WESTERN

JR Country Club, Sandman Inn, 180 W. Georgia St. near Cambie (tel. 681-2211).

Downtown Vancouver's leading country nightclub, this establishment draws leading Canadian bands to play in the rustic atmosphere of the Old West. Radio station CJJR broadcasts from here nightly and plays popular records between live sets.

Open: Mon–Sat 4pm–1:30am. *Prices:* Drinks $3.45. *Admission:* Mon–Thurs free, Fri–Sat $3. *Bus:* 242. *SkyTrain:* Stadium.

Cheyenne Social Pub, Lynnwood Hotel, 1515 Barrow St. (Main St. at Mountain Hwy.), North Vancouver (tel. 988-6161).

This North Shore watering hole has live country music Thursday through Saturday nights, with such local favorites as Pat Conroy, Bootleg, and the Honky Tonk Heroes among the regular performers.

Open: Mon–Sat 11am–1:30am, Sun noon–midnight. *Prices:* Drinks $3. *Admission:* Free. *Bus:* 210 or 239.

Boone County Cabaret, 801 Brunette Ave., Coquitlam (tel. 525-3144).

Many of the Vancouver area's best country-and-western night

spots are in the suburban Lower Mainland, in such towns as Surrey, Langley, and Abbotsford. This one, not far off Trans-Canada Highway 1, is among the closest to the city—and one of the most popular. Free dance lessons are offered at 8pm Monday, Tuesday, and Thursday.

Open: Mon–Sat 7pm–2am. *Prices:* Drinks $3.40. *Admission:* Fri–Sat $3. *Bus:* 151.

DISCOS

Amnesia, 99 Powell St. at Columbia, Gastown (tel. 682-2211).

This huge multilevel club has six bars, 10 video screens, and one of Vancouver's largest dance floors. The DJ plays Top 40 and "oldies," keeping the volume just low enough to allow conversation. The decor is chic, with theatrical lighting and artistic touches.

Open: Mon and Wed–Sat 8pm–2am. *Prices:* Drinks $3.50. *Admission:* Cover charge varies. *Bus:* 8 (Cordova St.).

Graceland, 1250 Richards St. between Davie and Drake, back alley entrance (tel. 688-2648).

One of Vancouver's more bizarre night spots, Graceland bears little or no resemblance to Elvis's Memphis mansion. A very outré establishment appealing to modern counterculturalists, it offers loud dance music in an abstract atmosphere of avant-garde works by local painters.

Open: Mon–Sat 8pm–2am. *Prices:* Drinks $3.50. *Admission:* Cover charge varies. *Bus:* 8, 10, or 20 (2 blocks west at Granville Street).

Luv-A-Fair, 1275 Seymour St. at Davie (tel. 685-3288).

"Outrageous" might be the best word to describe this disco. The usual crowd here ranges from acrylic mohawks to drag queens to stoned-out college students. It features a great dance floor, an outstanding sound system, and imported European new-wave music and rock videos.

Open: Mon–Sat 9pm–2am. *Prices:* Drinks $4. *Admission:* Mon–Thurs $2, Fri–Sat $3. *Bus:* 8, 10, or 20 (1 block west on Granville).

Pelican Bay, Granville Island Hotel, 1253 Johnston St. (tel. 683-7535).

The perpetual-motion machine hanging from the ceiling hints at what is occurring on the dance floor beneath, where well-dressed yuppies and yuppie-wannabes mingle. The disco is a restaurant in the early evening, when a piano lounge (open Tues–Sat) lends itself to conversation; there are complimentary hors d'oeuvres from 4:30 to 7pm. Parking is free.

Open: Mon–Sat 11am–1:30am; disco from 10pm. *Prices:* Drinks $3.50. *Admission:* Free. *Bus:* 51.

Shampers, Coast Plaza at Stanley Park, 1733 Comox St. at Denman (tel. 688-7711 or 684-6262).

The West End's most popular disco, Shampers is actually open all day—for light lunch until 5pm, for piano-bar music until 9pm, and finally disco until 2am. The evening menu features pasta.

Open: Mon–Sat noon–2am, Sun noon–midnight. *Prices:* Drinks $3.50. *Admission:* Sun–Thurs free, Fri–Sat $2. *Bus:* 8.

Sneaky's on Hornby, 595 Hornby St. at Dunsmuir (tel. 681-9561).

In a business where trendiness is everything, it's astonishing to learn that Sneaky's has been in business since 1972. Recently redesigned, it has two seating areas—one bright, the other romantically dim. A late-twenties and thirties age group frequents this fifth-floor disco.

Open: Mon–Sat 7pm–2am, Sun 7pm–midnight. *Prices:* Drinks $4. *Admission:* $4. *Bus:* 15 or 19. *SkyTrain:* Burrard.

---

3. The Bar Scene

Looking for quiet conversation, or perhaps a game of darts? There are large number of fine neighborhood pubs throughout Vancouver and Lower Mainland. Many of the pubs have live music some nights; licensing laws require them to close by 11pm, however.

Bimini, 2010 W. 4th Ave. near Maple St., Kitsilano (tel. 738-2714).

An immensely popular pub with two seating levels, patrons come here to mingle and converse, watch sporting events on TV, or listen (but not dance) to small bands.

Open: Daily 11am–11pm. *Prices:* Drinks $2.50. *Bus:* 4.

Darby D. Dawes, 2001 MacDonald St. at W. 4th Ave., Kitsilano (tel. 731-0617).

A favorite among university students, Darby's inviting English pub atmosphere is the venue for a jazz pianist at lunchtime and rock groups Thursday through Saturday nights.

Open: Daily 11am–11pm. *Prices:* Drinks $2.50 *Bus:* 4.

Dover Arms, 961 Denman St. at Nelson, West End (tel. 683-1929).

Another neighborhood pub in the English mold, this one draws literati from the densely populated West End, not far from Stanley Park or English Bay Beach.

Open: Daily 11am–11pm. *Prices:* Drinks $2.50. *Bus:* 8.

Molly Hogan's, 1445 E. 41st. Ave. at Knight St., Kensington (tel. 324-1400).

A bit off the beaten track, this is an essential watering hole for pub-lovers. The pub has a timber-camp atmosphere of rough wood furnishings and logging equipment on the walls. It's a place where the working class and students rub shoulders and enjoy it.

Open: Daily 11am–11pm. *Prices:* Drinks $2.50. *Bus:* 22.

Stamp's Landing, 610 Stamp's Landing, False Creek (tel. 879-0821).

The yachting crowd, especially those who live on their boats in the False Creek Marina, pack into this pub adjacent to Monk McQueen's restaurant. There's never a dull moment.

Open: Daily 11am–11pm. *Prices:* Drinks $2.50. *Bus:* 50 (1/4 mile south on W. 6th Ave.).

The Rusty Gull, 175 E. 1st St. at St. Andrew's Ave., North Vancouver (tel. 988-5585).

Barely three blocks from Lonsdale Quay, this is a bar for gourmet beer drinkers. It has 10 brews on tap, mostly from local cottage producers—including its own Rusty's Best Bitter. There's frequent live entertainment.

Open: Daily 10am–midnight. *Prices:* Drinks $2.50. *SeaBus:* Lonsdale Quay.

The John B Neigbourhood Pub, 1101 Austin Ave. at Marmont St., Coquitlam (tel. 931-5115).

Voted Vancouver's number-one pub in 1989, this establishment 14 miles east of downtown offers "businessmen's lunches" and free pub dinners from 3:30 to 6:30pm daily. It has a piano bar, dance music nightly, satellite TV for sports events, and stocks 20 local and imported beers. There's a dress code after 7pm.

Open: Daily 11am–11pm. *Prices:* Drinks $2.50. *Bus:* 152.

Checkers, 1755 Davie St. at Denman (tel. 682-1831).

At this friendly bar in the West End, patrons can either sit near the bandstand where the music is often classic rock, or withdraw to a less noisy corner for conversation. The decor is black-and-white, like a checkerboard.

Open: Daily 11am–11pm. *Prices:* Drinks $3. *Bus:* 8.

Heritage House Hotel, 455 Abbott St. at Pender, Gastown (tel. 685-7777).

One of the city's more popular gay bars; the lounge and pub on the main floor attract both men and women. Downstairs, there's a lesbian bar open Tuesday to Saturday; only women are admitted Friday and Saturday.

Open: Mon–Sat 11am–2am, Sun noon–midnight. *Prices:* Drinks $3.50. *Bus:* 19.

The Odyssey, 1251 Howe St. near Davie (tel. 689-5256).

A big dance club for Vancouver's sizable gay population, the Odyssey has live entertainment every Tuesday and Wednesday night. A disc jockey spins records the rest of the week. Friday is for men only.

Open: Tues–Sat 8pm–2am. *Prices:* Drinks $3.50. *Bus:* 8 or 401.

---

4. More Entertainment

Vancouver has become the western capital of Canada's film industry, and in many regards a northern outpost for American film producers. At least half a dozen major-network television programs are filmed here, among them "MacGyver" and "21 Jump Street," and a growing number of major studios are setting movies in and around the city. Some insiders have dubbed Vancouver "Hollywood North."

Wherever movies are shot, of course, they are also screened. Vancouver has no shortage of screens, especially along a one-block strip of Granville Mall between Robson and Smithe streets. The two biggest cinema groups are:

Famous Players, 16 theaters (tel. 681-4255). Downtown are the **Capital 6,** 820 Granville St. (tel. 669-6000), and the **Plaza,** 881 Granville St. (tel. 681-5567).

Cineplex Odeon, 13 theaters (tel. 687-1515). Downtown are the eight-cinema **Granville Theatre** complex, 855 Granville St. (tel. 684-4000), and the new **Royal Centre** complex, 1055 W. Georgia St. at Burrard (tel. 669-9791).

Ticket prices are normally $4 to $5 for adults, with student and senior discounts. Reduced prices sometimes apply to matinee performances.

Foreign, art, and "cult" films tend to be the domain of three theaters:

Pacific Cinemathèque, 1131 Howe St. between Helmcken and Davie (tel. 688-FILM or 688-3456).

Serious movie buffs only, please. Important foreign films are screened in series, along with outstanding but unknown North American features. This is also the headquarters cinema for the Vancouver Film Festival, held every September and October here and at the Hollywood, Paradise, Ridge, and Vancouver East theaters.

Admission: Adults $4, students and seniors $3; double features, $1 extra. Annual membership $5; includes one-time half-price admission. *Bus:* 401.

Ridge Theatre, 3131 Arbutus St. at W. 16th Ave., Arbutus Ridge (tel. 738-6311).

Here's where you're likely to catch the first Vancouver release of a Cannes Film Festival award winner, a new uncut print of an old classic, an unpublicized rock-music movie, or a sensational underground sleeper. This theater offers the city's first induction-loop system for hearing-impaired persons.

Admission: Adults $5, students $4, seniors $2 (free Mon), children 12 and under $2, all seats $2.50 Tues. *Bus:* 18.

Vancouver East Cinema, 2290 Commercial Drive at E. 7th Ave. (tel. 253-5455).

An associate of the Ridge, the Van East books similar types of films, but tends to appeal to a more hard-core film-buff audience with international-film and issue-oriented series. There are children's matinees every other Sunday afternoon at 2pm.

Admission: Adults $5.50, students seniors, and disabled, $2. Children's matinees, all seats $2. *Bus:* 21.

GAMBLING CASINOS

During the past few years, changes in government regulations have permitted the introduction of public gambling in British Columbia—with certain restrictions, to be sure. The use of dice remains banned, ruling out many games of chance. The law also stipulates that no gaming room shall contain more than 15 tables, that bets are limited to a maximum of $5, and that a percentage of all proceeds must go to charities.

As a result, Vancouver boasts a sprinkling of perfectly legal casinos. They are not concentrated in a strip, but scattered all over town and the suburbs. None of them offers a floor shows or other diversions, and the decor is usually modest and devoid of glamour.

Among the casinos are:

Great Canadian Casino, 2477 Heather St. and West Broadway at the Holiday Inn.(tel. 872-5543).

The largest Vancouver-area casino with its several branches around the Lower Mainland, this casual establishment features blackjack, roulette, and sic-bo.

Open: Daily 6pm–2am. *Bus:* 9.

Royal Diamond Casino, 1195 Richards St. at Davie (tel. 685-2340).

Informal and very friendly, the Royal Diamond is within easy walking distance of most downtown hotels. Its games include blackjack, roulette, and Canadian craps.

Open: Daily 6pm–2am. *Bus:* 8, 10, or 20 (2 blocks west at Granville St.).

Vancouver Casino, 611 Main St. at E. Georgia St. (tel. 253-4263).

With its main casino located at the south end of Chinatown, the Vancouver Casino attracts an international crowd—especially to sic-bo. It also has blackjack and roulette tables.

Open: Daily 6pm–2am. *Bus:* 8 or 19.

XI

GETTING TO KNOW VICTORIA

1. ORIENTATION
2. GETTING AROUND
3. VICTORIA FAST FACTS

Victoria, it is said, is "more English than the English." British Columbia's provincial capital and second-largest city (pop. about 250,000) perpetuates a colonial ambience that is largely absent in Vancouver, its cosmopolitan cousin across the Strait of Georgia.

Here, the venerable Parliament Buildings and the Empress hotel face directly upon the magnificent natural harbor. Flower baskets line the streets, and colorful gardens make the spring and summer seasons especially joyful. The climate is milder—and drier—than Vancouver's. Perhaps best of all, the city is amazingly easy to get around, especially for those who enjoy walking.

1. Orientation

ARRIVING
There are three principal ways to reach Victoria—by air, by sea (from Washington State), or by sea and land (from Vancouver or Washington). Most visitors prefer the marine connection.

By Air
At **Victoria International Airport,** four major airlines—Air Canada, Canadian, Horizon, and Ward Air—provide Victoria with direct connections to Seattle, Vancouver, Calgary, Edmonton, Saskatoon, Winnipeg, and Toronto.

Numerous provincial commuter airlines also serve the city, including several with floatplanes that land in Victoria's Inner

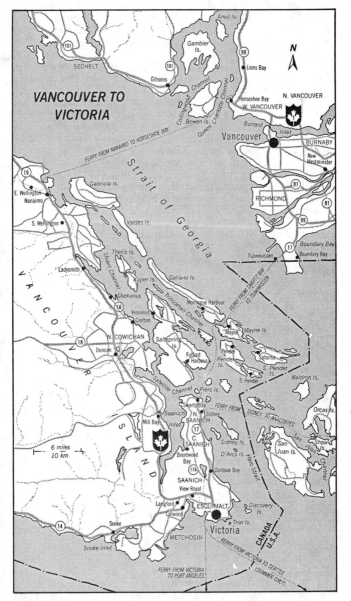

Harbour many times daily. Among them are **Air B.C.** (tel. 604/ 388-5151) and **Harbour Air** (tel. 604/688-1277), both from Vancouver, and **Lake Union Air** (tel. toll free 800/826-1890), from Seattle.

Helijet Airways (tel. 604/382-6222 in Victoria, 604/273-1414 in Vancouver) has helicopter service between downtown Vancouver and Victoria 15 times daily on weekdays, four times on weekends. The round-trip fare is $186 Monday through Friday, and $129 Saturday and Sunday.

The airport is about 16 miles (26 km) north of downtown, adjacent to Sidney near the northern tip of the Saanich Peninsula. For airport information, call 356-6600.

Customs restrictions for Victoria are the same as for Vancouver (see Chapter IV, "Getting to Know Vancouver," under "Orientation: Arriving"). The Victoria International Airport Customs office is open 8am–midnight daily (tel. 604/356-6644). **Revenue Canada Customs & Excise** (tel. 604/388-3531) is open 24 hours daily. For questions about reentering the United States, U.S. Customs in Victoria can be called at 604/384-3314.

From the airport, the four-lane Patricia Bay Highway (Rte. 17) speeds straight south into downtown Victoria. The **Airporter Shuttle Bus** (tel. 383-7311) covers the distance in about 30 minutes; buses leave every half hour from 8:15am to 11:45pm. One-way fare is $9 for adults, $6 for seniors and students. A limited number of hotel courtesy buses also serve the airport.

Average taxi fare from Victoria International to downtown is about $30.

Several auto-rental firms have desks at the airport with vehicles ready for drivers. They include **Avis** (tel. 604/656-6033), **Budget** (tel. 604/656-3731), **Hertz** (tel. 604/656-2312), **Sears** (tel. 604/656-3731), and **Tilden** (tel. 604/656-2541). It's best to make reservations well ahead of time, especially during busy periods.

By Train

You could only arrive by train if you've taken a ferry from the British Columbia mainland to Nanaimo or Courtenay. Then you could board the **Esquimalt & Nanaimo Railway,** a service of VIA Rail Canada.

The train leaves Courtenay, about 130 miles (210 km) northwest of Victoria, at 1:15pm daily, arriving in Nanaimo about two hours later, and completing the final half of the journey at 5:45pm. Trains leave Victoria daily at 8:15am, arriving Nanaimo at 10:40am and Courtenay at 12:50pm. One-way fare from Victoria to Nanaimo is $14 for adults, $12.50 for seniors and students, $7 for children 2 to 11; to Courtenay, one-way fare is $26 for adults, $23.40 for seniors and students, $13 for children.

The E&N Station is at 450 Pandora Ave. at the Johnson Street Bridge (tel. 604/383-4324 or toll free 800/665-8630).

By Bus

It's hard to imagine a bus terminal more centrally located than Victoria's. **Victoria Depot** (tel. 604/385-4411) is at 710 Douglas St., at the corner of Belleville Street, directly behind the Empress hotel, between the new Victoria Conference Centre and the Royal British Columbia Museum.

Pacific Coach Lines operates between here and Vancouver—a

3½-hour trip, including the ferry portion (see next listing). Service is hourly from 6am to 9pm between June 23 and October 9; every two hours from 6am to 8pm the rest of the year. **Island Coach Lines,** with Seattle–Victoria–Vancouver Island runs, is also based here.

By Car and Ferry

Because Victoria is on an island, those who drive to the city must first put their vehicle aboard a ferry. Three separate ferries serve the city:

BC Ferries (tel. 604/386-3431 or 604/656-0757) has three routes across the Strait of Georgia from the British Columbia mainland. The most direct for Vancouver–Victoria travelers is the 24-mile Tsawwassen–Swartz Bay route. Though schedules change seasonally, 95-minute sailings through the Gulf Islands operate more or less continually between 7am and 9pm daily. Tsawwassen is a 30- to 40-minute drive south of Vancouver; Swartz Bay is about the same distance north of Victoria, a straight drive down the Patricia Bay Highway.

Also appealing to many Vancouver–Victoria travelers is the Horseshoe Bay–Nanaimo route—a 30-mile, 95-minute run operating on a schedule similar to the Tsawwassen ferry's. Its mainland terminal is adjacent to West Vancouver; Nanaimo is 68 miles (110 km) north of Victoria on Trans-Canada Highway 1.

A third ferry route connects Powell River, some 100 miles north of Vancouver, with Comox on Vancouver Island. Infrequently taken by tourists, it operates four times daily.

The fare on all three routes is the same: $4.75 per driver or adult passenger, $2.25 for children 5–11, $17 for a car, $22.50 for an RV.

Washington State Ferries (tel. 604/381-1551, 604/656-1531, or toll free 800/542-7052) operate twice daily in summer, once daily September through May, between Anacortes, 90 minutes' drive north of Seattle, and Sidney, 30 minutes' drive north of Victoria. The trip (via Friday Harbor in Washington's San Juan Islands) takes about three hours; the fare (in U.S. dollars) is $31.05 for car and driver, $6.05 per passenger in summer; $5 less for vehicles off-season. From Sidney—where boats arrive between 11:30am and noon every day year-round, and about 5pm as well in summer—the Patricia Bay Highway affords direct access to Victoria.

Black Ball Transport (tel. 604/386-2202) crosses the Juan de Fuca Strait between Victoria and Port Angeles on Washington's Olympic Peninsula. The ferry M.V. *Coho* runs four times a day from mid-May through September; twice a day mid-March to mid-May and in October and November; and once daily December to mid-March. Fares (in U.S. dollars) are $23 for car or RV and driver, $5.75 per adult passenger, $2.90 per child 5 to 11. The often-rough 22-mile (36-km) transit takes about 1 hour, 35 minutes. A bonus is that the boat docks right in Victoria's Inner Harbour, within 350 yards (300m) of the Empress hotel.

Canada accepts all valid U.S. driver's licenses. Proof of insurance is required in the event of an accident (see Chapter II, "Before

You Leave Home," under "Insurance"). Make sure you have your vehicle registration with you. Seat belts are mandatory in British Columbia.

By Ship

Aside from the ferries, there's a proper ship you can take your car on, thanks to the **B.C. Stena Line.** Both the *Vancouver Island Princess* and *Crown Princess Victoria* have a casino and live entertainment, a Scandinavian-style buffet and à la carte dining, a duty-free shopping center, and a children's play area. One or both sail daily year round from Seattle to the Ogden Point Docks at the mouth of Victoria Harbour, a quick taxi ride or bus trip from downtown. The summer schedule (mid-June through Labor Day) calls for departures from Seattle at 8am, 1pm, and 7pm, arriving in Victoria some 4½ hours later. Off-season sailings depart Seattle at 10am and Victoria at 5:30pm every day.

Fares (in U.S. funds) are as follows: in summer (mid-June through Sept), car and driver $49 one-way; adults $29 one-way, $39 round-trip; seniors $25 one-way, $34 round-trip; children ages 5 to 15 $14 one-way, $19 round-trip; carload round-trip, $119. In winter, (Nov–Mar), car and driver $29 one-way; adults $18 one-way, $24 round-trip; seniors $14 one-way, $19 round-trip; children $8 one-way, $12 round-trip; carload round-trip, $89. Fares during shoulder seasons (mid-May through mid-June, and Oct) run midway between the summer and winter price levels.

For information and reservations, contact the B.C. Stena Line at 390 Belleville St., Victoria, BC V8V 1W9 (tel. toll free 800/323-5984) or at 101 Alaskan Way South, Pier 48, Seattle, WA 98104 (tel. toll free 800/962-5984).

For foot travelers only, a quicker way from the Seattle waterfront to Victoria's Inner Harbour is aboard the *Victoria Clipper,* a 300-passenger, 130-foot water-jet–propelled catamaran. There's no casino aboard this sleek vessel, but attendants provide first-class food, beverage, and duty-free shopping services for voyagers who don't want to leave their seats.

The trip to the Wharf Street terminal—near the Visitor's Information Centre—takes precisely 2½ hours. From mid-May to mid-September, the *Clipper* leaves Seattle at 8:30am and 3:30pm, docks in Victoria for an hour, then leaves British Columbia's capital city at noon and 7pm. The rest of the year, there's one sailing daily —at 8:15am from Seattle, 5pm from Victoria. Summer fares for adults are $42 one-way, $69 round-trip; for children and seniors, $36 one-way, $59 round-trip. Off-season fares for adults are $33 one-way, $55 round-trip; for children and seniors, $27 one-way, $44 round-trip. There are discounts for advance purchase.

For information and reservations, contact **Clipper Navigation** at 1000-A Wharf St., Victoria, BC V8W 1T4 (tel. 604/382-8100) or at 2701 Alaskan Way, Pier 69, Seattle, WA 98121 (tel. 206/448-5000 or toll free 800/888-2535).

For **customs** information, see Chapter IV, "Getting to Know Vancouver," under "Orientation: Arriving." For specific questions, consult the **Victoria Harbourmaster** (tel. 604/388-3578) anytime, or the **Inner Harbour Customs Dock** (tel. 604/388-3330 from 8am–4:30pm; 604/388-3339 after 4:30pm). **Revenue Canada Customs & Excise** (tel. 604/388-3531) is open 24 hours daily.

During the summer months, many cruise-ship companies also include Victoria on their itineraries for brief shore leaves.

INFORMATION

The **Tourism Victoria Information Centre,** 812 Wharf St. (tel. 382-2127), is your single best source of tourist information. Located beneath the art deco tower on the Inner Harbour, across the causeway from the Empress hotel, it is the province's largest info center. Staff offer assistance in planning sightseeing, transportation and tours, fishing and whale-watching charters, entertainment, and (perhaps most of all) accommodation. Visitors having trouble finding a place to stay can call the center's reservation hotline (tel. 604/382-1131 or toll free 800/663-3883 from throughout North America). The info center is open daily from 9am to 8pm May through September, 9am to 5pm the rest of the year.

Tourism Victoria's executive offices are on the 6th floor at 612 View St., Victoria, BC V8W 1J5 (tel. 604/382-2160).

Visitors planning trips outside of the immediate Victoria area —say, elsewhere on Vancouver Island, or to the Gulf Islands—can get help from the **Tourism Association of Vancouver Island,** 405 Bastion Square, Suite 302, Victoria, BC V8W 1J1 (tel. 604/382-3551).

CITY LAYOUT

Victoria sits on the extreme southeastern tip of Vancouver Island, the largest island on the Pacific coast of North America. Its spectacular doorstep is the Juan de Fuca Strait, a 15-mile-wide (24-km) sleeve of the Pacific Ocean that separates the island from Washington's snow-capped Olympic Peninsula. The city lies far closer to the United States than it does to mainland Canada. But downtown Victoria doesn't face the open water of the strait. Instead, it nestles around its cozy Inner Harbour, which defines the central city's western edge.

Get your bearings from the **Empress hotel,** the city's social focal point since the 1920s. This palatial grande dame is of such regality that you may get the impression the town was built around her as an afterthought. Standing with your back to the hotel, you're looking across little James Bay at the **Inner Harbour,** a wonderful bustle of yachts, ferries, fishing boats, launches, and seaplanes.

On your left rises the green-domed stone majesty of the **Parliament Buildings,** housing the legislative apparatus of British Columbia. Just east of it, and south of the Empress, is the outstanding **Royal British Columbia Museum.** On your right, Government Street slices through Victoria's main shopping and entertainment area. This is **downtown** and **Old Town,** a pair of districts so tightly entwined that it's hard to tell where one stops and the other begins—a mix of arcades, small squares, picturesque alleys, and wide commercial streets.

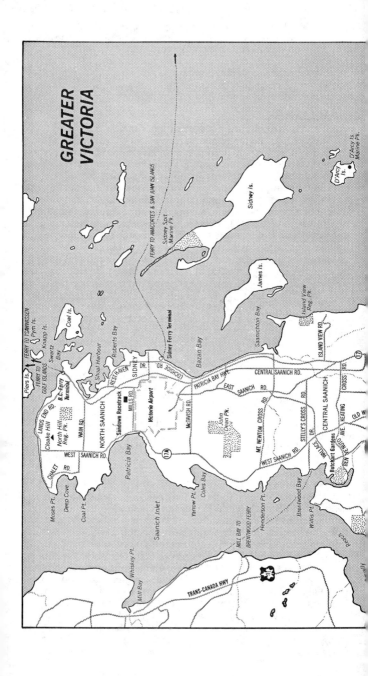

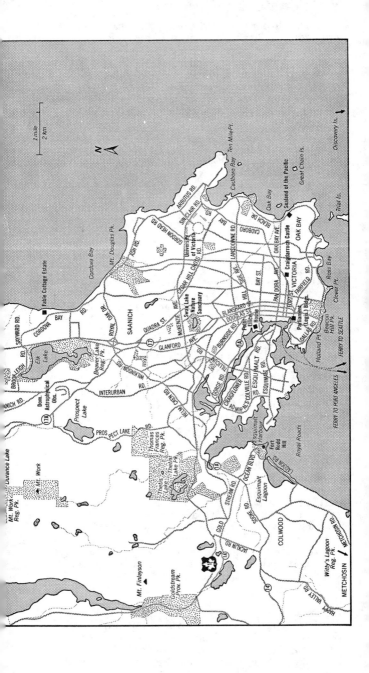

Farther to the north and east stretches what is known as **Greater Victoria,** more like a patchwork of townships and villages held together by parks and gardens. East lies **Oak Bay,** northeast the **University of Victoria,** and due north on the **Saanich Peninsula,** the enchanting **Butchart Gardens,** the airport, the town of **Sidney,** and the ferry terminal at **Swartz Bay.** West of downtown, across the Inner Harbour, is the industrial suburb of **Esquimalt,** and another 20 miles (32 km) west, the seaside community of **Sooke.**

Main Arteries and Streets

Government Street is paralleled to its east by two major north-south thoroughfares: Douglas Street and Blanshard Street. Douglas, in fact, is 7 miles long, extending from the Juan de Fuca Strait on the south shore of Victoria to the community of Saanich, 4 miles north of downtown. There, it becomes the Patricia Bay Highway, which proceeds all the way to Swartz Bay.

To the west of Government Street, Wharf Street winds along the Inner Harbour shore as far as Market Square, a quaint shopping complex. A major city landmark between Government and Wharf streets is Bastion Square, said to occupy the site of Victoria's pioneer fort. It's located behind the Central Post Office on View Street.

Chinatown, with its center at Fisgard Street at Government, eight blocks north of the Empress, marks the northern edge of Old Town. It's actually so small that many locals call it "China Block." City government functions are located just east, on Pandora Avenue. Pandora (one-way west) and Fort Street (one-way east) are the main thoroughfares to the affluent suburb of Oak Bay. The Johnson Street Bridge, at the west end of Pandora, crosses the Inner Harbour to Esquimalt.

South of the Empress, Government and Douglas streets are crossed by Belleville Street, a short but important thoroughfare that fronts James Bay. Along with adjacent Quebec Avenue, which parallels it a block to the south, it is the site of many Victoria hotels.

Finding an Address

Victoria's streets are numbered from the city's southwest corner, near the Ogden Point Docks, numbers get higher as you go north and west. Numbering on Douglas Street, for example, begins with zero at Dallas Road, which weaves along the city's south coastline, and reaches 3200 at Tolmie Street, at the northern city limit. Fort Street starts with its 500 block at Wharf Street, and is in the 1900 block by the time it crosses the city line into Oak Bay. If you're following Government Street north from James Bay to Chinatown, you'll go from the 700 block to the 1700 block.

Maps

Free, detailed city maps are handed out by the Tourism Victoria Information Centre. They're excellent, showing all roads in Victoria and arterials out of town. Stewart Maps & Guides publishes the best central-city map I've seen; Davenport's Greater

Victoria map is excellent for getting around the Saanich Peninsula. Check for either at local bookstores.

---

2. Getting Around

BY PUBLIC TRANSPORTATION

The buses of the **Victoria Regional Transit System** (BC Transit) operate about 18 hours each weekday (6am–midnight), with only slightly shorter hours on weekends. The system has 113 diesel-powered buses that carry 14 million people a year on 30 routes from Swartz Bay in the north to Sooke in the west. Information is available from a 24-hour automated "Busline" (tel. 382-6161).

Unless you're taking the bus well out of the city proper, you'll pay a one-zone fare of $1 for adults, 60¢ for seniors, students, and children. Two-zone fares are $1.25 and 75¢. Unlimited one-day bus passes are $3 for adults, $2 for seniors, students, and children, and can be obtained (along with schedules) from Tourism Victoria and dozens of merchants throughout the area.

Routes popular with tourists include no. 2 (Oak Bay, Sealand of the Pacific), no. 5 (downtown, James Bay, Beacon Hill Park), no. 14 (Victoria Art Gallery, Craigdarroch Castle, University of Victoria), no. 24 (Anne Hathaway's Cottage), no. 30 (James Bay night route from downtown), no. 61 (Sooke), no. 70 (Sidney, Swartz Bay), no. 74 (Butchart Gardens), and no. 75 (Fable Cottage).

Handicapped persons can book door-to-door rides by calling 727-7811.

BY TAXI

Victoria has 22 separate cab companies, so you should never have long to wait. Outside of downtown, though, a phone call is a surer thing than a streetcorner wave. Try **Blue Bird Cabs** (tel. 382-4235) or **Crown Taxi** (tel. 381-2242).

Fares are reasonable: Within downtown, you can expect to travel for under $3, except during rush-hour traffic and during the wee hours, when you'll pay drivers double time. Typical fare to the airport, 16 miles (26 km) distant, is about $30.

Something a bit more upscale? Give a call to **Classic Limousine** (tel. 386-5466), which offers hourly rates.

BY CAR

Having a car in Vancouver can be a great convenience, despite that city's heavy rush-hour traffic. Having a car in Victoria, on the other hand, often seems superfluous. So much of the B.C. capital can be enjoyed on foot, after all!

Some folks opt to rent a car for a single day to take in Butchart Gardens, Fable Cottage Estate, and similar up-island attractions. If you're among them, consider **Victoria Rent-a-Roadster,** 843 Douglas St. (tel. 604/361-7300). It's not cheap, but how many opportunities do you have to scoot around in a classic reproduction of a 1929 Ford Model A? The rental price of $24.95 for the first hour, $15 per additional hour, includes mileage, gasoline, and insurance. For a little extra, the operators will even throw in a picnic lunch for two!

Auto rental firms represented in downtown Victoria include **Avis,** 843 Douglas St. (tel. 604/386-8468), **Budget,** 757 Douglas St. (tel. 604/388-5525), **Dollar,** 1060 Yates St. (tel. 604/385-7777), **Hertz,** 901 Douglas St. (tel. 604/388-4411), **Metro Toyota,** 3106 Douglas St. (tel. 604/386-3516, **Sears,** 843 Douglas St. (tel. 604/388-9939), **Tilden,** 767 Douglas St. (tel. 604/386-1213), and **Victoria Nissan,** 3361 Oak St. (tel. 604/382-7227). **Joy Vacations,** 2343 Hamiota St. (tel. 604/598-6001), has recreational vehicles, ideal for lengthy up-island excursions.

Seasonal motorcycle and moped rentals can be had at **Harbour Scooters,** 843 Douglas St. or 1223 Wharf St. (tel. 385-2314), and **Budget Cycle-Time,** 327 Belleville St. or 727 Courtney St. (tel. 388-7874).

All major downtown hotels have parking lots for guests, with varying daily charges. There is parking on Gordon Street at Broughton, View Street between Douglas and Blanshard, Johnson Street just west of Blanshard, Yates Street just north of Bastion Square, and at The Bay, Fisgard Street at Blanshard.

Metered street parking is in high demand downtown, and is strictly enforced (for this reason, you should carry a pocketful of Canadian coins). Unmetered parking on side streets may be a long trek from where you're headed. Read signs carefully: If you park in a designated rush-hour lane, you can expect to be towed.

Driving rules are very similar to those in the United States. Remember, though: You'll have to deal with the metric system. Speeds and distances are in kilometers, gas is sold by the liter. You're permitted to turn right on a red light after you've come to a full stop. Seat belts are mandatory; children under 5 must be in car seats; helmets are compulsory for motorcyclists.

Members of the American Automobile Association (AAA) can get information and assistance from the **British Columbia Automobile Association,** 1075 Pandora Ave. (tel. 382-8171). They can provide emergency road service to AAA members (tel. 386-2264, in the northern Saanich Peninsula, or 656-6911, 24 hrs. a day).

ON FOOT

As previously stated, Victoria is a marvelous walking city. Stroll where you will; if you need suggestions, see this book's chapter on Victoria walking tours. An early-morning or dusk-hour wander around the Inner Harbour shoreline is particularly recommended.

BY BICYCLE

With Victoria's relatively flat terrain, two wheels can get you around the city very easily. Even the busiest city streets can be safely negotiated by cautious riders.

For seasonal rentals, check with **Budget Cycle-Time,** 327 Belleville St. or 727 Courtney St. (tel. 388-7874); **Explore Victoria,** 1007 Langley St. (tel. 381-2453); or **Harbour Scooters,** 843 Douglas St. or 1223 Wharf St. (tel. 385-2314).

3. Victoria Fast Facts

AIRPORT: Victoria International Airport, 16 miles (26km) north of the city center, handles more than 60 flights a day from Vancouver, Seattle, and other cities. See "Orientation: Arriving," above in this chapter, for details.

AREA CODE: 604.

AUTO RENTALS: Numerous car-rental agencies serve Victoria, both at the airport and downtown. See "Orientation: Arriving" and "Getting Around," above in this chapter, for details.

BABY-SITTERS: Major hotels usually can arrange baby-sitting service on short notice, though a day's advance notice is preferred.

BANKS: Most banks are open 10am to 3pm Monday through Thursday, 10am to 6pm Friday.

BUSES: The buses of the Victoria Regional Transit System will take you virtually anywhere you want to go. Call 382-6161 for information. The bus depot for Pacific Coach Lines and other long-distance service is at Bellevile and Douglas streets, next to the new conference center. See "Orientation: Arriving" and "Getting Around," above in this chapter, for details.

BUSINESS HOURS: Typical business hours are 8am to 5pm Monday through Friday, with lunch break from noon to 1pm. Shop hours vary, but many stores remain open from 9:30am to 5:30pm Monday through Thursday and Saturday, and 9:30am to 9pm Friday. Some may be open Sundays in summer.

BUSINESS SERVICES: Most major hotels offer secretarial, fax, and other services for a fee. Otherwise, **Central Business Services,** 1011 Fort St. (tel. 388-7355), is well equipped.

CLIMATE: Victoria, protected from southerly *chinook* breezes by Washington's Olympic Range, gets far less rainfall than Vancouver—just 26 inches annually, including fewer than 3 inches between May and August. More than one-third of the rain falls in December and January. Average temperatures range from a balmy 72°F (22°C) in July to a chilly 43°F (6°C) in January. See Chapter III, "Before You Leave Home," for details.

CURRENCY: The **Victoria Conference Centre Currency Exchange,** 724 Douglas St. (tel. 384-6631), specializes in exchanging money.

DENTIST: Major hotels may have a dentist on call. A major dental-health center is the **Cresta Dental Centre,** 3170 Tillicum

Rd. at Burnside St. (tel. 384-7711); it's a couple miles from downtown, but is associated with the **Abacus Dental Centre** at 1207 Douglas St. (tel. 382-7603).

DOCTOR: Hotels typically have a doctor on call. A doctor is on call 24 hours for consultation at 383-1193, and will make referrals where appropriate.

DOCUMENTS REQUIRED: See Chapter II, "Before You Leave Home," for details.

DRUGSTORES: **McGill & Orme,** 649 Fort St. (tel. 384-1195), is open 8am to 8pm Monday through Saturday; it has several dispensaries around the city, and has an emergency phone forwarding service. **Shopper's Drug Mart,** 1222 Douglas St. (tel. 384-0544), has even longer hours, including Sunday.

ELECTRICITY: As in the U.S., 110 volts, alternating current.

EMERGENCIES: Dial 911 for fire, police, ambulance, and poison control.

EYEGLASSES: Try **London Drugs, 911** Yates St. (tel. 381-1113) and 1320 Douglas St. (tel. 386-7578); or **Tru-Valu Optical,** 1708 Douglas St. (tel. 386-6622). If you wear lenses, contact **Nordic Contact Lenses,** 1105 Pandora Ave. (tel. 388-1325).

HAIRDRESSERS: Many major hotels have their own salons, and there are others along stylish streets and in shopping arcades. Tourism Victoria recommends the **Queen Victoria Inn,** 655 Douglas St. (tel. 388-5912); **Terry's Beauty Salon,** 1207 Douglas St. (tel. 383-2334); and **Margo Beauty Studio,** 1644 Hillside Ave. (tel. 595-2424).

HOLIDAYS: See listing in Chapter II, "Before You Leave Home."

HOSPITALS: The **Fairfield Health Centre,** 841 Fairfield Rd. (tel. 389-6300), is just three blocks east of the Empress hotel. **Royal Jubilee Hospital,** 1900 Fort St. (tel. 595-9200, emergency 595-9212), is also nearby, not far from Oak Bay. **Victoria General Hospital,** 35 Helmcken Rd. (tel. 727-4212, emergency 727-4181), is in the western suburb of View Royal. There's also **Saanich Peninsula General Hospital,** 2166 Mount Newton Cross Rd. (tel. 652-3911), about 13 miles (20 km) north of the city, and the **Queen Alexandra Hospital for Children,** Finnerty Cove off Arbutus Rd. (tel. 477-1826).

INFORMATION: See "Orientation," above in this chapter.

LANGUAGE: English and French are the official languages of Canada. In British Columbia English is the predominant language.

LAUNDRY/DRY CLEANING: You can either leave your

clothes to your hotel valet service, and pay the price, or drop them off at **Mr. One Hour Dry Cleaners,** 1019 Cook St. (tel. 388-5058). There are also numerous Laundromats around the city.

LIQUOR LAWS: See Chapter IV, "Getting to Know Vancouver."

LOST PROPERTY: Consult the Victoria Police (tel. 384-4111). If you think it may have disappeared on public transportation, call B.C. Transit's lost-and-found line (tel. 382-6161).

MAIL: The main **Victoria Post Office,** 1230 Government St. (tel. 388-3142), occupies most of the block at the southwest corner of Government and Yates streets. It's open 8:30am to 5:30pm weekdays. Merchants with the Canada Post symbol in their windows offer basic services Monday through Saturday. Remember to use Canadian postage stamps, not the U.S. variety!

MAPS: You can get good city and regional maps from information centers, bookshops, automobile clubs, service stations, and even hotel desks.

MONEY: See Chapter IV, "Getting to Know Vancouver."

NEWSPAPERS: *The Daily Colonist,* established in 1858, is the city's most widely read newspaper. A broadsheet, it is published every morning but Monday (the staff takes Sunday off). Its principal competition is the *Victoria Times,* a Monday-to-Saturday evening paper. Both are sold on newsstands and in many hotel lobbies. *Monday Magazine,* a weekly entertainment paper, comes out (wouldn't you know it?) on Thursday.

PHOTOGRAPHIC NEEDS: **London Drugs,** 911 Yates St. (tel. 381-1113) and 1320 Douglas St. (tel. 386-7578), has an excellent camera department. For more specific requirements, including repairs, try **City Photo Centre,** 1227 Government St. (tel. 385-5633).

POLICE: Dial 911 in emergency; property crime can be reported at 383-1313 in Victoria, 592-2424 in Oak Bay, 385-3311 in Saanich.

RADIO AND TELEVISION: AM radio stations include 900 CJVI (classic rock), 1070 CFAX (easy listening), and 1200 CKDA (soft rock). FM stations include 92.1 CKKQ (album rock), 98.5 CFMS (easy listening), and 105.1 CFUV (jazz, classical, alternative music).

CHEK (channel 6), a Canadian network affiliate, is Vancouver Island's only broadcast television station; Rogers Cable (channel 11) does community programming. Victoria viewers also receive all Vancouver and Seattle television broadcasts, including those of the Public Broadcasting System of the United States.

RELIGIOUS SERVICES: The variety should suit nearly

everyone's needs. Among places of worship within walking distance of most downtown hotels are **Christ Church Cathedral,** 912 Vancouver St. at Quadra and Courtney (tel. 383-2714); **Central Baptist Church,** 833 Pandora Ave. (tel. 385-7786); **Cathedral of St. Andrew** (Roman Catholic), 740 View St. (tel. 388-5571); **Grace Lutheran Church,** 1273 Fort St. (tel. 383-5256); **Glad Tidings Pentecostal Church,** 842 North Park (tel. 384-7633); **St. Andrew's Presbyterian Church,** 680 Courtney St. (tel. 384-5734); and **James Bay United Church,** 511 Michigan St. (tel. 384-5821). Nearby are Charismatic, Eastern Orthodox, Evangelical, Methodist, Mormon, Nazarene, Seventh-Day Adventist, Unitarian, Unity, and other Christian denominations.

Major non-Christian places of worship near downtown include **Congregation Emanu-El,** 1461 Blanshard St. (tel. 382-0615); the **Buddhist Dharma Centre of Victoria,** 1149 Leonard St. (tel. 385-4828); and the **Punjabi Akali Sikh Temple,** 2721 Graham St. (tel. 386-1081).

RESTROOMS: See Chapter IV, "Getting to Know Vancouver."

SAFETY: See Chapter IV, "Getting to Know Vancouver."

SHOE REPAIRS: Try **Stevenson's Shoe Clinic,** 714 Fort St. (tel. 383-8615), or a major department store.

TAXES: See Chapter IV, "Getting to Know Vancouver."

TAXIS: See "Getting Around," above in this chapter.

TELEPHONES: See Chapter IV, "Getting to Know Vancouver."

TIME: See Chapter IV, "Getting to Know Vancouver."

TIPPING: See Chapter IV, "Getting to Know Vancouver."

TRANSIT INFO: See "Getting Around," above in this chapter.

USEFUL TELEPHONE NUMBERS: Royal Canadian Mounted Police, 380-6161 . . . Emotional Crisis Centre, 386-6323 . . . Sexual Assault Centre, 383-3232 . . . Poison Control Centre, 595-9211 . . . Help Line for Children, dial 0, ask for Zenith 1234 . . . SPCA animal emergency, 385-6521 . . . Better Business Bureau, 386-6348 . . . Lawyer Referral Service, 382-1415 . . . B.C. road conditions, 387-3192.

WATER: You can drink it everywhere.

WEATHER: See "Climate," above, and "When to Go" in Chapter II. For current forecasts, call 656-3978; for a marine forecast, dial 656-7515; for an aviation forecast, call 356-6630.

XII

VICTORIA ACCOMMODATIONS

1. VERY EXPENSIVE HOTELS
2. EXPENSIVE ACCOMMODATIONS
3. MODERATELY PRICED HOTELS
4. BUDGET ACCOMMODATIONS

Vancouver has a wide choice of fine accommodations in all price ranges. They predominate in two areas. Most deluxe hotels nestle around the Inner Harbour at James Bay, while a high concentration of moderately priced motels flank Gorge Road, northwest of downtown. Accommodation standards are high, and visitors appreciate the little touch of England found in many of the hotels.

In this listing, I have organized accommodations by price range. Categories are based on summer rates in standard rooms for two persons: **very expensive** ($150 a night and up), **expensive** ($100 to $150), **moderately priced** ($50 to $100), and **budget** (under $50). These quotes are in Canadian dollars, and do not include the 10% provincial sales tax. Neither do they take into account any individual or group discounts that may be available.

Reservations are important at any time, and essential during the June-to-September summer season and other holiday periods. If you arrive without a reservation and have trouble finding a room, Tourism Victoria (tel. 382-1131 or toll free 800/663-3883) will try to help—but you may have to settle for something miles from downtown, perhaps out on the Saanich Peninsula.

A possible solution when times are tight is to get in touch with a bed-and-breakfast agency. Each of the following tries to match visitors and hosts with similar interests:

All Season Bed & Breakfast Agency, Box 5511, Station B, Victoria, BC V8R 6S4 (tel. 604/595-BEDS or 595-2337).

Canada-West Accommodations Bed & Breakfast Registry, 1804 Cook St., Victoria, BC V8V 3P6 (tel. 604/388-4620).

Garden City Bed & Breakfast Reservation Service, Box 6161, Station C, Victoria, BC V8P 5N7 (tel. 604/479-9999 or 479-1986).

All are members of the **British Columbia Bed & Breakfast Association,** P.O. Box 593, 810 W. Broadway, Vancouver, BC V5Z 4E2, an umbrella agency formed at the request of Tourism British Columbia for promotion and quality control. Each member home is inspected with regard to cleanliness, comfort, courtesy, and service to ensure high standards. Numerous other B&Bs, unaffiliated with agencies, also are members of the provincial association. Some of them are discussed in the subsequent listings.

B&B rates vary widely, but begin as low as $30 single, $40 double, and may range to $100 or more for special suites. Indicate your preferred price range when making reservations. Fireplaces, Jacuzzi baths, and heated swimming pools may be available in the higher price categories. Credit cards normally are accepted.

1. Very Expensive Hotels

• **The Empress,** 721 Government St., Victoria V8W 1W5 (tel. 604/384-8111; toll free 800/828-7447 in the United States, 800/268-9420 in Ontario and Quebec, 800/268-9411 in other provinces; fax 604/381–4334). 462 rooms, 20 suites. A/C MINIBAR TV TEL.

In many regards, the Empress *is* Victoria. The crowning achievement of early 20th-century architect Francis Rattenbury, the stately, ivy-banked, graystone chateau on the Inner Harbour opened for business in 1908. Ever since, it has created the first impression of Victoria for anyone arriving by sea. Celebrities from Rudyard Kipling and the King of Siam to John Wayne and Bob Hope have stayed here, and Queen Elizabeth II has been a frequent visitor. In 1988–89, the hotel—a Canadian Pacific property—closed for 5 months while undergoing a $45 million renovation. Its new lobby features a three-story-high ceiling supported by imposing pillars, a green Oriental carpet on a black marble floor, and a jade railing along the stairway to the mezzanine deck.

It's impossible to describe a typical guest room—there are 96 different configurations. All have an appropriately Victorian appearance, with richly restored antique furnishings and special features such as balloon curtains. The more deluxe rooms have harbor views; the more moderately priced face the new Victoria Conference Centre. In the renovation, 14 cozy "Romantic Attic" honeymoon view suites were added; accessible only by a private stairway, they have love seats and four-poster canopy beds. The renovation also added rooms for hearing-impaired persons, with a strobe-light alarm system.

Dining/Entertainment: There's sophisticated dining in the classically elegant Empress Dining Room, open daily for dinner and Sunday brunch. It offers finely crafted woodwork, custom-designed china table settings, and evening harp music. In summer, meals are also served in the spectacular Crystal Room, with its mirrored ceiling. More casual meals are served downstairs all day in the Garden Cafe, a contemporary bistro. The Bengal Lounge, with a curry lunch buffet Monday through Saturday, retains the ambience of British India. But the Empress is perhaps most famous for its afternoon teas: Seatings are four times daily, mid-September to mid-May, in the Tea Lobby, and eight times daily, mid-May to mid-September, in the art deco Palm Court, a twenties masterpiece with a Tiffany glass dome. Tea (with crumpets and scones, of course) runs $13.95 per person, and there's a dress code. Call for reservations.

Services: Room service 7am to 11pm, concierge, valet cleaning, secretarial service, massage service. Business-class guests get upgraded amenities, including Continental breakfast.

Facilities: Indoor swimming pool, health club with weight/exercise room, sauna, and whirlpool; shopping arcade including Native art gallery, men's and women's clothing stores, chocolate and china shops. Adjoins Victoria Conference Centre with meeting/banquet space for up to 1,500 people.

RATES: Early May to mid-Oct, $130–$170 single, $155–$195 double; mid-October to early April, $65–$85 single, $80–$100 double; suite year round $200–$635. AE, CB, DISC, DC, ER, MC, V. Parking: $8 underground, $12 valet. *Bus:* 5.

- **Hotel Grand Pacific,** 450 Quebec St. at Oswego, Victoria V8V 1W5 (tel. 604/386-0450; toll free 800/663-7550; fax 604/383-7603). 126 rooms, 24 suites. A/C MINIBAR TV TEL

Built like a turn-of-the-century French château, the Grand Pacific opened its doors in August 1989. Already, major renovations are planned by 1992, including construction of a 150-room, 11-story building with a restaurant and harborside park. For now, the hotel is an elegant but unpretentious showcase for its Canadian owners' collection of antiques and Asian art. It has two wings—an 8-story no-smoking West Wing, and a 6-story East Wing.

The rooms feature rich wood decor and subdued color schemes with floral trim. Each has a balcony, two sinks (one in the vanity), and brass fittings in the bath. Junior suites have French doors separating the bedroom and sitting room, as well as a walk-through bath. Each executive suite features a marble bathroom floor, a double Jacuzzi, a fireplace, three balconies, and a wet bar.

Dining/Entertainment: The Dining Room seats 160 for three meals daily, including a buffet breakfast. Its pastel decor, big bay windows, and brass chandeliers will be retained when it is converted to a meeting space in a year or two. Trophy's Club & Bar offers light dining and a lounge with a piano bar.

Services: Room service, concierge, valet cleaning, courtesy limousine.

Facilities: Athletic club with 25-meter indoor pool, separate kids' pool, weight room, aerobics classes, racquet courts, sauna, whirlpool, massage therapist, equipment sales. Fully equipped business center.

RATES: June–Sept, single or double with mountain view $155–$180, with harbor view $175–$200, suite $210–$400. Oct –May, $105–$120 single, $115–$130 double, suite $140–$300. AE, CB, DC, ER, MC, V. Parking: free. *Bus:* 30 (to Superior and Oswego sts.).

- **Abigail's Hotel,** 906 McClure St. at Quadra, Victoria V8V 3E7 (tel. 604/388-5363). 16 rooms. A/C

A four-story, gabled Tudor building surrounded by a beautiful garden, Abigail's is the quintessential small European-style luxury inn. This friendly, no-smoking hotel is only a four-block walk east of the Empress, but it seems like another world.

The rooms seem made to order for honeymooners or other young lovers. Decorated in pastel colors, they have crystal chandeliers with dimmer switches, stained-glass windows, fresh flowers, and goose-down comforters. Most have either a private Jacuzzi or a deep soaking tub; some also have fireplaces and/or four-poster canopy beds. Maybe best of all, there's no TV (a few have radios) or telephone (there's a pay phone in the lobby). Once you're here, you've escaped from the "real" world. But be sure to check in before 10pm—that's when the doors are locked, and unless you already have your room key, you won't get in.

Dining/Entertainment: A filling breakfast is served in the sun room between 8 and 9am. There's an afternoon "social hour" from 4 to 7pm in the library, with complimentary mulled wine and snacks. The library's piano and games table make it popular with guests.

Services: Concierge, complimentary umbrellas.

RATES (INCLUDING FULL BREAKFAST): Year round $100–$196 single or double. MC, V. Parking: free. *Bus:* 1.

- **The Beaconsfield Inn,** 998 Humboldt St. at Vancouver Street, Victoria V8V 2Z8 (tel. 604/384-4044). 12 rooms. A/C

An impressively restored Edwardian mansion dating from 1905, this companion hotel to Abigail's was originally commissioned as a wedding gift. Named for the London hotel said to have been King Edward VII's lover's rendezvous, it is centrally located just two blocks from Beacon Hill Park. The Beaconsfield boasts rich mahogany paneling, antique furnishings on hardwood floors, and delicate stained-glass window trim. The cozy library has wall-to-wall books.

All rooms have private baths (most with Jacuzzis or soaking tubs), down comforters, and impressive antiques. Some also have fireplaces, but as at Abigail's, none has televisions or phones, and there's no smoking allowed. Every room is unique; Lillie's Room features a wood-encased and canopied clawfoot bathtub. (If there's a guest overflow, three Victorian rooms with fireplaces and Jacuzzis are available at the nearby Humboldt House, 867 Humboldt St., a secluded and romantic retreat under the same ownership).

Dining/Entertainment: A full breakfast is served daily in the sun room, and there's an afternoon social hour—offering port, sherry, fruit, and cheese—in the library. The library also has a games table.

Services: Concierge, complimentary umbrellas.

RATES (INCLUDING FULL BREAKFAST): Year round $100–$196 single or double. MC, V. Parking: free. *Bus:* 1 or 2.

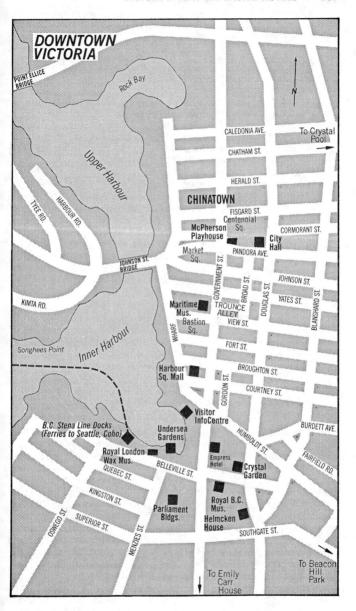

DOWNTOWN VICTORIA

POINT ELLICE BRIDGE

Rock Bay

Upper Harbour

HARBOUR RD.

TYEE RD.

JOHNSON ST. BRIDGE

KIMTA RD.

Inner Harbour

Songhees Point

B.C. Stena Line Docks (Ferries to Seattle, Coho)

Royal London Wax Mus.

QUEBEC ST.

KINGSTON ST.

OSWEGO ST.

SUPERIOR ST.

MENZIES ST.

Parliament Bldgs.

BELLEVILLE ST.

Undersea Gardens

Visitor InfoCentre

Harbour Sq. Mall

Empress Hotel

Crystal Garden

Royal B.C. Mus.

Helmcken House

SOUTHGATE ST.

To Emily Carr House

To Beacon Hill Park

FAIRFIELD RD.

BURDETT AVE.

HUMBOLDT ST.

GORDON ST.

COURTNEY ST.

BROUGHTON ST.

FORT ST.

VIEW ST.

WHARF

TROUNCE ALLEY

Bastion Sq.

Maritime Mus.

GOVERNMENT ST.

BROAD ST.

DOUGLAS ST.

YATES ST.

JOHNSON ST.

BLANSHARD ST.

Market Sq.

McPherson Playhouse

PANDORA AVE.

City Hall

CORMORANT ST.

Centennial Sq.

FISGARD ST.

CHINATOWN

HERALD ST.

CHATHAM ST.

CALEDONIA AVE.

To Crystal Pool

N

2. Expensive Accommodations

- **Laurel Point Inn,** 680 Montreal St., Victoria V8V 1Z8 (tel. 604/386-8721; toll free 800/663-7667; fax 604/386-9547). 130 rooms, 72 suites. A/C TV TEL

A magnificent property surrounded by immaculately tended gardens, Laurel Point occupies a promontory that juts into the Inner Harbour where visiting vessels make their final turn toward downtown. The spacious hotel added a new 72-room wing and a spectacular Japanese garden in 1989. The Asian art influence persists throughout the hotel, especially in the sculpture and ceramics mounted in glass-enclosed nooks in the hallways.

The rooms—every one of which offers a harbor view from a small balcony—have a simple beauty not often seen in hotel rooms. Some might find the light maple decor and beige-and-cream color scheme stark; others will see in it a Scandinavian or perhaps a Shinto touch. There's a photo mural of historical Victoria on one wall. Especially notable is the deep marble bathtub.

Dining/Entertainment: Cafe Laurel, an open lobby bistro with hanging baskets, wicker furniture, and antique cookware on its walls, serves three meals daily. Cook's Landing lounge has a nightly piano bar and large windows facing the harbor. A popular Sunday luncheon buffet is served in the ballroom.

Services: 24-hour room service, concierge, valet laundry, courtesy van.

Facilities: Indoor/outdoor swimming pool, Jacuzzi, sauna, exercise bicycles, gift shop, and meeting/banquet space for up to 250.

RATES: May–Sept, $115–$135 single, $130–$150 double, $175–$190 junior suite, $225–$400 full suite. Oct–Apr, $100–$120 single or double, $155 junior suite, $200–$400 full suite. Children under 12 free in parents' room. AE, CB, DC, ER, MC, V. Parking: free. Bus: 30 (to Montreal and Superior Sts.).

- **Chateau Victoria Hotel,** 740 Burdett Ave. at Collinson St., Victoria V8W 1B2 (tel. 604/382-4221; toll free 800/663-5891; fax 604/380-1950). 63 rooms, 117 suites. A/C FRIDGE TV TEL

This 18-story hotel was erected in 1975, on the former site of "the bird lady's house." Victoria Jane Wilson lived in a big white manor on the hill above the Empress. When she died in 1949 at the age of 76, she bequeathed a substantial sum to assure the lifelong support of her beloved parrot, Louis. The loquacious bird continued to live in the house until his caretaker's death in 1966, at which time he was moved to a retirement home. Unsubstantiated rumors have it that he's still alive, and may be over 100 years old. In any case, his spirit (and his mistress's) are alive at the Chateau. A major renovation was completed here in spring 1990.

Two-thirds of the rooms are elegant one-bedroom suites, with curtained French doors that separate sitting room from bedroom. Every suite has a kitchenette with a microwave oven, coffeemaker, and small refrigerator. Impressionist lithographs hang on the walls, bleached-oak furnishings include a working desk, an armoire, and a king-size or two queen-size beds. All have balconies, full-length-mirror closets, and built-in hairdryers. Seven floors are for non-smokers only.

Dining/Entertainment: The Parrot House Restaurant, Victoria's only rooftop room, is open for three meals daily, including continental dinners. Victoria Jane's Lounge offers light lunches Monday through Saturday.

Services: Room service, concierge, valet laundry, airport transfer, courtesy van, secretarial services, baby-sitting referral.

Facilities: Skylit indoor swimming pool, whirlpool bath. Business center, and meeting space for up to 50.

RATES: May–Sept, $150 single or double, $180–$200 suite; Oct–Apr, $140 single or double, $170–$200 suite. AE, CB, DC, ER, MC, V. Parking: free. *Bus:* 2.

- **Executive House Hotel,** 777 Douglas St. at Humboldt and Collinson, Victoria V8W 2B5 (tel. 604/388-5111; toll free 800/663-7001 in British Columbia and the U.S. Northwest, 800/663-7563 elsewhere in Canada; fax 604/385-1323). 94 rooms and 85 suites. A/C FRIDGE TV TEL

This gleaming tower overlooking the Victoria Conference Centre is full of pleasant surprises. Starting with the cozy lobby with its unusual wood-and-metal chandelier hanging over a 16-spoked table, the ambience makes it feel like a transplanted piece of home.

The rooms are very spacious, from studio-size "superiors" to one- and two-bedroom suites. Suites have kitchens with stoves and refrigerators, well-lit vanities, generous closet space, and small balconies. Studios have small fridges and standard furnishings, including a desk. Pastel shades are a common thread in the decor.

Dining/Entertainment: Barkley's Grill Room rates as one of Victoria's finest restaurants, with steaks and seafood in the $15-to-$20 range for dinner. The restaurant has an airy colonial-manor atmosphere, with nautical prints on the walls. Adjoining is the Polo Lounge, its decor reflecting the sport it's named for. Bartholomew's Grille, a pub-style restaurant on the lower arcade floor, serves three meals daily amid Tiffany-style lamps and antiques. It shares the floor with Bart's Pub and Doubles Oyster Bar, local hot spots.

Services: Room service, concierge, valet laundry, courtesy pick-up from the Inner Harbour.

Facilities: Health spa with exercise room, Jacuzzi, steam room, sun bed, massage therapist. Meeting space for up to 70.

RATES: May–Sept, $100–$110 single, $110–$120 double, $130–$140 one-bedroom suite; Oct–Apr, rates are 20%–50% less, depending upon season and availability. AE, CB, DC, ER, MC, V. Parking: $2. *Bus:* 2.

- **Harbour Towers Hotel,** 345 Quebec St. at Oswego, Victoria V8V 1W4 (tel. 604/385-2405; toll free 800/663-5896; fax 604/385-4453). 99 rooms, 86 suites. A/C TV TEL

A look of simple elegance greets arrivals at the 12-story Harbour Towers, the headquarters hotel for the annual Victoria Jazz Festival. Light jazz music wafts year round beneath the glass chandeliers of the marble-floored lobby. The natural lighting and soft colors give it a sort of Mediterranean appearance.

All rooms have floor-to-ceiling sliding windows, especially appreciated in rooms with a harbor view. Decor is primarily of beige and navy-blue hue. Every room has a vanity and clock radio; some have minibars. Suites have kitchens with two-burner stoves, microwave ovens, and small refrigerators. Seven deluxe penthouse suites even have fireplaces and stereo systems. No-smoking rooms are available.

Dining/Entertainment: The Impressions Cafe serves three meals daily in an "California-style" art deco atmosphere. Steak and seafood dinners are in the $14 to $18 range. The Lobby Lounge, open nightly, has a solo musician playing Thursday through Saturday evenings, and a local jazz group performs Sunday afternoons.

Services: Room service 6:30am to 1am, concierge (full-time in summer), courtesy van, baby-sitting service. "Royal Treatment" rooms include Continental breakfast, upgraded amenities, minibar, hairdryer, vanity, newspaper, free local calls.

Facilities: Indoor swimming pool, sauna, whirlpool. Beauty salon, gift shop. Meeting space for up to 300.

RATES: May–Sept, $150 single, $170 double, $210 one-bedroom suite, $275–$290 larger suite. Oct–Apr, $120 single, $130 double, $160 one-bedroom suite, $220–$275 larger suite. AE, CB, DC, ER, MC, V. Underground parking: free. *Bus:* 30 (to Superior and Oswego sts.).

- **Huntingdon Manor Inn,** 330 Quebec St. at Oswego, Victoria V8V 1W3 (tel. 604/381-3456; toll free 800/663-7557; fax 604/381-3456 ext. 403). 65 rooms, 50 suites. A/C TV TEL

"Leave your laughter by the fire, ere you take the high road." That 18th-century message from a Cambridgeshire coach house sets the mood for this gracious inn, named for the home town of Oliver Cromwell, England's "lord protector." Built in 1981, patterned after an Edwardian manor, it carries the atmosphere of a British hunting lodge with its antique-filled, tartan-carpeted lobby and rich wood appointments. The staff even wears red riding jackets.

Each blue-carpeted standard room has two double beds with lacy floral spreads, brass lamps and a clock-radio on the nightstands, an armoire with TV, a working desk, and standard amenities. The two-story Gallery Suites have bedroom lofts, gabled ceilings, and full kitchen facilities.

Dining/Entertainment: The Hunters Club Lounge has a fox-and-hounds decor, a big fireplace, and an outside deck. Light meals are served here; a full English breakfast is offered guests in the upper parlor.

Services: Valet laundry, guest Laundromat, free local calls, complimentary newspaper delivered to rooms.

Facilities: Indoor whirlpool and sauna. Car rental. Meeting space for up to 30.

RATES: May 15–Oct 15, $98–$130 single or double, $107–$225 suite. Oct 16–May 14, $68–$92 single or double, $77–$159 suite. Off-season rates include breakfast. AE, CB, DC, ER, MC, V. Underground parking: free. *Bus:* 30 (to Superior and Oswego sts.).

- **Inn on the Harbour,** 427 Belleville St., Victoria V8V 1X3 (tel. or fax 604/386-3451). 73 rooms, 5 suites. A/C TV TEL

This very friendly hotel opposite the M.V. *Coho* ferry terminal has a vaguely nautical theme in its decor. In the lobby is a scale model of H.M.S. *Royal Sovereign,* a 17th-century English vessel; its restaurant and lounge are named for the H.M.S. *Swiftsure,* the last of the tall sailing ships to serve duty in the Pacific (1882–1890).

Half of the rooms face the Inner Harbour, with fine views of the oceangoing activity. Standard units are in forest-green and floral prints, with standard furnishings and a step-up bathtub. Eighteen have kitchenettes, including a stove and refrigerator.

Dining/Entertainment: The Swiftsure Restaurant offers three meals daily, with dinners in the $11–$17 range. The handsome Swiftsure Lounge also serves light meals, and features a sushi bar. In summer, there's an outdoor barbecue on the sundeck.

Services: Room service, valet laundry, courtesy van, secretarial service, safe-deposit boxes.

Facilities: Indoor/outdoor swimming pool, sauna, whirlpool. Meeting space for up to 100.

RATES: June 15–Sept 30, $93–$103 single, $98–$108 double, $103–$113 twin. May 1–June 14, $63–$71 single, $68–$76 double, $80–$90 twin. Oct–Apr, $53–$58 single, $48–$63 double, $63–$68 twin. Children under 12 free with parent. AE, DC, ER, MC, V. Parking: free. *Bus:* 5 (to Belleville and Government sts.).

- **The Victoria Regent Hotel,** 1234 Wharf St. near Yates, Victoria V8W 3H9 (tel. 604/386-2211; toll free 800/663-7472; fax 604/386-2622). 15 rooms, 47 suites. A/C MINIBAR TV TEL

When an optimistic developer started this building in the late 1970s, he foresaw it as the future Victoria convention center. That plan crumbled, so he converted it to a condominium hotel. Today, it consists in part of individually owned time-share units, a few of which are permanent homes. The hotel, with its wedding-cake architecture, is unmistakable from the water, as it juts into the Inner Harbour.

The units include 15 studios, 15 one-bedroom suites, 30 two-bedroom suites, and two deluxe 3-bedroom penthouse suites with fireplaces, stereo systems, and bedroom Jacuzzis. All units are very large. There are full kitchens in each suite, equipped with stove, well-stocked refrigerator, toaster, stoneware, tables for four, even a dishwasher. All have king-size beds, hideaway sofas, working desks, clock radios, and serigraph art on the walls.

Dining/Entertainment: The Water's Edge Restaurant, on the ground floor is a converted suite that actually extends into the water. It serves three meals daily in summer, breakfast and lunch only in winter.

Services: Concierge, courtesy limousine, guest Laundromat, morning newspaper, baby-sitting referrals, secretarial service.

Facilities: Boat charters. Meeting space for 20.

RATES: May 16–Oct 31, $135 single or double, $205 one-bedroom suite, $275–$375 two-bedroom. Nov 1–May 15, $90 single or double, $125 one-bedroom, $175–$295 two-bedroom. No charge for children under 16 with parent. AE, DC, MC, V. Underground parking: free. *Bus:* 23 or 24 (at Johnson St. Bridge).

- **The Bedford,** 1140 Government St. at View St., Victoria V8W 1Y2 (tel. 604/384-6835; toll free 800/661-9255). 40 rooms. A/C MINIBAR TV TEL

An elegant small hostelry in early-20th-century European

style, this hotel in the heart of Old Town is a real find. Built in 1930, it was formerly the Bastion Inn; but in 1987 and 1988 it was thoroughly gutted and renovated under the direction of the Heathwood Resorts group. Today, the colorful flowerpots on the ledges above Government Street can only hint at its true charm. Guests are encouraged to leave the children at home.

As with many older inns, the rooms vary considerably in size, shape, and decor. Most share a pastel green-and-mauve color scheme, brass accents, stocked bookshelves, down comforters, and luxurious amenities. A dozen have fireplaces and sliding doors linking them to private Jacuzzis.

Dining/Entertainment: The Terrace Room serves three gourmet meals daily in summer, breakfast and lunch in winter, and afternoon tea year round. Garrick's Head Pub has pub meals 11am–11pm every day in summer, daily except Sunday in winter. The pub has a piano sing-along Thursday through Saturday nights, and locally brewed beer all the time.

Services: Concierge, valet laundry, free local phone calls, morning coffee and newspaper, overnight shoeshine.

Facilities: Meeting space for up to 80.

RATES (INCLUDING FULL BREAKFAST AND AFTERNOON TEA): May 19–Oct 31, $120 deluxe, $170 with fireplace; Nov 1–May 18, $95 deluxe, $135 with fireplace. AE, CB, DC, ER, MC, V. *Bus:* 5.

- **The Captain's Palace,** 309 Belleville St. at Oswego, Victoria V8V 1X2 (tel. 604/388-9191). 16 suites in two buildings.

This small Victorian hotel-restaurant, originally built in 1897 as the home of a prominent merchant and his family, has been restored and preserved in remarkably faithful fashion. From the foyer, with its hand-painted, ceramic-tiled fireplace and its rich wood paneling, to the crystal chandeliers hanging from frescoed ceilings, to the stained-glass windows and velvet tapestries, it is like a period museum. Even the staff is clad as liveried butlers or pinafored maids. Don't miss the $12,000, $1/12$-scale dollhouse replica of this mansion in the second-floor sitting room!

Every suite is fully furnished with estate antiques, right down to the carpeted private baths. There are no elevators, of course, but the stairs add to the charm! Some rooms have harbor views; others feature private parlors.

Dining/Entertainment: Breakfast, lunch, afternoon tea, and dinner are served in several lovely ground-floor rooms. Dinner prices are in the $15-to-$20 range; oyster stew, Neptune's sole, Cornish game hen, and Yorkshire beef bites are among the favorites.

RATES (INCLUDING FULL BREAKFAST): Apr 15–Oct 15, $110–$155 single or double; Oct 16–Apr 14, $65–$110. AE, DC, MC, V. Parking: free. *Bus:* 5 (to Belleville and Government sts.).

- **Holland House Inn,** 595 Michigan St. at Government, Victoria V8V 1S7 (tel. or fax 604/384-6644). 10 rooms. TV TEL

Owned by noted avant-garde artist Lance Olsen, this impeccably clean and tidy home is a veritable fine-art museum. The work of Olsen, sculptor David Toresdahl, and other B.C. artisans is on display throughout the home. Located fewer than two blocks behind the Parliament Buildings, it isn't Dutch at all: The three-story manse surrounded by a white picket fence was built in 1934 by an Englishman named Holland.

All rooms are furnished with antiques, and have private baths, wood floors, and four-poster beds with goose-down comforters. Two have wood-burning fireplaces, but smokers are requested to pursue their hobby on outside balconies.

Dining/Entertainment: Gourmet breakfasts—the likes of German apple pancakes or baked eggs with Brie and ham—are served between 7 and 10am to the strains of classical music in the Gallery Lounge. Jazz is the order of the afternoon in the lounge, and on six winter weekends, live classical recitals are offered.

Services: Room service.

RATES: June–Sept, $100–$165 single, $110–$175 double. Oct–May, $30 less. AE, DC, MC, V. *Bus:* 5 (to Superior and Government sts.).

• **Swans Hotel,** 506 Pandora Ave. at Store St., Victoria V8W 1N6 (tel. 604/361-3310). 12 suites (35 rooms). TEL

"I may be an ugly duckling now, but I'll soon be a swan!" Hans Christian Andersen's fable inspired the name given this converted 1913 feed warehouse when historic preservationist Michael Williams decided to turn it into a hotel-restaurant-brewery complex in 1988. Today, it's one of Old Town's best-known buildings. Buckerfield's Brewery produces a half dozen highly regarded British-style draft ales.

Williams's private collection of contemporary Canadian art hangs in the pub and in many of the rooms, which are like two-level artists' ateliers—two bedrooms upstairs, living area (with hideaway couch) below. They're great for families, as they have fully equipped kitchens and tables for six. The smaller units have ocean views; some have patios.

Dining/Entertainment: Swans Cafe is open for lunch and dinner daily; gourmet entrées are priced from $11 to $14. The often-crowded pub serves beers brewed on the premises.

Services: Guest laundry.

RATES (INCLUDING CONTINENTAL BREAKFAST): June 16–Oct 15, $120 double; Oct 16–June 15, $95 double; $10 per additional person. AE, MC, V. *Bus:* 23 or 24.

• **The Boathouse,** 746 Sea Drive, RR #1, Brentwood Bay V0S 1A0 (tel. 604/652-9370). 1 unit. FRIDGE TEL

Jean and Harvey Merritt's quaint bed-and-breakfast cottage is exactly what it claims to be: a converted boathouse, built on pilings in the Saanich Inlet, literally a stone's throw from the famed Butchart Gardens. It's rich in wildlife, including seals, herons, bald eagles, otters, and raccoons, and is a great spot for a romantic getaway.

The charming red cabin is reached down a long—make that *very* long—flight of stairs behind the Merritts' hillside home. Inside are a hideaway sofa bed, dining table, kitchen area with small refrigerator and toaster oven, gas furnace, and a reading alcove looking out on the floating dock. Full toilet and shower facilities are in a separate bathhouse a short way back uphill.

Dining/Entertainment: All the makings for a delicious Continental breakfast are provided the previous evening.

Facilities: Use of boat.

RATES (INCLUDING CONTINENTAL BREAKFAST): $105 year round. MC, V. Parking: free.

---

3. Moderately Priced Hotels

- **Carlton Plaza Hotel,** 642 Johnson St. at Broad, Victoria V8W 1M6 (tel. 604/388-5513; toll free 800/663-7241; fax 604/388-5343). 98 rooms, 5 suites. `A/C` `TV` `TEL`

Built in 1912 as the St. James Hotel, this heritage property has gone through many incarnations. The most recent began in 1989 when it was gutted and renovated to the tune of $1.5 million. Now a Best Western hotel, its rooms feature soft pastel decor and standard amenities and furnishings. Forty-one have fully equipped kitchens.

Dining/Entertainment: The Garden Cafe serves three meals daily except Sunday. Continental breakfast is served in the Island Bar and Lounge, off the lobby.

Services: Room service, valet laundry.

Facilities: Beauty salon, jeweler, gift shop. Meeting space for up to 80. Fitness club with weights and Jacuzzi under construction.

RATES (INCLUDING CONTINENTAL BREAKFAST): June–Sept, $75–$115 single or double, $130 suite; Oct–May, $60–$90 single or double, $100 suite. Children under 12 free with parent. AE, DC, ER, MC, V. Valet parking: $4. *Bus:* 5.

- **The Courtyard Inn,** 850 Blanshard St. at Courtney, Victoria V8W 2H2 (tel. 604/385-6787; fax 604/385-5800). 64 rooms. `A/C` `TV` `TEL`

Across the street from the law courts, this two-story hotel is built around a paved garden courtyard that sparkles in summer with wildflower baskets and safari umbrellas. Rooms are colorfully appointed, with all standard furnishings and amenities, including well-lit vanities. The quietest rooms either face the courtyard or are on the upper floor, with double-glazed windows.

Dining/Entertainment: The Court dining room serves breakfast daily, lunch weekdays, and gourmet dinners ($7–$14) nightly except Sunday. The Chambers lounge offers burgers and pub meals at lunchtime in a club atmosphere of Olde English prints and china. The Old Bailey pub, in the basement, is authentically British: Visiting rugby and cricket players make it their headquarters.

Services: Coin-op guest laundry, courtesy van.

Facilities: Indoor swimming pool, sauna; hair salon, gift shop. Meeting space for up to 80.

RATES: May 1–Oct 14, $80–$85 single, $85–$90 double; Oct 15–Apr 30, $65 single, $70 double, $55 single or double on weekends. AE, DC, ER, MC, V. Underground parking: free. *Bus:* 1.

- **The Dominion Hotel,** 759 Yates St. at Blanshard, Victoria V8W 1L6 (tel. 604/384-4136; toll free 800/663-6101; fax 604/382-6416). 101 rooms. `TV` `TEL`

Victoria's oldest surviving hotel dates from 1876. Today, it is a lovely family-oriented heritage property with rich woods, marble floors, brass trim, and red-velvet upholstery on antique chairs, following a $7 million restoration. Rooms have more modern appointments, but keep the flavor of times past with ceiling fans, brass lamps, and steam rooms. There are dozens of room types; all have been fully renovated in the past few years.

Dining/Entertainment: Central Park is an excellent gourmet restaurant, serving Continental and nouvelle dinners in a turn-of-the-century atmosphere for $13 to $17. The Lettuce Patch coffee shop offers three meals a day. The intimate Gaslight Lounge features carved solid-oak paneling, while the Barbary Coast Lounge is a bustling sports bar done in 19th-century San Francisco style.

Services: Room service, valet laundry.

Facilities: Barber shop.

RATES: May–Sept, $79–$89 single, $89–$99 double. Oct–Apr, $39.50–$44.50 single, $44.50–$49.50 double. Children under 16 free in parent's room. AE, DC, ER, MC, V. Parking: free. *Bus:* 10, 11, or 14.

- **Oak Bay Beach Hotel,** 1175 Beach Drive, Victoria V8S 2N2 (tel. or fax 604/598-4556). 45 rooms, 5 suites. A/C TV TEL

This Elizabethan-style inn sits on the Haro Strait, 3½ miles (5.5 km) east of downtown Victoria. Beautiful gardens extend to the shoreline; guests get an eyeful of Washington's San Juan Islands and snow-capped Mount Baker. The hotel is pure elegance, starting with the Grand Lobby—a huge living room with a century-old baby grand piano, priceless antiques, a big fireplace, even singing canaries. Every room is different; all boast pieces from hotelier Bruce Walker's personal antique collection. Rooms are priced according to size and view. The third-story junior suites are impressive, with canopy beds, bay windows, and balconies facing the sea.

Dining/Entertainment: The elegant Tudor Room by the Sea serves three meals, including Sunday brunch, and afternoon high tea daily. Gourmet West Coast cuisine dinners range from $14 to $28. The Snug, a cozy English pub, serves light meals and desserts. In summer, a salmon barbecue is offered in the garden nightly.

Services: Room service, valet laundry, morning coffee and newspaper, complimentary scheduled shuttle service.

Facilities: Upscale gift shop, cruises and charters aboard hotel's private yachts. Meeting space for up to 150.

RATES: May–Sept, $65–$98 standard, $148–$168 deluxe, $168–$200 junior suite, $235–$375 executive suite. Oct–Apr, 10% less. AE, CB, DC, ER, MC, V. Parking: free. *Bus:* 2.

- **Royal Scot Inn,** 425 Quebec St. between Menzies and Oswego, Victoria V8V 1W7 (tel. 604/388-5463; toll free 800/663-7515; fax 604/388-5452). 28 rooms, 150 suites. A/C TV TEL

A converted apartment house, the Royal Scot is a modern motel just a half block from the Parliament Buildings. In winter, it's favored by prairie province retirees escaping sub-zero climes. Standard room furnishings include walk-in closets, dressing tables, and VCRs (there's an in-house video rental). All suites have fully equipped kitchens. Deluxe suites have a room divider separating the bedroom from the living room; some have balconies. Luxury suites have separate bedrooms, with queen-size rather than double beds.

Dining/Entertainment: Piper's Restaurant, offering outdoor seating in summer, serves three meals daily plus high tea. Steak or seafood dinners run from $9.25 to $15.95.

Services: Room service, valet laundry, guest laundromat, free local calls, courtesy van.

Facilities: Indoor swimming pool, sauna, Jacuzzi, exercise room, gift/sundries shop, video rental. Meeting space for up to 55.

RATES: May 16–Sept 30, $89–$99 single or double, $110 deluxe suite, $125 luxury suite, $150–$225 other suites. Oct 1–May 15, $65–$75 single or double, $88 deluxe suite, $98 luxury suite, $115–$175 other suites. Discounted weekly and monthly rates. MC, DC, ER, MC, V. Parking: free. *Bus:* 5 (to Belleville and Government sts.).

- **The Coachman Inn,** 229 Gorge Rd. East at Washington St., Victoria V8A 1L1 (tel. 604/388-6611; fax 604/388-4153). 60 rooms, 12 suites. A/C TV TEL

This conveniently located Gorge Road motel is friendly and attentive. All rooms have outside entrances and queen-size beds; 28 have fully equipped kitchens. There's ample closet space, along with standard furnishings and amenities. Horse-and-hounds pictures hang on the walls.

Dining/Entertainment: The Post House Restaurant serves three meals daily. Squire's Lounge offers pub fare, and has an outside deck for warm afternoons. It is a major venue for darts tournaments, including the Victoria International Darts Challenge in late October. A Dixieland jazz band plays Sundays from 4 to 7pm year round.

Services: Coin-op guest laundromat, seasonal shuttle service.

Facilities: Indoor swimming pool, sauna, video-game room. Meeting space for up to 125.

RATES: July 1–Sept 15, $75–$95 single or double, $109 suite. May 16–June 30 and Sept 16–30, $65–$85 single or double, $89–$99 suite. Oct 1–May 15, $49–$69 single or double, $75–$82 suite. Children under 12 free with parent. AE, MC, V. Parking: free. *Bus:* 10.

- **Ramada Inn,** 3020 Blanshard St. near Finlayson, Victoria V8T 5B5 (tel. 604/382-4400; toll free 800/268-8998; fax 604/382-4053). 98 rooms, 25 suites. A/C TV TEL

Victoria's entry in the international Ramada chain is appealing to many for its location: adjacent to Mayfair Shopping Centre, Victoria's largest mall, and across the street from city-maintained Topaz Park and tennis courts. The lobby is sparse but spacious, the rooms nicely appointed. Twenty-two new suites have kitchenettes.

Dining/Entertainment: Redd's Roadhouse Restaurant has all-day casual dining; the menu includes pastas and Mexican food. Its upper floor is Redd's Pub, popular as a sports bar.

Services: Room service, valet laundry.

Facilities: Exercise room, Jacuzzi, sauna, gift shop, hair salon. Meeting space for up to 250.

RATES: May–Sept, $95 single, $99 double, $115–$125 suite; Oct 1–April 30, $69 single, $75 double, $89–$95 suite. Children under 18 free in parent's room. AE, DC, MC, V. Underground parking: free. *Bus:* 30 (Mayfair Centre) or 70 (Douglas St.).

- **Helm's Inn,** 668 Superior St. near Douglas, Victoria V8V 1V2 (tel. 604/385-5767; fax 604/385-2221). 23 units. A/C TV TEL

This gaily painted motel, just a half block from the Royal B.C. Museum, is popular among budget watchers who like to stay close to the center of action. Sixteen of the spacious rooms have kitchen units, making them especially appealing to families. The interior decor is eye-catching: blue trim around peach-colored doors, purple carpets, and a big grandfather clock on the stairway.

Services: Complimentary newspaper and morning coffee.

RATES: May 15–Oct 14, standard $75–$79 single or double, with kitchen $85–$90, one-bedroom suite $100–$105; Oct 15–May 14, standard $47 single or double, with kitchen $52, one-bedroom suite $59. MC, V. Parking: free. *Bus:* 30.

- **Scotsman Motel,** 490 Gorge Rd. East at Garbally St., Victoria V8T 2W4 (tel. 604/388-7358). 47 rooms. A/C TV TEL

Run by a hospitable husband-wife team, this motel has a tropical white gleam on the outside and a lobby rather incongruously decorated with hefty Scottish battle-axes. The rooms all have standard furnishings and amenities, with waterbeds available on request. More than half have kitchen facilities.

Services: Coin-op laundry.

RATES (INCLUDING CONTINENTAL BREAKFAST): $44–$49 single or double, $59–$74 twin. MC, V. Parking: free. *Bus:* 30.

---

4. Budget Accommodations

- **The James Bay Inn,** 270 Government St. at Toronto St., Victoria V8V 2L2 (tel. 604/384-7151). 50 rooms.

An early Edwardian manor built in 1907, this budget favorite was the last home of famed painter Emily Carr, a Victoria native. Its lobby features Gay Nineties decor. Rooms are simple and old-fashioned, but quite adequate for travelers who don't demand luxury. Daytona's restaurant serves three light meals daily; the Unwinder is a well-patronized basement neighborhood pub.

RATES: Singles $23–$32 (shared bath), $38–$42 (private bath); doubles $29–$38 (shared bath), $48–$52 (private bath). MC, V. Parking: free, but limited. *Bus:* 5 or 30 (to Government and Superior sts.).

- **Hotel Douglas,** 1450 Douglas St. at Pandora Ave., Victoria V8W 2G1 (tel. 604/383-4157). 67 rooms. A/C TV TEL

This old brick building across the street from City Hall is clean and basic. Its small lobby has no seating, but there's a bar on one side, a coffee shop on the other. Regular rooms are adequately furnished with modern bathrooms and nondenominational religious texts framed on the walls.

RATES: Singles $30 (shared bath) and $45 (private bath); doubles $35 (shared bath) and $50 (private bath). Children under 6 free in same bed with parents. MC, V. *Bus:* 1, 6, 14, or 30.

- **Sussex Apartment Hotel,** 1001 Douglas St. at Broughton, Victoria V8W 2C5 (tel. 604/386-3441). A/C TV TEL

An old-fashioned apartment hotel, the Sussex has a coffee shop, a barber shop, and several stores—a smoke shop, a bookshop, and a native crafts shop—on its ground floor. Guests choose between studio rooms or small apartments with kitchenettes. All are well maintained, simple, and clean.

RATES: $42–$48 single, $48–$54 double. Weekly/monthly rates available except May 15–Aug 31. MC, V. Parking: free. *Bus:* 1, 4, 5, or 30.

- **Maple Leaf Inn,** 120 Gorge Rd. East at Albany St., Victoria V9A 1L3 (tel. 604/388-9901). 64 rooms. A/C TV TEL

Like an alpine transplant, this resembles a chalet with a swimming pool, sauna, and sun deck. About half the units have their own kitchens (for just $10 extra). All have queen-size beds, or waterbeds on request. There's free morning coffee, a coin-op laundry.

RATES: $40–$48 single, $44–$54 double. MC, V. Parking: free. *Bus:* 10.

- **University of Victoria,** Housing and Conference Services, P.O. Box 1700, Victoria V8W 2Y2 (tel. 604/721-8395). A/C

Victoria's major university opens its dormitories to visitors for four summer months, when classes are not in session. All rooms have single or twin beds and basic furnishings. Bathrooms, pay phones, and TV lounges are on every floor; linens, towels, and soap are provided. Each building has a coin-op laundry. Guests may use campus cafeterias, dining rooms, and athletic facilities, including swimming pool, weight room, squash and tennis courts.

RATES (INCLUDING FULL BREAKFAST): May 1–Aug 31 only, $19.75 single, $32 double. Parking: free. *Bus:* 4 or 14.

- **YM-YWCA of Victoria,** 880 Courtney St. at Quadra, Victoria, V8W 1C4 (tel. 604/386-7511). 31 beds. A/C

Though the same building provides facilities for both sexes, the residence is for *women only.* A big brown brick building with a spacious lobby and green leather settees, the Y has a cafeteria (closed on Sunday), a swimming pool, and a cozy TV lounge. There are shared bathrooms and pay telephones on each floor.

RATES: June–Aug, $23 single, $36 double. Sept–May, discounted rates. Rents payable in advance. MC, V. *Bus:* 1.

- **Victoria Hostel,** 516 Yates St. near Wharf St., Victoria V8W 1K8 (tel. 604/385-4511). 102 beds.

Located in the heart of Old Town, this friendly youth hostel has everything the traveler really needs. Facilities include two kitchens (stocked with utensils) and a dining room, TV lounge with VCR, game room, common room, library, laundry facilities, and hot showers. Most beds are in dormitories, but there are a couple of family rooms.

RATES: $10 International Youth Hostel members, $15 nonmembers. Cash only. *Bus:* 23 or 24 (at Johnson St. Bridge).

XIII

VICTORIA DINING

1. A VERY EXPENSIVE RESTAURANT
2. EXPENSIVE RESTAURANTS
3. MODERATELY PRICED RESTAURANTS
4. BUDGET RESTAURANTS

What is true of cuisine in Vancouver is likewise true in Victoria. British Columbia's capital city isn't quite as cosmopolitan as its larger cousin, but the variety of food is still impressive—and here, it often comes with an added touch of English hospitality. Afternoon high teas are more "the thing" in Victoria than in Vancouver.

The following listing is organized by price range: **very expensive** (entrées average more than $20 Canadian per person), **expensive** ($15 to $20), **moderately priced** ($10–$15), and **budget** (less than $10). There's no tax on restaurant meals in British Columbia.

Restaurant hours vary. Lunch hour is typically noon to 1pm; in the evening, British Columbians rarely dine before 7pm, later in summer. Reservations are recommended at most restaurants, and are essential at the most popular. They may not be accepted, however, at some budget and even some moderately priced establishments.

1. A Very Expensive Restaurant

• **Sooke Harbour House,** 1528 Whiffen Spit Road, Sooke (tel. 642-3421). *Prices:* Appetizers $6.50–$15; entrées $19.50–$28. MC, V.

Victoria's finest restaurant isn't in Victoria. It's 23 miles (37 km) west near the seaside town of Sooke. Acclaimed as "the best restaurant in Canada" by the *Toronto Star,* the Sooke Harbour House offers diners a homey atmosphere, a spectacular view, and incomparable West Coast–style preparations of local seafood and organically farmed produce. A rambling white house on a bluff overlooking mile-long Whiffen Spit, the restaurant consists of a huge living room (with seating around a blazing fireplace in winter) and two adjoining rooms. Despite its acclaim, it's a come-as-you-are sort of place: Guests are encouraged to come in beach shorts or holiday casuals, if they choose.

Fredrica and Sinclair Philip, who opened Harbour House in 1979, buy from local fishermen, use no beef, and employ three full-time gardeners to help keep their large vegetable and herb patch thriving. The menu changes daily, according to available foods. My dinner at the Sooke Harbour House was as typical (and as satiating!) as any. My starter was shrimp bisque with roe; then abalone sautéed with pear butter and bronze fennel. My entrée of snapper and large shrimp was grilled with spinach, parsley, chive, and nasturtium crème fraîche, and served with beets, parsnip, and wild rice. I concluded with a salad of a half-dozen local greens with a raspberry hazelnut dressing, and a blackberry-and-riesling sabayon with coffee ice cream and hazelnut cookie.

The Philipses also have an adjoining 13-room bed-and-breakfast inn. Every room has a different configuration and nature theme; furnishings and art are specially chosen or custom-designed. All rooms have fireplaces, private balconies, and phones; many have hot tubs or Jacuzzis. Rates—which include breakfast, lunch, and an evening decanter of port wine—are $145–$230, with two small rooms for $95 and $105.

Open: Dinner daily from 6pm. *Reservations:* Essential. *Parking:* Free. *Bus:* 61. WEST COAST

---

2. Expensive Restaurants

• **Harbour House Restaurant,** 607 Oswego St. at Quebec Ave. (tel. 386-1244). *Prices:* Appetizers $3.95–$7.50; entrées $12.90–$24.95. AE, MC, V.

Good traditional North American cooking in a friendly, upscale environment is the forte at the Harbour House, set beside Quadra Park just off Belleville Street. Owner Harry Loucas, originally from the eastern Mediterrean island nation of Cyprus, emphasizes service: In fact, he personally greets each arriving customer and thanks him or her on departure. Waiters in bow tie and cummerbund bustle past tables bedecked with white linen, candles, and fresh flowers, delivering impeccable service and pausing long enough to discuss the menu and international wine list—and events of the world—with guests.

The menu is divided about evenly between meats and seafoods. Diners might start with the restaurant's excellent spinach salad, then dine on the generous salmon au champagne, served with three vegetables. Steak Stefanie (in a Grand Marnier sauce) is another favorite.

Open: Lunch, May–Sept only 11:30am–5pm, dinner daily 5–11:30pm year round. *Reservations:* Recommended. *Parking:* On street. *Bus:* 30 (to Superior and Oswego sts.). CANADIAN

• **The Latch Restaurant,** 2328 Harbour Rd., Sidney (tel. 656-6622). *Prices:* Appetizers $5.95–$9.95; entrées $13.50–$19.50 dinner, $6.50–$10.50 lunch. AE, DC, MC, V.

Five minutes from the Swartz Bay ferry terminal, a half-hour from downtown Victoria, is this timbered home on a point of land extending into the Strait of Georgia. Built in 1926 as the private summer retreat of B.C. Lt. Gov. Walter Nichol, it was dubbed "The Latch" by guests who found that every door had been fitted with a latch in place of doorknobs. Today, the private drive leads through expansive gardens with views across the strait and Sidney marinas.

The five dining rooms still have their original fir, beech, and cottonwood paneling. Three of the rooms are entirely private, and may be requested for no additional charge. Diners may start with a creative appetizer, such as papaya with brandied shrimp, and follow with Caesar salad, prepared tableside. Entrées are imaginative preparations of traditional favorites: rack of lamb provençale glazed with hot English mustard, bouillabaisse marseillaise, breast of pheasant périgourdine, ragout of veal tenderloin and wild mushrooms. Homemade desserts, like Brazilian torte or baked Alaska, are served with coffee beside the fireplace in the cozy drawing room.

Open: Lunch Sun–Fri noon–4pm, dinner daily 5–11pm. *Closed:* Labour Day, Christmas, and Jan. 3. *Reservations:* Requested. *Parking:* Free. *Bus:* 70 (Resthaven Drive). CONTINENTAL

- **Chauney's Restaurant,** 614 Humboldt St. near Government St. (tel. 385-4512). *Prices:* Appetizers $5–$8; entrées $15–$22 dinner. AE, MC, V.

Subdued luxury is the watchword at this near neighbor of the Empress. Swelling settees, soundless carpets, soft lighting, and a general air of total devotion to the pleasures of gastronomy, Mozart, and budding artists. The paintings and stained-glass windows represent the owner's commitment to promoting the city's artisans; the portraits of distinguished patrons are specially commissioned. Live classical entertainment is likewise presented by young Victoria musicians.

Though the art might sometimes be unacclaimed, the menu is very well established. Local seafood is carefully separated from imported delicacies. You can start with oysters Florentine and follow up with king crab Pernod. For dessert, try possibly the richest and most alcoholic baba au rhum on the island.

Open: Lunch Mon–Fri 11:30am–2:30pm, brunch (April–Oct) Sat–Sun 11am–2:30pm; dinner daily 5–11pm. *Reservations:* Suggested. *Parking:* Covered lot two blocks north at Gordon and Broughton sts. *Bus:* 5. CONTINENTAL

- **La Ville d'Is,** 26 Bastion Square (tel. 388-9414). *Prices:* Appetizers $5.45–$7.45; entrées $5.25–$8.25 lunch, $13.45–$19.85 dinner. AE, MC, V.

An ancient Breton legend tells of a magical island city-kingdom inundated 1,500 years ago by divine powers because of royal debaucheries. The kingdom's name—and its rarely experienced Breton cuisine—have survived at this intimate two-story brick restaurant tucked away behind the Maritime Museum.

Brittany native Michel Dutteau has preserved the seafood cuisine of his homeland in such hors d'oeuvres as pâté aux moules (mussels) and cotriade de Cornouailles (fish chowder); and entrees like lotte à l'Armoricaine (monkfish in garlic, cognac, and Macon wine) and soufflé de homard (lobster soufflé with prawns). For non lovers of fish, there's a lapin chasseur (marinated rabbit in red-wine sauce). Chocolate mousse is a dessert favorite. Lunch specialties include seafood vol-au-vent and crêpe crab Mornay.

Open: Mon–Sat 11:30am–2pm and 5:30–10pm. *Reservations:* Suggested. *Parking:* Covered lot at Yates and Langley sts. *Bus:* 5. BRETON

• **Larousse,** 1619 Store St. between Pandora Ave. and Fisgard St. (tel. 386-3454). *Prices:* Appetizers $3.50–$5.50; entrées $10.50–$20.50. AE, MC, V.

The neighboring North Park Gallery provides the exquisite art for the walls of this small, health-conscious restaurant. It attracts a professional and arty clientele who enjoy a soothing dining experience, aided by the light piped-in classical music.

Chef-owner Girard Hivon also considers himself an artist: "Chicken is the blank palette of the chef," he says. Thus, dishes like chicken Pondicherri (in a spicy cashew purée) and sénégalaise (in peanut and chili sauce), prepared in French overseas style, are two of his favorites. He also offers several superb veal dishes (there's no beef on the menu); smoked trout Larousse (poached in mustard, cream, and fresh basil sauce); and a couple of tangy vegetarian casseroles. Fresh fruit sorbets make a fine dessert, as does Larousse gâteau: coffee sponge layer cake with chocolate crème de cacao and orange Triple Sec cream fillings. Hivon purchases all ingredients locally, including herbs, berries, and edible flowers, and cooks with safflower oil and minimal salt.

Open: Wed–Sun 6–11pm. *Reservations:* Requested. *Parking:* On street. *Bus:* 23 or 24 (to Johnson St. Bridge). FRENCH COLONIAL AND PROVENÇAL

• **Chez Daniel,** 2524 Estevan Ave. near Heron St. (off Beach Rd.), Oak Bay (tel. 592-7424). *Prices:* Appetizers $5–$9, entrées $15–$22. MC, V.

This tiny restaurant—10 tables in two rooms—is the personal domain of Daniel Rigollet, chef de cuisine and maître rotisseur. There's a comfortable, intimate feeling here, enhanced by the classical music in the air.

Rigollet likes to experiment, based on whatever fresh ingredients are available, and he does so by keeping his recipes flexible. If they're fresh, start with mussels in a rich cream-and-chive sauce; otherwise, consider the consommé Germiny (with sorrel, cream, and egg yolk). Outstanding entrées include lamb with ginger in a cream sauce, duck with chestnuts and sea asparagus, salmon with vermouth and cream, and filet mignon à la moelle. The wine list was honored at the 1988 Vancouver International Wine Festival, and the desserts (including flambéed crêpes) are no less deserving.

Open: Tues–Sat 5:30–10pm; also Mon in summer. *Reservations:* Highly recommended. *Parking:* Free. *Bus:* 1. FRENCH NOUVELLE

• **Chez Pierre,** 512 Yates St. at Wharf St. (tel. 388-7711). *Prices:* Appetizers $4.75–$6.25, entrées $15.95–$19.95. AE, MC, V.

In the very heart of Old Town is this small, delightfully authentic French eatery, a magnet for those who know about Gallic food and the tourists they tell about it. Through the wrought-iron gates is an atmosphere of charming French provincial decor.

The escargots are superb as an appetizer, while the rack of lamb and the canard à l'orange (duck in orange sauce) continue to draw rave reviews from patrons. B.C. salmon, Dover sole, and scallops highlight the seafood list. Desserts are prepared fresh daily.

Open: Dinner Mon–Thurs 6–10pm, Fri–Sat 6–11pm. *Reservations:* Requested. *Parking:* Parking lot at Yates and Langley streets. *Bus:* 23 or 24 (to Johnson St. Bridge). FRENCH

- **Pablo's Dining Lounge,** 225 Quebec St. at Pendray (tel. 388-4255). *Prices:* Appetizers $4.50–$6.50, entrées $13–$18. AE, DC, MC, V.

Housed in a beautifully refurbished Edwardian home near Laurel Point, this restaurant is as famous for its food as it is for its Spanish coffee, presented with a kind of ritual fire dance by Pablo Hernandez himself—quite scary if you're unprepared for the spectacle. Hernandez, who came to Canada from Spain via London, is quite a showman.

The lobster here is live, and you can pick out your own feast. The paella valenciana is Victoria's best. If you've had enough of seafood, go for the Saltspring rack of lamb, the chateaubriand forestière, or the marinated chicken tikka. Dessert and coffee are served in the Loft Room, where there's live entertainment Wednesday through Saturday nights.

Open: Dinner daily 7–11pm. *Reservations:* Recommended. *Parking:* Free. *Bus:* 30 (to Montreal and Superior sts.). FRENCH AND SPANISH

3. Moderately Priced Restaurants

- **Causeway Restaurant and Cafe,** 812 Wharf St. (tel. 381-2244). *Prices:* Appetizers $4.95–$7.95; entrées $5.95–$9.25 lunch, $10.95–$17.95 dinner. AE, MC, V.

This restaurant may have the best view to dine by in Victoria. Located on the Inner Harbour across Government Street from the Empress, it occupies the lower floors of the same building as the Tourism Victoria Information Centre. By day, diners can enjoy the comings and goings of ferries and fishing boats, yachts and seaplanes in James Bay; by night, the spectacle of the Empress and the Parliament Buildings, lit by thousands of lights, is unforgettable.

There are really two restaurants here. The formal restaurant, green with plants, focuses on local seafood—oysters Rockefeller, baked salmon in phyllo pastry, baby coho stuffed with shrimp, whole cooked crab in lemon and butter. Meatier dishes like New York steak and chicken cordon bleu share the menu. Beneath, the promenade café serves lighter fare in a casual atmosphere; in summer, the doors open wide to a 24-seat outdoor deck. Both restaurant and café have full bars.

Open: Restaurant: breakfast, May–Sept only 7–11am; lunch 11:30am–4pm daily; dinner Sun–Thurs 4:30–9pm, Fri–Sat 4:30–10pm, in summer Sun–Thurs 4:30–10pm, Fri–Sat 4:30–11pm.

Café: Daily 7am–11pm in summer, 7am–5pm in winter. *Reservations:* Recommended in restaurant. *Bus:* 5. WEST COAST CONTINENTAL

- **Camille's,** 45 Bastion Square (tel. 381-3433). *Prices:* Appetizers $4.95–$5.95, entrées $9.95–$16.95. MC, V.

This find in the basement of Victoria's Old Law Chambers is a delightful and romantic experience. Tiffany lamps and wood partitions, accented by the original brick walls, lend it an atmosphere of mystery and intimacy.

The menu is more imaginative than mysterious. You might start with fish-and-flower terrine (salmon and red snapper with lemon-avocado sauce), or "simply splendid prawns" with artichoke hearts and a blackberry dressing. Suggested entrées include chicken mango; pork loin stuffed with Frangelico, peach, and hazelnut; broiled filet mignon served with a port and cranberry demiglaze; or prawns flambéed tableside in onions, garlic, and Pernod. The homemade desserts are completely scrumptious.

Open: Dinner 5:30–10pm daily. *Reservations:* Recommended. *Parking:* Lot at Langley and Fort sts. *Bus:* 5. WEST COAST

- **Herald Street Caffè,** 546 Herald St. near Government St. (tel. 381-1441). *Prices:* Appetizers $4.50–$6; entrees $5.50–$7.75 lunch, $9.25–$14.95 dinner. AE, MC, V.

Exceptionally popular among young artistic types, this casual Old Town restaurant, a block north of Chinatown, is in fact a gallery of local art: all of it for sale. But the beautiful fresh flower arrangements, potted palms, and hanging lamps wouldn't keep the intelligentsia—some in jeans, some in jacket and tie—coming if the food weren't also good.

The bistro is noted for its pastas: fettuccine, spinach linguine, canneloni, and others, made fresh daily and served many ways. Try it with steamed mussels in coconut milk, or with shrimp, puréed ginger, and roasted cashews. Other entrées include chicken sautéed with marinated black currants and blackberry Cabernet, and a fish steamer (local whitefish with Cantonese black beans and vegetables, served with curried yogurt or creamy garlic).

Open: Lunch Mon–Thurs 11:30am–3pm, Fri–Sat 11:30am–4pm, Sun (brunch) 10am–3pm; dinner Mon–Thurs 5:30–midnight, Fri–Sat 5:30pm–3am, Sun 5:30–11pm. *Reservations:* Not accepted (expect lines). *Parking:* On street. *Bus:* 4, 10, or 14 (Douglas St.). NOUVELLE AND PASTA

- **Metropolitan Diner,** 1715 Government St. between Fisgard and Herald (tel. 381-1512). *Prices:* Appetizers $4–$7, entrées $10–$15 dinner. MC, V.

Talk about eclectic! But then, there are clues. The moment you enter, you'll realize this is a stylish, upscale restaurant, not a diner; and Victoria isn't exactly a metropolis, either.

It's the menu—some describe it as a blend of California, the Continent, and the Far East—that has tongues wagging. How about trout stuffed with banana? Fettuccine in a lobster-cream champagne sauce? Rabbit with juniper berries? Duck-and-pink-peppercorn pizza? It may raise eyebrows, but it all works. So do the delicious desserts, like the oddly named "chocolate bag."

Open: Lunch Mon–Fri noon–2pm; dinner Sun–Thurs 5:30pm–midnight, Fri–Sat 5:30pm–1am. *Reservations:* Recommended. *Parking:* On street. *Bus:* 4, 10, or 14 (Douglas St.). NOUVELLE

- **Rattenbury's,** 703 Douglas St. at Belleville (tel. 381-1333). *Prices:* Appetizers $3.50–$5.50; entrées $5.95–$8.50 lunch, $12.95–$16.95 dinner. MC, V.

Housed in the south wing of the famed Crystal Gardens, and named for the architect who built the adjacent Empress hotel, Rattenbury's might be construed as a relic. Quite the opposite is true: It's a modern, upscale restaurant, boasting a pleasant outdoor eating area where diners can watch the city stroll by.

Those outdoor seats are especially popular in summer, when barbecued salmon (marinated in pesto, grilled over charcoal) is the meal of choice. Anytime, Rattenbury's has such light lunchtime fare as homemade soups, papaya with shrimp salad, crêpes, quiche, and burgers; and gourmet dinners such as prime rib, steak Oscar, halibut Pacifica, and seafood Thermidor. There's also a children's menu. Dessert? Try the Nanaimo bars.

Open: Lunch daily 11:30am–4pm; dinner Sun–Thurs 4–10pm, Fri–Sat 4–11pm. *Reservations:* Recommended at dinner. *Parking:* Parkade at Empress hotel. *Bus:* 5 or 30. FAMILY STYLE

- **Chandlers,** 1250 Wharf St. at Yates (tel. 386-3232). *Prices:* Appetizers $3.95–$4.95; entrées $8.45–$24.95; oyster bar $4.95–$8.95. AE, MC, V.

You can't miss this building—its north wall is painted with an exquisite mural, depicting the orcas (killer whales) of the surrounding waters. Readers of *Best of Victoria* magazine voted it their favorite seafood restaurant. Originally a ship chandlery (thus the name), it has a sporty decor, with hardwood floors and green trim. Historic photos of the Port of Victoria hang on the walls, and light rock music plays continuously.

Full dinners are served upstairs, with entrees like barbecued tiger prawns, teriyaki salmon, and Caribbean lobster tail. But Shawkey's Raw Bar & Grill, a ground-floor oyster bar, seems to be crowded all the time. At least a half dozen different West Coast and East Coast oysters are offered daily, along with Dungeness crab, grilled halibut, steamed Manila clams, seafood Caesar salad, and specialty sandwiches (like the salmon croissant).

Open: Lunch daily 11:30am–5pm; dinner Mon–Thurs 5–10pm, Fri–Sat 5–10:30pm, Sun 5–9:30pm. *Reservations:* Suggested. *Parking:* Covered lot at Yates and Langley sts. *Bus:* 23 or 24 (to Johnson St. Bridge). SEAFOOD

- **The Grand Central Cafe,** 555 Johnson St. opposite Market Square (tel. 386-4747). *Prices:* Appetizers $3.95–$7.50; entrées $9.95–$14.95 dinner. MC, V.

The best time to visit this spacious, elegant old brick structure is in summer, when the beautiful rear courtyard—with its classic fountain surrounded by flowering plants—is open for dining. Then the crowds come out for the splash of sunshine, just like in New Orleans.

That's what Cajun food is all about: a little zing, a little spice.

You can start with Cajun oysters or sincronizade, a tortilla dish, then fill up on blackened swordfish, chicken Rochambeau, or jambalaya. If you're still hungry, have a slice of Key lime pie. For a "lighter" meal, enjoy the famous six-spice bread with the soup of the day: "If one's not enough, the next one's on us!"

Open: Lunch Mon–Sat 11:30am–2:30pm, Sun (brunch) 11am–2:30pm; dinner Sun–Thurs 5:30–10pm, Fri–Sat 5:30–11pm. *Reservations:* Recommended. *Parking:* On street. *Bus:* 23 or 24 (to Johnson St. Bridge). CAJUN

• **Holyrood House,** 2315 Blanshard St. at Bay (tel. 382-8833). *Prices:* $7.75 lunch, $15.25 dinner, $11.50 Sunday brunch. MC, V.

Named for the royal palace in Edinburgh, this unique baronial building serves as the clubhouse of the Sons of Scotland and the Caledonian Society. Though it was built only in 1957, it has an atmosphere of medieval times—especially with its decor of Scottish antiques and artifacts, among them the only known replica of a 13th-century Sir William Wallace sword. Authenticity carries to the two dining rooms: the Scotia Lounge has a motif of highland tartans; the Tartan Room (for nonsmokers) has a red tartan floor.

Come here when you're hungry—service is buffet-style, all-you-can-eat. Savor the Scottish steak pie (without kidneys) or haggis, or stick to a more North American regimen of international salads, homemade soups, ham, turkey, roast beef, and salmon.

Open: Lunch Tues–Thurs 11:30am–2pm, Sun (brunch) 11am–2pm; dinner Fri–Sun 5–9pm. *Reservations:* Not taken. *Parking:* Free. *Bus:* 6 (to Bay and Quadra sts.). SCOTTISH

• **Pagliacci's,** 1011 Broad St. near Broughton (tel. 386-1662). *Prices:* $8–$14. MC, V.

A happy and convivial mixture of Italian restaurant and New York nightclub, with possibly the most enthusiastic clientele in town, Pagliacci's is outrageously popular. Tables are so close together that you can spoon your neighbor's soup, and the vibes are so good that you hardly need the laid-on entertainment. The casual atmosphere here is perfect for people-watching. The bad news is, it's always crowded, and you may have to wait in line for the privilege; the good news is, people-watching's just as good in line! (When owner Howie Segal, a transplanted New Yorker, threw a party at Beacon Hill Park for his eatery's 10th anniversary, 25,000 people came!)

The food, perhaps surprisingly, is *not* secondary to the ambience. Delicious pastas and crêpes, and entrées like chicken Marsala and veal parmesan, make zesty meals. Late-night arrivals often enjoy a cup of cappuccino and one of Pagliacci's melt-in-your-mouth desserts.

Open: Daily 11:30am–12:30pm. Light menu 3–6pm. *Reservations:* Not accepted. *Parking:* Covered lot at Gordon and Broughton sts. *Bus:* 5 (Government St.) or 30 (Douglas St.). ITALIAN/JEWISH

• **Millos,** 716 Burdett Ave. near Penwell St. (tel. 382-4422 or 382-5544). *Prices:* Appetizers $3.95–$14.95; entrées $6.45–$10.95 lunch, $12.95–$20.95 dinner. AE, MC, V.

This windmill (*millos*) of fun is just a half block from the Victoria Conference Centre. Its white Mediterranean decor spills across five seating levels; there's a full mural of the Parthenon on one wall, Grecian urns with dried flower arrangements against another, dolls and curios around a central fireplace. Three folk dancers invite the audience to join them weaving around the floor Friday and Saturday nights, and a belly dancer entertains an hour later (nightly in summer).

Owner George Mavrikos has seen to it that the food is genuine and the portions generous. The dolmades (stuffed grape leaves) and saghanaki (sharp cheese fried in butter and flambéed in brandy) are fine starters. Entrées include moussaka, lamb or halibut souvlaki, and kota kapama (a chicken casserole); non-Greek dishes are also on the menu, like baby back ribs and New York steak. For dessert, consider yogurt with walnuts and honey.

Open: Lunch Mon–Fri 11:30am–4:30pm; dinner daily 4:30pm–11pm. *Reservations:* Recommended. *Parking:* Adjacent. *Bus:* 2. GREEK

- **Hunan Village,** 546 Fisgard St. (tel. 382-0661). *Prices:* Appetizers $2.25–$7.95; entrées $5.95–$9.50; three-course meal (for two) $18.65–$26.70. MC, V.

The cuisine of the south central Chinese province of Hunan is not intended for tender palates. Like that of its western neighbor, Szechuan, Hunanese food is quite spicy; but if it's prepared well, delicate flavors will still come through.

Here, in a room that has eschewed the ostentation of some Chinese designers for simple elegance, it *is* prepared well. Try the hot-and-sour beef or chicken, the braised rock cod, the harvest pork, or the kung pao shrimp.

Open: Lunch Mon–Sat 11am–4pm; dinner Mon–Sat 4–11pm, Sun 5–11pm. *Reservations:* Accepted. *Parking:* On street. *Bus:* 4, 10, or 14 (Douglas St.). HUNANESE

- **Ocean Phoenix Restaurant,** 509 Fisgard St. (tel. 382-2828). *Prices:* Appetizers $4.50–$9.95; entrées $4.95–$22.95; three-course dinner (for two) $15.95–$45.70. MC, V.

It's unusual in North America to see the shrine of a Taoist god so prominently displayed in a restaurant, as it is here. Perhaps that's a good sign: No chef or server is likely to falter when they're being watched so closely.

One way to determine the quality of a Chinese restaurant is to see if it has shark's-fin or bird's-nest soup on the menu. Ocean Phoenix has both. It also has mash-winter-melon-and-dry-scallop soup, fish-maw soup with shredded chicken, duck-web hot pot, braised abalone with sea cucumber, crab in ginger and onions, and diced pork with walnuts. Talk about authentic!

Open: Mon–Sat 11am–11pm, Sun 11am–10pm. *Reservations:* Accepted. *Parking:* On street. *Bus:* 4, 10, or 14 (Douglas St.). CANTONESE

- **Le Petit Saigon,** 1010 Langley St. near Fort St. (tel. 386-1412). *Prices:* Appetizers $2.50–$6.95; entrees $5.50–$14.95 dinner, $4.95–$6.95 lunch. MC, V.

Vietnamese cuisine is a harmony of East and West—Chinese-inspired tempered by a century of French influence. Here, the light, subtle tastes are exquisitely done. Spring rolls, shrimp salad, brochettes, hot-and-sour seafood soup, shrimp on sugar cane, crêpes, lamb curry—you can't go wrong.

Open: Lunch Mon–Fri from 11am, dinner daily from 5pm. *Reservations:* Accepted. *Parking:* Covered lot adjacent. *Bus:* 5 (Douglas St.). VIETNAMESE

• **Taj Mahal,** 679 Herald St. near Douglas (tel. 383-4662). *Prices:* Appetizers $2.25–$13.95; entrées $6.25–$14.95. AE, DC, MC, V.

The domes and minarets of the exterior, while not exactly mimicking Shah Jahan's Agra tomb, hint at an exotic dining experience within—and that's what you get. It could be New Delhi, as servers in saris walk gracefully through a decor of imported Indian arts and crafts.

The food is superb: beef vindaloo, lamb biryani, fish masala, chicken tikka, mouth-watering tandoori dishes baked in a proper clay oven. There's also a menu for vegetarians. Everything is prepared according to the diner's palate: spiced mild, medium, hot, or very hot. For the latter category, you'd best be a native.

Open: Lunch Mon–Fri 11:30am–2pm, Sat noon–2:30pm; dinner daily 5:30–10:30pm. *Reservations:* Recommended. *Parking:* Covered lot at The Bay, one block east. *Bus:* 4, 10, or 14 (Douglas St.). NORTH INDIAN

• **Da Tandoor,** 1010 Fort St. near Vancouver St. (tel. 384-6333). *Prices:* Dishes $6.95–$11.95. MC, V.

An elaborately beautiful restaurant with a small dining patio in front, this one's near the east end of Antique Row. The interior gleams with ornamental copperware, in an aromatic atmosphere of spices and incense, with soft, melancholy sitar strains in the background and quietly impeccable service.

The menu is vast and takes some studying. There are cold and hot appetizers like shrimp pakora (marinated in yogurt and ginger), a hearty mulligatawny soup, and plates of Indian tidbits called samosas. Tandoori oven–baked dishes are the specialty, but the chicken curry with ground cashew nuts is also excellent, as is the saag gohst, a lamb preparation. There's a vegetarian lunch buffet with the likes of eggplant bharta and malai kofta, and a choice of Indian desserts like ras malai (sweetened cheese with almonds).

Open: Lunch Tues–Fri 11:30am–2:30pm, dinner Tues–Sun 5–10:30pm. *Reservations:* Recommended. *Parking:* On street. *Bus:* 1. NORTH INDIAN

---

4. Budget Restaurants

• **La Bohème,** 537 Johnson St. opposite Market Square (tel. 385-3551). *Prices:* Tapas $3.75–$7. AE, MC, V.

This former bookstore, antique shop, and art gallery has been reborn as a very Bohemian coffeehouse (downstairs) and an elegant country home (upstairs). The binding link is Rumanian violinist Lache Cercel, who wanders through and entertains. The cold and hot tapas are the order of the day—try Mimi's favorite (cold breast of chicken morsels in a curried peanut sauce with mango chutney) or Sachiko (egg fettuccine in a sauce of coconut milk, bananas, curry, and shrimp). Wines, beers, and liqueurs are served.

Open: Daily 11am–midnight. Upstairs dining room open Mon–Fri noon–3pm, 5:30–10:30pm; Sat 3–10:30pm. *Bus:* 23 or 24 (to Johnson St. Bridge). NOUVELLE

- **James Bay Tea Room,** 332 Menzies St. at Superior (tel. 382-8282). *Prices:* Dinners $7.15–$10.50. MC, V.

Portraits of Queen Elizabeth II and her father, King George VI, hang on the walls of this small white frame house behind the Parliament Buildings. It's English through and through. Hearty breakfasts, like eggs and bangers, are served daily. Lunch features steak-and-kidney pie, Welsh rarebit, and Cornish pasties. A dinner favorite is roast beef and Yorkshire pudding; nightly specials are priced no higher than $8.50. Afternoon tea includes scones with whipped cream and jam.

Open: Breakfast Mon–Sat 7am–11:30am, Sun 8am–12:30pm; lunch Mon–Sat 11:30am–1:30pm; tea daily 1–4:30pm; dinner daily 4:30–9pm. *Reservations:* Recommended. *Bus:* 5. ENGLISH

- **Six Mile Pub,** 494 Island Hwy. (Colwood exit), View Royal (tel. 478-3121). *Prices:* $4.50–$6.95. MC, V.

First opened in 1855 as the Parson's Bridge Hotel, this pub boasts the longest-established liquor license in British Columbia. The current building, erected in 1898, has a loyal local clientele. It has a dark Tudor interior and an outdoor courtyard, and serves standard pub fare as well as deli-style sandwiches.

Open: Daily lunch 11:30am–2pm, dinner 6–9pm; pub open Mon–Sat 11am–1am, Sun 11am–midnight. *Parking:* Free. *Bus:* 50. ENGLISH PUB

- **Wah Lai Yuen,** 560 Fisgard St. (tel. 381-5355). *Prices:* Three-course dinner (for two) $11.50–$19.75. Cash only.

This is a thoroughly local café—Formica tables, an open kitchen, no attempt at creating an atmosphere. There's no need: The food speaks for itself. One man's suggestion for a satiating meal: braised minced-beef soup, prawns with black-bean sauce, sweet-and-sour pork, tofu with mixed vegetables, and steamed rice.

Open: Mon–Sat 10am–9pm, Sun 10am–7pm. *Bus:* 4, 10, or 14 Douglas St.). CANTONESE

- **Wong's,** 548 Fisgard St. (tel. 381-1223). *Prices:* Three-course dinner (for two) $12.75–$25.30. MC, V.

Twenty-six steps above the rest of Chinatown, this spacious dim sum palace obviously believes in fortune and luck: The linen, hanging lanterns, and other trim are all symbolically red, and the placemats elucidate the Chinese zodiac. Luncheon diners enjoy dim sum, the Oriental answer to petits fours; at dinnertime there's a good choice of the likes of garlic black-bean beef, scallops with pea pods, and oysters with ginger and onions—as well as chow mein, chop suey, and other San Francisco-style favorites.

Open: Lunch daily 10am–3pm; dinner Mon–Thurs 4:30pm–

12:30am, Fri–Sat 4:30pm–1:30am, Sun 4:30pm–10pm. *Bus:* 4, 10, or 14 (Douglas St.). DIM SUM/CANTONESE

- **Don Mee Restaurant,** 538 Fisgard St. (tel. 383-1032). *Prices:* Three-course dinner (for two) $12.50–$22.70. MC, V.

A four-foot, gold-colored laughing Buddha, holding auspicious offerings of fruit in his upstretched arms, greets visitors at the foot of the stairs leading to this large and elegant room. Established in the 1920s, Don Mee's has updated its decor (lots of glass) and musical selections (Streisand, Chicago), but still serves such tasty basic fare as dim sum, chop suey (13 kinds), and sweet-and-sour spareribs.

Open: Lunch Mon–Fri 11am–2:30pm, Sat–Sun and holidays 10:30am–2:30pm; dinner Mon–Thurs 5–10:30pm, Fri–Sat 5pm–1:30am, Sun 5–10pm. *Bus:* 4, 10, or 14 (Douglas St.). CANTONESE AND SZECHUAN

- **Café Mexico,** 1425 Store St. (tel. 386-5454). *Prices:* Appetizers $2.75–$15; entrées $4.95–$9.50. MC, V.

A low-lit brick room decorated with lots of greenery and souvenirs from south of the (U.S.) border, this casual restaurant at Market Square is popular with a younger set. Rock music plays not-so-softly in the background, while the kitchen serves up the usual fare of enchiladas, tacos, burritos, chiles rellenos, chimichangas, and fajitas. One dish worth requesting is vista del mar, a grilled flour tortilla topped with prawns and scallops in a wine-cream sauce, covered with melted cheese, avocado, and sour cream.

Open: Sun–Thurs 11:30am–11pm, Fri–Sat 11:30am–midnight. *Bus:* 23 or 24 (to Johnson St. Bridge). MEXICAN

- **Fogg n' Suds,** 711 Broughton St. near Douglas (tel. 383-BEER). *Prices:* Appetizers $2.50–$7.95; entrées $3.95–$9.95. AE, MC, V.

One of a growing chain of B.C. pub restaurants, Fogg n' Suds boasts an international menu: American hamburgers, Mexican nachos, Italian pastas, Japanese yakitori, Greek calamari, German schnitzel . . . for instance. The pub is named in part for Phileas Fogg (of *Around the World in 80 Days*), but the "Suds" take priority: Canada's largest beer list has some 250 brews from 36 countries. (Customers get "passports" stamped for each new beer they consume.) The Victoria restaurant is one of the chain's most elegant, with rich wood decor.

Open: Mon–Sat 11am–1:30am, Sun 11am–midnight. *Bus:* 1, 2, or 5 (Douglas St.). INTERNATIONAL

XIV

WHAT TO SEE AND DO IN VICTORIA

1. THE TOP ATTRACTIONS
2. MORE ATTRACTIONS
3. KIDS' VICTORIA
4. ORGANIZED TOURS
5. SPORTS AND RECREATION

There are three primary elements to Victoria sightseeing: its parks and gardens; its British heritage, much of it reflected in historic homes and buildings; and its excellent museums. Chances are, you'll have bits of all of them in each day of sightseeing.

SIGHTSEEING STRATEGIES

If You Have One Day

Victoria has three essential sights, and today you'll want to see them all. Start with the sights, sounds, even smells, of the Royal British Columbia Museum, Western Canada's finest. Cross Belleville Street to the Empress, the city's world-famous hotel, for lunch or (if you've reserved ahead) an early-afternoon tea. Then head north, up the Saanich Peninsula, to spectacular Butchart Gardens (you can travel there by city bus, tour bus, or private car). These gardens are so memorable, you may want to stay for dinner.

If You Have Two Days

Put on your walking shoes: Victoria is custom-made for the footloose. On the morning of your second day, explore the Inner Harbour area, including the Parliament Buildings, the Royal London Wax Museum, the Undersea Gardens, and the Crystal Garden. Lunch at a restaurant or hotel café overlooking the bustle of boats on James Bay. Then start up Government Street to spend the afternoon touring Downtown and Old Town, with their charming shops and attractions, such as the Maritime Museum (on Bastion Square) and Chinatown. See Chapter XV, "Walking Around Victoria."

If You Have Three Days

Spend days one and two as described above. On your third day, take the one-mile walk (via Antique Row) or a short bus ride (no. 11) out Fort Street to Craigdarroch Castle, the city's most remarkable Victorian mansion. Nearby is the Art Gallery of Greater Victoria, worth an hour's exploration. Then continue east to fashionable Oak Bay for lunch and the remainder of the afternoon. Sealand of the Pacific is at the Oak Bay Marina. If you're driving, return along Beach Drive and Dallas Road for gorgeous seascapes across the Juan de Fuca Strait.

If You Have Five Days or More

There's lots more to see and do in and around Victoria—heritage homes, small galleries, beautiful parks and gardens. But why not get out and discover Vancouver Island? Dive into the spectacular wilderness, hiking in Pacific Rim National Park or Strathcona Provincial Park, whale-watching from Tofino or Ucluelet, fishing at Port Alberni or Campbell River. Or go low-key, and drive to the Native Heritage Centre, the British Columbia Forest Museum, lovely Lake Cowichan, and numerous parks and beaches. For further information, contact the Tourism Association of Vancouver Island, 405 Bastion Square, Suite 302, Victoria, BC V8W 1J1 (tel. 604/382-3551). Another option: Ferry to B.C.'s Gulf Islands or Washington's San Juan Islands, all of them isolated jewels with quiet life-styles.

1. The Top Attractions

Butchart Gardens, 800 Benvenuto Ave., Brentwood Bay, Central Saanich (P.O. Box 4010, Station A, Victoria, BC V8X 3X4) (tel. 652-4422 or 652-5256 for 24-hour recording).

These internationally acclaimed gardens on an arm of the Saanich Inlet, 13 miles (21km) north of Victoria, must not be missed. Comprising 50 acres of a 130-acre (53 ha) private estate, they are considered one of the world's great horticultural achievements. It's hard to believe they had their humble beginning in a limestone quarry.

Robert Butchart, a pioneer Canadian manufacturer of Portland cement, established a home on Tod Inlet in 1904. When he exhausted the limestone deposit near their house, his wife, Jenny, hatched a plan to relandscape the eyesore. Importing topsoil by horse and cart from nearby farmland, she slowly converted the quarry into a stunning showcase known today as the Sunken Garden. So impressed was Mr. Butchart that he populated the garden with birds—ducks, peacocks, and trained pigeons. The Butcharts added a Japanese Garden in 1908, an Italian Garden a few years later, and an English Rose Garden in 1929.

As the fame of the gardens grew, the Butcharts left the cement business and turned their house into an attraction of its own, with a bowling alley, indoor saltwater swimming pool, paneled billiard room, and self-playing Aeolian pipe organ. They named their estate Benvenuto, the Italian word for "Welcome." It now houses offices and the Dining Room restaurant.

The gardens today are owned and administrated by a Butchart grandson, R. Ian Ross. More than half a million visitors tour them each year. Over 1 million plants, in some 700 varieties, ensure uninterrupted bloom from March through October; in winter, the landscaping and shrubbery itself is awesome. Even then, there are plenty of blossoms in the Show Greenhouse.

From June through September, when the gardens are illuminated at night, there's free evening entertainment every night— comedy musical revues, puppet shows, and Saturday-night fireworks. The gardens are also lit during the Christmas season (Dec 1–Jan 6).

Facilities include two year-round restaurants—the Dining Room for gourmet lunches and dinners, afternoon tea, and the summer Benvenuto Buffet; and the Blue Poppy, offering family dining in a flower-filled greenhouse. The Coffee Bar serves snacks and beverages outdoors during the summer season. The Seed & Gift Store is one of the best spots in Victoria to find quality souvenirs. Wheelchairs, baby carts, cameras, and umbrellas are on loan to visitors.

Open: Daily Jan–Feb and Oct–Nov 9am–4pm, Mar–Apr 9am–5pm, May 9am–6pm, June and Sept 9am–9pm, July–Aug 9am–11pm, Dec 9am–8:30pm. *Admission:* Apr–Oct $9.50 adults, $5 students 13–17, $1 children 5–12: Nov–Mar $5 adults, $3 students, 50¢ children. *Bus:* 74.

Royal British Columbia Museum, 675 Belleville St. near Government (tel. 387-3701; recording 387-3014).

This outstanding museum documents the human and natural history of the province in a series of masterful displays.

Start with natural history on the second floor. Learn about fossil prehistory and regional landforms and vegetation. Then enjoy the vast and impressive dioramas—a coastal rainforest, a seacoast, and the Fraser River delta. Each presents typical flora and fauna of the ecozone; the seacoast exhibit even includes live tidepool dwellers.

The third-floor history section is a place to linger for hours. You'll work backward from present day to Native Canadian prehistory, and it's a stunning journey! At the top of the escalator, you can compare artifacts of each decade since the 1920s. Then you enter the brick streets and wooden sidewalks of Old Town (1870–1920), a re-created townscape where you will see silent films at the Roxy Theatre, hear a train rumble through the Port Moody station, and smell the cinnamon in the baker's kitchen of the Grand Hotel. Late 19th-century industry is depicted in dioramas or working models of a farm, salmon cannery, sawmill, coal mine, and gold-sluicing operation. The reconstructed hull of Capt. George Vancouver's H.M.S. *Discovery* is the centerpiece of the presentation on exploration and the fur trade.

Native Canadian history and culture take up the other half of the top floor. The exhibition starts with an audiovisual presentation and an exhibit explaining archeologists' methods of studying ancient cultures. Detailed displays, including some dioramas, portray aspects of the peoples' daily lives—highlighted by a sound-and-light show that makes cosmological myths come alive through masks. As you enter the gallery of coastal tribes' art, including totem poles and a longhouse, note the scale model of a Haida village—it took five years to create. Finally, you'll learn about the influence of white settlement on indigenous culture.

The 535-seat Newcombe Auditorium, on the ground floor, presents a marvelous series of evening programs that has included speakers such as (in 1989–90) Sir Edmund Hillary and scientist and TV personality Dr. David Suzuki. On the adjacent grounds, the Provincial Archives house a wealth of historical documents and photographs; Thunderbird Park hosts demonstrations of tribal totem-pole carving; and 19th-century St. Ann's Schoolhouse is open for inspection.

A tearoom (serving light meals) and an excellent gift shop are located on the main floor.

Open: Daily May–Sept 9:30am–7pm, Oct–Apr 10am–5:30pm. *Closed:* Christmas Day and New Year's Day. *Admission:* Two-day passes, $5 adults, $3 seniors and students 12 to 17, $1 children 6 to 11, free for children under 5. *Bus:* 5, 17, 28, or 30.

2. More Attractions

MUSEUMS AND GALLERIES

Art Gallery of Greater Victoria, 1040 Moss St. near Fort St. (tel. 384-4101).

Located in a historic mansion in the stately Rockland district, the gallery is one of the most important in Canada. Its six halls present permanent collections and temporary exhibits by leading Canadian contemporary artists, important North American and European artists from the 15th to the 20th centuries, and traditional and contemporary Asian artists. In particular, it houses an extensive collection of Japanese and Chinese art, featuring the only Shinto shrine on display in North America.

The gallery is a collector's piece in its own right. The 1889 Spencer Mansion is a Victoriana-lover's dream. Among its eccentricities is a fireplace faced with rare Minton tiles—each one telling part of the legend of King Arthur.

The Gallery Shop has fine art books and reproductions, while Art Rental and Sales offers original work by regional artists. Prior permission is required to photograph.

Open: Mon–Wed and Fri–Sat 10am–5pm, Thurs 10am–9pm, Sun 1–5pm. *Closed:* Mondays, Thanksgiving to Easter. *Admission:* $3 adults, $1.50 seniors and students 12 to 17, free for children under 12. No charge Thurs 5–9pm. *Bus:* 10, 11, or 14.

Royal London Wax Museum, Belleville St. at Menzies, Inner Harbour (tel. 388-4461).

If you've never been to a wax museum, or even if you have, this one is fun. Wax figures of the rich and famous (as well as some poor and infamous) have been crafted at world-famous Tussaud's in London and transported here for display.

The cast includes British royalty, past and present (including Charles and Di); great composers, authors, inventors, and other intelligentsia; Storyland characters, among them Snow White and the Seven Dwarfs, Alice in Wonderland, and the Wizard of Oz; a Galaxy of Stars, including Elvis Presley and Marilyn Monroe with her petticoat flapping in the wind; a Hall of Religion, with great spiritual figures of the ages; and the requisite Chamber of Horrors, a gruesome dungeon of guillotines and Algerian hooks, complete with sound effects.

The exit from the gift shop (don't get too enthusiastic here) leaves you in a parking lot. Circle to your right to return to the main entrance on Belleville Street.

Open: Daily May–Sept 9am–9pm, Oct–Apr 9am–6pm. *Admission:* $5 adults, $4 seniors and students 13 to 19, $2.50 children 5 to 12, free for children under 5; family $18. *Bus:* 5, 27, 28, or 30.

Miniature World, 649 Humboldt St., at the Empress (tel. 385-9731).

An unusual attraction, to say the least, Miniature World began in the late 1960s as the hobby of circus performers Don and Honey Ray. Fascinated by miniatures, they bought them all over the world when they toured, and assembled them into lifelike dioramas when they got back home.

Today, this lilliputian extravaganza in the basement of the Empress has more than 40 displays, depicting everything from historic battles to fairy tales, from the cross-Canada railroad to the world of Charles Dickens, and from an incredible 24-room dollhouse (right down to tiny Delft fireplace tiles) to a circus, with seven animated acts and a midway, that really works!

Open: Daily May–Sept 8:30am–10pm, Oct–April 9:30am–5:30pm. *Admission:* $6 adults, $5 students 12 to 17, $4 children 5 to 11, free for children under 5; 15% family discount. *Bus:* 5, 27, 28, or 30.

Maritime Museum, 28 Bastion Square at Langley St. (tel. 385-4222).

A wealth of artifacts and models connected with British Columbia's nautical history are on display here. They include a 36-foot dugout canoe; two famous vessels, the *Tilikum* and the *Trekka;* and various ship models, naval uniforms, photographs, journals, and other artifacts. The museum is housed in the former B.C. provincial courthouse, built in 1889.

Open: Mon–Sat 10am–4pm, Sun noon–5pm. *Admission:* $4 adults, $3 seniors, $1 students 6 to 18, free for children under 6. *Bus:* 5.

Emily Carr Gallery, 1107 Wharf St. near Fort St. (tel. 387-3080).

Western Canada's most acclaimed artist was a Victoria native. This gallery preserves many of her works, including hundreds of her paintings of totem poles. She was renowned for capturing the early-20th-century life-styles of coastal tribes.

Open: May–Sept. daily 10am–8pm; Oct–Apr, Mon–Sat 10am–5pm. *Admission:* Free.

Classic Car Museum, 813 Douglas St. at Humboldt (tel. 382-7180).

Sixty years of vintage automobiles are on display at this small museum behind the Empress. The sheer functional beauty of some of those Rollses, Jaguars, Chryslers, and ancient Auburns makes some folks itch to get behind the wheels. Also on display are the Crown Jewels of England—in replica, of course.

Open: Daily 9am–6pm. *Admission:* $5 adults, $3 children. *Bus:* 4, 5, 27, 28, or 30.

HISTORIC SITES

Craigdarroch Castle, 1050 Joan Crescent near Fort St. (tel. 592-5323).

This splendid stone mansion on a low hill in the Rockland district was built in 1887–1889 by Robert Dunsmuir, a Scottish immigrant who made a fortune in coal. He spared no expense on what was essentially a status symbol to announce, to all who cared to notice, that he was the richest and most important man in British Columbia. Dunsmuir died shortly before the house was completed; his widow, Joan, lived there until her death in 1908. Subsequently, it became a veterans' hospital and the seat of Victoria College, the school board, and a conservatory of music. In 1979, the Castle Society began to reconstruct the interior as it appeared in the Victorian Age. The society has obtained many of the Dunsmuirs' original paintings and furnishings.

From the outside, Craigdarroch Castle—the name means "rocky oak place" in Gaelic—carries overtones of Dunsmuir's ancestral homeland. Heavy stonework of granite, marble, and sandstone has been shaped into a picture of Elizabethan chimneys soaring above Roman arches, corbeled turrets, and a French Gothic roofline. Within are four floors and 39 rooms with 18 fireplaces, each one different. The finest oak, walnut, mahogany, cedar, spruce, and other woods were used to panel the walls and ceilings, and to create the complicated parquet flooring. Throughout the castle, light is diffracted by art nouveau stained and leaded windows—one of North America's finest collections.

Open: Daily May–Sept 9am–7:30pm, Oct–Apr 10am–4:30pm. *Admission:* $3 adults, $2.50 seniors and students 12 to 17, by donation for children under 12. *Bus:* 11 or 14 (Fort St.).

Helmcken House, 675 Belleville St. (tel. 387-3440 or 387-4697).

The oldest house in British Columbia open to the public, this 1850s residence of a pioneer doctor is a slice of upper-middle-class life 140 years ago. It contains period furnishings and Dr. Helmcken's medicine chest, a superb antique collection brought from England in the colony's early days. The house is located adjacent to the Royal B.C. Museum, in Thunderbird Park. Administered by Victoria Heritage Properties.

Open: Mid–May to mid–Oct, daily 10am–5pm; also Dec 1–31 for Christmas program. *Admission:* Donation. *Bus:* 5, 27, 28, or 30.

Carr House, 207 Government St. at Simcoe (tel. 387-4697).

Situated just a couple blocks from Beacon Hill Park, this quaint 1860s house is notable as the birthplace, in 1871, of artist-author Emily Carr. Demonstrations and furnishings attempt to re-create her life-style. Administered by Victoria Heritage Properties.

Open: Mid–May to mid–Oct, daily 10am–5pm. *Admission:* By donation. *Bus:* 5 (Niagara St.).

Point Ellice House, 2616 Pleasant St., near the Bay Street Bridge (tel. 387-5953 or 387-4697).

British Columbia's largest collection of Victoriana—antiques and furnishings from three generations—are found in this beautiful home. It is surrounded by a magnificent garden, which includes roses planted in the 19th century and still blooming today. Administered by Victoria Heritage Properties.

Open: Mid-May to mid-Oct, daily 10am–5pm. *Admission:* Donation. *Bus:* 14.

Craigflower Farmhouse, 110 Island Hwy., Admirals and Craigflower rds. View Royal (tel. 387-3067).

One of Vancouver Island's first farmhouses, this building was constructed in 1856. It has been painstakingly restored with many period furnishings from Scotland, home of its original owners. Staff in period costume conduct demonstrations of crafts and life-styles, many of them inviting visitor participation. Nearby, the Craigflower Colonial Schoolhouse, oldest standing school building in western Canada, has been restored to its 1855 appearance. Administered by Victoria Heritage Properties.

Open: Mid-May to mid-Oct, daily 10am–5pm. *Admission:* Donation. *Bus:* 14.

Fort Rodd Hill National Historic Park, 501 Belmont Rd., Colwood (tel. 380-4662).

The fort on Rodd Hill was constructed between 1895 and 1900 to protect Royal Navy ships in Esquimalt Harbour against an attack from the sea. After the British garrison was withdrawn in 1906, it became a Canadian base, and remained active for another 50 years. Three separate batteries with gun emplacements make up the defense system.

Open: Daily in summer 8am–8pm, in winter 8am–4:30pm. *Admission:* Free. *Bus:* 52 (transfer from 50).

Fisgard Lighthouse National Historic Site, 501 Belmont Rd., Colwood (tel. 380-4662).

The first permanent light on the Pacific coast of Canada was built in 1860. It still guides vessels through the entrance to Esquimalt Harbour, principally to the navy base in Constance Cove on the opposite shore.

Open: Daily in summer 8am–8pm, in winter 8am–4:30pm. *Admission:* Free. *Bus:* 52 (transfer from 50).

PARKS AND GARDENS

Crystal Garden, 731 Douglas St. at Belleville (tel. 381-1213).

A lush tropical garden in an all-season greenhouse, Crystal Garden is a fascinating example of adaptation for historic preservation.

Across the street from the Victoria Conference Centre, the structure was built in 1925 to hold the largest saltwater pool in the British Empire. Johnny Weissmuller once set a world swimming record here. Ballrooms hosted big-band dances here, and a promenade of flowers hosted many small exhibitions. Soaring maintenance costs forced closure in 1971, but a public outcry prompted the provincial government to invite restoration bids. Crystal Garden reopened about 1980 in its present form.

Today, 47 species of birds live under the glass roof in a garden filled with hundreds of rare and exotic trees, shrubs, and flowers. Flamingos and macaws roam freely; other species are in a half dozen aviaries. A family of pygmy marmosets, "the world's smallest monkeys," other primates, reptiles, and a pair of wallabies fill out the menagerie. Colorful koi fish play in the waters of a stream that runs through the middle of the garden.

Afternoon tea is served daily on the promenade deck ($6.95 plus admission), and a mall of souvenir shops faces Douglas Street.

Open: Daily 10am–9pm. *Admission:* $5.50 adults, $3.50 children 6 to 16, free for children 5 and under. *Bus:* 4, 5, 27, 28, or 30.

Undersea Gardens, 490 Belleville St., Inner Harbour (tel. 382-5717).

A gently sloping stairway takes visitors to a glass-enclosed viewing area at the bottom of the Inner Harbour. There, at eye level, they see some 5,000 marine creatures feeding, playing, hunting, and mating. Among them are sharks, wolf eels, poisonous stonefish, flowerlike sea anemones, and salmon. The highlights are the underwater performances of scuba divers; the star of the show is a huge, nightmarish, but remarkably photogenic octopus named Armstrong.

Open: Daily 10am–5pm. *Admission:* $5.50 adults, $4.50 seniors, $4 students 12 to 17, $2.50 children 5 to 11, free for children under 5; family $14.95. *Bus:* 5, 27, 28, or 30.

Sealand of the Pacific, 1327 Beach Ave., Oak Bay (tel. 598-3373).

Canada's biggest and best oceanarium is located at the Oak Bay Marina. Its hourly shows are superb, especially the orcas (killer whales) that leap, "talk," and splash on command; and the California sea lions, clown princes of the marine world. There are fine exhibits of fur seals and sea otters. In the underwater reef pools, you can view razor-toothed eels, sharks, and salmon. There's also an eerie octopus grotto with Pacific eight-armers measuring 6½ feet across. You can get as close a look as you're liable to want through thick underwater windows.

Open: Mid–June to early Sept, daily 10am–9pm; mid–Mar to mid–June and early Sept–Oct, 10am–5pm; Nov to mid–Mar, Wed–Sun 10am–5pm. *Admission:* $6 adults, $4.50 students 12 to 17, $2.50 children 5 to 11, free for children under 5. *Bus:* 2.

Fable Cottage Estate, 5187 Cordova Bay Rd., Saanich (tel. 658-5741).

This magnificent and enchanting oceanfront estate consists of 3½ acres (1.5 ha) of themed floral gardens laid out around the Fable Cottage. The former residence, whose gingerbread roof makes it look like something out of a fairy tale, is a treasure house of family heirlooms and handcrafted furnishings. The gardens surrounding it have ponds, wishing wells, hidden pathways, a rippling stream, and stunning examples of floral design highlighted by surprising animations of child-size elves and gnomes. A garden tea pavilion serves snacks and refreshments.

Open: Late March–October, 9:30am–dusk. *Admission:* $5.75 adults, $5.25 seniors, $3.75 for ages 5 to 17, $2.75 for children 4 and under. *Bus:* 75.

Beacon Hill Park, between Southgate St. and Dallas Rd., Douglas and Cook sts. (tel. 381-2532).

Victoria's major city park covers 154 acres (62 ha), stretching from just behind the Royal B.C. Museum south ¾ mile to the Juan de Fuca Strait. Within it are groves of trees, gardens, wildflowers, trails, about a mile of pebble beach, and at least a half dozen ponds —all of them wildlife sanctuaries. Notable among the trees are Garry oaks, unique to this coast of Vancouver Island. A lookout on top of Beacon Hill offers a marvelous view across the strait to Washington's Olympic Mountains. The park also contains what is said to be the world's tallest totem pole (128 ft./39m) as well as a children's farm, aviary, tennis courts, bowling green, putting green, cricket pitch, wading pool, playground, picnic area, and a memorial to Scottish poet Robert Burns.

Open: Daily, dawn to dusk. *Admission:* Free. *Bus:* 5.

MISCELLANEOUS ATTRACTIONS

English Village, 429 Lampson St. near Wychbury, Esquimalt (tel. 388-4353; toll free 800/663-6106).

This authentic reproduction of an entire Elizabethan village— William Shakespeare's 16th-century Stratford-upon-Avon—includes the Olde England Inn hotel and restaurant. Shakespeare's birthplace has been replicated, along with the Plymouth Tavern, Garrick Inn, Harvard House, God's Providence House, and numerous other buildings, not the least of which is the Olde Curiosity Shoppe. Anne Hathaway's Cottage, the thatched, beamed, and shingled house of Shakespeare's wife, seems to be the main attraction, fully furnished with period antiques. The inn itself is a museum: The entry hall is replete with suits of armor, ancient weaponry, banners, and a huge copper-canopied fireplace. A fine restaurant serves teas and gourmet English food like Cumberland broth and rabbit pye (the original spelling).

Open: Daily in summer 9am–9pm, in winter 10am–5pm. *Admission:* $4 adults, $2.50 seniors and students 8 to 17, free for children under 8. *Bus:* 24.

Dominion Astrophysical Observatory, 5071 West Saanich Rd., Saanich (tel. 388-0001).

Located atop Little Saanich Mountain just west of Elk Lake, about 10 miles (16km) north of Victoria, this observatory offers stargazers a stunning view of the universe on clear Saturday nights. The view from the top during the day is also worth the drive.

Open: Mon–Fri 8:30am–4:30pm. Observations Sat 9–11pm only. *Admission:* Free.

Government House, 1401 Rockland Ave. near Lotbiniere (tel. 387-2080).

The official residence of the lieutenant governor, who represents the British Crown in British Columbia, is not open to the public—but the grounds are! Lovers of parks and gardens find that the manicured lawns, flowering shrubs, and flower beds make a wonderful place for a stroll.

Open: Daily dawn to dusk (grounds only). *Admission:* Free. *Bus:* 1.

Royal Roads Military College, 2050 Sooke Rd., Colwood (tel. 380-4508).

There may have been no reason for James Dunsmuir to one-up his late father, Robert Dunsmuir, who built Craigdarroch Castle in 1889. Nevertheless, early in the 20th century, James commissioned noted architect Samuel Maclure to build him a mansion to end all Victorian mansions. Completed in 1908, "Dunsmuir Castle" was indeed enormous—three times the size of Craigdarroch. The grounds, 650 acres at Hatley Park, 8 miles (13km) southwest of Victoria, were so extensive that a crew of over 100 maintained them. Today a military college has taken over Dunsmuir's home—sometimes called Hatley Castle—but the gardens and grounds are open to the public.

Open: Daily 10am–4pm (grounds only). *Admission:* Free. *Bus:* 52, 53, or 61.

Parliament Buildings, 501 Belleville St., Inner Harbour (tel. 387-3046 or 382-2127).

Architect Francis Rattenbury designed and constructed these buildings in 1897, commemorating the diamond jubilee of Queen Victoria's reign. Lit in the evening by more than 3,000 light bulbs, the buildings are nearly as remarkable a landmark as the Empress hotel. Free tours of the complex are offered weekdays by reservation, except when the house is sitting.

The British Columbia legislature bears a certain resemblance to the British House of Commons, at least in the ceremonial trappings. The Speaker sits on a kind of canopied throne. He is escorted by a sergeant-at-arms. The symbol of his authority is a golden mace—now purely ornamental, but originally a very handy implement to use on the heads of obstreperous members who "disturbed the assembly."

Open: Mon–Fri 9am–5pm. *Admission:* Free. *Bus:* 5, 27, 28, or 30.

3. Kids' Victoria

A few suggestions on how to entertain the children during your Victoria stay:

Land of the Little People, 321 Belleville St., Inner Harbour (tel. 385-1735).

Laid out in a charming garden setting is a series of toy delights: a collection of dollhouses, a model railroad (you can run it yourself), an English village green, a pond with Japanese koi fish, a 1900s-style Main Street, and a superb model of London's Tower Bridge. In between are waterfalls, Japanese dwarf bonsai trees and shrubs, a wishing pond, and a Belgian chocolate factory.

Open: Daily 10am–7pm. *Admission:* $2.75 adults, $2 seniors and students 12 to 16, free for children under 12 with parent. *Bus:* 5, 27, 28, or 30.

Other attractions have been discussed in the previous pages:

Beacon Hill Children's Farm, in Beacon Hill Park (see "More Attractions: Parks and Gardens," above), offers a petting zoo, pony rides, and other activities with young farm animals.

Crystal Garden (see "More Attractions: Parks and Gardens," above), with its free-flying macaws and footloose flamingos make it an exciting destination.

Fable Cottage Estate (see "More Attractions: Parks and Gardens," above) is like a fairy tale come true, with its gingerbread-roofed house and animated elves peeking through the garden.

Miniature World's animated circus (see "More Attractions: Museums and Galleries," above) is the icing on the cake for kids who have already marveled at the scenes of battles, the railroad diorama, the reborn fairy tales, and the great dollhouse.

The **Royal British Columbia Museum** (see "The Top Attractions," above) provides a fascinating learning experience. Children especially like the natural-history dioramas, the re-created Old Town, the hull of Captain Vancouver's ship, and the sound-and-light show on Native Canadian myths.

Some children like the **Royal London Wax Museum**'s Storyland (see "More Attractions: Museums and Galleries," above). Others prefer the Chamber of Horrors. You probably already know which one your kids will like best.

Sealand of the Pacific (see "More Attractions: Parks and Gardens," above) is a great place to spend an afternoon, watching the trained killer whales and the hilarious sea lions.

Undersea Gardens (see "More Attractions: Parks and Gardens," above) are a window into another world. Here, the youngsters can stare down a toothy wolf eel or gawk at Armstrong the giant octopus.

If you're staying more than a few days with the children, you'll want to get your hands on a copy of *Kids! Kids! Kids! and Vancouver Island,* written by Daniel Wood and Betty Campbell.

And then there are the times you'd like a day of your own — and the kids might, too. **Child's Eye View,** 520-620 View St. (tel. 384-7228), is a child-care service that will take your youngster on small-group excursions to many of the attractions mentioned above. The professional staff will pick up the children at your hotel, give them lunch, and cover all admissions and transportation for $45 a day ($30 mornings only, $25 afternoons only).

4. Organized Tours

Perhaps you're one of those travelers who prefers to let someone else handle your sightseeing arrangements. Transportation, admissions, timing, and narration are things you'd prefer not to worry about. Listed below are several of the tours available.

All Seasons Fun Tours, Box 5396, Station B, Victoria V8R 6S4 (tel. 604/383-3828).

Custom-made tours in a private luxury van; $38 per hour per party, $10 additional for videotaping.

C to C Tours, Box 6308, Station C, Victoria V8P 5M3 (tel. 604/727-2736).

Educational topical tours in a luxury van; 3½–4 hours, $30–$35 per person. Trips depart at 9am and 2pm, focusing on gardens, castles, artists, and shopping. A summer-night trip to Butchart's Gardens departs at 6:30pm.

Gray Line of Victoria, 700 Douglas St., Victoria V8W 2B3 (tel. 604/388-5248; toll free 800/663-8390).

Grand City Tour, 1½ hours, $10.50 adults, $5.25 children. Schedule varies by season, from half-hourly 9:30am–7pm in mid-summer to once daily (at 2pm) Nov 1–Mar 10.

Butchart Gardens, 3 hours, $21 adults, $17 juniors, $10.50 children. Schedule varies by season, from hourly 9am–4pm in midsummer (with a dinner tour at 5pm and an evening tour at 7pm) to once daily at 12 noon in early Nov and late Mar. No tours mid–Nov to mid–Mar.

Other seasonal tours take in English Village, Point Ellice House, Craigdarroch Castle, Fable Cottage Estate, Sealand, lower Vancouver Island, and the Gulf Islands.

Heritage Tours, 180 Goward Rd., RR #7, Victoria V8X 3X3 (tel. 604/474-4332).

Tours of the city, Butchart Gardens, and Craigdarroch Castle in British Daimler limousines. Rates start at $45 per hour, but are per vehicle, not per person. The limo can hold up to six adults. May–Sept only.

---

5. Sports and Recreation

SPORTS

Victoria isn't a hotbed of action for spectators. The **University of Victoria** men's and women's basketball teams are consistent contenders for the Canadian national collegiate championship. Ice hockey, of course, is a major draw, especially the **Victoria Cougars,** who play a winter-long minor-league schedule in the Western Hockey League against teams from B.C., Alberta, Washington, and Oregon. The Cougars play from November to March at the Victoria Memorial Arena, Blanshard and Caledonia streets. Games are at 7pm; call 604/384-1522 for tickets.

RECREATION

Victoria and Vancouver Island *are* tremendous places to be if you're an outdoors lover. The following listing can only provide a sampling of what's available.

Beaches

In this Canadian sun belt, the most popular is **Willows Beach,** along the Esplanade in Oak Bay. It has a park with a playground and snack bar. A good approach is by Dalhousie Street, off Cadboro Bay Road. Other excellent beaches are at **Gyro Beach Park** on Cadboro Bay near the University of Victoria; **McNeill Bay** near Gonzales Point, Victoria's southeasternmost cape; and **Saxe Point Park** and **MacAulay Point Park,** both in Esquimalt. The inland lakes have fine freshwater swimming, as well: Try **Elk Lake,** on Patricia Bay Road 7 miles (11km) north of downtown Victoria; and **Thetis Lake,** about 6 miles (10km) west. Be aware that at the latter, nude sunbathers often seek out secluded spots.

Bicycling

This is a favorite way of getting around Victoria. A favored route for visitors is the 8-mile (13km) **Scenic Marine Drive,** following Dallas Road and Beach Drive along the city's south shore, then returning to downtown via Oak Bay Avenue. For rental locations, see Chapter XI, "Getting to Know Victoria: Getting Around."

Boating

Numerous operators have vessels for charter hire, "bareboat" rental, or skippered rental, for periods from a few hours to several weeks. Check **Pedder Bay Marina,** Pedder Bay Drive, Metchosin (tel. 478-1771); and **Brentwood Inn Resort,** 7171 Brentwood Drive, Brentwood Bay (tel. 652-3151).

Sailors can listen to a taped marine forecast by calling 656-7515. Those unfamiliar with local waters, or unsure of their own skills, might want to consult **Horizon Yacht Centre,** 1327 Beach Drive, at Oak Bay Marina (tel. 595-2628), or the **Canadian Power Squadrons,** 1608 Quadra St. (tel. 383-6677).

Canoeing/Kayaking

The lakes and indented coastline of southeastern Vancouver Island are ideal for the paddle sports. Even more thrilling—for ocean kayaking, in particular—are the offshore Gulf Islands. A growing number of outfitters package trips for visitors. Some of the best are offered by **Gulf Island Kayaking,** RR #1, Galiano Island, BC V0N 1P0 (tel. 604/539-2442). The **Victoria Canoe and Kayak Club** (tel. 382-1077) can provide full information on how and where to get started.

Diving

Both coasts of Vancouver Island have excellent diving. The strong tidal currents around the Gulf Islands, and further south where the Strait of Georgia meets the Juan de Fuca Strait, create an ideal environment for rich and varied marine life, including abalone, scallops, sea cucumbers, forests of kelp, and much more. Along the coast of Pacific Rim National Park, west of Victoria, a stretch of sea known as "the graveyard of the Pacific" has literally dozens of shipwrecks, most from the late 19th and early 20th centuries.

Information, equipment, and diving courses are available from **Ocean Centre,** 800 Cloverdale Ave. (tel. 386-7528); **Frank**

White's Scuba Shop, 1855 Blanshard St. (tel. 385-4713); and the **Brentwood Bay Dive Shop,** 1205 Verdier St., Brentwood Bay (tel. 652-1933).

Fishing

Vancouver Island has some of the best saltwater and freshwater fishing in the world. Many of the lakes are regularly stocked with rainbow and cutthroat trout and steelhead, while char, kokanee, brown trout, and trophy-size smallmouth bass are also common. In the Victoria area, Elk and Beaver lakes (8 miles/13km north via Patricia Bay Rd.) and Shawnigan Lake (39 miles/63km northwest via Hwy. 1 and Shawnigan Lake Rd.) are especially well stocked.

Saltwater fish include all species of salmon (chinook, coho, pink, sockeye, and chum), halibut, ling cod, rockfish, and snapper.

You need a license to fish in British Columbia if you're 15 (for tidal waters) or 16 (for freshwater or nontidal waters). Regulations change frequently, as dictated by fish conservation studies, so current rules should be checked in the annual B.C. Fishing Regulations Synopsis. No license is required for catching shellfish, though size restrictions apply.

The B.C. Department of Fisheries (tel. 388-3252 during office hours) has a 24-hour phone line open spring, summer, and fall (tel. toll free 800/663-9333). It gives recorded information of interest to every fisherperson: openings, closings, and restrictions, where the big ones are hitting and what lures they're hitting on.

Numerous fishing operators have charters available. Their packages typically include hotel pickup, fishing license, tackle, and a light lunch. Rates vary, but can typically run $75 per person per half-day charter.

Golf

Golf seems tailor-made for Victoria. The mild climate, the Scottish-English heritage, and the rolling landscape combine to make this an extremely popular year-round sport for residents and visitors alike.

Public courses in or near the city include **Cedar Hill Municipal Golf Course,** just 2 miles (3.2km) from downtown at 1400 Derby St. (tel. 595-3103), and **Mount Douglas Golf Course,** 4225 Blenkinsop Rd. (tel. 477-8314), about 3½ miles (5.6km) away. Numerous other public courses are north, up the Saanich Peninsula, or west, toward Sooke.

Leading private clubs, which may have reciprocal privileges with other North American clubs, include **Victoria Golf Club,** 1110 Beach Drive, Oak Bay (tel. 598-4321); **Uplands Golf Club,** 3300 Cadboro Bay Rd., Oak Bay (tel. 592-7313); **Gorge Vale Golf Club,** 1005 Craigflower Road, Esquimalt (tel. 386-3401); and **Royal Colwood Golf & Country Club,** 629 Goldstream Rd., Colwood (tel. 478-8331).

Hiking

There are some fine trails in **Thetis Lake Park** and **Goldstream Provincial Park** near Victoria. But serious backpackers head to huge (810-square-mile/2,100km²) **Strathcona Provincial Park** (200 miles/320km north of Victoria via Hwys. 1 and 19 to Campbell

River, then west on Hwy. 28), or to **Pacific Rim National Park** (65 miles/105km west via Hwy. 14 to Port Renfrew). Strathcona's Forbidden Plateau is speckled with alpine lakes, but the Pacific Rim's **West Coast Trail,** extending 48 miles (77km) from Port Renfrew to Bamfield, is the target of many experienced hikers. Established long ago as a lifesaving trail for shipwrecked sailors, it is rugged and often wet, and takes a week end-to-end at an average pace. Whales can frequently be seen from the trail. (Bamfield, at the trail's western terminus, is reached by ferry from Port Alberni).

Victoria's **West Coast Outdoor Recreation Society,** 204-3293 Douglas St. (tel. 604/388-6632), provides a general information service to hikers planning to tackle the trail. The society also operates a "need-a-partner" computer data bank, and offers summer outings.

Hunting

See Chapter VII, "What to See and Do in Vancouver," for information on hunting licenses and regulations in B.C.

Ice Skating

The most centrally located rink is **Victoria Memorial Arena,** 1625 Blanshard St. (tel. 384-0444). Others are located at the **George R. Pearkes Recreation Complex,** 3100 Tillicum Rd. (tel. 388-6664); the **Oak Bay Recreation Centre,** 1975 Bee St. (tel. 595-7946); and the **Juan de Fuca Recreation Centre,** 1767 Island Hwy., Colwood (tel. 478-8384). Skates are generally available for rent.

Sailboarding

This new sport—which combines surfboard and sail—is better known as windsurfing. You may see occasional adventurers dodging boats on the Inner Harbour, but novices are usually advised to try **Elk Lake,** eight miles (13km) north of Victoria, and experts are steered to **Lake Nitinat** in Pacific Rim National Park, some 100 miles (160km) northwest via Lake Cowichan.

Beginning and advanced instruction is offered by **Active Sports,** 1620 Blanshard St. (tel. 381-SAIL). Board rentals start at $10, beginner lessons (including board and wet suit) at $25. A unique sailboarding simulator helps first-timers get their balance and learn to set the sail before they ever enter the water.

Sailing

Lessons are offered by Victoria Sailing School, 1010 Wharf St. (tel. 384-7245), and **Horizon Yacht Centre,** 1327 Beach Drive, at Oak Bay Marina (tel. 595-2628). Many boat charter operators also have sailboats available for rent by experienced sailors.

For a short sail around the Inner Harbour in a Crown 23 craft, try **Sunshine Sail** (tel. 380-7582). Yachts cruise daily except Saturday 10am to sunset. Rates are $10 per person per hour for four-person cruises, $20 per hour for a solo sailor. The minimum is two hours. Children under 5 are free.

If you're contemplating a sail to the Gulf Islands, check with **Aboard/Ashore Sailing Vacations,** 120-645 Fort St. (tel. 604/382-0332). For $155 to $175 per person per day, you get not only the boat, but also a skipper and crew, plus meals and accommodation en route.

Skiing

The mountains in central Vancouver Island rise to over 7,200 feet (2,200m). At this latitude (50°N), that's plenty high enough for a snow cover—and good skiing. The Comox Valley, for instance, gets an astonishing annual snowfall of about 472 inches (1,200cm).

The major resort is **Mt. Washington,** P.O. Box 3069, Courtenay, BC V9N 5N3 (tel. 604/338-1386), in the Comox Valley 5 hours' drive north of Victoria. The third largest area in British Columbia, it has a 1,600-foot (492m) vertical drop and 20 groomed runs for novices, intermediates, and experts, serviced by four chair lifts and a beginners' tow. The area also has 19 miles (31km) of track-set nordic trails, connecting to Strathcona Provincial Park. Full-day rates are $26 for adults, with equipment rentals $16 daily. Open daily in winter. Snow report: 338-1515.

Nearby **Forbidden Plateau,** 2050 Cliffe Ave., Courtenay, BC V9N 2L3 (tel. 604/334-4744), is the island's oldest ski resort, having opened in 1950. It has a 1,150-foot (354m) vertical and 12 groomed runs, with one chair lift, three T-bars, and a rope tow. Full-day adult rates are $20; complete equipment rentals are $14. Open Friday, Saturday, and Sunday in winter. Snow report: 338-1919.

The nearest ski area to Victoria is **Mount Arrowsmith,** P.O. Box 265, Port Alberni, BC V9Y 7M7 (tel. 604/723-9592). It's "only" 120 miles (193 km) from the British Columbia capital, a solid 3½-hour drive in winter. Arrowsmith caters primarily to novices, with a 1,000-foot vertical, six runs, two T-bars and a rope tow.

Near the north end of Vancouver Island, **Mount Cain,** P.O. Box 1225, Port McNeill, BC V0N 2R0 (tel. 604/281-0244 or 956-3792), also offers novice alpine and cross-country skiing.

There are several ski shops in Victoria. For rentals, sales, and service, try **Snow Magic,** 485-C Burnside Rd. East (tel. 383-5655), or **Manfred's Ski Shop,** 1684 Douglas St. (tel. 380-1010).

Swimming

Crystal Pool, 2275 Quadra St. (tel. 383-2522), is Victoria's largest aquatic facility, with a 50-meter lap pool, a separate children's pool, diving pool, sauna, whirlpool, weight and aerobics rooms, and a cafeteria-lounge. It's open 18 hours a day.

Other good public pools are at **Juan de Fuca Recreation Centre,** 1767 Island Hwy., Colwood (tel. 478-8384); **Oak Bay Recreation Centre,** 1975 Bee St. (tel. 595-7946); **Esquimalt Pool,** 527 Fraser St. (tel. 386-6128); **Gordon Head Recreation Centre,** 1744 Feltham Rd. (tel. 477-1871); and, of course, the **YM-YWCA,** 880 Courtney St. (tel. 386-7511).

All Fun Recreation Park, 650 Hordon Rd. (tel. 474-4546 or 474-3184), is 8 miles (13km) northwest of Victoria, off Millstream Road. In addition to a ¾-mile waterslide complex, it has a mini-golf course, bumper boats, go-kart track, games parlor, RV park, gift shop, and ice cream caboose. The Western Speedway drag-racing track is adjacent.

Whale Watching

Most of this takes place on trips from Tofino or Ucluelet, about halfway up Vancouver Island's west coast. But there is one firm that takes visitors on trips of 1½ to 3 hours from Victoria's Inner Harbour into the Gulf Islands or San Juan Islands, with sightings of orcas (killer whales) and porpoises likely during season (May–Sept). **Sea Coast Expeditions and Research,** 1655 Ash Rd., (tel. 477-1818) has biologist guides aboard its Zodiac boats during their 20- to 50-mile trips. Rates are $25 to $50 for adults (kids under 14 half-price), or $75 for a *guaranteed* whale sighting. Sea lions and marine birds are always around.

WALKING AROUND VICTORIA

1. Inner Harbour

Logically and geographically, the best launching pad for sightseeing is the **Tourism Victoria Information Centre** (1), at Wharf and Government streets on the Inner Harbour. With a highly knowledgeable staff, unfailing helpfulness, and an immense stock of maps, timetables, brochures, and pamphlets, the center can save valuable holiday time and shoe leather, as well as tipping the visitor off to local sights he or she might otherwise have missed.

Walk south, along the causeway facing James Bay. On your left is the **Empress** hotel (2) (see Chapter XII, "Victoria Accommodations"). As you follow the harbor shore west, you look south at Victoria's other major landmark, the **Parliament Buildings** (3) (see Chapter XIV, "What to See and Do in Victoria"). Beside the province's legislative center lies **Heritage Court** (4), a superb combination of concrete buildings and native plant gardens which you enter by stepping over the petrified prints of a dinosaur. The **Netherlands Carillon,** a gift from the Dutch nation, rises like a slender white column 88 feet (27m) from the mall floor, carrying bells weighing 10,612 pounds (4,813kg).

Opposite the legislative lawns, at Belleville and Menzies streets, you'll spot some horse-drawn carriages in front of **Confederation Garden** (5). From 10am to 11pm, they offer relaxed tours of this corner of Victoria for up to six people. Rates per carriage (not per person) are $1 per minute, up to an hour. The centerpiece of the garden, a monument to Canadian confederation, is a huge bronze sculpture displaying the coats of arms of the 10 provinces and the federal coat of arms.

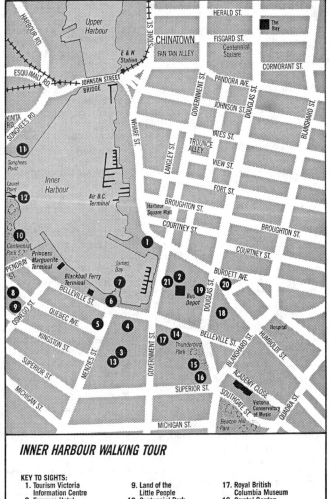

INNER HARBOUR WALKING TOUR

KEY TO SIGHTS:

1. Tourism Victoria Information Centre
2. Empress Hotel
3. Parliament Buildings
4. Heritage Court
5. Confederation Garden
6. Royal London Wax Museum
7. Undersea Gardens
8. Heritage Village
9. Land of the Little People
10. Centennial Park
11. Songhees Point Development
12. Fisherman's Wharf
13. James Bay Inn
14. Thunderbird Park
15. Helmcken House
16. St. Ann's Schoolhouse
17. Royal British Columbia Museum
18. Crystal Garden
19. Victoria Conference Center
20. Classic Car Museum
21. Miniature World

Across Belleville Street are two of Victoria's major tourist attractions—the **Royal London Wax Museum** (6) and the **Undersea Gardens** (7). (See Chapter XIV for details on both.) Behind the wax museum is the terminal of Black Ball Transport's M.V. *Coho,* a ferry which plies the international route to Port Angeles, Washington. Further down the harbor shore is a terminal owned by B.C. Stena Lines, which runs daily service to Seattle. (See Chapter XI, "Getting to Know Victoria," for information on arriving by ship.) Opposite the latter terminal, on the south side of Belleville, is the Captain's Palace hotel and restaurant, with its adjacent **Heritage Village** (8) and **Land of the Little People** (9) (see Chapter XIV).

Centennial Park (10), a lovely and painstakingly maintained stretch of city-owned shoreline, includes Laurel Point and Laurel Point Inn with its views of the Empress to the east and outer Victoria Harbour to the west. On the shore opposite the promontory rises the new **Songhees Point Development** (11). Once an industrial zone, this area will soon boast two new luxury hotels, condominium towers, restaurants, pubs, and a walkway through the encircling park.

Follow the main thoroughfare west through a series of staggered junctions and you'll come to **Fisherman's Wharf** (12) at St. Lawrence and Erie streets. Home to Victoria's largest concentration of fishing boats, this is a great place to catch the flavor of the maritime industry—and buy fresh seafood—when the fleet is in.

Return one block north on St. Lawrence and turn east on Superior Street. Continue through three residential blocks to the corner of Menzies Street. The **James Bay Inn** (13), on your right, is one of Victoria's oldest hotels, dating from 1907. It was the last home of famed artist Emily Carr. Across Menzies, you're in the government district, with the Parliament Buildings on your left and various provincial office buildings on your right.

Turn north (left) on Douglas Street. About halfway down the block, bear left into **Thunderbird Park** (14), notable for its awesome wooden totem poles. Here you'll find two important 1850s heritage buildings—the **Helmcken House** (15), home of a pioneer doctor, and **St. Ann's Schoolhouse** (16)—and beyond them the **Royal British Columbia Museum** (17) (see Chapter XIV for details on these attractions).

Continue north on Douglas across Belleville Street. On your left is the city bus depot, where connections are made to Vancouver (via ferry) and to other Vancouver Island destinations. On your right is the **Crystal Garden** (18), once the British Empire's largest saltwater swimming pool, now a lovely greenhouse full of tropical vegetation and birds (see Chapter XIV).

Across the street, north of the bus depot, is the new **Victoria Conference Centre** (19), 720 Douglas St. (tel. 386-6338). Opened in 1989, this attractive two-level structure accommodates groups up to 1,500 people. It was designed with an eye to history as well as to efficiency, since it adjoins the famous Empress hotel. The gardens and foyer, both open to the public, display fine art by provincial artists, including a totem pole commissioned by master carver Tony Hunt. (Look for Qwawina, the raven, on top; Sisiutl, the double-headed serpent, in the middle; and Nanis, the grizzly bear, holding a halibut at the bottom.) Nineteen stores make up a shopping plaza around the perimeter of the conference center; they include arts, fashion, jewelry, and other gift outlets.

At the northeast corner of Douglas and Humboldt streets is the **Classic Car Museum** (20). Turn left on Humboldt; halfway down this block, in a side door of the Empress hotel, is **Miniature World** (21). (See Chapter XIV for details on both these attractions). The info center—this walk's starting point—is another half block ahead.

---

2. Downtown/Old Town

The Tourism Victoria Information Centre (1) is also the launching pad for this walk. Head north on Government Street, a quaint, somewhat narrow thoroughfare lined with shops. The oldest brick building in British Columbia, the **Windsor Hotel building** (2) (1858), survives at the northeast corner of Courtney Street (901 Government St.); today, its bricks have been timbered over, and it houses gift shops. Canadian Customs is at the intersection's southwest corner; the two-story Harbour Square Mall shopping plaza is at the northwest corner.

The corner of Broughton and Government streets, another block north, marks the southeast corner of the former **Fort Victoria** (3), constructed by the Hudson's Bay Company in 1843 as the western headquarters of the company's fur-trading empire. Located within the area now bounded by Government and Wharf streets, Broughton Street and Bastion Square, it featured 22-foot (7m) cedar pickets and two octagonal bastions. It was torn down in 1858 when the Fraser River gold rush led to a real-estate boom.

Just past View Street, a little byway cuts off on the right, running one block west to Broad Street. This is **Trounce Alley** (4), where bearded miners and roisterous mariners once clustered to spend their gold on female entertainment. A lot of paint, soap, and affection has gone into making this wee lane a kind of welcome mat. Lit by gas lamps, hung with heraldic crests, ablaze with flower baskets and potted shrubs, Trounce Alley now offers jewelry, fashions, edibles, and souvenirs.

From Broad Street, circle back west down View Street into **Bastion Square** (5). In the late 19th century, this area was bustling with waterfront hotels, saloons, and warehouses. Today it's an enchantingly restored pedestrian mall, with the raucousness ironed out and the face-lifted old buildings crammed with restaurants, offices, and art galleries. On the site now occupied by the **Maritime Museum** (6) (see Chapter XIV, "What to See and Do in Victoria") was the police barracks, where convicted murderers were publicly hanged and buried. Their bones may still lie beneath the paving of the square.

You can get a good feel for the city's historic preservation efforts by strolling through some of Old Town's alleyways. From Bastion Square, turn north up Commercial Alley. Cross Yates Street, and a few steps further west, turn north again up Waddington Alley. On the other side of Johnson Street is **Market Square** (7), a shopping center made up of beautifully restored historic buildings. Its 40 stores include seven restaurants, numerous arts-and-crafts shops, bookstores, boutiques, and gift shops. They occupy two levels surrounding an open-air terrace, popular for lunching any time of year, but especially on summer weekends when bands and individual musicians often perform to an appreciative audience.

On its western side, Market Square faces the **Johnson Street Bridge** (8), the main link between downtown Victoria and the Esquimalt peninsula. The VIA Rail/Esquimalt & Nanaimo Railroad terminal is just across Store Street. Go north two blocks on Store; across Herald Street, on the left, is the **Harbour Public Market** (9), the city's major market for fresh produce.

Return down Store Street one block and turn east on Fisgard Street. You're now in **Chinatown** (10)—known to many facetious Victoria residents as "China block." In fact, it occupies about a block and a half of Fisgard. Nevertheless, this is Canada's oldest Chinatown, established in 1858 when the first Chinese arrived as gold seekers and railroad workers; at one time it covered six city blocks and had a permanent population of around 3,000. Today, most of the buildings are restaurants and gift shops, but three features are of special interest.

Spanning Fisgard on the west side of Government Street is the **Gate of Harmonious Interest** (11). Built in 1981, its lavish detail, including dragon-head moldings, symbolized the completion of a major revitalization of the Chinatown area. Extending one block south from Fisgard, about 50 yards west of the gate, is **Fan Tan Alley** (12), the narrowest street in Canada. Not more than 4 feet wide in places, this was the main entrance in the late 19th century to a maze of streets that comprised "Little Canton." Opium smoking, gambling, and prostitution were rampant behind its doors. At the east end of Chinatown, halfway down the block between Government and Douglas streets, the **Chinese School House** (13) (built in 1907), with its tiled pagoda-style roof, recessed balconies, and "lucky" colors of red and gold, is the best surviving example of early Chinatown architecture.

Centennial Square (14), a 1962 urban development project, occupies the block south of Fisgard. Surrounding a modernistic fountain and the **Floral Knot Garden** (15), a replica of one in England's Hampton Court, are the restored 1878 **City Hall** (16), the **Victoria Police Department** (17), a carpark, shopping arcade, senior citizens' recreation center, and the **McPherson Playhouse** (18) (tel. 386-6121). Victoria's main performing arts center occupies the former Pantages Theatre, a vaudeville establishment restored to its 1912 baroque Edwardian style.

From City Hall, at the southeast corner of Centennial Square, proceed east one block on Pandora Avenue. The building at the southeast corner of Blanshard Street is **Congregation Emanu-El Synagogue** (19), built in 1863 and now a national historic site. It is the oldest surviving Jewish temple both in Canada and on the west coast of North America.

Were you to continue farther east on Pandora, you'd encounter a downtown "church row"—Baptist, Methodist, Gospel, and Seventh-Day Adventist places of worship within the next two blocks. Instead, turn south on Blanshard, down "cinema row" and past the impressive **St. Andrew's Roman Catholic Cathedral** (20) at the corner of View Street. Turn east (left) one block further, on Fort Street, onto **Antique Row** (21). Extending for three blocks to

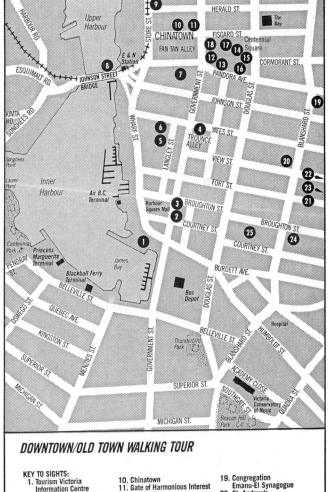

DOWNTOWN/OLD TOWN WALKING TOUR

KEY TO SIGHTS:
1. Tourism Victoria Information Centre
2. Windsor Hotel Building
3. Fort Victoria site
4. Trounce Alley
5. Bastion Square
6. Maritime Museum
7. Market Square
8. Johnson Street Bridge
9. Harbour Public Market
10. Chinatown
11. Gate of Harmonious Interest
12. Fan Tan Alley
13. Chinese School House
14. Centennial Square
15. Floral Knot Garden
16. City Hall
17. Victoria Police Department
18. McPherson Playhouse
19. Congregation Emanu-El Synagogue
20. St. Andrew's Roman Catholic Cathedral
21. Antique Row
22. Pioneer Square
23. Christ Church Cathedral
24. Royal Theatre
25. Central Library

Cook Street, the concentration of shops here carries everything from 19th century furniture, crystal, and paintings to rare stamps, coins, and books. Just a few blocks beyond Cook, it approaches the

Art Gallery of Greater Victoria and **Craigdarroch Castle** (see Chapter XIV).

Turn right off Antique Row at Quadra Street. A short block south is **Pioneer Square** (22), one of the oldest cemeteries in British Columbia. Hudson's Bay Company fur traders, ship captains and crew members from British Royal Navy vessels lie beneath the sandstone markers. Guided tours of this graveyard as well as of Ross Bay Cemetery, between Dallas and Fairfield roads, are offered Sundays most of the year by the Old Cemeteries Committee (tel. 384-0045). **Christ Church Cathedral** (23), seat of the bishop of the Roman Catholic Diocese of British Columbia, overlooks the park at Quadra and Courtney streets.

Now head back to the starting point by walking west on Courtney. Look north toward Broughton as you cross Blanshard; the **Royal Theatre** (24) (tel. 385-6515), on the right side of the street, is the home of the Victoria Symphony and host to many touring and local groups. In the next block on Courtney is Victoria's **Central Library** (25). When Courtney hits Government Street, turn left, and you're at the info center again.

XVI

VICTORIA SHOPPING

1. Best Buys

Visitors to Victoria generally find their greatest shopping joys in traditional English goods, both antique and modern, and in British Columbian arts and crafts.

As in Vancouver, the cornerstones of shopping are the two big department stores, **The Bay** (Hudson's Bay Company) and **Eaton's.** The Bay, 1701 Douglas St. between Fisgard and Herald sts. (tel. 385-1311), is long established as Victoria's leading department store; of course, it was the Hudson's Bay Company that founded the city! Eaton's has a major outlet in a suburban shopping mall, but its showcase is the new **Victoria Eaton Centre** (tel. 381-4012), which occupies most of two city blocks between Government and Douglas, Yates and View streets. Eaton's (tel. 382-7141) and 17 shops opened here in March 1989; another 158 shops and restaurants were ready for the buyers' onslaught in summer 1990. The unique architecture of this four-story complex incorporated several late-19th-century buildings and includes two small park areas with fountains and reflecting pools, as well as a rooftop garden patio.

As for shopping streets: **Government Street** from Humboldt to Yates, a five-block stretch, is the prime area to seek out British goods and Canadian crafts. **Fort Street** from Blanshard to Cook is known as "Antique Row" for the number of collectibles shops and auction houses in those three blocks. **Lower Johnson Street,** in the two long blocks from Wharf to Douglas streets, has earned a reputation for the trendy and avant-garde. And **Oak Bay Village,** especially Oak Bay Avenue from Foul Bay Road to Monterey Street (six blocks), so resembles a British shopping district—with its hanging flower baskets and Tudor-style storefronts—that it is referred to as "behind the Tweed Curtain."

Downtown, in addition to the Victoria Eaton Centre, there are two important shopping centers. **Harbour Square,** on two levels between Government and Wharf, Courtney and Broughton streets, houses 25 shops selling women's and men's fashions, jewelry, and a variety of imports, plus a small food court. **Market Square,** at the harbor end of Johnson and Pandora streets, is a charming historic restoration containing 40 shops (see Chapter XV, "Walking Around Victoria"). Within a short drive or bus ride of downtown are three large shopping malls—**Mayfair Shopping Centre,** 3147 Douglas St. between Tolmie, Finlayson, and Quadra (tel. 383-0541); **Hillside Shopping Centre,** 1644 Hillside Ave. at Shelbourne St. (tel. 595-7154); and **Tillicum Mall,** 3170 Tillicum Rd. at Burnside Rd. West (tel. 381-7123).

Hours vary from shop to shop, but Thursdays (for some) and Fridays (for all) are late shopping nights in downtown Victoria. Expect shops to be open from 9:30am to 5:30pm Monday through Wednesday and Saturday from 9:30am to 9pm Thursday and Friday, and (in touristed areas) from noon to 5pm Sunday.

1. Best Buys

ANTIQUES: On Antique Row (Fort St.), start at the 1100 block (Cook St.) and work back toward downtown. The most authentic collectibles are at the east end of the row, and they're often missed by people who start their search at the Douglas Street end. Antique dealers here will happily recommend other shops if they don't have what you're looking for. Two places especially worth a look are **Kilshaw's Auctioneers,** 1115 Fort St. (tel. 384-6441), for estate sales, and **Vanhall's Antiques,** 1023 Fort St. (tel. 382-7643), for silver.

ART: There are fine galleries all over the city. Some to consider: **North Park Gallery,** 1619 Store St. (tel. 381-3422); **Herald Street Artworld,** 655B Herald St. (tel. 384-3766); **Marshall Gallery,** 1636 Cedar Hill Cross Rd. (tel. 477-1242); **Handloom Gallery,** 641 Fort St. (tel. 384-1011), for Canadian crafts work; and the shop at the **Art Gallery of Greater Victoria,** 1040 Moss St. (tel. 384-4101).

BOOKS: **Munro's Book Store,** 1108 Government St. (tel. 382-2464), is not only a Victoria landmark, but the city's most important book dealer with over 30,000 titles. **Poor Richard's Books,** 968 Balmoral Road (tel. 384-4411), offers current and rare editions in an old brick heritage house.

Specialty stores include **Baba Fine Art Books,** 634 Humboldt St. (tel. 382-4262); **Everywomans Books,** 641 Johnson St. (tel. 388-9411); and the **Magic Bean Buyer Bookstore,** for children, at Market Square, 560 Johnson St. (tel. 384-0411).

CHINA AND CRYSTAL: This is a major item in Victoria—Waterford crystal, Royal Worcester bone china, and so forth. Check **Victoria Limited Editions,** 919 Fort St. (tel. 386-5155); **Sidney Reynolds,** 801 Government St. (tel. 383-3931); **Montague Bridgman,** 1005 Broad St. (tel. 386-4588); and **Eaton's** at Victoria Eaton Centre (tel. 382-7141).

CRAFTS: Government Street has the greatest concentration of shops dealing in traditional Northwest Coast Native Canadian and Eskimo arts and crafts. Native to Vancouver Island are long-wearing Cowichan sweaters, handspun from undyed raw wool. Look also for woodcarved masks, boxes, and bowls; jewelry of silver, gold, jade, and black argillite; soapstone and ivory sculptures;

weaving, leatherwork, and basketry. Among the outstanding shops are **Canadian Impressions,** 811 Government St. (tel. 383-2641), and **Quest,** 1023 Government St. (tel. 382-1934).

FASHIONS: We're talking British and European imports, and Canadian designers. Government Street and its side streets are the best places to look for both men's and women's fashions. Try **George Straith,** 921 Government St. (tel. 384-6912); **W & J Wilson Ltd.,** 1221 Government St. (tel. 383-7177); **Anthony James,** 1225 Government St. (tel. 381-2152); and **Hughes Ltd.,** 564 Yates St. (tel. 381-4405). Outstanding for men's fashions are **Couvelier,** 620 Humboldt St. (tel. 382-3312); and **B1 & Company,** 1008 Broad St. (tel. 386-1622). Women should check out **Shanelle,** 614 Trounce Alley (tel. 381-2131); **Sunday's Snowflakes,** 1000 Douglas St. (tel. 381-4461), and **Gibson's Ladies Wear,** 708 View St. (tel. 384-5913). If you're in the market for Scottish tartans, **Prescott and Andrews,** 817 Government St. (tel. 384-2515), may have what you need.

FOOD: What do you look for in a British town? Why, tea and chocolates, of course! **Murchie's,** 1110 Government St. (tel. 383-3122) has custom blends of all major British teas plus its own chocolates made on the premises. Chocoholics may also love **Rogers Chocolates,** 913 Government St. (tel. 384-7021); **Bernard Callebaut,** 635 Broughton St. (tel. 380-1515); and **Coco's Chocolates,** 722 Broughton St. (tel. 384-2262).

JEWELRY: The most interesting pieces are those crafted by Native Canadian artisans in silver, gold, British Columbia jade, or black argillite, a semiprecious stone mined only in the Queen Charlotte Islands. For this type of jewelry, see "Crafts," above. For more traditional work, visit **Nugget Jewellers,** 2nd floor, 824 Johnson St. (tel. 385-8444).

PUBLIC MARKET: The **Harbour Public Market,** 1810 Store St. (tel. 384-8155), is just north of Chinatown. Produce, fish, and meat stalls, take-out food booths, and craft and clothing boutiques have turned a former warehouse into a bustling marketplace.

SOUVENIRS: There are plenty of shops with the requisite junk. My favorites for quality and variety are side by side, a few steps east of Government Street: **Drover's Cottage,** 623 Fort St. (tel. 385-1312), and **Scaramouche Gallery,** 635 Fort St. (tel. 386-2215).

XVII

VICTORIA NIGHTS

1. THE PERFORMING ARTS
2. THE CLUB AND MUSIC SCENE
3. THE BAR SCENE
4. MORE ENTERTAINMENT

Though a relatively small city, Victoria has a surprisingly active nightlife. There's a strong emphasis on "high" culture, including theater, symphony, and opera; but jazz music is also very big, and the city has its share of pubs, discos, and rock clubs.

The **Community Arts Council of Greater Victoria,** 620 View St., Suite 511 (tel. 381-ARTS or 381-2787) keeps an up-to-date list of current and future events scheduled in the city. So does **Tourism Victoria,** 812 Wharf St. (tel. 382-2127). Tickets for most events can be obtained from the box office of the **McPherson Playhouse, 3** Centennial Square, Pandora and Government sts. (tel. 386-6121), or at Tourism Victoria. Current listings can be found in the two daily newspapers, *The Daily Colonist* and the *Victoria Times;* in *Monday Magazine,* a weekly tabloid published on Thursdays; and in the bi-monthly *Arts Victoria.*

Throughout the summer, there's free entertainment around the shore of James Bay, in Market Square, in Beacon Hill Park, and wherever else people congregate. And numerous festivals bring out-standing artists of all pursuits to parks and performing arts centers at little or no charge. They include jazz festivals in April and June, the classical-oriented Victoria International Festival in July and Au-gust, and the avant-garde Fringe Festival in September.

The following is a quick-reference list of major performance spaces in Victoria, with box office telephone numbers. Details are provided in the listings below.

McPherson Playhouse	(tel. 386-6121)
Royal Theatre	(tel. 386-6121)
University Centre Auditorium	(tel. 721-8299)
Belfry Theatre	(tel. 385-6815)

1. The Performing Arts

MAJOR CONCERT/PERFORMANCE HALLS

McPherson Playhouse, 3 Centennial Square, Pandora Ave. and Government St. (tel. 386-6121).

This 800-seat baroque Edwardian theater, restored in 1962, was built in 1914 as the Pantages Theatre for vaudevillians. Today, it is the home of the Victoria Symphony Orchestra, the Pacific Opera Victoria, and numerous other musical and theatrical groups. Free noon-hour concerts are presented throughout the year.

Open: Box office, Mon–Sat 9:30am–5:30pm, and 6–9pm on all performance days. *Prices:* Vary according to performance. *Bus:* 23, 24.

Royal Theatre, 805 Broughton St. at Blanshard (tel. 383-9711; box office, 386-6121).

Built in the first decade of the 20th century and renovated in the late 1970s, the Royal is operated by the McPherson. It complements the larger venue's programs as a locale for concerts, dance recitals, and touring stage plays.

Open: Box office at McPherson Playhouse (see above), Mon–Sat 9:30am–5:30pm, and 6–9pm on all performance days. *Prices:* Vary according to performance. *Bus:* 1 (Courtney Street).

Another important performance hall is the **University Centre Auditorium** at the University of Victoria, Finnerty Rd. (tel. 721-8299). One of the most acoustically sound in Canada, this auditorium seats 1,233 for concerts, plays, dance performances, and lectures.

THEATER

The theater is very active in Victoria, with several companies mounting regular productions throughout the year. Most prominent is the **Belfry Theatre,** 1291 Gladstone St. at Fernwood (tel. 385-6815). This acclaimed group—it represented Canada in the Olympic Arts Festival in Calgary in 1988—performs a five-play season from October to April in its own small and intimate playhouse. Programs span the gamut of serious theater; contemporary Canadian playwrights are preferred, but the Belfry has also produced works by Eugene O'Neill, Harold Pinter, and Stephen Sondheim. Artistic director Glynis Leyshon directs ShowFest at Niagara-on-the-Lake, Ontario, in summer. The belfry's box office is open Monday through Friday from 9am to 5pm. Tickets cost from $6.50 to $13 for adults; senior and student discounts are available.

The **Intrepid Theatre Company,** 620 View St., Suite 602 (tel. 383-2663), produces the annual **Victoria Fringe Festival,** held for nine days in late September. It offers more than 200 performances in comedy, drama, music, dance, mime, and puppetry. This is where counterculture joins the mainstream. Themes range from absurd and/or existential to leading-edge avant-garde. No production charges over $5 for tickets, but none are sold until an hour before show time.

The **Victoria Theatre Guild,** 805 Langham Court Rd., Rockland (tel. 384-2142), presents a fall-to-spring season of musicals, dramas, and comedies at the Langham Court Theatre. Prices are $9 for adults, $8 for seniors and students.

The **Capital Comedy Theatre,** 1299 Tracksell Ave. (tel. 382-5750), stages its productions on an irregular basis at the McPherson Playhouse.

The University of Victoria's **Phoenix Theatres,** Sinclair Rd. at Finnerty (tel. 721-8000), serve up a year-round potpourri of productions at two campus theaters, plus two repertory plays June through August at the campus Faculty Club.

The **Kaleidoscope Theatre,** 715 Yates St. (tel. 383-8124) has drawn raves internationally for its work with young audiences (3 to 18 years). Kaleidoscope has both a resident company and a touring company, and runs a professional theater school for kids 4 to 84.

Theatre Inconnu, based in Market Square (tel. 380-1284), is an avant-garde troupe that performs in the shopping plaza and elsewhere around town on an irregular basis.

OPERA

The nationally acclaimed Pacific Opera Victoria, 1316B Government St. (tel. 385-0222; box office, 386-6121), mounts three productions annually—in September, February, and April—at the McPherson Playhouse. In the 1989–90 season, it presented Rossini's *La Cenerentola,* Tchaikovsky's *Eugene Onegin,* and Gilbert and Sullivan's *The Pirates of Penzance.* Pre-performance lectures are given nightly by opera scholars on the McPherson mezzanine. Tickets are obtained at the box office at McPherson Playhouse (see above), and cost from $12 to $33.

The **Victoria Operatic Society,** 798 Fairview Rd. (tel. 381-1021), established in 1945, presents a year-round schedule of operettas and light musicals at McPherson Playhouse. Typical prices are $12 and $14 for adults, $8 and $10 for children 12 and under.

ORCHESTRAL AND CHORAL MUSIC

The year's big event is the **Victoria International Festival,** held from the second week of July through the third week of August. Symphony concerts, classical recitals, ballet performances, baroque concerts, and other events featuring dozens of world-renowned musicians are presented at the McPherson Playhouse, Royal Theatre, University Centre Auditorium and Recital Hall, Christ Church Cathedral, and the co-sponsoring St. Michael's University School. Prices of events vary, but a 19-concert subscription ticket can be obtained for just $94.50 ($83 for students). Get tickets from the McPherson Playhouse box office (tel. 386-6121); for further information, write the festival coordinators in care of St. Michael's University School, 3400 Richmond Rd., Victoria, BC V8P 4P5 (tel. 604/595-4522).

The **Victoria Symphony Orchestra,** 846 Broughton St. (tel. 385-6515), enters its 50th season in October 1990, with nearly 50 dates scheduled over the following seven months. Most series are performed at the Royal, including "Masterworks" (its main classical series), "Seagram Pops," and "Concerts for Kids." Two other shorter series are offered at the University Centre Auditorium: "Bach to Mozart" and "20th Century Spectrum." Tickets cost from $7.50 to $18 for adults, with a $1 discount for seniors and students.

The 72-member **Greater Victoria Youth Orchestra** (tel. 477-3870), featuring performers aged 12 to 24, was founded in 1986. Already, its alumni are performing with provincial symphony orchestras in eastern Canada and studying at conservatories from Vienna to Yale. The group plays November and March concerts at the University Centre Auditorium, and makes occasional other appearances. Tickets are $6 for adults, $3 for seniors and students.

The **Island Chamber Players,** 851 Pendele Place (tel. 385-6973), perform a September-to-April season of seven concerts at North Park Gallery, 1619 Store St. Tickets are $12 for adults, $10 for students and seniors.

Other notable groups are the **Victoria Choral Society,** whose year culminates in a Christmas-week performance of Handel's *Messiah* with the VSO at the Royal Theatre; the **Victoria Savoyard Society,** which stages about three Gilbert & Sullivan operettas each year; the **Victoria Conservatory of Music,** 839 Academy Close (tel. 386-5311), a professional music school one block east of the Royal B.C. Museum, which presents student recitals; and the **University School of Music,** which offers free concerts by faculty and students every Friday at 12:30pm, plus a full schedule of evening performances.

DANCE

Numerous amateur companies and dance studios present recitals and full-scale performances throughout the year. In addition, companies from across North America frequently perform—usually at the Royal Theatre.

2. The Club and Music Scene

NIGHTCLUBS AND CABARETS

Harpo's, 15 Bastion Square (tel. 385-5333).

Victoria's best intimate showcase for high-profile artists, short of a concert hall, overlooks the waterfront above Wharf Street. A wide variety of artists, from jazz (Joanne Brackeen Trio) to blues (Koko Taylor) to progressive rock (the Oyster Band) to African (Native Spirit) perform behind a fine dance floor.

Open: Mon–Sat 7pm–2am. *Prices:* Drinks $3.50. *Admission:* $3–$13, depending upon act. *Bus:* 5 (Government St.).

ROCK MUSIC

There are a limited number of downtown clubs serving up live rock music on a regular basis.

The Forge, 919 Douglas St. in the Strathcona Hotel (tel. 383-7137), is probably the biggest and best. Hard or progressive rock bands provide the beat for a crowd that ranges from new wavers to blue-collar workers. It's open nightly, with a $3 cover charge.

The Rail, 2852 Douglas St. at the Colony Motor Inn (tel. 385-

2441), is a pub-style spot for hard rockers. The **Banana Moon Nite Club,** 770 Yates St. near Blanshard (tel. 389-0666), has "classic rock and boogie" bands nightly except Sunday, when there's a musicians' jam.

JAZZ, BLUES, FOLK

It's easier to find good live jazz in Victoria than hot rock. To begin with, there are two major jazz festivals here each year—the **TerrifVic Dixieland Jazz Festival** (tel. 381-5277), over four days in late April, and the **Jazz Fest** at Market Square (tel. 386-2441), spreading over nine days in late June. The Dixieland event brings more than a dozen bands from as far away as the British Isles, Latin America, and (of course) New Orleans to perform at venues all over the city, and there's free shuttle service between sites in a double-decker bus. Three-day badges for all performances are $50. The Jazz Fest leans more toward swing, bebop, fusion, avant-garde, riffs, and licks; in 1989, it drew over 150 musicians from 10 countries. Noon-hour and evening performances are focused on Market Square's central courtyard.

The **Victoria Jazz Society** (tel. 388-4423) is a clearinghouse of information on jazz activity throughout the greater Victoria area. It often sponsors performances by visiting artists at Harpo's, Hermann's Dixieland Inn, and the Royal Theatre. And when he's in town, Victoria's own world-famous jazz flutist, Paul Horn, can often be convinced to concertize.

The following establishments present regular evening jazz:

Hermann's Dixieland Inn, 753 View St. near Blanshard (tel. 388-9166), is like a 1950s time warp. This low-lit jazz club has photos and posters all over its walls, and old trumpets and trombones practically against the ceiling. It specializes in Dixieland jazz, with occasional fusion or blues. Meals are not really gourmet, but feature very generous portions of home cooking. Hermann's is open Monday through Friday from 11:30am to 2am, Saturday 3pm to 2am. Full meals cost $9.95 to $11.95, drinks $3, and usually there is no cover charge.

Pagliacci's, 1011 Broad St. (tel. 386-1662), has an eclectic variety of music most evenings, from Latin jazz to big band, jazz fusion to Balkan folk songs. **La Bohème,** 537 Johnson St. (tel. 385-3551), serves up entertainment, ranging from jazz fusion to classical, at 9pm Tuesday through Saturday. Both establishments are reviewed in Chapter XIII, "Victoria Dining."

For lovers of acoustic music, the **Victoria Folk Music Society** (tel. 386-9530 or 386-0737) hosts a weekly performance at 8pm Sunday in Norway House, 1110 Hillside Ave. Admission is $2.

COUNTRY AND WESTERN

The selection here is limited. But the **Esquimalt Inn,** 856 Esquimalt Rd. (tel. 382-7161), fills a need for C&W lovers. There's live music here seven nights a week, and jam sessions starting at 3pm Saturdays and Sundays. Take bus 23.

DISCOS

The names change, the places change, but there are always discos with canned dance music. Most are open Monday through

Saturday until 2am, Sunday until midnight. Some of the hot spots at this writing are:

Club California, 1318 Broad St. (tel. 382-1331). An upstairs club with a large dance floor and big-screen rock videos, it's open nightly, with frequent theme nights.

Julie's Cabaret, 603 Pandora Ave. at Government St. (tel. 386-3631). This techno-funk disco shares quarters with Monty's Pub in Victoria Plaza. Open nightly; $3 cover.

Merlin's, 1208 Wharf St. (tel. 381-2331). A waterfront club that attracts an early-twenties crowd, it has regular theme nights, including a Thursday ladies' night with male dancers. There's a $3 cover after 9:30pm on weekends.

Pier 42, 1605 Store St. at Pandora (tel. 381-7437), is in the basement of Swans Pub (and under the same management). An older clientele dresses well—and sometimes lines up—to dance to sixties and seventies oldies and Top 40 hits. Open Tuesday through Saturday nights only, from 7pm; $2 cover.

Spinners, 858 Yates St. near Quadra (tel. 381-5442), is an under-19 dance club (heavy in 13- and 14-year-olds) with a stiff cover charge: $5 Wednesday and Thursday, $6.50 Friday and Saturday. Open till midnight.

Sweetwaters Niteclub, Market Square off Store St. (tel. 383-7844), is an elegant singles club that features classic tracks and anything else worth dancing to. There's no cover, but you must expect a line seven nights a week.

---

3. The Bar Scene

It's only natural that a town as British as Victoria should have some outstanding pubs. In particular, don't fail to visit at least one of its brew pubs, which manufacture their own beers and ales. Remember, licensing laws require pubs to close by 11pm.

Spinnakers Brew Pub, 308 Catherine St. near Esquimalt Rd. (tel. 386-BREW or 386-2739).

This full-mash brew house overlooks Victoria Harbour on the west side of the Songhees Point Development. A great place for a light meal or an evening ale, it draws a mixed clientele of local old-timers and young professionals. Brewmaster Jake Thomas buys his malted barley from Great Britain and cultures his own yeast in the laboratory. He has 30 different recipes, among which the favorites are Spinnaker ale, Mitchell's Extra Strong Bitter, and Empress stout. Phone ahead if you'd like to tour the brewery. A new upstairs restaurant was scheduled to open in summer 1990. Live music is often presented evenings.

Open: Daily 11am–11pm. *Prices:* Meals from $4.75, beers from $2. *Bus:* 23 (Esquimalt Road).

Swans Pub, 506 Pandora Ave. at Store St. (tel. 361-3310).

Housed in a converted 1913 feed warehouse, this hotel-café-brewery complex (see Chapter XII, "Victoria Accommodations") is extremely popular with the city's young professional crowd. The pub serves a half dozen British-style draft ales brewed on the premises at Buckerfield's Brewery, and the adjoining Swans Cafe serves lunch and dinner daily.

Open: Daily 11am–11pm. *Prices:* Entrées $11–$14, beers from $2. *Bus:* 23 or 24.

Pig & Whistle, 634 Humboldt St. (tel. 383-2413).

This cheerily romanticized English pub next to the Empress hotel has a London "bobby" standing guard and Cockney-style entertainment in the form of Pearly Kings and Queens, musicians and comedians. To ease you into the sing-alongs, the lyrics of such perennials as "Me Old Man's a Dustman" and "She Was One of the Early Birds" come printed on the menu.

Open: Daily noon–midnight. *Prices:* Entrées $8–$13. *Bus:* 5.

---

4. More Entertainment

GAMBLING CASINOS

See Chapter X, "Vancouver Nights," for general information concerning gambling in British Columbia. Victoria has a sprinkling of legal casinos scattered around the city. Don't expect Las Vegas or Atlantic City: None of them offers a floor shows or other diversions, and the decor is modest and devoid of glamour. The main games are blackjack, roulette, and sic-bo.

Among the casinos are **Casino Victoria,** 716 Courtney St. near Douglas (tel. 380-3998), and the **Great Canadian Casino,** Red Lion Inn, 3366 Douglas St. near Ardersier (tel. 384-2614). Both are open from 6pm to 2am every night.

METRIC CONVERSIONS

Canadians use the metric system of weighing and measuring, and if you are prepared for it, you can avoid confusion.

LENGTH

1 millimeter = 0.04 inches (*or* less than 1/16 inch)
1 centimeter = 0.39 inches (*or* just under ½ inch)
1 meter   = 1.09 yards (*or* about 39 inches)
1 kilometer = 0.62 mile (*or* about ⅔ mile)

To convert **kilometers to miles,** take the number of kilometers and multiply by .62 (for example, 25km × .62 = 15.5 miles). To convert **miles to kilometers,** take the number of miles and multiply by 1.61 (for example, 50 miles × 1.61 = 80.5 km).

CAPACITY

1 liter = 33.92 ounces
       = 1.06 quarts
       = 0.26 gallons

To convert **liters to gallons,** take the number of liters and multiply by .26 (for example, 50 l × .26 = 13 gal). To convert **gallons to liters,** take the number of gallons and multiply by 3.79 (for example, 10 gal × 3.79 = 37.9 l).

WEIGHT

1 gram   = 0.04 ounce (*or* about a paperclip's weight)
1 kilogram = 2.2 pounds

To convert **kilograms to pounds,** take the number of kilos and multiply by 2.2 (for example, 75kg × 2.2 = 165 lbs). To convert **pounds to kilograms,** take the number of pounds and multiply by .45 (for example, 90 lb × .45 = 40.5kg).

TEMPERATURE

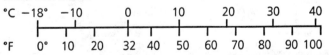

To convert **degrees C to degrees F,** multiply degrees C by 9, divide by 5, then add 32 (for example $9/5 × 20°C + 32 = 68°F$). To convert **degrees F to degrees C,** subtract 32 from degrees F, then multiply by 5, and divide by 9 (for example, $85°F − 32 × 5/9 = 29°C$).

INDEX

GENERAL INFORMATION

SIGHTS AND ATTRACTIONS

Vancouver

Victoria

ACCOMMODATIONS

Vancouver

AIRPORT
Abercorn Inn (*M*), 65
Delta Airport Inn Resort (*E*), 58–9
The Delta River Inn (*E*), 59
Executive Inn (*M*), 64
Stay'n Save Motor Inn (*M*), 64

BED & BREAKFAST AGENCIES
A Home Away From Home Bed & Breakfast Agency, 44
Born Free Bed & Breakfast of B.C., 44
British Columbia Bed & Breakfast Association, 44
Canada-West Accommodations Bed & Breakfast Registry, 44
Copes' Choice Bed & Breakfast Accommodations, 44
Old English Bed & Breakfast Registry, 44
Town & Country Bed & Breakfast in B.C., 44
Vancouver Bed & Breakfast Ltd., 44
WestWay Accommodation Registry, 44

DOWNTOWN
Abbotsford Hotel (*M*), 61
Burrard Motor Inn (*M*), 61
Delta Place Hotel (*VE*), 45
Four Seasons Hotel (*VE*), 45, 48
The Georgian Court Hotel (*E*), 53
The Hotel at the YMCA (*B*), 67
Hotel California (*B*), 65
Hotel Georgia (*E*), 54

Hotel Vancouver (*VE*), 48–9
Hyatt Regency Vancouver (*VE*), 49
Kingston Hotel (*B*), 66
Le Meridian (*VE*), 49–50
Nelson Place Hotel (*B*), 66
New World Harbourside (*VE*), 50–1
Pan-Pacific Hotel Vancouver (*VE*), 51
Quality Inn, 54
Sandman's Inn (*M*), 61
St. Regis Hotel (*B*), 66
Wedgewood Hotel (*E*), 53–4
YMCA (*B*), 66

EAST OF DOWNTOWN
2400 Motel (*B*), 68
Burnaby Cariboo R.V. Park (*B*), 68
Cariboo Motel and Trailer Park (*B*), 68
Exhibition Park Travelodge (*M*), 63

GASTOWN/CHINATOWN
Backpackers Youth Hostel (*B*), 68
Dominion Hotel (*B*), 67
Niagara Hotel (*B*), 67
Patricia Hotel (*B*), 67

NORTH SHORE
Canyon Court Motel (*M*), 65
Capilano Motor Inn (*M*), 65
Capilano R.V. Park (*B*), 69–70
Globetrotter's Inn (*B*), 69
Grouse Inn (*M*), 65
Lonsdale Quay Hotel (*E*), 60
Park Royal Hotel (*E*), 60

KEY TO ABBREVIATIONS: *B* = Budget; *E* = Expensive; *M* = Moderately priced; *VE* = Very Expensive

Victoria

RESTAURANTS

Vancouver

INTERNATIONAL
Earl's, South of Downtown (*B*), 110
Fogg n' Suds, South of Downtown (*B*), 110
Monte Cristo Restaurant, Downtown (*B*), 104
Picasso Cafe, South of Downtown, (*M*), 100–1
Sea Level Bistro, West End (*B*), 106

ITALIAN
Al Forno, Gastown/Chinatown (*B*), 107
Cafe Il Nido, Downtown (*M*), 88
Cafe Roma, North Shore (*M*), 102
Corsi Trattoria, North Shore (*M*), 101–2
Il Giardino di Umberto, Downtown (*E*), 77
Old Spaghetti Factory, Gastown/Chinatown (*B*), 107
Piccolo Mondo, Downtown (*E*), 77
Presto Panini Cafe, Downtown (*B*), 103
Settebello, West End (*B*), 105
Tommy O's Off Broadway, East of Downtown (*M*), 95
Umberto Al Porto, Gastown/Chinatown (*M*), 93
Zeppo's Trattoria, South of Downtown (*M*), 99–100

JAMAICAN
A Taste of Jamaica, Downtown (*B*), 104

JAPANESE
Frankie's Inn, North Shore (*B*),
Ichibankan, West End (*M*), 91–2
Japanese Deli, Gastown/Chinatown (*M*), 94
Kamei Sushi Restaurant, Downtown (*E*), 79
Naniwa-ya Seafood Restaurant, Downtown (*E*), 78–9
Restaurant Suntory, Downtown (*VE*), 74
Tojo's Restaurant, South of Downtown (*E*), 85

KOREAN
New Seoul, East of Downtown (*B*), 109

MEDITERRANEAN
Umberto's Fish House, Downtown (*E*), 76

MEXICAN
Pepita's, West End (*M*), 92

NATIVE CANADIAN
Quilicum Native Indian Restaurant, West End (*M*), 89

NOUVELLE
Alma Street Cafe, South of Downtown (*M*), 96–7
Angelica, South of Downtown (*E*), 83
Bishop's, South of Downtown (*E*), 82–3
Sami's California Cafe, South of Downtown (*M*), 98

PIZZA
Al Forno, Gastown/Chinatown (*B*), 107

PROVENCALE
Le Mistral Restaurant, Downtown (*E*), 76–7

SCANDINAVIAN
The Scanwich, Downtown (*B*), 103

SEAFOOD
The Amorous Oyster, South of Downtown (*M*), 97
Bridges, South of Downtown (*M*), 97
The Cannery, East of Downtown (*M*), 94–5
Dover Seafood, West End (*B*), 104–5
Joe Fortes Seafood House, Downtown (*M*), 87
A Kettle of Fish, Downtown (*M*), 87
Monk McQueen's, South of Downtown (*E*), 83–4
Naniwa-ya Seafood Restaurant, Downtown (*E*), 78–9
The Only (Fish & Oyster Cafe), Gastown/Chinatown (*B*), 107
Papillote Fish & Game House, South of Downtown (*E*), 84
Robson Grill, West End (*M*), 89–90
Seven Seas Seafood Restaurant, North Shore (*M*), 101
Soft Rock Cafe, Kitsilano (*M*), 179
Steamers and Stews, Downtown (*B*), 102
Tsui Hang Village, Downtown (*M*), 88–9
Umberto's Fish House, Downtown (*E*), 76

SOUTHWESTERN
Santa Fe Cafe, South of Downtown (*M*), 98–9

SPANISH
Chateau Madrid, Downtown (*M*), 88
La Bodega, Downtown (*B;* tapas), 103–4
Las Tapas, Downtown (*B;* tapas), 103

Victoria

NOW, SAVE MONEY ON ALL YOUR TRAVELS!
Join Frommer's™ Dollarwise® Travel Club

Saving money while traveling is never a simple matter, which is why the **Dollarwise Travel Club** was formed 31 years ago. Developed in response to requests from Frommer's Travel Guide readers, the Club provides cost-cutting travel strategies, up-to-date travel information, and a sense of community for value-conscious travelers from all over the world.

In keeping with the money-saving concept, the annual membership fee is low—$18 for U.S. residents or $20 for residents of Canada, Mexico, and other countries—and is immediately exceeded by the value of your benefits, which include:

1. Any TWO books listed on the following pages.
2. Plus any ONE Frommer's City Guide.
3. A subscription to our quarterly newspaper, *The Dollarwise Traveler*.
4. A membership card that entitles you to purchase through the Club all Frommer's publications for 33% to 50% off their retail price.

The eight-page *Dollarwise Traveler* tells you about the latest developments in good-value travel worldwide and includes the following columns: **Hospitality Exchange** (for those offering and seeking hospitality in cities all over the world); **Share-a-Trip** (for those looking for travel companions to share costs); and **Readers Ask . . . Readers Reply** (for those with travel questions that other members can answer).

Aside from the Frommer's Guides and the Gault Millau Guides, you can also choose from our Special Editions. These include such titles as *California with Kids* (a compendium of the best of California's accommodations, restaurants, and sightseeing attractions appropriate for those traveling with toddlers through teens); *Candy Apple: New York with Kids* (a spirited guide to the Big Apple by a savvy New York grandmother that's perfect for both visitors and residents); *Caribbean Hideaways* (the 100 most romantic places to stay in the Islands, all rated on ambience, food, sports opportunities, and price); *Honeymoon Destinations* (a guide to planning and choosing just the right destination from hundreds of possibilities in the U.S., Mexico, and the Caribbean); *Marilyn Wood's Wonderful Weekends* (a selection of the best mini-vacations within a 200-mile radius of New York City, including descriptions of country inns and other accommodations, restaurants, picnic spots, sights, and activities); and *Paris Rendez-Vous* (a delightful guide to the best places to meet in Paris whether for power breakfasts or dancing till dawn).

To join this Club, simply send the appropriate membership fee with your name and address to: Frommer's Dollarwise Travel Club, 15 Columbus Circle, New York, NY 10023. Remember to specify which single city guide and which two other guides you wish to receive in your initial package of member's benefits. Or tear out the next page, check off your choices, and send the page to us with your membership fee.

FROMMER BOOKS
PRENTICE HALL PRESS
15 COLUMBUS CIRCLE
NEW YORK, NY 10023
212/373-8125

Date_____

Friends:

Please send me the books checked below.

FROMMER'S™ GUIDES

(Guides to sightseeing and tourist accommodations and facilities from budget to deluxe, with emphasis on the medium-priced.)

☐ Alaska $14.95	☐ Germany $14.95
☐ Australia $14.95	☐ Italy $14.95
☐ Austria & Hungary $14.95	☐ Japan & Hong Kong $14.95
☐ Belgium, Holland & Lux-	☐ Mid-Atlantic States $14.95
embourg $14.95	☐ New England $14.95
☐ Bermuda & The Bahamas $14.95	☐ New York State $14.95
☐ Brazil $14.95	☐ Northwest $14.95
☐ Canada $14.95	☐ Portugal, Madeira & the Azores $14.95
☐ Caribbean $14.95	☐ Skiing Europe $14.95
☐ Cruises (incl. Alaska, Carib, Mex, Ha-	☐ South Pacific $14.95
waii, Panama, Canada & US) . . $14.95	☐ Southeast Asia $14.95
☐ California & Las Vegas $14.95	☐ Southern Atlantic States $14.95
☐ Egypt $14.95	☐ Southwest $14.95
☐ England & Scotland $14.95	☐ Switzerland & Liechtenstein $14.95
☐ Florida $14.95	☐ USA $15.95
☐ France $14.95	

FROMMER'S $-A-DAY® GUIDES

(In-depth guides to sightseeing and low-cost tourist accommodations and facilities.)

☐ Europe on $40 a Day $15.95	☐ New York on $60 a Day $13.95
☐ Australia on $40 a Day $13.95	☐ New Zealand on $45 a Day $13.95
☐ Eastern Europe on $25 a Day . $13.95	☐ Scandinavia on $60 a Day $13.95
☐ England on $50 a Day $13.95	☐ Scotland & Wales on $40 a Day $13.95
☐ Greece on $35 a Day $13.95	☐ South America on $35 a Day $13.95
☐ Hawaii on $60 a Day $13.95	☐ Spain & Morocco on $40 a Day $13.95
☐ India on $25 a Day $12.95	☐ Turkey on $30 a Day $13.95
☐ Ireland on $35 a Day $13.95	☐ Washington, D.C. & Historic Va. on
☐ Israel on $40 a Day $13.95	$40 a Day $13.95
☐ Mexico on $35 a Day $13.95	

FROMMER'S TOURING GUIDES

(Color illustrated guides that include walking tours, cultural and historic sites, and other vital travel information.)

☐ Amsterdam $10.95	☐ New York $10.95
☐ Australia $9.95	☐ Paris $8.95
☐ Brazil $10.95	☐ Rome $10.95
☐ Egypt $8.95	☐ Scotland $9.95
☐ Florence $8.95	☐ Thailand $9.95
☐ Hong Kong $10.95	☐ Turkey $10.95
☐ London $8.95	☐ Venice $8.95

TURN PAGE FOR ADDITONAL BOOKS AND ORDER FORM

0690

FROMMER'S CITY GUIDES

(Pocket-size guides to sightseeing and tourist accommodations and facilities in all price ranges.)

☐ Amsterdam/Holland........$8.95		☐ Montréal/Québec City $8.95		
☐ Athens...................$8.95		☐ New Orleans $8.95		
☐ Atlanta...................$8.95		☐ New York.....................$8.95		
☐ Atlantic City/Cape May $8.95		☐ Orlando......................$8.95		
☐ Barcelona.................$7.95		☐ Paris $8.95		
☐ Belgium $7.95		☐ Philadelphia..................$8.95		
☐ Boston $8.95		☐ Rio $8.95		
☐ Cancún/Cozumel/Yucatán ..$8.95		☐ Rome $8.95		
☐ Chicago $8.95		☐ Salt Lake City $8.95		
☐ Denver/Boulder/Colorado		☐ San Diego $8.95		
Springs.................$7.95		☐ San Francisco $8.95		
☐ Dublin/Ireland............$8.95		☐ Santa Fe/Taos/Albuquerque $8.95		
☐ Hawaii $8.95		☐ Seattle/Portland...............$7.95		
☐ Hong Kong $7.95		☐ Sydney $8.95		
☐ Las Vegas $8.95		☐ Tampa/St. Petersburg $8.95		
☐ Lisbon/Madrid/Costa del Sol. .$8.95		☐ Tokyo $7.95		
☐ London...................$8.95		☐ Toronto......................$8.95		
☐ Los Angeles...............$8.95		☐ Vancouver/Victoria............$7.95		
☐ Mexico City/Acapulco $8.95		☐ Washington, D.C...............$8.95		
☐ Minneapolis/St. Paul.......$8.95				

SPECIAL EDITIONS

☐ Beat the High Cost of Travel . . .$6.95		☐ Motorist's Phrase Book (Fr/Ger/Sp)....$4.95	
☐ Bed & Breakfast—N. America $11.95		☐ Paris Rendez-Vous...............$10.95	
☐ California with Kids $14.95		☐ Swap and Go (Home Exchanging) $10.95	
☐ Caribbean Hideaways $14.95		☐ The Candy Apple (NY with Kids) $12.95	
☐ Manhattan's Outdoor		☐ Travel Diary and Record Book $5.95	
Sculpture.............$15.95			

☐ Honeymoon Destinations (US, Mex & Carib) $14.95

☐ Where to Stay USA (From $3 to $30 a night) $10.95

☐ Marilyn Wood's Wonderful Weekends (CT, DE, MA, NH, NJ, NY, PA, RI, VT) $11.95

☐ The New World of Travel (Annual sourcebook by Arthur Frommer for savvy travelers) . .$16.95

GAULT MILLAU

(The only guides that distinguish the truly superlative from the merely overrated.)

☐ The Best of Chicago $15.95		☐ The Best of Los Angeles...........$16.95	
☐ The Best of France.........$16.95		☐ The Best of New England $15.95	
☐ The Best of Hong Kong $16.95		☐ The Best of New York.............$16.95	
☐ The Best of Italy $16.95		☐ The Best of Paris................$16.95	
☐ The Best of London........$16.95		☐ The Best of San Francisco $16.95	
	☐ The Best of Washington, D.C. $16.95		

ORDER NOW!

In U.S. include $2 shipping UPS for 1st book; $1 ea. add'l book. Outside U.S. $3 and $1, respectively.
Allow four to six weeks for delivery in U.S., longer outside U.S.

Enclosed is my check or money order for $_____

NAME_____

ADDRESS_____

CITY_____ STATE _____ ZIP _____

0690